Pan-Asianism and Japan's W

The Palgrave Macmillan Series in Transnational History

Series Editors: **Akira Iriye** (Harvard University) and **Rana Mitter** (University of Oxford)

This distinguished series seeks to: develop scholarship on the transnational connections of societies and peoples in the nineteenth and twentieth centuries; provide a forum in which work on transnational history from different periods, subjects, and regions of the world can be brought together in fruitful connection; and explore the theoretical and methodological links between transnational and other related approaches such as comparative history and world history.

Published by Palgrave Macmillan:

Pan-Asianism and Japan's War 1931–1945

Eri Hotta

First published in hardcover in 2007 by PALGRAVE MACMILLAN®
in the United States—a division of St. Martin's Press LLC, 175 Fifth
Avenue, New York, NY 10010.

Where this book is distributed in the UK, Europe and the rest of
the world, this is by Palgrave Macmillan, a division of Macmillan
Publishers Limited, registered in England, company number
785998, of Houndmills, Basingstoke, Hampshire RG21 6XS.

Palgrave Macmillan is the global academic imprint of the above
companies and has companies and representatives throughout the
world.

Palgrave® and Macmillan® are registered trademarks in the
United States, the United Kingdom, Europe and other countries.

ISBN: 978-1-137-27035-1

Library of Congress Cataloging-in-Publication Data

Hotta, Eri, 1971–
    Pan-Asianism and Japan's war 1931–1945 / Eri Hotta.

            p. cm.—(Palgrave Macmillan transnational
            history series)
        Includes bibliographical references.
        ISBN 978-0-230-60103-1 (alk. paper)
        1. Japan—Foreign relations—1912–1945. 2.
    Regionalism—Asia. 3. Japan—Foreign relations—Asia. 4.
    Asia—Foreign relations—Japan. 5. Greater East Asia Co-
    prosperity Sphere. 6. Sino-Japanese Conflict,
    1931–1933. 7. Sino-Japanese War, 1937–1945. 8. World
    War, 1939–1945—Japan. I. Title.

    DS889.5.H68 2008

    327.510509'044—dc22   2007021604

A catalogue record of the book is available from the British Library.

Design by Scribe Inc.

First PALGRAVE MACMILLAN paperback edition: January 2013

10 9 8 7 6 5 4 3 2 1

To my parents,
Kimiko and Kensuke Hotta

Contents

Preface

Unlike some defeated ideologies, such as fascism, Pan-Asianism has faded from the contemporary historical imagination. Yet in the early twentieth century, it had a powerful hold on elites around Asia, especially in Japan, India, and to some extent in China. Fuelled by a powerful idea of community between Asian nations defining themselves against the colonialist West, Pan-Asianism appeared to have immense cultural power a century ago. Yet just a few decades later, the "spiritual" concepts defined by works such as Okakura Tenshin's *Ideals of the East* were distorted by the Japanese militarist government into a brutal ideology of imperialism that seemed fixated on conquering, rather than liberating, Asia.

Despite this disturbing past, the present day has seen a revival of interest in the concept of "Asia." From the "Asian Values" debate of the 1990s to the rapprochement between China, India, and Japan in the early twenty-first century, the idea that this region has values and aims in common has once more gained currency. What better time, then, to explore again an earlier attempt to understand "Asia" across the boundaries of its nation-states and to understand how the ideals of an earlier age had gone so very wrong?

Eri Hotta's book is a powerful addition to this series in transnational history. Using a theoretically sophisticated approach and a wealth of evidence, she makes a claim crucial to understanding Pan-Asianism: that it was not one idea, but at least three. A core of ideas ran through Pan-Asianism throughout its life, in particular, a vision that a regional identity could somehow mediate between emergent nationalisms and provide a convincing counterargument to the challenge of Western dominance. Yet among its Japanese exponents, the ideas of cooperation central to the concept's founders gave way to a racially charged politics of dominance in which Pan-Asianism became a tool to deny, rather than to encourage, the freedom of many of its Asian neighbors. Yet at the same time, many Asian peoples did find the rhetoric of Pan-Asianism had potency as well, drawing on its assumptions to forge their own ideas of liberation. These ambiguities are explored with brilliance and subtlety in this book.

Hotta's work, like all the best history, also opens up as many questions as it answers. Pan-Asianism, as she observes, has been followed by other attempts to forge cross-regional, transnational communities. This book has significant implications not just for understanding imperialism and its ideologies in the receding past but also for understanding the nature of international society beyond the nation-state today.

Rana Mitter
Akira Iriye
Oxford, May 2007

A Note on Names, Translations, and Sources

This book follows the Japanese convention of placing the surname before the given name in referring to Japanese names. For example, Prime Minister Tōjō's full name is expressed as Tōjō Hideki. As an exception, this convention is reversed when identifying the Japanese authors of publications written in English. For example, Ogata Sadako, when she is cited in the context of her English publication, is referred to as Sadako Ogata.

For Japanese words, macrons are used to indicate long vowels, with a long vowel approximately constituting twice the length of the short one in pronunciation. Notable exceptions to this rule are such widely recognized names as Tokyo, Osaka, and Kyoto, which could be spelled Tōkyō, Ōsaka, and Kyōto. In addition, the spellings of Japanese names and words in book titles are preserved as in the original even when macrons are applicable.

Well-known historical Chinese names and terms, such as Sun Yat-sen, Chiang Kai-shek, Chiang Tso-lin, Pu Yi, Kwantung Army, and Kuomintang are spelled as they most frequently appear in contemporaneous English literature.

The translations of Japanese sources are all mine unless otherwise specified.

The place of publication for all the Japanese sources cited and consulted is Tokyo, except when indicated otherwise.

Acknowledgments

It is with much pleasure that I express my thanks to those who helped and inspired me during the writing of this book. First of all, I am indebted to the series editors Akira Iriye and Rana Mitter for taking on my book. The former is a historian whom I have always admired. The latter supervised my doctoral dissertation, from which this book heavily draws. I have cherished the opportunity to work with them both.

During my stay in Oxford, I benefited greatly from the guidance and encouragement of Avi Shlaim, whose faith in my ability to pursue this topic never wavered from the very beginning. Jonathan Wright and Adam Roberts put me on the right course whenever I turned to them for help. James Piscatori was a great source of inspiration. His view on Pan-Islamism helped me sharpen the conceptual aspects of my work at a most critical time.

Arthur Stockwin and Naoko Shimazu offered constructive advice on my doctoral dissertation. Sheldon Garon read an earlier version of the manuscript. Katharine Wilson and Noga Arikha helped polish the manuscript with their discerning eyes. Their invaluable comments were much appreciated throughout the course of revising the manuscript.

The late Haruko Sumitomo was instrumental in bringing my attention to the life of her elder brother Saionji Kinkazu. Both Masako Saitō and Muneo Ōhashi kindly shared with me their private collections of papers and books on two people featured in the book: Saitō Hiroshi and Hamaguchi Osachi, their father and grandfather, respectively. Conversations with them enriched my overall understanding of these fascinating characters.

Friends and colleagues, such as Ikumi Okamoto, Fuyubi Nakamura, Tokiko Nakamura, Christopher Szpilman, Christopher Goto-Jones, Robert J. C. Young, Ankhi Mukherjee, Jacqueline Atkins, and Gwen Robinson, all helped me in this endeavor at various times when I needed their support. I would also like to thank Alessandra Bastagli, Christopher Chappell, and Brigitte Shull at Palgrave Macmillan for their help in finishing the manuscript.

Finally, I would like to thank my family—my parents, to whom the book is dedicated, as well as my sister, Mari Toyoda, and brother, Daisuke

Hotta—for their love and unconditional support throughout the entire process of researching and writing this book. But the book simply would not have come into being without the untiring encouragement, apt criticism, and unlimited help I have received from my husband, Ian Buruma.

Introduction:
Pan-Asian Ideology and the Fifteen Years' War

In the beginning was Manchuria. The Japanese Kwantung Army's seizure of China's northeast provinces in 1931 catapulted Japan into an era of warfare that lasted until the country's unconditional surrender to the Allied forces in August 1945. Numerous battlefield dramas, such as Japan's military conflict with China starting in 1937 (the "China Incident"), its costly battle with the Soviet army at Nomonhan in 1939, and its surprise attack on Pearl Harbor in 1941, all ended in the loss and the destruction of the Empire, leading some Japanese scholars to term this period the "Fifteen Years' War."[1]

At the height of its wartime expansion in early 1942, Japan claimed for itself an extensive area of land in the Asia-Pacific, reaching far north to the Aleutian Islands and south to the European colonies of Southeast Asia. The extraordinary story of Japan's Fifteen Years' War and its fleeting but enormous empire is much-chronicled, yet remains little understood. This book argues that the key to understanding this empire-building war lies in the transnational ideology of Pan-Asianism. Throughout this war, Pan-Asianism—the doctrine that called for "Asian" unity formulated by Asian intellectuals since the end of the nineteenth century—played an integral and critical role in Japan's wartime policy formulation. Even while Japan's international behavior appeared to show wild policy swings and its decision-making body was forever fragmented, there was in fact a consistent core of ideological thought underpinning the development of

1

that policy. Moreover, the ideology enabled the country to mobilize its population in a comprehensive fashion. Without Pan-Asianism, Japan might well not have taken the path from Manchuria to Pearl Harbor, to Southeast Asia, and to its ultimate defeat in 1945.

During the period of its expansion, Pan-Asianism was always palpable in Japan's articulation of its foreign policies and purposes, albeit in varying forms and degrees. In the early 1930s, Pan-Asianism became associated with the country's foreign policy in its enunciation of the "Asiatic Monroe Doctrine." Over the course of the 1930s, Pan-Asianism as a matter of official policy came into increasingly sharper focus in its puppet state Manchukuo, followed by the declaration of the construction of a "New East Asian Order" and the "Greater East Asia Co-Prosperity Sphere" as Japan's war aims in Asia and the Pacific. Indeed, the recurring ideological theme of Japan's expansion in the Fifteen Years' War was Pan-Asianism.

Pan-Asianism and the Fifteen Years' War

But first, what exactly is Pan-Asianism? And moreover, what is the reason for calling this period between 1930 and 1945 the Fifteen Years' War?

A standard Japanese dictionary definition holds that "Pan-Asianism is an assertion that Asian nations should unite under *Japanese leadership* to resist Western Great Powers' invasion of Asia." It goes on to explain the historical transformation of Pan-Asianism from a civic rights-based liberal internationalist idea popular in the 1870s and 1880s into an "embellishment of Japanese imperialism."[2] Because of its association with Japan's expansionism and its multiple roles at different moments in history, Pan-Asianism is a historical and value-loaded concept that seems to resist simple categorization. To my mind, the above-line of definition that embeds Japan's leadership as an inherent component of Pan-Asianism blurs the conceptual focus of this curiously paradoxical "transnational nationalist" ideology. The assumption that all Asians constituted a single group, in large part originating in Japan's democratic rights movement as well as the turn-of-the-century aesthetic and artistic movement among Asian intellectuals, had appealed to and influenced Japan's political elites of many stripes prior to 1931. Such a sentiment was reinforced by the 1905 Japanese victory over Russia, which was regarded by many, inside and outside of Japan, as a triumph of an Asian people over a white one.

Japanese leadership of an Asiatic union might very well have been on the minds of some Pan-Asianists from the ideology's inception, but it would be wrong to assume that there ever was any agreement on this issue. On the contrary, Japanese and non-Japanese Pan-Asianists alike had varying ideas about the types of Pan-Asian alliance to be achieved, the methods to be employed, and the alliance leadership to be established. To be sure, Japanese leadership became a very important condition for Japan's own wartime rendition of Pan-Asianism. But it was not a consistent precondition for *all* the manifestations of Pan-Asianism that have emerged over the course of its history. Therefore, it is critical not to confuse the concept with the history. In order to analyze the development of Pan-Asianism properly, one must at first dislodge Pan-Asianism from its overwhelmingly negative consequences.

Moreover, it is not satisfactory to characterize Pan-Asianism as a mere "assertion" as the dictionary definition does. I regard Pan-Asianism as an "ideology" and not simply as an "assertion," "opinion," or even "belief." By claiming that Pan-Asianism is an "assertion," one might diminish or overlook the actual political consequences of what was once a very potent and real ideology. For the same reason, many nationalist movements and other variants of nationalism in the modern era should be understood as ideological doctrines rather than mere assertions or beliefs.[3]

This study, then, refers to an ideology that highlights the fundamental self-awareness of Asia as a cohesive whole, be this whole determined geographically, linguistically, racially, or culturally. Pan-Asianism also assumes that Asia is weak, and that something must be done to make it stronger so that it may achieve recognition by the West. This line of thinking was never an improvised concept, created to provide an *ex post facto* justification for Japan's expansionist war that started in 1931. Rather, Japan's intellectuals and political elites, as well as many of their Asian colleagues, had come to embrace the idea of Asian linkages for quite some time before 1931. Within this broad framework, many Japanese Pan-Asianists, aware of their country's unique position as almost the only Asian country that had escaped colonization, came to believe that Japan had a special mission to save weak Asia from Western domination.

As far as the Fifteen Years' War is concerned, the emergence of the term can be traced to the mid-1950s, when liberal and leftist intellectuals tried to discredit Japan's wartime claim as the liberators of Asia.[4] To them, the war began in 1931, with the Japanese takeover of China's northeastern provinces, and continued uninterrupted until the end of the Pacific

War. The proponents of the term "Fifteen Years' War" treat the Pacific War (1941–45) as the inclusive part of Japan's "war of aggression" that encompassed both the Manchurian Incident (1931) and the *de facto* war with China that started in 1937. By doing so, they reject the conservative rendition of the Pacific War as Japan's "war of no alternative." Conversely, conservatives insist that Japan, an essentially peace-loving power, was encircled and pushed into war by Western imperialists and their pawns. For that reason, the term *"Daitōa Sensō"* (Greater East Asia War), the official name given to Japan's war against the West and the China Incident in December 1941, is the preferred term for the hardest core of those conservatives.

Because of their anti-Communist stance, conservatives were helped by the U.S. occupation and Cold War policies that supported them to steer Japan clear of the Soviet threat in the name of creating a stable ally in the East. Even after the fall of the Soviet Union, many Cold War concerns in East Asia remain vis-à-vis Communist China and North Korea. This enables them to invoke power-political arguments and Japan's unique position, as the only country to have experienced nuclear attacks (with the focus on *"our* suffering" and not "the suffering we inflicted on others"), for the further consolidation of their power base, in effect ducking the accountability question of war in the conservative mainstream of Japan's political discourse.

The question of what to call the war, and which "war" to study, therefore, tends to reflect the hopelessly polarized debate of war history and its unexamined political baggage. The postwar leftist historians and public school teachers in the powerful Teachers' Union (*Nikkyōso*) are countered by the opposite extreme of those who categorically glorify the war, who are often found among conservative politicians and bureaucrats. As such, two dominant and equally dogmatic perspectives have long polarized and stifled the emergence of a more nuanced understanding of the Fifteen Years' War in Japan. The leftist and liberal perspective is referred to by conservatives as the *Tokyo Saiban-shikan* (Tokyo Trial Historical Perspective), suggesting that it represents the perspective of the victor rather than Japan's own. The interpretation that exalts Japan's part in the war, on the other hand, is referred to as the *Kōkoku-shikan* (Imperial Nation Historical Perspective), because of its ultranationalist claim that Japan's war was a holy and just war carried out through the selfless devotion to the emperor and to save Asia from colonialism by making it more like Japan.

Hence there is much in a name. Even beyond any political associations, the alternative term to the "Fifteen Year's War," the "Pacific War" (*Taiheiyō Sensō*), which began with the Japanese attack on Pearl Harbor, poses the obvious problem of unjustly neglecting other theatres of war in East and Southeast Asia. Nonetheless, the "Pacific War" has become a widely used term in postwar Japan without much popular resistance. In the meantime, the concept of the "Fifteen Years' War" has largely remained an academic and historiographical phrase insulated from popular debate, incapable of directly influencing the nature of public discourse concerning Japan's expansionism, since such a public discourse was often stymied and discouraged as an unwelcome distraction from the more immediate concerns of international politics.

In the early 1980s, some Japanese scholars began to advocate the use of "Asian and Pacific War" (*AjiaTaiheiyō Sensō*) to modify what they regarded as the overly simplistic, U.S. perspective-dominant, and geographically limiting "Pacific War." While appealingly encompassing in its geographical scope, however, this term too fails to capture two essential aspects of the war in question. First, the Asian and Pacific War does not fully convey the protracted and prolonged nature of Japan's active military commitment abroad. In spite of the claim that relative calm prevailed and that there were no overt military operations in North China for four years from mid-1933 onward, guerrilla warfare between Japanese and Chinese forces did continue even during that period.

Certainly, the existence of guerrilla war alone would not refute the view that there was indeed a hiatus in intense military activity. Moreover, it is also true that the Kwantung Army's attempt to incite a wide-scale war had already started in 1928, with the Japanese assassination of the Manchurian warlord Chang Tso-lin. Indeed, some scholars offer valid criticism against the term "Fifteen Years' War" on that basis and reject the legitimacy of the Manchurian Incident of 1931 as the war's starting point. Sandra Wilson thus poses the question: "Should we therefore have an 18-year war from 1928 to 1945?"[5]

However, all these arguments against the Fifteen Years' War thesis, in the end, miss the most important point. They take for granted the analytical focus of war as exclusively confined to a situation of somatic violence, without specifying what exactly constitutes a war in the first place.

This point highlights another important aspect of this war, which is its heavily ideologically driven character. If one were to define "war" as a situation of conflict, both physical *and* psychological, between two or more social—often, but not always, state—actors, there emerges a convincing argument for resurrecting the idea of the Fifteen Years' War in a less partisan incarnation. The term "Pacific War" simply does not capture the lasting character of Japan's struggle to locate itself in the changing and volatile international environment. Such a struggle provided the necessary preconditions for the evolution of Pan-Asianism into Japan's official war ideology. It was with the Manchurian Incident of 1931 that Japan was propelled for the first time onto the course of a Pan-Asianist crusade with the initiative of the Pan-Asianist Colonel Ishiwara Kanji.[6] Japan's subsequent state- and nation-building of Manchukuo, its legitimization and escalation of the unofficial war with China that started without a coherent purpose, and its attack on Pearl Harbor and mobilization of the whole of Japan for the construction of the Co-Prosperity Sphere, all referred to the same and consistent ideological core of Pan-Asianism despite the *ad hoc* nature of tactical planning. Thus the role of Pan-Asianism went far beyond the commonly perceived one of legitimizing Japan's war. Rather, Pan-Asianism was an integral part of making and prolonging that war. And for that reason, I opt to employ the term "Fifteen Years' War" in this book fully to express the peculiar character of Japan's battles in both material and nonmaterial spheres.

Justification . . . or Reason for War?

To be sure, the suggestion that Pan-Asianism was much more than an *ex post facto* explanation for Japan's ultranationalist designs and that it was an ideology with palpable political consequences is bound to be controversial. This is so because there is little doubt that the Japanese claim of creating a Pan-Asian utopia, invoked under various propagandistic banners (most infamous of which was the "Greater East Asia Co-Prosperity Sphere"), was an unqualified failure. Therefore, Japan's self-appointed Asian leadership may be viewed cynically as a retroactive euphemism for self-interested exploitation. And, in fact, that is often what it was in practice. At the very least, the manner in which many Japanese not only proclaimed but also acted upon their vision of Pan-Asian reform suffices to defy the all too easily accepted notion of ideology, popularized by E. H. Carr, as providing "a cloak for national policy."[7]

Without the Pan-Asian ideology, it is indeed difficult to appreciate the dangerous earnestness with which Japan went about its imperialist mission, once the government had resigned itself to the Manchurian *fait accompli* of 1931. Beyond the official rhetoric, the comprehensive fashion in which Japan mobilized its population for empire-building through rigorous programs of "re-education," first in Manchuria and later in Southeast Asia, reflects the force and pervasiveness of Pan-Asianism. Time and again, the Japanese occupiers talked of establishing an Asia for Asians: efforts were made with the utmost seriousness to open educational institutions, including elite schools and universities. They claimed that they were developing a new Asian culture in a way that integrated the virtues of both modern and ancient civilizations, and they built facilities for disseminating the new Asian culture, including movie studios, think tanks, printing presses, and cultural associations.[8]

Such comprehensive programs, which were often made into top priorities in Japan's occupation programs, were in Akira Iriye's words "the more grotesque examples of the cultural aspect" of Japan's war in Asia.[9] Notwithstanding the lack of effectiveness of such programs, the fact remains that Japan willingly saw far-reaching reformative implications in what they were doing. That the Japanese not only bothered to talk of grand Asian ideals but also engaged in rigorous social and cultural programs, even under the pressing conditions of war, makes it impossible to argue for the role of ideology as a mere "cloak for national policy."[10] Rather, it was a case of ideology becoming the national policy, providing fundamental continuity and cohesion in Japan's otherwise divided body politic, as well as galvanizing popular support for its war effort.

Typologies of Pan-Asianism

This is not to suggest, however, that Japan's Pan-Asianism did not undergo any changes in contexts, labels, and functions during the Fifteen Years' War. On the contrary, there were at least three major threads in Pan-Asianist thought, which will be discussed in more detail in Chapter 1. The first type of Pan-Asianism was of the kind that emphasized Asian commonalities in the vast philosophical dimension of Asian civilization, which included both China and India. The second type of Pan-Asianism could be defined as the kind that sought to create an alliance (*dōmei* or *renmei*) among Asian nations, frequently, but certainly not exclusively, within the narrower geographical and cultural confines of East Asian (or alternatively, "Sinic" or "yellow-race") nations. Finally, the third type signifies the kind of Pan-Asianism that would become ever more enmeshed with Japan's expansionist and ultranationalist thinking, declaring Japan to be the "Asian alliance leader" (*Ajia no meishu*) in a crusade to save the rest of Asia—again with fluctuating geographical boundaries—from Western imperialism. Categorization of these three strands of Pan-Asianism is crucial, as it enables us to trace systematically different assumptions and emphases that affected the meaning of Pan-Asianism at any given time, and in various individual and historical circumstances that emerged over the course of the Fifteen Years' War.

Existing Literature

In stark contrast to the primacy given to Pan-Asianism in Japan's political discourse before August 15, 1945, the notion that Pan-Asianism acted as a consistent and viable ideological force behind Japan's Fifteen Years' War has so far eluded systematic study. Even the most brilliantly executed historical accounts that examine and integrate nonmaterial aspects of Japan's war with more tangible material considerations tend either to trace the impact of nonmaterial factors only in a piecemeal fashion, or else, to take their importance too readily.[11] Such a lack is all the more confounding in the light of the plethora of diplomatic and military histories of this period, both in English and Japanese, that could potentially and mutually benefit from a further exploration of the role of Pan-Asianism as a propeller for Japan's war from 1931 to 1945.

To be sure, there is a body of important works, both classic and new, in the field of modern Japanese history that in one way or another underscores the significance of Japan's Pan-Asianism in the Fifteen Years' War. To name only a few important examples, in English-language scholarship historians have made invaluable contributions toward our understanding of Japan's Manchurian venture. From the perspective of the origins of the Fifteen Years' War, the classic work on Japan's policy in Manchuria in English is Mark Peattie's biographical study of Ishiwara Kanji.[12] Never a high-ranking officer, Ishiwara nonetheless played a pivotal role in Japan's China policy and is considered to be the mastermind behind the 1931 Manchurian Incident.

From the broader perspective of Japanese wartime imperialism, Louise Young's study on Japan's mobilization efforts for the building of Manchukuo, Japan's puppet state, is important.[13] Sandra Wilson's work also addresses the issue of Japan's imperialist mission in Manchuria, looking at the popular and societal responses to the country's call for comprehensive mobilization.[14] The two accounts put forward contrasting interpretations: the former argues that Japan's mobilization programs for Manchuria were carried out in a "total" fashion, while the latter shows the limited appeal of those very programs. Such different interpretations reveal the complexities and richness of studies on Japan's imperialism yet to be fully explored. On this point, the three volumes of studies on Japanese colonialism and imperialism edited by Peter Duus, Ramon Myers, and Mark Peattie effectively treat many of the most pertinent issues in the scholarship of Japanese imperialism.[15] In addition, works by historians such as Rana Mitter, Tak Matsusaka, Barbara Brooks, and Prasenjit Duara should be especially noted, as they deal specifically with the important topic of the Japanese presence in Manchuria, with varying interpretational and chronological foci.[16]

The state of the intellectual history of this period, too, needs to be noted, as it directly concerns our understanding of Japan's Pan-Asianism. A number of scholars have been paying much attention to the question of how leading Japanese thinkers attempted to reconcile Western ideas with Japanese politics. The works of William Miles Fletcher, Harry Harootunian, Tetsuo Najita, and Graham Parkes, which will be discussed in due course, all serve as important examples in this category.[17]

In Japanese scholarship, the topic of Pan-Asian ideology and Japan's expansionism becomes more convoluted, as it is firmly rooted in and complicated by the debate over the collective and inherited war guilt. Disagreements abound, however, this war has given rise to scores of significant historical accounts in Japanese over the years.[18] Especially, postwar generations of scholars, perhaps less personally constrained by the polemics of guilt and responsibility, have produced some works of significance. A primary example is Yamamuro Shin'ichi's award-winning study of Manchukuo.[19] It is an attempt at explaining the disastrous outcome of Japan's programs in Manchuria that sought to combine the irreconcilable. In it, Manchukuo, like Hobbes's Leviathan and Neumann's Behemoth, is likened to the Greek mythological monster Chimera, whose body consists of Pan-Asian ideology, Japan's ultranationalism, and the newly emerging modern China. Another noteworthy study by Matsumoto Ken'ichi, who is best known for his work on such colorful Pan-Asianist and ultranationalist figures as Kita Ikki and Ōkawa Shūmei, deals with the development of Pan-Asianism in Japan's politico-intellectual life.[20] Matsumoto's critical essay on the writings of Takeuchi Yoshimi, the China expert prominent during and after the war, is especially relevant to the present study. However, since Matsumoto's subtle analysis does not place the role of Pan-Asianism in the context of Japan's policy formulation specifically, it is only suggestive, not quite explanatory, of the force of Pan-Asianist tenets on the country's wartime intellectuals.

In any event, perhaps helped by an increasing interest in transnational history, Pan-Asianism has become something of a buzzword of late. And there have been truly important developments both in English and Japanese scholarship that have opened up new areas of inquiry for the subject, including perspectives from the postcolonial critique in literature, transnational and sovereignty studies, history of imperialism, as well as anthropology.[21]

Still, there remains a question over the puzzling absence of Pan-Asian ideology as a "consistent" analytical component of Japanese expansionism "throughout" the Fifteen Years' War in the existing literature. This oversight sits in dramatic contrast to the attention paid to the role of Emperor Hirohito and the imperial institution, another main ideological pillar propping up wartime Japan, which has remained a contentious topic in historical literature and continues to attract the interest of broader audiences.[22]

Arguably, this neglect of Pan-Asianism as a stand-alone analytical tool of historical study can be explained by the combination of two kinds of difficulties. First, there are theoretical difficulties associated with the study of ideational elements in the field of foreign policy analysis in international relations (IR), the discipline that this examination of "transnational nationalist" ideology of Pan-Asianism necessarily straddles. The most fundamental question from an IR perspective is whether "ideas"—and not just "material interests"—make war. Building on that question, more qualitative difficulties with the study of Pan-Asianism emerge within the narrative of the development of Japanese expansionism. The question thus becomes:

Did Pan-Asianism Make the Fifteen Years' War?

The study of Pan-Asianism in Japan's expansionist past carries with it a unique burden: the thankless task of presenting the perspective of the instigator as well as that of the loser of a devastating war. To be sure, what Japan made of Asia under various utopian declarations was rather a dystopia imposed by the imperialist and militarist aggressor. Japan as the self-professed Asian leader claimed to liberate the rest of Asia but increasingly lost credibility once the gap between rhetoric and practice became wider and more apparent as the war dragged on, causing enormous suffering and deaths of those Japan claimed to liberate. So, the proposition that Pan-Asianism was indeed a powerful driving force behind Japan's expansionism should not automatically imply that the country's conduct during the war was any more excusable.

The romanticism that such an all-encompassing ideology as Pan-Asianism evokes is indeed the pitfall into which some recent "revisionists" in Japan have fallen. Since the late 1990s, the contention that Japan waged the expansionist war in Asia and the Pacific for Pan-Asianism has been a central theme of Japan's war historical debate. Partly as a consequence of the economic downturn and of changing attitudes to the U.S.–Japan alliance in the post–Cold War era, there has been a marked rise in popular interest concerning the interpretation of the war. Some views are indeed alarming. For example, a major movie on the life of General TōjōHideki was released.[23] In it, the wartime prime minister on trial at the International Military Tribunal for the Far East in Tokyo is portrayed as a Japanese nationalist who also genuinely longed for the liberation of Asia from Western powers.

In this vein, the most troubling phenomenon in contemporary Japanese society is the remarkable popularity since the late 1990s of "philosophical" comic books by Kobayashi Yoshinori. Kobayashi's *manga*, compiled into a volume that has sold 560,000 copies within a year of its publication, shows Japan's wartime imperialism in an exceptionally self-glorifying light. "Can you die for your country?" is Kobayashi's provocative question to young readers, who had hitherto been unaccustomed to seeing Japan's war history explained in such a positive and readable way. Kobayashi declares that the Japanese army "bravely fought the white imperialists, who arrogantly regarded colored peoples as lowly primates," while emphasizing such Japanese combat successes in Southeast Asia as the "Fall of Singapore."[24]

The notoriety of Kobayashi's *manga* has elicited responses from many different perspectives, ranging from categorical dismissal to total agreement. Politics soon followed the popular debate, producing controversies with numerous ramifications. To name only a few, discussions have included debates on the rewriting of school textbooks, the government's decision officially to sanction the rising sun flag and the national anthem as the country's standard symbols, the still-intensifying debate over building up Japan's military capabilities, with or without a revision of the

U.S.-drafted pacifist constitution of 1947, as well as the legality and moral judgments over prime-ministerial visits to the Yasukuni Shrine, where Japan's war dead, including those prosecuted as war criminals at the Tokyo Trial, are enshrined. Debates have also been held about hitherto unacknowledged or half-acknowledged atrocities on Japan's part, including biological experiments conducted on prisoners of war, sex slavery, and massacres of local populations in various theatres of war, such as the Rape of Nanking in 1937. As with many other impassioned polemics, these debates often resemble parallel monologues rather than genuine dialogues.

Nevertheless, if there is *ipso facto* importance in the emergence of such alarming trends, it is that they have stimulated a broad-based Japanese desire to shed further light on the war. Until recently, the popular view in Japan tended to regard its expansionist war as an aberration that was chiefly blamed on the "militarists" who led the country (and the emperor) astray. The popular view that the war was an illogical development, though long dismissed in academia as well as in informed circles, as a less than convincing or wholesome explanation of the war, accounts for the complacency and lack of self-reflection of which Japan's conservative politicians as well as the Japanese nation as a whole are often accused by its neighbors.

In this interpretation, "events" somehow took hold of the nation and altered Japan's attitudes to foreign policy and security dramatically. In contrast to its exemplary internationalism as a signatory of the Versailles-Washington system in the 1920s, Japan began the 1930s with a new expansionist role by occupying Manchuria. Later, when the country's decision-making mechanism was hijacked by a group of militarists, Japan's claim to regional leadership took a decisive leap and initiated more aggressive "advances" into China and Southeast Asia. This was done under the banner of the "Co-Prosperity Sphere," which then led to the monumental blunder of waging a war against the United States. Clearly, there is a tremendous sense of comfort in viewing Japan's expansionist policy as a result of this deficient clockwork and of the actions of a certain group of power-hungry militarists, rather than as a consequence of a single master plan or a consistent set of goals. Yet by concentrating excessively on "what went wrong," one becomes so immersed in details and points of obvious disruption that one risks overlooking some fundamental currents of continuity. Japan's policymakers, as well as a much broader corps of those who actually mobilized for the war, succumbed to the temptation of Pan-Asianism. In that process of elevating Pan-Asianism as a national and state ideology, the role played by intellectuals of varying stripes before and throughout the Fifteen Years' War was significant. Pan-Asianism, espoused by many such unlikely allies of war, might have been beautiful in theory, but it was dangerously naïve as a war aim.

Central Questions

Despite the difficulties outlined above, the examination of Pan-Asianism in the Fifteen Years' War promises fascinating rewards of both practical and conceptual significance not confined to the field of Japanese history. At a practical level, the topic of ideology in wartime Japan offers a useful handle on the contemporary debate concerning Japan's alleged return to nationalism warranted by the popular "revisionist" interpretations of the far right. At a conceptual level, the study of Pan-Asianism and Japan's foreign policy cuts to the core of the old debate between those who argue for or against the importance of ideational elements in international politics, especially as it concerns analyses of war. Therefore, the central questions raised in this book are both specific and of a general nature. Specifically, what was the role of ideology in Japan's foreign policy in the Fifteen Years' War? And more generally, what does Japan's case tell us about the role of ideology in foreign policy?

Admittedly, the theme of continuity is necessarily an unsettling one as it strikes at the heart of the question of Japan's responsibility for the war. In this respect, there is an interesting parallel to be drawn between Japanese and German historiography. Most famously, Fritz Fischer in his 1961 *Griff nach der Weltmacht* (Grab for World Power)[25] has argued that Germany had expansionist aims and that World War I came about more by German design than by accident. The notion that the German elites deliberately opted for expansionism as an alternative to social democracy debunked the myths that Germany had engaged in a defensive war to escape the Great Power "encirclement," thereby, to the unease of many, linking the foreign policies of Wilhelmine and Nazi Germany.

Certainly, the idea that Japanese foreign policy in the Fifteen Years' War was marked more by continuity than change from the previous period is not a novel line of academic enquiry.[26] Furthermore, the continuity thesis is not tantamount to a purely intentionalist interpretation of Japanese expansionism in a manner advanced by the Fischerian school. On the contrary, the Manchurian Incident marked a decisive turning point for Japan's expansionism in the next decade and beyond. Up until then, Japan's approach to developing and safeguarding its Manchurian interests had been far more cautious and gradualist in character. Neither do I suggest here that Japan thenceforth pursued a policy of expansion steadfastly, grabbing every opportunity for conquest in a premeditated and systematic fashion. Nonetheless, the focal point of this study is that Pan-Asianism itself provided some basic undercurrents of continuity in Japan's otherwise fragmented policymaking body, and moreover enabled the comprehensive mobilization of its population. In this sense, the theme of continuity cannot be overemphasized.

In the following pages, the story of how Pan-Asianism shaped Japan's foreign policy will unfold in a roughly chronological order: each chapter will focus on a different theme in order to highlight the various functions of Pan-Asianism at different times and under varying circumstances. Chapter 1 seeks to set out the basic premises of this study by further defining Pan-Asian ideology. This will be followed by a more empirical discussion in Chapter 2 of the origins of Pan-Asianism, concentrating on the period prior to the Fifteen Years' War.

Chapter 3 examines Japan's shift in foreign policy orientation in the 1930s, from internationalism to Pan-Asianism, amid increasing economic uncertainty and domestic instability. Here, the ideological impetus of Pan-Asianism behind the Manchurian Incident of 1931, as well as the Incident's implications for Japan's international position, is duly considered. Following the military takeover of Manchuria, Japan set out to establish Manchukuo under the Pan-Asian slogan of "harmony of the five races." Chapter 4 examines Japan's peculiar imperialism in this puppet state that was the foremost embodiment of its Pan-Asianist experiment.

Far from Manchuria, Pan-Asianism entered the prime space of domestic politics in the second half of the 1930s, with the outbreak and the escalation of Japan's China War. This important period, characterized in many historical analyses by its "fascistic" turn, is the focus of Chapter 5. The first part of the chapter will provide a background to the period's looming sense of national crisis, with dramatic events unfolding both at home and abroad that contributed to the political and intellectual climate at that time. The discussion will include the intensification of the cult of Emperor Worship, as well as other potent political ideologies that competed and interacted with the chauvinistic rendition of Pan-Asianism, namely, fascism and Marxism. The second part of Chapter 5 will take a look at the role of intellectuals in this period. Our attention will turn especially to those intellectuals who participated in the legitimization of Japan's war through their activities in Prime Minister Konoe Fumimaro's brain trust known as the Shōwa Research Association (SRA). They helped the government reformulate Pan-Asianism as the country's official war aim of constructing a "New Order" and eventually a "Co-Prosperity Sphere," thereby further officializing and politicizing Pan-Asianism.

On the eve of Pearl Harbor, Pan-Asianism assumed an even more critical role in unifying Japan's otherwise divided policymaking body. Unlike the more *status quo*–oriented view of Pan-Asianism that was tolerant of national differences within "Asia," the type of Pan-Asianism that now gained a prominent place in Japan's political discourse was an ever more blatantly Japan-centric and revisionist ideology originally promulgated under the leadership of Konoe Fumimaro during the intensification of the China War. Chapter 6 examines how many literati, including even those who had previously regarded the China War as a deviation, began to embrace the view that Japan was indeed embarking on a war of "world historical significance" and of Pan-Asianist salvation, encouraged by the country's initial combat successes in the war against the West.

Chapter 7 looks at the Japanese Empire's last hours, paying special attention to the question of what propelled the country to continue professing its chauvinistic rendition of Pan-Asianism, even when its defeat was drawing ever nearer. In this final chapter, the main theme is Pan-Asianism in action, as observed in the struggle of Japan's cultural elites in attempting to reform the societies of the occupied territories. Often, those who engaged in the cultural programs did not necessarily accept the militarist and imperialist ideology of wartime Japan. However, their belief at least in the legitimacy of Japan's Pan-Asianist mission in the "Co-Prosperity Sphere" provided them with enough justification and drive to take active part in the occupation programs. This shows the overpowering and dangerous attraction of Pan-Asianism until the very end of the Fifteen Years' War.

Finally, a word about sources is due. As mentioned, the story of Japan's Pan-Asianism in the making of the Fifteen Years' War has so far been recounted only in a fragmented way, presumably owing to various technical as well as interpretational difficulties. One such difficulty is how exactly to construct a balanced picture from available materials. This book consults a range of policy-related primary source materials such as conference proceedings and memoranda. Essential as it is to this study, however, the examination of policy development alone would rarely suffice to tell the story of Pan-Asianism beyond the obvious fact of policy deliberation and adoption. Thus this book also attempts to draw from contemporaneous writings, journals, and diaries as well as some postwar memoirs of the people involved. The goal is to penetrate the deeper ideological layers of Pan-Asianism and show how it adapted to different requirements demanded by varying beliefs, ideas, events, and circumstances.

In the end, what follows is an account of an ideology that started, sustained, and even prolonged Japan's war from 1931 to 1945. The ideology of Pan-Asianism was paramount and pervasive in Japan's wartime thinking, acting as a guide to action, to policy, and ultimately to mobilization. Even when the ideology was not explicitly professed, I would argue that it was always present and implicit. But when the war finally ended, the ideology was much reduced and treated at best as a vacuous concept that had never amounted to anything and at worst as a disgraceful tool of Japan's wholly self-interested imperial conquest without any legitimate basis in transnational aspirations. Insistence on both views obviates a more nuanced understanding of history.

However, even if one does not accept either of those extreme positions, one is often confused by the historical ambiguities of the Pan-Asianist concept itself. This makes it difficult for some to appreciate Pan-Asianism's basic importance in the making of that very history. For instance, the critic and Chinese literature scholar Takeuchi Yoshimi (1910–77), who was himself a most ardent supporter of Japan's Pan-Asianist war aim during the Pacific phase of the war, reflected in a self-critical fashion in 1963:

> [W]hile difficult to define, one has to acknowledge that a spiritual mood that can only be called Pan-Asianism, and ideologies built upon it, did emerge at various points throughout Japan's modern history. But unlike such official ideologies as democracy, socialism, or fascism, Pan-Asianism does not contain any inherent value, and so cannot be perfectly self-sufficient. It necessarily appears as a concept dependant on other ideologies. Therefore, it is impossible to trace the historical development of Pan-Asianism *per se*. The notion that Pan-Asianism can be historically recounted is, perhaps, a biased perspective tainted with the ideology of historicism.[27]

I beg to differ. This study argues that from its birth in the late nineteenth century to its demise by the end of the Fifteen Years' War, the most basic claim of Pan-Asian ideology remained remarkably consistent. Pan-Asianism, even though it both competed with and interacted with other political constructs of both left and right, was not entirely the "dependent" ideology as Takeuchi claimed it was after the war.

The present book's concern is not limited to the demonstration of the importance of Pan-Asianism in the Fifteen Years' War. A better understanding of this historical episode in the history of this particular—and presumably "peculiar"—empire sheds a useful light on factors and forces that govern international politics to this day.

This is so because pan-nationalist ideology, such as Pan-Asianism, remains one of the most cogent but overlooked doctrines that have shaped and continue to shape the contemporary world. Pan-nationalism, as a paradoxical "transnational nationalist" ideology that aspires to transcend smaller nation-state boundaries, has come to play a prominent role in today's international politics, albeit often under different labels. These include regionalism, postcolonialism, and globalization that together constitute a post–Cold War international order. More directly, the sorts of grievances and ambitions that Japan's wartime Pan-Asian ideology tried to highlight have disturbingly familiar echoes, for example, in today's jihadist or Pan-Islamist rhetoric. In this cross-referential sense, the study aims to tackle, at its basic conceptual core, the broader, pervasive, and enduring question of the emotional engine behind other pan-nationalist movements in general. That in turn makes this study not only a story of a nation at war, but also of certain political ideologies with extraordinary staying power and all-encompassing appeal.

1
Conceptual Roadmap: Tea, China, and Leadership

Seen from the sweeping perspective of world history, Pan-Asianism was but one of the many products of the intellectual atmosphere of post- and counter-Enlightenment Europe that begot modern nationalism. Rationality and reason, the primary claims of the Enlightenment for a desirable human condition, came to be countered by urgent emotional need for blood, soil, and belonging. An elemental desire to belong to a group was said to be just as important as food, communication, and procreation. The notion of national spirit, which referred to the spiritual and organic basis for unity of a people or a nation, was to be one of the most influential political forces of the nineteenth and twentieth centuries.

The idea that the nation represented some sort of a "natural" or "organic" condition of human existence was critical in modern nationalist thinking. It provided a seemingly legitimate basis for a state, hence Ernest Gellner's succinct definition: "Nationalism is primarily a political principle, which holds that the political and the national should be congruent."[1] Such linking of "nation" and "state" effectively marked the beginning of a new category of political relations—international relations—by which is in fact meant "inter-state" relations, or a sovereignty-based international order. It sought to secularize the Westphalian state system, which still smacked of the conservative Holy Roman imperial order. Thus modern nation-state nationalism developed on the ruins of the medieval ecclesiastical order and feudalism in Western Europe.

Despite its avowedly secular outlook, however, modern nation-state nationalism was not only a political but also a normative principle with vast potential for serious internal contradictions. It posits that nations, like organisms, exist, and that they should have the right to determine

19

for themselves what sort of political communities they would like to form within a given territory. In this sense, nationalism is an ideology based on a moral principle asserting not only how the world is, but also how it ought to be. This meant that nationalism in territories under imperial and colonial rule had an even greater share of psychological as well as practical hurdles to overcome. When applied to their empires, Western imperialists were determined that they would not easily extend to others what they claimed for themselves as a natural right and organic condition for their own, such as the right to national self-determination and sovereignty. These inconsistencies were often justified, at the height of New Imperialism, in terms of *mission civilisatrice* and colonial discourse of race, Social Darwinism, and other scientific as well as pseudoscientific claims of progress.

Even in the "West" itself, the purportedly natural combination of blood-and-soil nationalism and secular values of modern state institutions was a potentially dangerous marriage. The "organic" nation represented counterevolutionary, counter-Enlightenment impulses while the "secular" state signified Enlightenment principles. The two categories did not always counterbalance one another. For example, Germany and Japan, both relative latecomers to the world of international power game, were from time to time tempted to emphasize the mythic and the irrational dimension of its nation to compensate for the lack of supposedly naturally emerging political will that seemed more securely institutionalized and readily observable in the British parliamentary system, French republic, or U.S. constitutional democracy.

Like numerous other nationalist movements and their variants outside the context of nation-state nationalism, pan-nationalism was a solidarity movement that developed in tandem, and often in conflict, with the emerging international order dictated by the great powers. Its utmost characteristic is clear in its etymology of the Greek prefix "pan," meaning "all." Overwhelmed, lesser groups were often compelled to seek strength in numbers—in their "trans"-nations—by claiming to transcend already existing political arrangements and nation-state boundaries for a greater union that would be fit enough to survive in the competitive environment of international politics. As such, pan-nationalism has been most prominent when the legitimacy of newly emerging nation-state boundaries was still being contested, as in the times of the disintegration of the Russian, Chinese, Ottoman, and Austro-Hungarian Empires and the decolonization of Western colonial empires in Asia, Africa, and America.

From this, there appear to be at least two identifiable features that are common to all pan-nationalist movements. First is the grand scale of the unions they aspired to, and second, their desire to combine separate and already existing arrangements by appealing to a yet greater cohesive factor. Therefore, pan-movements have been defined as "politicocultural movements seeking to enhance and promote the solidarity of peoples bound together by common or kindred language, cultural similarities, the same historical traditions, and/or geographical proximity. They postulate the nation writ large in the world's community of nations."[2] Examples of such pan-nationalisms are numerous and include Pan-Slavism, Pan-Germanism, Pan-Europeanism, Pan-Turanism, Pan-Americanism, Pan-Asianism, Pan-Arabism, Pan-Africanism, and Pan-Islamism.

Specifically, Pan-Asian nationalism or Pan-Asianism had innately contradictory elements. It at once represented a resistance to and acceptance of new conceptions of social distinctiveness born primarily, though not exclusively, of external origins. Therefore, at the very onset, the Pan-Asianist claim that Asia as a unique group constituted a viable counterbalance to the West required an intellectual challenge of internalizing those new conceptions among Asians themselves. The next step was to invoke the memory of the old and the lost. Where memories of old traditions did not suffice, early Pan-Asianists resorted to an imagined Asian past of great spiritual and geographical dimensions to legitimize their claims of a singular identity. After all, the power of history could only be rivaled by the power of imagination.

With such prevailing intellectual *milieux* in mind, this chapter examines the origins of Pan-Asianist thought, or more precisely "thoughts." Concentrating on the conceptual side of the ideology, that is, Pan-Asianism as a tempting theory more than problematic practice, the chapter traces how it evolved and developed prior to the outbreak of the Fifteen Years' War. The following sets out the starting assumptions of this study, a high-resolution roadmap, so to speak, to which one can readily refer later. The goal here is to demonstrate that the seemingly indefinable concept of "Pan-Asianism" can indeed act as a useful and consistent analytical tool for the Fifteen Years' War.

At the very basic level, Pan-Asianism was not simply an expression of antagonistic feelings toward the West, but an attempt precisely to overcome such negative, pent-up feelings. Although its emotional premises were clearly reactionary, and in some categories of Pan-Asianism, anti-Westernism was certainly part of it because of the very international power dynamic that produced such an ideology in the first place, Pan-Asianism's foremost objective was to assert a positive Asian distinctiveness, without categorically denouncing or dehumanizing its Hegelian Other. Importantly, Pan-Asianism of all persuasions, including the more Japanese chauvinistic rendition of it, did not reject modernity as a route to recovering Asian greatness. Pan-Asianism claimed that "Asia" existed as a cohesive whole and that it was a viable force to be reckoned with by the West. In spite of the ideology's changing functions and surrounding operational circumstances, Pan-Asianism was to remain more or less unchanged in such basic aspirations.

Pan-Asianism: "Pan," "Asia," and Other Contested Concepts

Pan-Asianism existed in various historical contexts while being repeatedly reinterpreted by groups and individuals who embraced it. The term is inevitably loaded with unresolved historical judgments, overwhelming most analysts with its blatant paradoxes and contradictions in practice. That is one of the main reasons why Pan-Asianism has not yet benefited from any consensus even as to its very existence, much less its meaning. Such a problem of elusive definition is necessarily intertwined with a problem of any discourse analysis executed in varying practices of translation, transliteration, and extrapolation. This lack of clarity in Pan-Asianism itself poses a great problem of consistency in what it is that one is actually analyzing.

Here, the general problem of what Douglas Howland terms "semantic transparency" in Japan's adoption and adaptation of Western political concepts emerges. He criticizes the way in which a clear meaning of ideas is often sacrificed when the historian identifies certain key terms as originating from "Western political discourse" and researches how they arrived at the present meanings, without considering that those concepts might have continued to evolve in different contexts, Japanese or Western, in multiple parallels though not necessarily in sync.[3] The fluidity of language and its meaning acquires even further layers of complexity as certain concepts are thrown back and forth between different linguistic and historical contexts. That is why we need to be particularly aware of what is being understood as "Pan-Asianism." Moreover, the heavily contested nature of the very term, in which the uniqueness of "Asia" was expressed in shifting and sometimes overlapping categories—be they "race," "language," "culture," "religion," or "spirit"—could potentially blur much needed analytical clarity. However, those difficulties do not render analysis impossible. For this reason, it is useful at this point to further define Pan-Asianism, along with other fundamental, yet very much contested concepts, that form the core of this book's discussion.

Pan-Asianism, which proclaimed the universal origins of some sort of an "Asian" group, consisted of two irreducible features irrespective of its changing contexts, functions, and manifestations. The first feature of the ideology was the notion that "Asia," be it a geographical, racial, or cultural body, existed. The second feature was the assumption that "Asia" needed to be liberated from Western imperialist domination and to balance the West in a viable manner. In other words, the ideology's basic contention emanates from a rather simple and straightforward awareness that there was a collective entity that could be called Asia and that there was something fundamentally wrong with Asia, which had to be put right. Around these two basic objectives of achieving self-awareness and external recognition Pan-Asianism is further elucidated as a type of discourse that sought to instill an Asian identity in Asians themselves in order to attain parity with the West, which had placed Asia in a humiliating secondary position in the politics of nation-states. This definition provides relatively less value-laden, more neutral, and most critical components of the ideology than its historical associations would tempt one to assume.

Despite the above definition, "Asia" (Ajia in Japanese [sometimes *Ashu*], which is usually synonymous with Tōyō, literally the eastern ocean but simply signifying the East) still remains a historical concept. As with any historical and evolving concept, including the "West" and "Europe," it is necessarily susceptible to varying interpretations and shifting boundaries. Nonetheless, it seems reasonable to say that whatever the alleged basis of Asian singularities, the nineteenth-century concept of "Asia" initially relied upon colonial suppositions and perceptions about its distinctiveness, expressed in the language of "race," "culture," "religion," and perhaps all inclusively, "civilization." In this sense, "Asia" was very much a product of centuries of social construction by outsiders rather than insiders. However, even more critically, once accepted by "Asians" themselves, "Asia" became not simply an externally imposed and artificial construct but an identity. As the constructivist axiom of "The world is in the eye of the beholder" dictates, the discourse of Pan-Asianism initially signified that process by which Asia started to take on a life of its own, as Asians themselves came to acknowledge the viability and vitality of its existence.

Indeed, in Prasenjit Duara's instructive analysis, this Pan-Asianist discourse was in large part about civilization and not just about nationalism and racism.[4] Here, "civilization" does not connote only the limited dimensions of advancement, whether it be measured by certain European social, political, technological, or indeed cultural standards, but refers to the existence of some higher, transcendental authority, as Christianity and later Enlightenment values were for Western civilization. Accordingly, Duara traces the genealogy of civilization and its alternative understanding away from the European civilization based on its own particular values by following the reasoning of Oswald Spengler's *Decline of the West* (and Toynbee's interpretation and popularization of it).[5] In this assessment, an alternative civilization, like its Western counterpart, derived its transcendental authority from the dialectic of spiritual, moral, and universal dimensions that were found in Confucian rationality, Buddhist humanism, and Hindu logic. Such spiritual authority acts as a civilizational universalizer, providing a "recognition function" between Other and Self or, in this instance, "East" and "West."[6] In the broad category of civilizational discourse of Pan-Asianism, race, nation-state nationalism, and obviously the "transnational nationalist" ideology of pan-nationalism too, all became built-in components of "Asian civilization." In this view, nationalism and racism were very much part and parcel of that new civilizational discourse.

However intangible or slippery such an emerging view of Asian distinctiveness was, Japan, as the first competitive Eastern player in the great power politics, began to be attracted to the potential mobilizing power of Pan-Asianism. This mounting sentiment came to be called *Han-Ajiashugi* (Pan-Asianism),[7] *Ajiashugi* (Asianism), or *Dai-Ajiashugi* (Great Asianism) and manifested itself in such political slogans and programs as "Asia is One," "the same letters, the same race," "the Asiatic Monroe Doctrine," a "New East Asian Order," and finally the "Greater East Asia Co-Prosperity Sphere" over the subsequent course of history.

Although such differing "labels" of Pan-Asianism are important and illuminating, dwelling excessively on the terminological differences when they clearly refer to the same basic features of Pan-Asianism would be fruitless. Lessons should be drawn from the recent debate on resurgent Islamism that suffers from such linguistic preoccupations without being able to address a more important question of what such terms as Pan-Islamism, Islamism, and Political Islam might have in common for the use of analytical consistency. Thus it seems sufficient to clarify in the beginning that those various Japanese terms for Pan-Asianism, be it *Han-Ajiashugi*, *Ajiashugi*, or *Dai-Ajiashugi*, constituted alternative terms for grappling with the same two main contentions—namely, that Asia as such existed and that Asia needed to be recognized. The resounding appeal of Pan-Asianism was the idea that strength in relation to its Other could be found in numbers. In that sense, Pan-Asianism appealed to effectively the same sentiments as any other pan-nationalisms, identifiable by their two most apparent common features: first, the grand scale of their wished-for unions and second, their desire to encompass separate and existing units by the yet greater cohesive factors that bind them, making them "transnational nationalisms."

What then was this "Asia," which was still an obscure and emerging construct, even—or rather, especially—for Asians themselves? According to the present geographic convention, a demarcation line between Europe and Asia starts from the Arctic Ocean along the east of the Ural Mountains, turning southwest along the Zhem to the north and the West of the Caspian Sea, eventually following the Kurma-Manych Depression into the Sea of Azov. And while its geographical boundaries have been repeatedly contested and modified, its size was always vast.

Ancient in its etymological origin, the term "Asia" had also undergone transformations in its meaning since the time of the ancient Greeks. According to *Encyclopædia Britannica*, "Asia" covers about 30 percent of the landed area of the earth, and the term was probably derived from the Assyrian word *asu*, simply meaning "east," or more broadly, the direction from which the light, or the sun, rises.

To a carefully qualified degree, one could apply Edward Said's Orientalist critique and its general power dynamic to the case of Asia as a whole. Considering the very etymological origins, it seems at the very least safe to accept the fundamentally "Western" inception of "Asia" as Europe's "East."[8] This is not to assume uncritically that "Asia" was a result of a uni-directional transference of knowledge from the West to the East. Nevertheless, there is some sense in attributing the origins and general character of such a discourse to that overwhelming power structure and the power-political realities of the past few centuries. In a similar vein, there is also some important truth to the view that Japan, too, created its own version of "Orientalism" in its ascent as a modern power, by claim-ing hegemony of discourse over other Asian nations, especially Korea and China.[9] However, from the perspective of this book, it is important to remember that Japan's hegemony in Asia before and throughout the

Fifteen Years' War, unlike Western imperialism, was never an established power relation but remained a contested and evolving idea vulnerable to outside attacks, both from the East and West. The multidirectional nature of the construction and dissemination of Asian discourse was self-evident in many instances, especially in the formulation of Pan-Asianism as will be shown in the following.

Another problem with viewing Asia solely as "Japan's Orient" is the very historical context in which nationalisms of other Asian nations were equally newly emerging, often internally divided entities in the larger discourse of modern nation-state nationalism. In claiming Asian leadership by at once distinguishing itself from and identifying with Asia, Japan also had to navigate the ocean of emerging Asian nationalisms in which it was not at all clear who, or which group, would be the one to determine its national self. This classic problem of national self-determination, that is, the identification of who is the self that determines, was a persistent challenge in Japan's Asian policies, especially vis-à-vis China but also in almost all other parts of Asia Japan occupied.

Going back to the origins of Asia, its vast size makes it difficult to identify a watershed moment for Western acquisition of knowledge about it, in the way the Napoleonic expedition to Egypt was for the Orient in Said's view (and here, the term "Orient" is employed to suggest precisely the way Said intends, which applies mostly to the Arab and Islamic Middle East). Nevertheless, it is reasonable to conclude that gradual and far-reaching European links to the outside world, as early as the time of the Arab seafarers and Marco Polo, had a part to play in the formation of Asia in Western cultural discourse, a process that accelerated precipitously in the age of New Imperialism. In the Anglophone world, ideas about the East were most readily and intensively formulated through the British Empire's sustained presence on the Indian subcontinent and its advance into as far east as the eastern coast of China and Japan.

Along with the emerging colonial discourse of this period, a prevalent subscription to a linear view of history developed. What compounded such a view was the rise of Social Darwinism and various scientific as well as pseudoscientific theories of race, which reinforced the justifications for Western colonial rule under which Asia came to be depicted as a culture or civilization synonymous with what was quintessentially exotic, incomprehensible, and racially (and thus inherently) inferior. Indeed, that sense of irreconcilability of Asia with Europe is proclaimed in one of the most celebrated phrases of the English language:

Oh, East is East and West is West, and never the twain shall meet,
Till Earth and Sky stand presently at God's great Judgment Seat;

Because of this opening passage, Rudyard Kipling's *The Ballad of East and West* (1889) is too often quoted out of context as a verse emphasizing differences between East and West. Moreover, misinterpreted as a suggestion of unconditional Western supremacy, the lines selected above have undeservedly earned the poet a racist label. Contrary to the popular reading, however, the paragraph continues:

But there is neither East nor West, Border, nor Breed, nor Birth,
When two strong men stand face to face,
though they come from the ends of the earth![10]

The ballad is about two soldiers from East and West coming to recognize in each other an identifiable sense of honor, heroism, and bravery, despite the differences in their physical appearances. It should then be read as an appreciation of humanity.

Perhaps more importantly, however, the unwavering fact remains that Kipling sees a world as deeply divided between East and West. In addition, he seems to imply, by "never the twain shall meet," that the sort of gap existing between the two camps is unbridgeable by any means. Neither does Kipling see East and West as perfect equals, as the title of another of his well-known verses *White Man's Burden* (1899) clearly shows.[11] If anything, the verse, which was written at the time of the Spanish-American War, demonstrated his genuine belief in the West's *mission civilisatrice*. Quite faithfully, then, Kipling's view mirrored the conventional and colonial perception of the time that gave rise to Pan-Asianism, in other words, the notion that the world was compartmentalized into two distinct—purportedly civilizational—camps. Furthermore, this binary world was in the end characterized by an utter "imbalance," rather than "balance," of power. In the classical balance-of-power sense, indeed, the lack of equilibrium in the world governed by relative material capabilities made even the ancient, proud, and gigantic East look like a burden on a white man's shoulder.

Given this perceptible imbalance, it was in the end understandable that pioneering Pan-Asianists and Asian nationalists (and the two groups were by no means mutually exclusive) should have thought the most convincing argument for the strength of Asian civilization to be lying in the qualitative world of art, spirituality, and aesthetics. The long-simmering

European interest in Eastern religions provided a ready basis for such a claim of Asian greatness. Indeed, the European understanding of Eastern spirituality, which developed in tandem with and sometimes in outright contradiction to the colonial discourse of racial inferiority of the colored peoples, went back at the very least to the eighteenth century. *Chinoiserie* was more than a fashion trend in furniture and porcelains adorning European salons and princely estates. Voltaire, in his criticisms of Catholicism, claimed the Chinese Confucian way of governance to be superior. The German Romantics and their fascination with Sanskrit scriptures led to the nineteenth-century wave of translations of Indian and other Eastern religious scriptures into various European languages.

In the minds of enthusiasts, Eastern religions and their emphasis on their seeming universalism appeared to suggest that they provided a desirable alternative to the dogmatism of Christianity as a world religion. Such an awareness coincided with the growing interest since the 1860s in the occult and spiritualism, particularly in the New World, which added to the popularity of various paranormal experiments including spirit-channeling, mind-swaying, and table-turning. That was yet another manifestation of an attempt to overcome what were increasingly being regarded as the shortcomings of Europe's religious orthodoxy and scientism.

The establishment of the theosophical doctrine by Helena Petrovna Blavatsky (1831–91) was in many ways a culmination of those different approaches to spirituality gaining popularity in the second half of the nineteenth century. The Theosophical Society, founded in New York in 1875 and publicized by its most effective spokeswoman Annie Besant (1847–1933) put forward the importance of intuitive insight and possibility of spiritual evolution in one's own lifetime as well as through reincarnation. The influence of Indian religiophilosophical traditions on the doctrine was immense. Conversely, theosophy's impact on the educated classes of India, where the society had moved its headquarters in 1878, were at once considerable, in turn affecting the spiritualist emphasis of the Pan-Asianist discourse to follow.

For Pan-Asianists in search of higher transcendental authority for the legitimization of the unity of Asia, aesthetics was another useful category. In the end, beauty was exempt from primarily quantitative and exacting standards of power politics. Western connoisseurs, too, responded in a positive manner to such a Pan-Asianist insistence on the excellence of Asian arts, as had been the case with the *Chinoiserie* trend earlier. The French Impressionists are known for their embrace of Asian, partic-ularly Japanese, arts. Anglophone poets, too, followed suit. Delighted to find "simple" beauty in Asian arts and deploring the increasingly "modern" and tainted conception of beauty in European arts, W. B. Yeats (1865–1939) wrote to Noguchi Yonejirō, his Japanese poet friend:

> I take more and more pleasure from oriental art; find more and more that it accords with what I aim at in my own work. The European painter of the last two or three hundred years grows strange to me as I grow older. . . . All your painters are simple, like the writers of Scottish ballads or the inventors of Irish stories. . . . I would be simple myself but I do not know how. I am always turning over pages like those you have sent me, hoping that in my old age I may discover how. . . . A form of beauty scarcely lasts a generation with us, but it lasts with you for centuries. You no more want to change it than a pious man wants to change the Lord's Prayer, or the Crucifix on the wall [blurred] at least not unless we have infected you with our egotism.[12]

The lack of modernity and the sense of inertia, identified as the primary weakness of Asia in power-political terms, were now increasingly viewed by some as its strength, at least in certain spiritual and artistic senses, irrespective of the actual validity of Yeats's claims about the resilience, consistency, or even simplicity of Asian aesthetics.

It is true that Pan-Asianism on the whole did not escape the immediate power-political considerations of Asia's weakness, as will be seen in Japan's attempt at fomenting modern Asian nationalisms under its leadership. Much as though Japanese Pan-Asianists might have seen the world in "realist" (i.e., material) terms, however, they ultimately had to refer to the subjective richness of Asian ideals and moral superiority over the West to assert Asian unity and greatness because Asia—and Japan as the leader of Asia—remained weak in the sense of relative capabilities. That is why Japan's eventual expansionist course became as much a quest for material survival as a topsy-turvy cultural mission coined in the language of greater Asian civilization, compelled by the development of international politics and history as well as Japan's reading, and increasing misreading, of its own position within it. All the same, the most critical source of strength of Pan-Asianism can be located in metaphysical, philosophical, and cultural arenas of intellectual endeavor, which all

Pan-Asianists claimed, or implicitly accepted, as the major sources of Asian civilization.

At this point, it is useful to remember the three types of Pan-Asianism offered at the beginning of this book. Each one of the three types of Pan-Asianism had different assumptions about the method to be employed and the alliance to be achieved. There was first and foremost a Pan-Asianism that emphasized Asian commonalities in the vast philosophical dimension of Asian civilization, encompassing even the two great civilizations of China and India, whose Asiatic features, its advocates claimed, were for instance embodied in the sophisticated art of appreciating and drinking tea. What made this Asia stick, despite its internal religious, linguistic, and cultural differences, was the peace-loving disposition of Asians who find joy in the everyday act of tea-drinking and even manage to bring it onto a higher spiritual and artistic plane.

Second, there was a type of Pan-Asianism that sought to create an alliance among Asian nations, frequently, but not exclusively, within the narrower geographical and cultural confines of East Asian (or alternatively, "Sinic" or "yellow-race") nations and adhering to the requirements of modern nation-state nationalisms. Finally, the third type of Pan-Asianism represented a strand that would become enmeshed with Japan's expansionist and ultranationalist programs, declaring Japan to be Asia's preordained alliance leader (*meishu*) in a crusade to save the rest of Asia from Western imperialism, again with varying geographical boundaries. These three major threads of Pan-Asianism—Teaist, Sinic, and Meishuron (Japan-as-a-leader thesis) Pan-Asianisms—are differentiated primarily by methodological specificities and the form of an eventual Pan-Asian union.

Teaist Pan-Asianism: Pan-Asianism as a Civilizational Discourse

The first type of Pan-Asianism is the movement readily associated with Okakura Kakuzō, a.k.a. Tenshin (1862–1913). This brand of Pan-Asianism has the most all-encompassing vision for both geographical and conceptual boundaries of Asia as a single group. While it first emerged in tangible written format slightly later than the following two types of Pan-Asianism, it is the most philosophically important, as well as the most historically illuminating, type of Pan-Asianism that affected all threads of thinking in the history of Pan-Asianism.

The movement was born out of an attempt by Asian intellectuals, writing frequently in English, to assert in literature, art, and critical writings a vision of a unitary East. In spite of the complete Western technological and material dominance in all aspects of life that awed and overwhelmed Asia, this thread of Pan-Asianism preached that Asia could achieve the goal of self-awareness and external recognition by asserting itself as a nonmaterialist pan-nation, which was nonetheless comparable, even possibly superior, to Europe in its cultural and philosophical substance.

Okakura, the art historian and critic, tirelessly advanced this view that the spiritualism and ancient wisdom of Asia could provide a corrective to the materialism of the West. He summed up his Pan-Asianist vision in the preamble of *The Ideals of the East* (1903):

> Asia is one. The Himalayas divide, only to accentuate, two mighty civilizations, the Chinese with its communism of Confucius, and the Indian with its individualism of the Vedas. But not even the snowy barriers can interrupt for one moment that broad expanse of love for the Ultimate and Universal, which is the common thought-inheritance of every Asiatic race, enabling them to produce all the great religions of the world, and distinguishing them from those maritime peoples of the Mediterranean and the Baltic, who love to dwell on the Particular, and to search out the means, not the end, of life.[13]

Contrary to the prevalent image of Pan-Asianism as a simple manifestation of raw and destructive antagonisms, such as anti-Westernism and anti-imperialism, these Teaist Pan-Asianist intellectuals did not present East and West as inherently hostile to one another. Rather, they found in the world of high culture a possibility of creating a common bond among Asians, and perhaps even more crucially, of gaining what they believed to be a deserved recognition from the West, that Asia was a civilization *par excellence*. As such, Teaist Pan-Asianists aspired to recognition without specifically calling for the achievement of material parity with the West, much less achieving it by military means. Moreover, although wary of an indiscriminate flow of Western influence, they acknowledged that the West might indeed have enough useful knowledge and ideas from which the East could very well benefit.

Okakura, whose *The Book of Tea* (1906) still enjoys some renown outside Japan, was himself a typical product of such a cosmopolitan East-West fusion.[14] Born into a silk merchant family in the port city of Yokohama, he was educated from an early age in English at a Christian mission school and later in classical Chinese and Japanese at a Buddhist temple, followed by a course of studies at the newly founded Tokyo Imperial University. Through his association with his philosophy professor Ernest Fenollosa, an avid collector from Massachusetts of Buddhist art, Okakura dedicated himself to the preservation and development of national traditions in Japanese art during his early professional career as an Education Ministry bureaucrat. He was eventually appointed as the director of the National Academy of Arts in Tokyo in 1890 at the age of twenty-eight.

In 1901, after having lost a factional battle within the academy, Okakura left for India, where he spent a year traveling and living in the household of Rabindranath Tagore (1861–1941). Tagore and Okakura saw themselves as brothers-in-arms, embracing many common interests and agendas, not the least of which was their preoccupation with the future of their respective national traditions and their dedication to all-round artistic education. At the Bengali poet's suggestion, Okakura wrote *The Ideals of the East* based on numerous conversations he had with Tagore and his disciples, including his nephew and independence activist Surendranath Tagore. Strongly echoing the philosophical outlook of Tagore along with that of Swami Vivekananda (1863–1902), a Bengali spiritual leader whom Okakura much admired and had traveled many miles to meet, the book marked the beginning of Okakura's role as a spokesman for Asian civilization. He was especially welcomed by Japanophile audiences in Boston, where he became the acquisitions adviser for the Chinese and Japanese collections at the city's Museum of Fine Arts in 1904.

Since the later phase of Okakura's career flourished in this function as a cultural and civilizational interlocutor for Bostonians, the development of his Pan-Asianist discourse as a result of his exchange with Indian elites is often overlooked or forgotten. However, the importance of his Indian filter, through which such concepts were rendered to him, and its influence on the very language in which he perfected his Pan-Asianist worldview, commands attention. For instance, Okakura's language closely paralleled Vivekananda's assertion that Asia produced giants in spirituality while the Occident produced giants in politics and science. For Vivekananda, as well as for Okakura, Eastern metaphysics must ultimately be deemed superior to Western science, but it would inevitably require some convincing. The similarities between the two become indisputable when Vivekananda posits his grim assessment of Western science, alluding to the Aristotelian model of cause-and-effect, to his English audience on his lecture tour:

The Eastern mind could not rest satisfied till it had found that goal, which is the end sought by all humanity, namely, Unity. The Western scientist seeks for unity in the atom or the molecule. When he finds it, there is nothing further for him to discover, and so when we find that Unity of Soul or Self. . . . When I see a chair, it is not the real chair external to my eye which I perceive, but an external something plus the mental image formed. Thus even the materialist is driven to metaphysics in the last extremity.[15]

This is not to say that Okakura was the first Japanese to be affected by the subcontinental rendition of Eastern-versus-Western metaphysics and spirituality. The idea that the birthplace of Buddhism provided the universalizer of Eastern civilization was already felt in the early Meiji period, when Japanese Buddhism looked to Sri Lankan and Indian Buddhist revivalism in the face of severe persecution by those who attempted to establish Shinto as modern Japan's new state religion. Anagarika Dharmapala (1864–1933), one-time theosophist, the founder of the Maha-Boddhi Society, and the foremost advocate of Sri Lankan nationalism, developed close ties with Japanese Buddhists in the 1880s and 1890s, visiting the country at length on four different occasions.[16] His Japanese colleagues included Takakusu Junjirō (1866–1945), a Sanskrit scholar and student of Max Müller at Oxford; Tanaka Chigaku (1861–1939), a former Buddhist monk whose reading of apocalyptic Nichiren Buddhism inspired many ultranationalists of the 1920s and 1930s; and Hirai Kinzaburō (1859–1916).

Hirai was a linguist, philosopher, Spiritualist, and educator, who in 1885 opened a private school called Oriental Hall in Kyoto. The school was meant to counter the popularity of Niijima Jō's Christian academy Dōshisha, which Hirai regarded as a dangerous educational institution aimed at wholesale Westernization. At the 1893 World's Parliament of Religions in Chicago, Hirai indicted the hypocrisy of American Christians by declaring:

If you remember the sense of excitement you felt when you gained independence from Britain's oppressive rule, why don't you please take the lead and lend a hand in the abrogation of the unequal treaties that are sapping Japan's national interest. . . . In fact, the Christian missionaries dispatched from your country witness our plight, but until now, they have never bothered to report the realities of our situation. Is this called Christian justice?[17]

This incident was reported with much enthusiasm and approval in the Japanese national newspaper *Asahi*, with a description: "[T]housands present agreeing with Hirai's indictment greeted him with a standing ovation, waving handkerchiefs and shouting 'Shame on you! Shame on you!' at Christian missionaries in the audience."[18]

That Japan, and by extension Asia, was a humiliated victim of Western arrogance had long been a prevalent sentiment. The rendition of the West as a mechanistic, materialistic, soulless, and aggressive civilization was also not new, as its genesis could be traced within the counterevolutionary line of nationalist argument advanced by the German Romantics and Russian Slavophiles within the peripheral West itself. As such, the idea of soulless and individualistic "West" and its hypocrisy were no news to Okakura's audience abroad, but already an established discourse before his clear articulation of his Teaist Pan-Asianism. The originality of Okakura therefore rested not in his awareness of the world's power imbalance, or in his reiteration of rather unoriginal characterizations about the two camps (for instance, the masculine "West" and feminine "East"), but rather in his suggestion of an entirely new way for Asia to overcome that imbalance in international relations. He wanted Asia to apply a fundamentally different definition of power lying beyond any tangible material measurements. In short, he tried to settle the lack of "hard power" with an abundance of "soft power." In his evocative rhetoric, he enunciated his belief that Asia was quite capable of resisting the temptation of being further "civilized" in the Western sense because Asia was, and always had been, a civilization on a par with Europe, and all that needed to happen was for both camps to come to terms with that already existing truth.

Thus Okakura's Pan-Asianism conjures up an image of an across-the-border peace movement of sorts. In such a view, Mahatma Gandhi, although he eventually came to reject Western influences categorically and thus clearly differed in that respect, shared a great deal in common with Okakura. Gandhi arguably realized the Teaist Pan-Asianist precepts in the *satyagraha* movement and turned them into a singular and nonviolent method of accomplishing awareness and recognition, in stark contrast to the Japanese chauvinist interpretation of Pan-Asianism that would fully develop over the course of the Fifteen Years' War.

In spite of his spiritual emphasis, however, in analyzing Okakura's Pan-Asianism as recorded in his English writings, it becomes clear that even his Pan-Asianism could not be separated entirely from Japan's ascent as a rapidly industrializing military power just as India's desire for independence and Bengali-led Indian nationalism influenced his Asian awareness. In *The Awakening of Japan* (1905), for instance, Okakura put forward what could easily be interpreted as an apologia for Japan's militarist turn. He wrote: "When we emerged from our sleep of three centuries international conditions were changed indeed!"[19] It was because "[e]vents were taking place in Asia which threatened our very existence" that Japan was compelled to resort to force, as "[n]o Eastern nation could hope to maintain its independence unless it was able to defend itself from outside attack."[20] For him, Korea was within Japan's lines of legitimate national defense perimeters, and it was because "the independence of the peninsula was threatened by China in 1894" that Japan was compelled to go to war.[21] And the same consideration of international emergencies, he insisted, operated as the *jus ad bellum* for the war with Russia starting in 1904.

In face of such passages, it would be farfetched to say that Pan-Asianism, even in Okakura's all-embracing art historical, philosophical incarnation, was an apolitical ideology dissociated from Japan's exclusive nationalism. Neither is his suggestion about Japan's age-old lack of desire for aggrandizement convincingly substantiated. Japan's proactive expansion can for instance be traced to Toyotomi Hideyoshi's 1592 Korean invasion, or more recently in the Meiji era, Saigō Takamori's 1873 proposal to send a punitive expedition to Korea. Furthermore, some would argue that Japan's nineteenth-century development of Hokkaido in the north can be attributed to a similar expansionist impulse.

In that sense, the Ruskinian plea of *l'art pour l'art* on a high order was clearly not the only abiding principle of this brand of Pan-Asianism. Nevertheless, it is worth noting that Okakura time and again made a point of saying that the use of force was not the *preferred*—though regrettably perhaps *necessary*—method of achieving political ends for Asia. Harking back to his thesis of the East's peace-loving proclivity even more strongly, his most celebrated work, *The Book of Tea*, put forward "Fain would we remain barbarians, if our claim to civilization were to be based on the gruesome glory of war. Fain would we await the time when due respect shall be paid to our art and ideals."[22] He further bemoaned: "When will the West understand, or try to understand, the East? We Asiatics are often appalled by the curious web of facts and fancies which has been woven concerning us. We are pictured as living on the perfume of the lotus, if not on mice and cockroaches,"[23] "[y]ou may laugh at us for having 'too much tea,' but may we not suspect that you of the West have 'no tea' in your constitution?"[24]

For Okakura, tea was a metaphor for the East's unwarlike constitution of which the West unwisely made light. But perhaps more importantly, Okakura's frustration with the *status quo* international order was doubly amplified and complicated by the very fact of Japan's own military aggrandizement, which increasingly conflicted with his own conception of Asian-ness and upon which topic he stopped commenting entirely, at least in writing, after *The Book of Tea*. However, Japan had no other choice, Okakura seemed to imply, when he concluded: "He [the West] was wont to regard Japan as barbarous while she [the East] indulged in the gentle arts of peace," but now that Japan had become a military power, "he calls her civilized since she began to commit wholesale slaughter."[25]

Another important facet of Teaist Pan-Asianism was that in such a sweeping vision of a unitary East, the most fundamental questions—who exactly was an Asian and what constituted the territorial and "racial" limits of Asia—were left undefined. The concept of Asian unity here allowed for elusive and shifting boundaries that amounted to a loose cluster of extensive but only vaguely generalizable attitudes toward life on the part of non-Western, nonwhite people. The result of this "West and the Rest" worldview was a somewhat ambiguous and internally inconsistent claim of Asia that potentially included all conceivable places, races, philosophies, and religions, provided they were not part of the seemingly unitary West. Thus the discussions of Pan-Asianism ranged in groups and geography not only from Japan to India but into the Arabian Peninsula and sometimes even Africa. Okakura summed up this expansive and elastic view of Asia as much in the following:

[I]t is also true that the Asiatic races form a single mighty web. We forget, in an age of classification, that types are after all but shining points of distinctness in an ocean of approximations, false gods deliberately set up to be worshipped, for the sake of mental convenience, but having no more ultimate or mutually exclusive validity than the separate existence of two interchangeable sciences. If the history of Delhi represents that Tartar's imposition of himself upon a Mohammedan world, it must also be remembered that the story of Baghdad and her great Saracenic culture is equally significant of the power of Semitic peoples to demonstrate Chinese, as well as Persian, civilization and art, in face of the Frankish nations of the Mediterranean coast. Arab chivalry, Persian poetry, Chinese ethics, and Indian thought, all speak of a single ancient Asiatic peace, in which there grew up a common life, bearing in different regions different characteristic blossoms, but nowhere capable of a hard and fast dividing line. Islam itself may be described as Confucianism on horse-back, sword in hand. For it is quite possible to distinguish, in the hoary communism of the Yellow Valley, traces of a purely pastoral element, such as we see abstracted and self-realized in the Mussulmân races.[26]

Thus for Okakura, Asia was about a common way of being based on love and peace, overriding even the ethnic and religious differences within, creating a common outlook on life that could uniformly be identified as "Asiatic" over far-reaching physical as well as psychological space.

This elasticity of Asian-ness was duly reflected in the geographic scope of Asia in Japanese thinking during the Fifteen Years' War. Japan's Asian boundaries shifted in accordance with war situations, first starting from Manchuria, then extending to North and South China, and finally into Southeast Asia and the Pacific. While the Japanese government's ultimate Pan-Asianist program of the "Greater East Asia Co-Prosperity Sphere" only reached as far west as the occupied areas of present-day Southeast Asia, its understanding of Asia easily extended as far as and even beyond the Indian subcontinent through to the Middle East and Africa, just as Okakura had earlier advanced.

Sinic Pan-Asianism: Pan-Asianism as a Basis for East-Asian Alliance

Narrower in geographic scope but more logically formulated than the above all-embracing vision of Pan-Asia were the ideas of a shared culture as a basis for a loose union, such as Chinese-Japanese solidarity. This second type of Pan-Asianism had already been established in Japan's intellectual discourse by the late nineteenth century, as some of the most illustrious characters within Japan's public life naturally took to the idea of "the same letters, the same race" (*dōbun dōshu*). The idea of this union (*dōmei* in Japanese, as in alliance of equals) connoted some sort of an inherent cultural bond among East Asian (*Tōa*), yellowed-skinned races (*ōshoku jinshu*). Hence "culture" and "race" were defined more often than not by the identifiably common features conferred by centuries of Chinese influences, rather than by the all-inclusive "Asian" philosophical and spiritual outlook on life that Okakura saw as a universalizer of Asian civilization, transcending even the Himalayan divide. The idea that those who used the same writing system should be considered the same race proved compelling enough for the educated strata of Japan, and even to some in China, understandably because of the simplicity of its argument. Especially, educated Japanese had long been devoted Sinophiles. They were almost invariably versed in classical Chinese poetry, Chinese arts, and Confucian ethics, in which field the Japanese had developed their own flourishing scholarship. Particularly notable was Japan's synthesis of Chu Hsi's teachings culminating in the neo-Confucianism formalized by Hayashi Razan (1583–1677) and also the ancient Wang Yang-ming Confucianism advanced by Ogyū Sorai (1666–1728), which became popular among the samurai class. Thus for Japan's educated class inheriting this Sinophilic tradition, the notion of forging a cultural and possibly political bond between China and Japan was at once reasonable and attractive.

In 1898, Japan's first party cabinet was formed under the premiership of Ōkuma Shigenobu. Ōkuma differed from previous leaders in his active pursuit of a friendly policy toward China. Thus his premiership created a perfect opportunity for those who supported the idea of *dōbun dōshu* to turn the concept into a tangible organization. Having secured governmental support, the two cultural organizations of the Same Letters Society (*Dōbunkai*) and the East Asia Society (*Tōakai*) merged to form the East Asian Society for People of the Same Letters (*Tōa Dōbunkai*). The society's stated objectives were fourfold. They were (1) to preserve and protect China, (2) to help improve the conditions of China and Korea, (3) to study the current affairs of China and Korea for the above purposes, and (4) to initiate a national debate.[27] One of the most notable accomplishments of this organization would be its spin-off organization: the Tōa Dōbun Shoin (East Asian Same Letters Academy), active in Shanghai from 1900 to 1945. It was a three-year higher school, partly supported by Japan's Foreign Ministry, that boasted diplomats, journalists, and politicians among its graduates. The school was particularly famous for its compulsory senior thesis project that required its students to embark on extensive research trips into the interior of China. Conversely, the society also ran preparatory schools in Japan for Chinese students seeking admissions to Japanese universities.

Besides such an educational endeavor, the broadness and ambiguous tone of the society's goals reflected a range of political agendas harbored by its members. Certainly, the members did not all have the same ideas about Japan's specific role in the society's essentially, but not exclusively, cultural undertakings. This was because the very topic of China generated conflicting views and policy preferences, which in turn colored their opinions about the format of a possible Sino-Japanese union of the future. In real political terms, the instability of China generated two dissenting views on Japan's foreign policy. It came down to the ultimate question of whether to align with the great powers or with the Chinese nationalists.[28] The real situation was not as clear-cut, of course, but Japan's China policy around the turn of the century nonetheless fluctuated between these two positions.

Consequently, the Tōa Dōbunkai membership encompassed a wide spectrum of views on the political future of China, and by extension, Japan's possible leadership role within East Asia. The society's first president was Prince Konoe Atsumaro (1863–1905), the father of Konoe Fumimaro (sometimes pronounced more formally as Ayamaro), who would become a central figure in the formulation of Japan's Pan-Asianist policy of the late 1930s. Educated at Bonn and Leipzig in the theory of constitutional government, the senior Konoe served as the head of the Peers Academy and the chairman of the House of Peers. The prince's privileged background made him an influential and widely traveled critic of Japan's foreign policy, and he made effective use of this position in his active, albeit short, life. He asserted his views on a Sino-Japanese alliance in a controversial 1898 article entitled "Let Nations of the Same Race Unite and Discuss Chinese Questions."[29] In it, Konoe called for an alliance of equals between China and Japan, criticizing that "In recent times, Japanese people have increasingly grown conceited owing to the country's victory [in the Sino-Japanese War] . . . [e]specially, those residing in various parts of China treat Chinese as Europeans do."[30]

While Konoe admitted that Japan was indeed more modernized than China, he warned that there was no legitimate basis for competition between the two countries of the same race. To him, "Asia's future, in the end, lies in the ultimate struggle between different races (*jinshu kyōsō*)," and even if "changes in situations [between Japan and Qing China] should occur due to temporary diplomatic strategies. . . . Chinese and Japanese would need to stand together against the arch-enemy of the white race."[31] Confrontational and anti-imperialist in its general tone, this article was introduced in *Die Frankfurter Zeitung* as a dangerous statement that might in turn intensify the widely held notion of "yellow peril" in Europe and the United States.[32]

There are at least three possible formative influences on Konoe's Pan-Asianism. In his early childhood, he was privately tutored in Chinese classics by Iwagaki Gesshū (1809–73). Iwagaki was not a conventional classicist, as he consciously tried to apply his scholarship to practical problems of economics, politics, and international relations. Iwagaki's adventure novel, written in 1875, was an account of a warrior from a fictitious country modeled on Japan, which defeats Britain, thereby liberating Qing China and India from their colonial yoke. The story ends as the country prepares to counter another impending threat from the north, Russia.[33]

The second influence on the formation of Konoe's Pan-Asianism was his direct exposure to European imperialism as a young adult. On passing through the Straits of Taiwan en route to Europe, he saw the Pescadores, situated between Chinese mainland and Taiwan. Seeing numerous French flags waving in the sky" after the Sino-French War (1883–85), he noted that "blue-eyed men have occupied the islands," and wondered in his diary if "those Westerners would encroach upon my country next."[34] Generally, it is not difficult to see how foreign travels and studies serve as a wake-up call for one's nationalist and pan-nationalist consciousness, with ready examples to be found in the community of Chinese students and exiles in Japan burgeoning after 1896. Such rising national consciousness led to the founding of the Chinese Revolutionary League (Tung Meng Hui) under the leadership of Sun Yat-sen (1866–1925) in Tokyo in 1905.

The third formative influence on Konoe was his friendship with Arao Sei (1859–96), around whose advocacy of the preservation of Chinese integrity Konoe developed a philosophical basis of his public activity. Arao was trained as an Army intelligence officer and in that capacity moved to China in 1886. Having secured the friendship of Kishida Ginkō (1832–1905), a China expert, journalist, and the proprietor of the Sino-Japanese trading company Rakuzendō, Arao came to know politically conscious Chinese as well as Japanese operators in China. Through his information-gathering activities, he became convinced that China was suffering from old age, and Japan's policy should aim at forging a strong commercial alliance between China and Japan to revive old China. This conviction eventually led him to resign from the armed service and establish the Institute of Sino-Japanese Economic Research (Nisshin Bōeki Kenkyūjo) in Shanghai in 1890. He was forced to close shop and return to Japan following the outbreak of the Sino-Japanese War (1894–95), but was nonetheless encouraged by the prospect of Japan's victory on the basis that the collapse of the corrupt *ancien règime* would surely resurrect China. In the same vein, he argued against the Japanese demand for indemnities and territorial concessions from China, stating that Japan, as an Asian neighbor, should not act like other imperialist powers. Such a move would, he argued, obstruct the fostering of a vibrant Sino-Japanese trading bloc. Arao's insistence on an equal Sino-Japanese alliance through development of trade resonated with Konoe's pragmatic and incremental approach to his Pan-Asianist ideals.

Aside from Konoe, another figure with notable Sinic Pan-Asianist sympathies in the original Tōa Dōbunkai membership was the future premier Inukai Tsuyoshi (1855–1932), who headed the East Asia Society, a precursor to the Tōa Dōbunkai. Sympathetic to modern Chinese and Asian nationalist aspirations, his commitment to helping out Asian nationalists was well-known. His house in Tokyo served as a haven for political refugees from all over Asia, including Indochina, India, and China. The son of a classical Chinese scholar and himself well-versed in Chinese classics, Inukai was immensely admiring of China's cultural legacies.

For him, the question of Japanese superiority in Asia was a simple fact of power politics to be reckoned with, but never the absolute determinant in the broader power configuration that surrounded the two countries of Japan and China. Such a view was in general agreement with that of Konoe. But Konoe saw the cultivation of friendships with the ruling elites of the existing Qing regime—for example, his class equivalent—as the most effective route to equal partnership, leading him to state that to "study the China Questions, one must associate not only with China's politicians and men of high aspirations (*yūshika*, or more commonly 'fighters') . . . but also with her upper class."[35] In contrast, Inukai saw a realization of modern Chinese nationalism as an imperative step toward such an equal partnership. To be sure, such differences in viewpoints reflected in part Konoe's short life that ended before the fall of the Qing dynasty. However, it is not difficult to imagine that the aristocratic Konoe preferred the preservation of the *status quo*, with its class system intact, more than Inukai, who directly supported revolutionary causes of other Asian nationalists.

Even so, upon reflection, Konoe and Inukai were more similar than not in their belief that a sense of Sino-Japanese solidarity could be nurtured without sacrificing the countries' respective nationalisms. Their ideological assumptions were encapsulated in such key words as "partnership," "alliance," "union," "racial struggle," and most pronouncedly "China," with the fundamental understanding that China provided an ancient cultural bond of strength, as well as a current political problem of weakness in East Asia.

Indeed all those concepts were at play in the writings of a popular cultural critic and writer Takayama Rinjirō a.k.a. Chogyū (1871–1902) at the turn of the century.[36] His 1898 article for the semimonthly *Taiyō*, of which he was the editor in chief opens with an arresting declaration: "Race is the greatest fact of history. Most of the existing cultural differences are based on racial differences."[37] Following a racial determinist line of argument, he depicted the world as divided into the broad "Aryan" and "Turan" racial camps, which more or less coincided with Okakura's perception of the East and the West.

While all-embracing in its geographical claim (e.g., Turkish, Hungarian, and Finnish peoples were purportedly extracted from the same Turan racial stock, as proven by their linguistic similarities, although Indians and Persians were excluded because of their Indo-European origin), Pan-Turanism, in Takayama's eyes, specifically identified Japan and China (even though the majority Han Chinese were usually excluded from various discussions of Pan-Turanism) to be of vital importance in resurrecting the past glory of the Turan race as a whole. He stated:

> Japan and the Chinese Empire, as the last nation-states of the Turan race, must embrace each other and lend support to each other, pledging to share in each other's fate. China is our only ally. . . . The racial struggle is the most critical struggle. . . . The Japanese nation should not determine its attitude by the sentiment of Japanism (*nihonshugi*) . . . when we observe the Far East question from a perspective of historical and racial struggle. . . . [T]he fate of the Turan people is a life-or-death problem for us the subjects of the Japanese Empire.[38]

While reminiscent of Okakura's claim in its geographical vastness, Takayama's specific focus on the necessity to unite Japan and China while respecting the existing smaller nationalisms and alliance-making found a closer ideological kin in the Sinic thread of Pan-Asianism embraced by Konoe and Inukai. Nevertheless, it would perhaps be giving too much credit to Takayama as a thinker to call him a Sinic Pan-Asianist. He is best known for his advocacy of "Japanism," which attempted to create a uniform moral system for Japan based on the nation, history, and state, making him more ideologically inclined to the third category of Pan-Asianism that extolled Japanese leadership in the Asian union. Besides, though hugely popular in his own time, he only had a few years of prominence in Japan's public discourse, making it doubly difficult to account for the development of his political view, which seems to have been still evolving at the time of his untimely death. Or, perhaps more cynically, he might have been the type of "thinker" who more or less attached himself to theories and languages that were deemed fashionable at any given time, Pan-Turanism and Sino-Japanese alliance both being perfect examples of such vogue. His half-baked and confused understanding of Pan-Turanism, which was the claim popularized by the Ottoman scholar and activist Ziya Gökalp (1876–1924) that Turkish, Mongolian, Finnish, Hungarian, Japanese, and other languages originated in the land of Turan northeast of Persia, itself corroborates this view.

In the end, Takayama's understanding of this already convoluted racialist ideology was premature at best. It nonetheless shows the prevalence of different pan-nationalist thoughts and their perilous transmutations within Japan's mainstream intellectual opinion. It also shows that Japanese understanding of racial determinism, like Okakura's understanding of Asian spirituality that interacted with the Bengali-led Indian nationalist discourse, had a non-Western source. It fed off the pan-nationalist doctrine laboriously arrived at by another aspiring modern power—Turkey. Therefore, while it is important to point out direct and more obvious Western influences conferred by the likes of Count de Gobineau and Houston Stewart Chamberlain on this line of thinking, one must not fail to acknowledge the confluence of ideas shared by the two non-Western powers in the making with similar grievances and ambitions. To certain Japanese intellectuals such an interaction was at once reasonable and reassuring.

Certainly, there were those who showed more determined dedications to the Sinic Pan-Asianist cause without resorting to fanciful racialist arguments. Reflecting a desire to see a stronger China, some took decisive actions to encourage modern Chinese nationalism. For example, Miyazaki Torazō, a.k.a. Tōten (1871–1922) born in the same year as Takayama, was a Byronian, or perhaps more accurately, Lafayettesque romantic. Inspired by the prospect of revolution in China, he spent a substantial period of his life assisting with Sun Yat-sen and Chinese nationalists, as a publicist, financier, supplier of arms, and combatants. Yamada Yoshimasa, touted as the first Japanese to have died for the Chinese Nationalist cause in the short-lived Wuchang Uprising (1911) led by Sun Yat-sen, shared Miyazaki's intense passions. Similar dedications were also displayed by Umeya Shōkichi, a film tycoon who established a precursor body to the giant movie studio Nikkatsu. Though not a combatant in the field, he gave up the bulk of his fortune to aid Sun Yat-sen's revolutionary ambitions.

Born to a noted progressive family active in the Freedom and People's Rights Movement (*Jiyū Minken Undō*) of the 1880s and 1890s, Miyazaki was educated at a mission school as well as a private school run by the journalist Tokutomi Sohō. His education in nineteenth-century European liberalism was a guiding light for his equally revolutionary activities in Korea and the Philippines. Like many other *Minken* believers who professed Pan-Asianism, he approached international politics in terms of the nineteenth-century European liberalism of Giuseppe Mazzini's persuasion, upholding the view that democratic rights could and should be accorded to individual nations. For this to happen, however, the nations suffering under imperialism must first be liberated and must determine their own destinies. In such a process of national awakening, he saw Japan as being able to provide practical support, as he tried to show by his own example. To this end, he wrote an autobiographical account of his revolutionary life and ideas—influential in both Japan and China—that widely spread the thoughts and aspirations of Sun Yat-sen, *My Thirty-three Years' Dream* (1902).[39]

Because of its recognition of really existing or nascent nation-state nationalisms within a greater pan-union, Sinic Pan-Asianism, which advanced collaboration and alliances with Japan's closest neighbors, rode the rising historical tide of such internationalist norms as national self-determination, international law, and sovereignty without much resistance. Thus proponents of this variety of Pan-Asianism could best be described as "pragmatic utopians." They attempted to configure various Asian nationalist aspirations to the international order, while still wholeheartedly accepting the fundamental Pan-Asianist grievances of "something is wrong" and "something must be done with Asia (and especially China)" to prepare for the ultimate racial struggle between the white and yellow peoples of the world, but perhaps in a more metaphysical than literal sense.

Meishuron Pan-Asianism: Pan-Asianism as a Japanese Crusade

Sinic Pan-Asianism viewed a strong future China as an extension of Japan's national interest vis-à-vis the West. Conversely, there were those who saw a weak China as an immediate threat to Japan's national and regional interests. This growing preoccupation was reflected in the call for Japan to take on a leadership role in "building" or "founding Asia" (*kōa*). Then, too, Uchida Ryōhei (1874–1937), an original member of Tōa Dōbunkai, was a notable revolutionary who aided, like Inukai and Miyazaki, Sun Yat-sen in his nationalist revolt. As the founder of the ultranationalist organization Kokuryūkai (Amur River Society, established in 1901), he had much in common with Tōyama Mitsuru (1855–1944), who had two decades earlier co-founded a similar far-right organization called Genyōsha (Dark Ocean Society). The Kokuryūkai was so named because of Uchida's view that Japanese should take control of the Amur River Basin in anticipation of a Russian advance to the south.

And so, in the beginning of the twentieth century, both Uchida and Tōyama rallied for a hard-line policy against Russia, while materially and physically supporting the causes of Asian nationalists. These included the Korean noble Kim Ok-kyun; Rash Behari Bose, a Bengali revolutionary in exile in Japan from 1915 because of an assassination attempt against the Viceroy of India Lord Hardinge; and most famously, Sun Yat-sen.[40]

Although allies in matters related to those persecuted nationalists, Uchida and Tōyama differed sharply from the more *status quo*-oriented Sinic Pan-Asianist thinking, which after all respected the self-determination and integrity of China, and accepted the existing international order and political realities dictated by the Western great powers. While the Sinic Pan-Asianists saw only a limited supportive function for Japanese nationalism within the context of modern Asian nationalisms, members of the Genyōsha-Kokuryūkai persuasion increasingly came to believe that the Japanese Empire had an active role to play in transforming China and other Asian nations in the image of Japan. And in trying to achieve those ends, they often resorted to violent means.

Indeed, the rising consciousness of Japan's leadership role in this Meishuron category of Pan-Asianism was tightly interlocked with international political events. In the late 1880s and 1890s, the Genyōsha was deeply involved in Korea's pro-reform Tonghak movement, whose millenarian and grass-roots activities precipitated the intervention of Qing China at the request of the Korean government, effectively leading to the Sino-Japanese War. In 1904, Yi Young-gu (1868–1912), a Tonghak leader who assisted Japan's war efforts against Russia by mobilizing his troops, and Song Pyŏng-jun (1858–1925), an interpreter for the Japanese Army Commander in Korea during the Russo-Japanese War, formed the pro-Japanese reformist political organization Ilchinhoe (Advancement Society or Isshinkai in Japanese) in 1904. The society identified with

Japanese success as a modern power, and positively interpreted Japan's defeat of Russia, unlike the pro-Russian and pro-Chinese government, and became the first successful mass-based political party in Korea.[41] Uchida, who in 1906 obtained a post on the staff of Itō Hirobumi, Japan's resident-general in Korea, acted as adviser to this movement, and worked to galvanize popular support for Japan's leadership in modernizing the country.

The Ilchinhoe shared many of Meishuron Pan-Asianist concerns about the future of Asia and its security that went beyond exclusive Korean nationalism. The society was greatly inspired by the theory of integration formulated by Tarui Tōkichi, who will be discussed further. It was also rightly preoccupied with the Russian threat from the north. As a preliminary step toward achieving an Asian federation, the society proposed to carry out a fundamental reform by expanding Korea's productive and agricultural industries. Such a plan also extended to a proposal that Yi lead half a million to one million Ilchinhoe members, along with civilian volunteers, to develop Manchuria in anticipation of a revolution in China, at which point they would declare a confederate state of Japanese, Koreans, Manchus, and Mongols to provide a bulwark against Russian advance. Such an advocacy for a multiethnic state supported and reinforced the ethnological and geolinguistic argument that Manchus were an ethnically distinct group closer to Japanese and Koreans than Chinese.

In many ways, the characterization of the Genyōsha and Kokuryūkai and their many spin-off societies simply as ultranationalist organizations is one-dimensional. While their paternalistic insistence on Japanese leadership cannot be denied, the followers of the Meishuron doctrine preferred to see both the Sino-Japanese and Russo-Japanese Wars as collaborative efforts with Korean modernizers to prevent Chinese and Russian imperialist advances. While the eventual Japanese annexation of Korea in 1910 revealed that their government acted on an old-style imperialist principle, the Genyōsha-Kokuryūkai revolutionaries spoke against the annexation, leading Uchida to indict the government, which in turn led to the dissolution of the Ilchinhoe. Almost a decade later, the March First (*Samil*) Independence Movement of 1919 eliminated any illusions about Korean compliance as the Japanese gendarmerie brutally suppressed nationwide protests and nonviolent calls for Korean national self-determination. In recounting the history of the Ilchinhoe and their dashed hopes of partnership with Japan, Uchida lamented, well after the deaths of Yi and Song, in 1932: "Those in the [Japanese] government themselves are corrupted by the Western philosophy of utilitarianism, and since the Meiji period, they have been mistreating Korea and China, . . . going right against the very Japanese spirit."[42]

Thus a certain type of life philosophy celebrating self-sacrifice, moral rectitude, dedication to goals, and purity of motives—still observable in present-day *yakuza* gangster mythology—were important features of Meishuron Pan-Asianists. Such a philosophy often attracted the type of basically well-meaning but impulsive and often reckless young men who drifted to the Asian mainland in search of great adventure, who came to be called *tairiku rōnin* (literally, a continental drifter, or a masterless samurai on the continent) and who formed an important part of ultranationalist/Meishuron Pan-Asianist organizations.

According to their particular meta-theoretical logic, even the resort to violence would be immune to and above the rule of law as long as their motives were pure, such as helping out the underdog and punishing the enemies. On the one hand, the Genyōsha had its immediate origins in various democratic rights-inspired revolutionary programs of the 1870s and 1880s, which attracted figures like Miyazaki. On the other hand, the coercive nature of their methods and their increasingly Japan-centric views tended to terrorize and antagonize the very people they claimed to help, eventually giving rise to the climate of fear, producing a counterproductive condition for the propagation of their purported ideals.

The excessive sense of Japanese-ness in the Meishuron argument had old roots. It followed from the nativist traditions of the late eighteenth century in which "national learning" (*Kokugaku*) scholars, such as Kamo no Mabuchi (1697–1769) and Motoori Norinaga (1730–1801) attempted to revive interest in Japanese cultural traditions. By rejecting the primacy of the Buddhist and Confucian heritage, *Kokugaku*—combined with the Mito School of nationalist teachings, which emphasized internal reform to resist foreign encroachments—acquired a xenophobic edge, finding its expression in the "Revere the Emperor, Oust the Barbarians" (*sonnōjōi*) movement on the eve of Japan's opening to the West.

The Meishuron moral code, justifying Japanese leadership in Asia and the use of force to achieve desirable ends, was articulated in the 1933 official publication by the Kokuryūakai. It summarized the philosophical works by such protonationalists of the late Edo period as Honda Toshiaki and Yoshida Shōin, who pondered the ways in which Japan would best survive in a hostile world. It states:

The very active spirit towards the outside world, kindled in the heart of those pioneers, suggested that the era had come in which the long suppressed traditional spirit (*dentōteki seishin*) would be resurrected. This in turn provides a glimpse into the coming of a governance that guarantees a future leap of the Imperial Nation of Japan.[43]

Hence the process by which the Genyōsha-Kokuryūkai came to embrace the mythic sense of Japan as Asia's alliance leader seemed well complete by the 1930s. In effect, dual characteristics came to predominate this final strand of Pan-Asianism: devotion to the Japanese Empire and grievance about a weak Asia. The argument ran that for Asia to be stronger, it must become more like Japan, which had managed to modernize without sacrificing the superior spirit of ancient Japanese values embodied by its imperial institution. This line of thought was to find powerful expressions in the words and actions of charismatic leaders such as Kita Ikki and Ishiwara Kanji. Still later, Japan's Pan-Asianist programs would exhibit an unmistakable ultranationalist impulse to "Japanize" (*nipponka*) its occupied territories and make all Asians into the Japanese Emperor's subjects (*kōminka*).

While the Meishuron argument constituted a critical component of Japan's wartime Pan-Asianism, it is important, however, to recognize that the idea of Japan holding a unique position in Asia was not only promoted by this category of Pan-Asianists alone. Even Prince Konoe Atsumaro, who much preferred a union of China and Japan based on a common Sinic culture, acknowledged that Japan was unique among the yellow peoples of Asia in having escaped Western domination. Wary of the same sort of arrogance that characterized the West, he preached in the wake of Sino-Japanese War that it was in both the cultural and material interest of Japan to preserve the integrity of the Chinese nation as the fountainhead of Asian greatness.[44]

Similarly, we have already seen how Okakura had to explain Japan's emergence as a modern military power in what was, to his way of thinking, the peace-loving, tea-drinking Asian civilization by appealing to reasons of national survival. Apart from such concerns, Okakura did not hesitate to extol Japan's superior perspective over other Asian nations. For instance, he claimed that the Way of Tea was forgotten by the Chinese, who had invented it, but was nurtured and further developed into a sophisticated art form in Japan. He also argued that "[i]t is in Japan alone that the historic wealth of Asiatic culture can be constructively studied through its treasured specimens" since Japan is the far eastern terminus as well as the meeting point of Asian treasures.[45] Therefore, all three types of

Pan-Asianism implicitly shared the assumption of Japanese superiority in all spiritual, cultural, and material spheres.

Despite the marked ultranationalist turn in Japan's formulation of Pan-Asianism in the 1930s, however, the more accommodating forms of Pan-Asianism based on philosophical and cultural commonalities of Asian peoples did not disappear completely. As the following chapters will demonstrate, different Pan-Asianist threads became further entangled. And while Meishuron Pan-Asianism came to occupy a prominent place in Japanese politics of the late 1930s, a more critical fact remains in the final analysis. Japan's less radical leaders might have had misgivings about the militant aspects of Meishuron Pan-Asianism. But in the end, they, too, held a basic understanding about Asia's deplorable weakness and Japan's singular position in Asia. This enabled Japan's divided government eventually to launch various Pan-Asianist programs, even when its leaders might not have immediately agreed on *how* to achieve *what* sort of a Pan-Asian union. In other words, Pan-Asianists of different shades and colors were of one mind on the question of *why* they were Pan-Asianists, which was that "Asia was one" and "Asia was weak," and utterly and unconditionally at that. As a result, they concurred that something had to be done about it and that it ultimately had to be done by Japan, who was in a relatively better-off position than the rest.

Perhaps most critically, none of the three categories of Pan-Asianism was an entirely anti-modernist ideology. Even Meishuron Pan-Asianists, who celebrated chauvinistic and traditionalist concepts such as Shinto and Bushido (Way of the Samurai) and were thus decidedly anti-Western in their attitude, did not reject modernity as part of the Asian claim for greatness. Rather, the argument went that the modern Japanese state's greatness, symbolically enshrined in its imperial institution as a source of both ancient and modern achievements of the nation, had to be transplanted to the rest of Asia. By remaking Asia in the image of Japan, where the spiritual and the modern co-existed, Asia could reclaim its ancient civilizational greatness without selling itself out to the West. Much like the way postcolonial leaders, such as Gamal Abdel Nasser, Suharto, Mao Zedong, and Fidel Castro, sought modernity in their interpretations of socialism and communism rather than in Western capitalism, Pan-Asianism had a certain appeal for those who preferred to achieve modernity without being compromised by what were in their eyes overtly Western values.

* * *

While the above three types aim to provide some helpful organizing principles behind Pan-Asianist thinking, they neither purport to be all-inclusive nor definitive. They show neither the finer differences within one category nor the ways in which the different types might have interacted, especially over an extensive period. That different types of Pan-Asianism overlapped and that individual Pan-Asianists placed varying emphases on different types of Pan-Asianism at different times suggests that there were reinforcements as well as conflicts within what one is tempted simply to term "Pan-Asianism." Rather than dwelling on the already convoluted terminological differences—including *Han-Ajiashugi*, *Ajiashugi*, or *Dai-Ajiashugi*—the three categories would enable us to analyze the motives, intent, and goals of certain Pan-Asianism with more clarity and consistency.

To be sure, those Pan-Asianists already discussed only suggest some of the most representative and identifiable cases, who more or less embraced a relatively consistent set of preferences for a particular type of Pan-Asianism over the other types, for the reasons of their convictions, character, or time. There were those who simply went along with the kind of Pan-Asianism that seemed most suitable to Japan's foreign policy goals or intellectual vogue of the time, as was probably true in the case of Takayama Chogyū. Even more blatant is the example of Tokutomi Sohō(1863–1957), who started off his career as a popular rights advocate in the 1880s and successively grew to be one of the most passionate spokesmen for Japan's expansionist policies, finally ending up as a postwar critic of Japan's wartime Pan-Asianism in his long and prominent journalistic career, which developed hand in hand with Japan's search for a respectable position in the world.

However, even Tokutomi's case does not suggest that he was less of a Pan-Asianist than, say, Uchida Ryōhei, who was a consistent Meishuron advocate. Since the basic aspirations of Pan-Asianism are morally righteous and unobjectionable, and especially since Teaist Pan-Asianism is the least systemized ideology that could have acted as furniture of the mind, Pan-Asianism must have attracted a huge following. Any number of those engaged in Japan's political discourse can be said to be Pan-Asianists of one kind or another. It is not the ambition of the following chapters to recount as many of them, but to select the most relevant cases to account for the focus of each chapter.

Another difficulty of categorization of Pan-Asianism emerges in the case of Pan-Asianism that does not exactly fit any of the three types. This was the case, for example, with the kind of Pan-Asianism put forward by the renowned political activist and adventurer Tarui (Morimoto) Tōkichi (1850–1922). In his 1893 pamphlet (originally drafted in 1885) *Daitō Gappōron*, which was written entirely in classical Chinese for the purpose of distribution throughout East Asia and which had an enormous influence on the Ilchinhoe leader Yi Young-gu, he introduced an idea of regional integration as a form of Pan-Asianism.[46] Tarui argued that a confederacy (*gappō*) of Japan and Korea would possibly later merge with Qing China "to unite and defeat the self-interested white race intent on devouring us, the yellow race."[47] In seeing the future course of world history in terms of a "white" versus "yellow" racial struggle, Tarui's logic was consistent with the fundamental Pan-Asianist preoccupation, especially of the Sinic strand. But the most original point of his argument centered upon a complete fusion of political organs between Korea and Japan, an aim that was unspecified and unforeseen in any of the three types of Pan-Asianism already examined.

In Tarui's view, the common features of East Asian nations originated from "the familial system that provides fundamental building blocks of a nation."[48] He claimed that this stood in stark contrast to "the individual system," seen in the West, which was why Western people were lacking in "human love and feelings."[49] Countering the argument that it was not in Japan's national interest to enter into an equal merger with Korea, he proclaimed that "From ancient times, so-called nations, nation-states, and states have signified different things [over time], meaning that they are socially constructed terms (*shakai no go*)."[50] So, too, is "national interest." The anticipated economic burden on Japan from such a merger with Korea would, in his mind, be easily overcome by the mutual benefits of creating uniform state organs, and the distinctions between the two nations would be blurred. He envisaged "big-boned and strong Koreans learning from the advantages of our military system and together [with us] preventing a Russian threat."[51]

For Tarui, the commonalities of the Confucian family principle in Korea appeared strong enough preconditions on which to build one stronger nation; after all, he was at pains to point out, a "nation" was a malleable concept to begin with. Instead of highlighting the weakness of East Asia, and the need for unconditional Japanese leadership in creating a strong Asia, Tarui called for the creation of tangible institutions based on a common political culture of the family-state, which would further generate common norms and interests concerning merging national interests. This is reminiscent of a functionalist argument often seen in the more recent theory of European integration, where cooperative relations in one area (in Tarui's argument, common defense policy for Japan and Korea) would spill over to other areas, eventually creating a workable regional union.

Judging from the variety of views, it is clear that the three types of Pan-Asianism do not adequately explain all facets of Pan-Asianism, especially as their varying agendas and goals became increasingly marred by and entangled with one another and also with more immediate strategic interests during the war. Still, just as a rigid and inflexible application of categories is unwise, it would be equally, if not more, foolish to pretend that there is a consensus about "Pan-Asianism." That sort of conceptual as well as historical negligence would allow for the equally lax and categorical contention that Pan-Asianism was a euphemism for Japanese imperialism and nothing more. Having defined and established Pan-Asianism, the following task becomes one of unearthing its different aspirations, implications, and functions in the history of the Fifteen Years' War. A brief historical backdrop, however, is due before commencing the story of the Fifteen Years' War itself.

2

Prelude to the Fifteen Years' War

Japan's rude awakening to the modern world, following more than two centuries of self-imposed isolation under the Tokugawa Shōgunate, began with the arrival in 1853 of Commodore Matthew Perry in Edo Bay. The threat of Western domination propelled the new Meiji regime to modernize—and to various contested degrees—to Westernize. Japan nonetheless proved a quick study of Western norms, customs, and moreover, the principles of power politics that often superseded such shared norms and customs. Ingeniously encapsulating the country's rising consciousness of the Hobbesian world where anarchy ruled, a popular Japanese song of the 1880s went: "There is a Law of Nations, it is true, / but when the moment comes, remember, / the Strong eat up the Weak."[1]

Japan's tireless quest to end unequal treaties with the great powers continued into the 1890s. Japan's victory in the Sino-Japanese War (1894–95) delivered a blow to China, which many had believed until then to be Asia's "sleeping giant." The war's conclusion at Shimonoseki in turn intensified the great power competition for concessionary rights in China. From this, Japan gained its first colony, the island of Formosa (Taiwan), though only after the Triple Intervention by Russia, France, and Germany pressured Japan to return the Liaotung Peninsula, confirming in the Japanese mind hard realities of international politics. After its victory over Russia ten years later, again fought over the question of who would dominate Korea, Japan added protectorate rights in Korea, the Russian leasehold over the Liaotung Peninsula, Russia's railroad and mining rights in southern Manchuria, and sovereignty over the southern half of Sakhalin (Karafuto) to its colonial possessions.

However, even these tangible rewards and the hard-earned prestige gained at Portsmouth were not a good enough vindication for Japan's deep-seated sense of humiliation and wounded pride. Having been fed with a series of sensational reports of Japanese victory during the war, the public felt betrayed by the terms of peace, which did not even offset the enormous costs of war. Like the humiliating Triple Intervention a decade earlier, Portsmouth, too, appeared to confirm Japanese suspicions of Western imperialist conspiracy.

It was in the light of such developments on the Asian mainland that Pan-Asianism became an increasingly attractive principle of foreign policy for many Japanese. Pan-Asianism, as understood in Japan's political discourse, grew in close association with the country's material concerns and other prevailing political ideologies. The following account will try to make sense of such crisscrossing of various interests and viewpoints in the period prior to the book's main chronological focus. The discussion will first revolve around Pan-Asianism's influence on Japan's policy formulation, while highlighting other political concepts that informed that process in the meantime, including Japan's more blatantly nationalistic thoughts. It then attempts to evaluate how Pan-Asianism, which was after all one of the many political ideologies existing in Japan before the 1930s, competed and interacted with other political constructs, not in the least through the medium of those who simultaneously embraced any number of them, for the eventual place of prominence in Japan's wartime policy formulation and mobilization from 1931 to 1945.

Fukuzawa's *Datsuaron* and Its Mirror Image

As the first and only major non-Western power, Japan came to assume the paradoxical role of an imperialist, which had itself only narrowly and recently escaped from imperial conquest. This paradox has led Peter Duus to his brilliant characterization of Japanese in this period: "[A]s the internal interests demanded and external circumstances dictated, they would either run with the hare or hunt with the hounds."[2] Hence Japan was a singular sort of power in the making. Its rise served to inspire anticolonialist movements, but such a rise also involved acquisition of its own colonial territories and various treaty rights from its fellow Asians. To further complicate the picture, just as Japan was striving to secure a position in that existing international order, that very international order itself was undergoing phases of profound transformation. By the end of the nineteenth century, the tides of New Imperialism had engulfed much of the non-Western world, only to be contested within two decades by the newly emerging forces of post–World War I liberal internationalist principles, as well as the growing presence of future superpowers, as expressed in the two distinct modes of production and *modus vivendi* of Americanism and Bolshevism.

In analyzing its approach to this changing "West," Robert Scalapino's classic observation that Japan went through three significant Hegelian stages of thesis, antithesis, and synthesis remains compelling.[3] At first, the dominant attitude was one of outright rejection of things Western, followed by concerted efforts at speedy Westernization, reaching a final synthesis in the attempt at combining traditional and modern values, encapsulated in the concept of "the Best of Japan and the West Combined" (*wayō setchū*). This thesis-antithesis-synthesis transition is of particular interest in its Pan-Asianist implications. The newspaper column, in which Fukuzawa Yukichi (1834–1901) urged Japan to abandon Asia and be more like Europe, is often regarded as a blatant legitimization of Japan's imperialist designs in Asia. One of the leading Meiji intellectuals and the founder of the top private university Keiō Gijuku, Fukuzawa stated:

> Our nation cannot afford to wait for the enlightenment of our neighboring countries to happen, and to join in them in the effort of building Asia. Rather, we should avoid that situation and join in the fate of the civilized and enlightened West, dealing with China and Korea as Westerners do, without being bound by special protocols, simply because we are neighbors. If one keeps bad company, one cannot avoid being branded with a bad name. In my heart, I vow to sever ties with our bad friends in Asia's East.[4]

The above was written in 1885, the same year as Tarui Tōkichi's original draft of *DaitōGappōron*. (Tarui lost it as a result of his imprisonment after having been implicated in the Osaka Incident, in which Japan's progressive sympathizers of Korean independence unsuccessfully plotted a military uprising and smuggled arms.) Japan's China policy vis-à-vis Korea was becoming a primary foreign policy concern. Fukuzawa's proclamation of *nyū-ō datsu-a* or "Enter Europe and Exit Asia" seems to represent the exact opposite viewpoint of Tarui's proposal for a Great Eastern Confederation, with Fukuzawa representing the cold realism of power politics that begot Japan's later expansionism, and Tarui, the honorable idealism of Pan-Asianism.

However, such a dichotomous and retrospective reading of the two texts is overly simplistic. It is now generally accepted that Fukuzawa's short column was "rediscovered" and made famous by postwar historians and commentators attempting to locate philosophical roots of Japan's expansionism in its modernization.[5] Thus Fukuzawa's argument has to be understood in context. While religiously beholden to Western Enlightenment values and notion of progress, he did not see "civilization" in and of itself as a source of all good. Rather, his realist impulse led him to profess civilization as the surest way of preserving the integrity and autonomy of a nation-state. The argument was: "If one cannot help oneself, one should not bother helping others who are not willing to help themselves in the first place." Here, he is merely urging, though in a disturbingly paternalistic tone judged by twenty-first-century sensibilities, to abandon alliances that would needlessly sap Japan's strength and prestige.

In this sense, it would be misguided to read *datsuaron* (exit-Asia thesis) as a unilateral declaration of Japan's aggressive intent and expansionist designs in East Asia—"Exit Asia and Conquer It Instead"—as many have done in the postwar period. Fukuzawa saw that less involvement with weak Asia, the better. On the exact same issue, Tarui saw more involvement, the better. Fukuzawa posited that the strength of Japan, too, would be jeopardized if Japan stayed in Asia, making it vulnerable again to Western encroachments from which Japan itself had barely escaped. On the other hand, Tarui saw the source of Japan's strength in the combined forces of Asia, and especially of Korea and Japan. The overwhelming and common concerns for both were Japan's survival as a sovereign nation-state, without which almost the whole of Asia would be subjected to Western control.

In reality, Fukuzawa was no less of a Pan-Asianist than Tarui in his heartfelt awareness of the Asian neighbors' plight and his desire to take part in solving it. In supporting Korea's speedy modernization, Fukuzawa hosted and aided the reformist Korean noble Kim Ok-kyun, when he sought political refuge in Japan in 1880. He subsequently accepted Korean students at his school and dispatched his disciples to Korea to help establish newspapers, an essential tool of civilization in his mind. At the same time, he was a realistic Japanese nationalist in his assessment of Japan's still relatively weak position in the international system, which in his view made the country ill-equipped to take on Asian leadership. The major difference was that while Fukuzawa saw "civilization" as a tool for individual survival, Tarui favored "confederation" for the benefit of collective survival. But the difference ends there. Neither Fukuzawa nor Tarui can be likened to such early Meiji reactionaries as Saigō Takamori (1827–77), who advocated Japan's expedition against Korea in 1873 (*seikanron*), even though Tarui in his youth had been greatly inspired by *seikanron*.[6]

In 1887, two years after the appearance of Fukuzawa's *datsuaron*, the philosophical leader of the Freedom and People's Rights movement Nakae Chōmin (1847–1901), known for his translation of Jean Jacques Rousseau, penned a classic fiction that precisely encapsulated the dilemmas of Japan that both Fukuzawa and Tarui had attempted to overcome in their respective proposals. It was called *Sansuijin Keirin Mondō* (A Discourse by Three Drunkards on Government). In it, three men engage in a political debate over a bottle of sake. One of the three is a Westernizer, who believes in Western ideas of linear progress and democracy. Another is an advocate for traditional samurai values—a perfect continental drifter candidate—who thinks Japan's future lies in Asia rather than the West. The third man and the host of the party is Nankai-sensei (presumably Nakae's alter ego), who adores drinking as much as he likes discussing politics. He lends a moderating voice to the argument between Westernized gentleman and Asia-firster. Nankai-sensei's views are of a gradualist nature, reprimanding the two young men that they are only talking in abstract about things that do not really exist either in the West or in the East. Nankai-sensei suggests for Japan an admittedly trite course of concentrating on the strengthening of parliamentary democracy, commerce, diplomacy, and education. Finding their master's views rather dull and unsatisfactory, the two impatient youngsters complain. They would never return to discuss politics with him after this debate. One presumably left for the United States and the other for Shanghai. Alone, Nankai-sensei keeps on drinking.[7] All the three characters are notable, as they seem to embody different sets of viewpoints and preferences—and uncertainties—for the future of Japan that Fukuzawa, Tarui, and Nakae all tried to address in each of their works. Here, too, the Hegelian idea of thesis–antithesis–synthesis plays itself out.

Where exactly did Japan go next? The following decade witnessed the Japanese government opting *not* to invoke Pan-Asianism as a main framework of its foreign policy, generally following Fukuzawa's advice in keeping up appearances with the great powers. Japan stuck to the old imperialist game, and itself became an imperialist in Asia, even though there were individual Japanese Pan-Asianists and Pan-Asianist organizations operating outside of and occasionally within Japan's official capacity.

With increased national strength came a tempting opportunity for Japan to return to the company of Asia. In the minds of some, Japan now had the ability and responsibility to revive and lead Asia. According to Okakura's Teaist vision of "Asia is One," Pan-Asianism found in the strength of Asia's philosophical and artistic traditions the elevated claim to power comparable, even superior, to that of the West. In reality, Pan-Asianism became "ideologized," precisely because Japan was becoming stronger in real-political terms, and its views, therefore, carried more weight. The rising Japanese pride and confidence culminated in the assertion that Japan was a country in which various traditions of philology, Confucianism, as well as Western science found its most effective synthesis. Many even began to find good reasons for Japan's peripheral location, just as Okakura thought of it as a treasure house of Asian arts and their glorious terminus. The robustness of Japan's claim of representing the best of all worlds gave an additional momentum to its modernization and imperialism as well as its ambition of Asian leadership. Such a new understanding effectively set the stage for the ultimate ascent of the Meishuron category of Pan-Asianism.

Russo-Japanese War

The key moment for Japan's identification as Asia's *meishu* came in 1905, with its victory over Russia in the Russo-Japanese War. This impressed in the minds of other non-Western peoples that Europeans were neither invincible nor unassailable. The impact of the Japanese victory on Asian elites was amplified, as the news resonated with their own respective nationalisms and pride. As an impressionable teenager, Jawaharlal Nehru (1889–1964) described in his memoir, written during his imprisonment from mid-1934 to early 1936:

> The next important event [following his introduction to theosophy] . . . was the Russo-Japanese War. Japanese victories stirred up my enthusiasm and I waited eagerly for the papers for fresh news daily. I invested in a large number of books on Japan and tried to read some of them. . . . Nationalistic ideas filled my mind. I mused of Indian freedom and Asiatic freedom from the thralldom of Europe.[8]

The language of Asian solidarity, in defiance of the West, acquired a realistic and convincing edge because of this victory, interpreted by many in terms of an Asian versus European racial struggle. At the same time, Japan's victory consolidated the Western view of Japan as a serious power in the making worthy of admiration and support. In turn, Japan's own perception of its Asian leadership began to assume a crusading tone of assisting its less fortunate neighbors. Accordingly, Japan's Pan-Asianist sympathizers welcomed Indo-Chinese anticolonial nationalists, such as Phan Boi Chau and Prince Cuong De; Indian independence fighters such as Subhas Chandra Bose and Rash Behari Bose; and the Chinese nationalists, Liang Ch'i-ch'ao and Sun Yat-sen.

Particularly, Sun Yat-sen (1866–1925) left a significant mark on Japan's Pan-Asianist discourse of the pre–Fifteen Years' War period. Indeed, Sun and his Chinese nationalist colleagues were an integral part of the development of early Pan-Asianism, and Sun's importance in that function continued beyond his lifetime. Especially noteworthy was his 1924 speech delivered in Kobe on "Great Asianism" (*Dai-Ajiashugi*), in which he contrasted the West's "Forceful Way" (*hadō* in Japanese, *badao* in Chinese) to Asia's "Kingly Way" (*ōdō* and *wangdao*). The former suggested a coercive method enabled by modern arms and cold diplomacy, and the latter the Confucian concept of benevolence, perfected by Mencius, that had purportedly guided ancient emperors in governing the Central Kingdom. According to Sun, Japan, along with Turkey, had managed to master the material strength to become Asia's "watchguard."[9] However, the Twenty-One Demands, a diplomatic attempt by Japan during World War I to consolidate its foothold in China, and the terms of peace at Versailles, which directly gave rise to the May Fourth Movement (1919), appeared to confirm in the minds of Chinese nationalists that Japan was acting more in a Western fashion, failing to respect its Asian roots. Ironically for Sun, who intended this speech to be part indictment and part plea, urging Japan to reconsider upholding what he described as more morally righteous values of the East in its external behavior, its key concept of the "Kingly Way" would be later taken up by Japanese occupiers to legitimize their rule in Manchuria as an Asian, and purportedly more righteous, mode of governance.[10]

More Indian Links

Another Asian nationalist figure prominent around the time of Sun's speech was Rash Behari Bose (1886–1945). Though largely forgotten, his profound involvement with Japanese society, which spanned more than three decades, merits a few words of explanation. H. P. Ghose's observation that "Rash Behari Bose was, so to say, not an individual but an institution from which emanated inspiration and instruction"[11] may be an exaggeration. Yet the degree to which Bose's cause was absorbed into the orthodoxy of Japan's Pan-Asianist discourse and public life cannot be overemphasized. Born in northeastern Bengal, he engaged in anti-British terrorist activities from his youth, which forced him to flee India in 1915. He ended up in Japan, where he quickly befriended a group of influential Pan-Asianists of various stripes, such as the Genyōsha don Tōyama Mitsuru and Prime Minister Inukai Tsuyoshi. He also married into one of Tokyo's most progressive families. This family, the Somas, who owned one of the first and hugely successful Western-style brasseries called Nakamura-ya in the Shinjuku district of Tokyo, risked their positions and provided Bose with a safe haven when the British police kept pursuing him.

Bose was a prolific writer, acting as contributor and editor of anti-British journals such as *The New Asia* and *The Asian Review*. He also wrote a considerable number of books in Japanese on India, its struggle for independence, and its folklore.[12] Moreover, he established cultural associations and study groups such as the Indian Society, Indo-Japanese Friends Society, and a hostel for Asian students staying in Tokyo called "Villa Asians," which he personally managed from 1933 to 1941.

Here, as studied by Hyung Gu Lynn, the prevalence of voluntary associations (or more accurately *hanmin hankan dantai*—semiprivate, semipublic organizations legally recognized in Japan's public life) and their overlooked importance, especially before the intensification of the Fifteen Years' War, in building coalition influences on the mainstream of Japanese politics must be noted. Bose's cultural, educational, and lobbying activities, too, were tightly interlocked in such a power dynamic of cross-institutional networks underpinning more obvious institutional structures of the Japanese government such as political parties and bureaucracies.[13]

Through his activities in those organizations, Bose's role in promoting Japan's Pan-Asianist discourse became considerable. Bose, like some other influential thinkers/agitators of his time including Ōkawa Shūmei, saw Pan-Asianism as providing a more egalitarian alternative to the existing international order of the Versailles-Washington system. For example, Bose helped to organize the August 1926 Conference of All Asian Peoples in Nagasaki, Japan's first Pan-Asian meeting with representatives from China, India, Afghanistan, Indochina, the Philippines, and Japan. At the conference, Bose criticized the internationalism of the League of Nations:

> We know some criticize today's meeting saying there is no need to establish another international union because we have one. But the two internationals are completely different in their nature. The one is for the benefit of five hundred millions of the whites and the other is for one hundred and a half millions of Asian peoples. For thousands of years, the Easterners were a very superior people in civilization, spiritually and materially. . . . The Union now [*sic*] we are going to shape a new form of our Eastern civilization. Its basis is on the pure faith and love for Asia. Let us unite and do our best to establish this union at all cost and let us make a big contribution to the happiness of all humanity in propagating our aims and objects all over the world![14]

Like many members of Japan's ultra-right, Bose's confrontational style and his proclivity for radicalized methods to resolve international and domestic grievances were soon to be given an extra push as the worldwide depression dealt a blow to Japan's fledgling great power status in the 1930s. The fact that Bose's position depended on the support from Japan's more radicalized group of Pan-Asianists determined the course of his career as a "collaborator" with Japan's wartime regime. During the war, Bose sat on the boards of many cultural and political organizations of a Pan-Asianist persuasion, continued to deliver lectures, write pamphlets, and maximize his rare and well-connected position, primarily to educate and enlighten the Japanese audience on India's cause and its desire for independence.

In retrospect, Bose's identification of Indian independence with Japan's wartime imperialism produces some unsettling ramifications. Had he decided to part ways with the Japanese, once Japan's aggressive conduct in China and Southeast Asia became obvious, his reputation as a "half-legendary and half-mysterious"[15] independence fighter might have been preserved. And that was exactly what other prominent Indian exiles in

Japan, such as Ananda Mohan Sahay and Raja Mahendra Pratdap, opted to do after the outbreak of the Pacific War. In comparison, Bose's choice was clearly more problematic. He was a primary figure in the 1942 Conference of Asian Nations held in Osaka. In the following year, he participated in the Indian Independence Conference held in Bangkok and became the president of the Indian Independence League. He was also the first head of the Indian National Army, established in Singapore by General Mohan Singh under the auspices of Japan's occupation forces; he was later succeeded by Subhas Chandra Bose. By directly attaching his ultimate goal of India's independence to Japan's war, Bose, by the end of his life, stood not only physically, but also ideologically isolated from the mainstream of Indian nationalism.[16] However, his role in the production and dissemination of Pan-Asianist discourse in Japan should not be neglected, as the recognition and active support of Bose's struggle gave a realistic and appealing edge to the Pan-Asianist claim that Japan and India were truly partners fighting the same war for Eastern civilization.

Thus not entirely independent of concerns outside of Japan's exclusive and state-centric interests, and well before the 1930s, Pan-Asianism had come to enjoy the legitimacy of a viable political construct within Japan, speedily and dramatically particularizing a more vague discussion of common traditions in the philosophical, artistic, and cultural realms into the practical and the power political. But with increasing Japanese confidence and conviction came the risk of losing the more benevolent, tolerant, and, in Okakura's words, "Asian" aspects of Pan-Asianism, expressed in such phrases as "love for the Ultimate and Universal" as "the common thought-inheritance of every Asiatic race."[17]

Agitators and Reformers

However impressive, Japan's quick rise as a military power put the country under various social, economic, and psychological pressures that eventually led to an emergence of several strands of extreme egalitarianism, traditionalism, and ultranationalism. They all interacted in different ways with the notion of Pan-Asianism. One of the main ideologies carrying extensive pseudotraditional overtones was a Japanese brand of national socialism that was comparable to that of Nazi Germany in its reliance upon the evocation of myths and racial superiority. Kita Ikki (1883–1937), deemed the most effective advocate of Japanese national socialism, articulated his political vision in *Outline of Plans for the Reconstruction of Japan* (1919). Sometimes dubbed the Japanese *Mein Kampf* and written in Shanghai at the time of the May Fourth Movement, this essay is said to have prompted various ultranationalist groups, such as the Ketsumeidan (Blood Brothers Band) led by apocalyptic Nichiren Buddhist monk Inoue Nisshō and the Sakurakai (Cherry Blossom Society) composed of young army officers, to bring terror to Japan's high politics in the 1930s. Kita's thesis advanced a swift transformation of Japan into an entirely new country that could lead the revival of Asia, which had once been represented by "a high *Asian* civilization of Greece" to stand against Western imperialism.[18]

The *Outline*, which was the last of his three revolutionary tracts, based its claim on the dichotomy of radical reform at home and missionary expansion abroad that conspicuously resonated with the Meishuron strand of Pan-Asianism. It is generally believed that his charismatic appeal to young officers, who resorted to murderous tactics in the 1930s, was so great that the government regarded him as the inspirational mastermind behind the failed coup of February 26, 1936. This led to his arrest and, ultimately, to his execution in August 1937.

This conventional narrative notwithstanding, Kita and his ideas need to be approached carefully. Although much has been written about this eccentric figure, most famously by his biographer Tanaka Sōgorō, there in fact remain more questions than answers as to his actual significance in history.[19] Christopher Szpilman persuasively argues that Kita as both theorist and activist is vastly overestimated. The contradictions one sees in his life, such as his indictment of capitalist evils while shamelessly receiving handsome sums from a *zaibatsu* conglomerate, or his detached view of the Japanese emperor in his advocacy of the emperor-organ theory while blindly idolizing the Meiji emperor, that had been favorably considered by his followers and admirers to be a sign of the complexities of his thoughts and multiple ideological allegiances, are revealed to be a sign of absence of any original thinking. In other words, Kita "had little interest in an abstract pursuit of truth. He strove for effect. He wrote to impress, to shock, to frighten and terrorize," embodying "Japan's persistent tradition of political intrigue, blackmail and extortion."[20] As an activist, his followers were a mere handful, and after withdrawing from the ultranationalist society Yūzonsha co-led by Ōkawa Shūmei and Kamekawa Mitsutarō, he neither formed nor joined another such organization, living in reclusive isolation devoted to the practice of Nichiren

Buddhism. Szpilman's explanation provides an important and refreshing corrective to historical accounts that on the whole seem to render conflicting but equally overvaluing verdicts on Kita, without being able to decide what he actually achieved.

However, the most remarkable fact still remains despite the above corrective, that Kita has in fact been able to sustain such mythical importance in Japanese history. That is perhaps because in spite of everything, including the lack of original thinking and consistency of political programs, Kita's charismatic appeal was indeed genuine. His execution also gave an indispensable final touch to his myth, making him a martyr to the cause of both right and left immune to mundane criticism. As an object of admiration, then, his influence during his lifetime (primarily channeled *via* his devoted follower Nishida Mitsugi) could not have been negligible, even though his actual influence on specific political actions was probably far less and more indirect than the conventional wisdom holds. In a crude sense, then, whether or not the ultranationalist admirers of the 1930s understood Kita correctly becomes less important. The critical point is that they all *thought* they did.

Aside from his personal charisma, moreover, there was perhaps enough in his words and deeds to convince his admirers and critics alike of all generations of Kita's importance. His earlier incarnation might provide us with a clue. Kita's first book, *Discourse on Body Politic and Pure Socialism* (*Kokutairon oyobi Junsei Shakaishugi*, 1906), in which he argued for the world government and declared that Japan's body politic already provided conditions for socialism, was highly ideological. It found its kin in the extreme egalitarianism of the anarchist-socialist Kōtoku Sūsui (1871–1911), who was implicated in the Osaka Incident and was finally executed for his part in the Great Treason Incident, a 1910 plot to assassinate the emperor. Also, Kita proved to be not just a bookish self-taught theorist. He was dispatched to Shanghai at the time of the 1911 Revolution, acting as a liaison for the Kokuryūkai and supporting Song Jiaoren while finishing his second book *Unofficial History of the Chinese Revolution* (*Shina Kakumei Gaishi*, 1916) that attacked Japan's imperialist policy on the Asian mainland. Kita was again in China from 1916 to 1920, witnessing the rising Chinese resentment against Japan and its culmination in the May Fourth Movement, leading him to write the *Outline*, calling for radical restructuring of the Japanese state. Arguably, his Pan-Asianist sympathies, not merely expressed in words but deeds, provided some consistencies to the otherwise incoherent and conflicting set of claims, and acted as a proof, for those who looked for it, of the purity of his motives and his seeming authenticity as a serious thinker-*cum*-activist.

Ōkawa Shūmei (1886–1957) is another important figure frequently compared to Kita in his eccentricity and influence on Japan's ultranationalism.[21] Ōkawa, a scholar of Sanskrit and Islamic studies, whose interest in Asia was first triggered by Henry Cotton's *New India or India in Transition* (1907), was supposedly an active supplier of arms to Indian revolutionaries based in Japan such as R. B. Bose. Inspired by his idol Rabindranath Tagore, he located the source of Asian strength in the primordial realm of agriculture. To the extent that he was concerned with Asia well beyond the borders of the Sinic sphere of influence, he should be regarded as the more rightful inheritor of the Teaist brand of Pan-Asianism than any other pseudotraditionalist players of his time or since. All the same, his platform also embraced volatile and metatheoretical mysticism with a Japanese nationalist—and increasingly "ultra" nationalist—stamp. He insisted that the strengthening of absolute sovereignty of the emperor, the resolution of the Manchurian-Mongolian Problem (i.e., "How should Japan secure its foothold in the region?"), and radical internal reform were integral parts of Japan's survival. Thus in his view of Japan's part in Asia, he agreed with his former colleagues in Rōsōkai and Yūzonsha, who became mainstream opinion makers after the outbreak of the Pacific War, and with Tokutomi Sohō Kanokogi Kazunobu (1884–1949), and Tsukui Tatsuo (1901–89), who together spearheaded Japan's propaganda efforts through the Great Japan Patriotic Association of the Press (Dai-Nippon Genron Hōkokukai), established in 1942.

Agrarianism was another line of pseudotraditionalist ideology that interacted with Ōkawa's view of Asia as a primarily agricultural and spiritual civilization. This school of thought was advanced by Ishikawa Sanshirō (1876–1956), an anarchist, Gondō Seikyō (1868–1937), a Kokuryūkai member, and Tachibana Kōzaburō (1893–1974), a Christian socialist-turned-ultranationalist. Drawing from Robert Owen's and Peter Kropotkin's rural utopianism, and also harking back to the late Tokugawa teachings of rural self-sufficiency advocated by Ninomiya Kinjirō (Sontoku), agrarianism pitted city against country, industry against farming, and Japan—and the East—against the West. As far as Japan's policies in the 1930s were concerned, there is a view that the agrarian ideology did not have a palpable effect on the country's conduct. This view posits that agrarianism essentially acted against peasant interests, keeping the peasant frugal and contented without bothering to alter the basic structure of the state to be based on farming.[22] Nevertheless, such a view neglects the role of agrarian ideology as a driving force behind certain factions of the Japanese Army. The Army was overwhelmingly of rural origin, with many of its young soldiers coming from the areas that were hardest hit by the great depression as well as agricultural failures that followed the boom years of World War I. That was precisely why the movement that was initially inspired by egalitarian principles of socialism and anarchism began to attract a following among ultranationalists on the far right.

This is not to suggest that the marriage of egalitarian principles and ultranationalism was an inevitable development of the 1930s. But the heightened sense of national crisis of the period provided enough preconditions that allowed for the twin call for internal reform and expansion abroad to take hold of the imagination of enough fanatics who were not afraid to kill and to die for a particular cause. In a similar vein, the attraction of Marxists to Pan-Asianism is also understandable. They, too, preferred a radical change, and many of them saw Asian unity as a preliminary step toward world revolution. It was also in such an egalitarian understanding of socialism that Japanese women before 1931 found room for their voice in their country's public life. Feminist-socialists like Kanno Suga and Itō Noe, both of whom died along with their respective lovers (Kanno with Kōtoku Shūsui for the Great Treason Incident of 1910, and Itō with Ōi Kentarō in his murder by the police in the wake of the Great Kantō Earthquake of 1923) are apt examples. Fukuda (Kageyama) Eiko (1865–1927), who was imprisoned at the age of twenty for her part in the pro-Korean reform Osaka Incident, later matured into a social reformer promoting Asian women's causes, partly through her journal *Sekai Fujin* (World Women, 1907–09), a bimonthly that aimed to introduce social issues concerning Asian women, such as calling for support of female Chinese students studying in Japan, improvement of social acceptance of international marriages (for example, between Japanese and Koreans or Japanese and Chinese), and dispatching female teachers to China to help boost literacy. However, theirs was an uphill struggle. Their progress was dealt a blow by the fall of Minseitō cabinet following the Manchurian Incident, stifling many of its progressive agenda, including universal suffrage for another fifteen years, relegating women to secondary and supportive, though by no means negligible, roles in the total mobilization for the Fifteen Years' War.

Emperorism

More likely than not, many of those who espoused radical egalitarian principles would not have approved of Japanese imperialism. And yet, Japan's war cannot be understood without reference to the cult of the emperor which was as all-encompassing an ideology as Pan-Asianism. Together with Pan-Asianism, Emperorism fused different threads of radical and pseudotraditionalist political ideas of the 1920s and 1930s. The very notion that the Japanese state was an extension of the imperial family, or a nation of families composed of the Imperial Household at the top, was never the monopoly of this particular period of social agitation. Rather, it had been the official agent of Japan's state-building project since the Meiji era. On this point, Bertrand Russell in 1945 aptly observed, in conjunction with his critique of Robert Filmer's *Patriarcha: Or The Natural Power of Kings*, that Japan was quite unique in the modern world to suppose that political power should be in any way assimilated to that of parents over children.[23]

This family-state principle, based on the claim that the emperor descended from the Sun Goddess Amaterasu with the rest of the Japanese constituting branches of the same family, was in fact invented in 1868. In trying to locate the source of European power, the Japanese state-builders perhaps overestimated the role of Christianity as providing a sociopolitical glue for the cohesion of European states. Rather than adopting Christianity, Confucianism, or Buddhism, which were all foreign in origin, they concluded that State Shinto, a politicized version of ancient and animistic rites, was a suitable alternative for the modern Japanese state. Hence they moved the emperor who had been, for hundreds of years, a marginalized and politically powerless figure in the ancient capital of Kyoto to the new capital of Tokyo and installed him as the highest living deity of reinvigorated Shintoism. Thus the modernization and the *raison d'être* of the Japanese state had ever since depended upon the unifying power of that nationalist creation myth.

Especially, ultranationalist militants in certain quarters of the armed services held that they had the sacred mission of serving and protecting the emperor. Hand in hand with the intensification of the Fifteen Years' War, even more radicalized followers of this ideology came to believe that the Imperial Way equaled the morally righteous way for Asia as a whole, and should thus prevail over Western influences, thereby directly linking the claim of Japan's *meishu* role to the ultimate ambition of constructing a "Co-Prosperity Sphere." This is why the two ideological pillars of Emperor Worship and Pan-Asianism, though not immediately apparent, were heavily dependent on each other, making it impossible to explain Japan's expansionism with just one or the other.

Pan-Asianism Takes Root

Japan's international experience of the period immediately preceding the Fifteen Years' War is important in understanding the incorporation of Pan-Asianism in Japan's policy discourse of the 1930s. To its joy and pride, having moved against German footholds in China during World War I, Japan was rewarded with a seat as one of the "Big Five" powers at the Paris Peace Conference (1919).[24] Japan nonetheless came out of that conference deeply dissatisfied with certain terms of the postwar settlements. Especially upsetting for Japan were disagreements over the Covenant of the League of Nations and the futile debate about the inclusion of clauses guaranteeing racial equality and religious freedom.[25]

Immediately following the Peace Conference, the perceived—though perhaps not entirely tangible—concessions, which Japan accepted at the Washington Conference (1921–22), became another source of national discontent. Japan agreed to a naval arms limitation that left the fleet inferior in strength to those of the United States and Britain, deepening a sense of humiliation and influencing the climate of popular opinion against the great powers. The domestic economic downturn, caused in large part by the worldwide depression and protectionist trade barriers of the great powers, provided Japan with yet more reasons to be frustrated with the Anglo-American-dominated international order.

Prince Konoe Fumimaro (1891–1945), the son of Konoe Atsumaro and a three-time prime minister, who was to preside over the promulgation of the "New East Asian Order" statement as a vital component of Japan's foreign policy in 1938, voiced his complaint about the state of international system politics in 1918. Shortly before his embarkation as a member of the delegation to Paris, Konoe published an emotive essay entitled "Reject the Anglo-American Peace."[26] Attacking the proposal for the League of Nations as "the ideology of sustaining the *status quo*," he identified Japan's mission as one of articulating its support for "the eradication of economic imperialism and the unbiased, equal treatment of the yellow race."[27]

The post–World War I settlement lent a degree of urgency to Japan's Pan-Asianism, as it seemed to confirm the deep-seated Japanese suspicion that the West was still unwilling to recognize Asia on an equal footing. In his representative work "Various Problems Concerning Resurgent Asia" (1922), Ōkawa Shūmei propounded that the colonization of Asia by Europeans came as a doleful result of the separation between the spiritual and the social spheres of human life.[28] Asia concentrated on the attainment of internal, reflective, and indeed spiritual freedoms; but in doing so, it had failed to apply the acquired knowledge to the smooth running of their societies. But the Japanese victory over Russia inspired the rest of Asia, and, moreover, World War I intensified Europe's class struggle and Asia's national struggle. In the minds of those who espoused radical doctrines, this development intimated the advent of a brighter future for the whole world. Regarding the Peace of Paris as a scheme of desperate *status quo* powers to resist that unstoppable historical tide, Ōkawa declared:

> Asian nations must first and foremost gain freedom. A free Asia must then be thoroughly and firmly unified. How to achieve that freedom and unity is the most pressing Asian concern. Today's Asia is a slave to Europe. What sort of an ideal could a slave possibly have?[29]

To achieve Asia's freedom, Ōkawa even saw an alliance with the Soviet Union (which was partly Asian anyway in his view) as a tempting possibility. He believed that the combined force of socialist revolution in Europe and the revival of Asia alone could alter the course of world history in the end.

The emergence of such pronounced Pan-Asianist perspectives in Japan's political discourse and the intensification of international politics into the 1930s were significant. They suggest that one can grasp Pan-Asianism in all its richness and subtlety only within the context of a kaleidoscopic interchange of various events and ideas on an international scale. Likewise, the way this ideology is enmeshed in Japan's perception of its international role reveals that numbers and figures are often neither the most immediate nor the most accurate measurements in a causal analysis of war origins—rather, ideas are.

Indeed, the pattern of a convergence of interests seen between Japan's ultranationalism and its Pan-Asianism is a testament to Hannah Arendt's classic analysis of Bolshevism in *The Origins of Totalitarianism*.[30] Arendt contended that the temporary success of Bolshevism owed more to the mixture of Russian national interests, and indeed Pan-Slavism, than to any other ideology or political movement. Especially in the arena of foreign policy, Soviet Russia's totalitarian aims were frequently linked to the pursuit of some incontrovertible Russian interests couched in the slogans and vocabulary of Pan-Slav ideology.[31] This insight is important, since it shows the sheer resilience of nationalism as a universal doctrine: even though Russian Communists claimed, and presumably genuinely believed, that the restructuring of the entire international system into a world system was their ultimate goal, they, too, could not escape from the assumptions of nation-states as the constitutive units of that very system they tried to overthrow. Similarly, more and more Japanese, amid the country's struggle to secure a place for itself in the very same international system that seemed neither perfect nor egalitarian, came to be tempted by Meishuron Pan-Asianism that legitimized Japan's dominant position in their vision of Asia. Pan-Asianism of the 1930s came to hold specificities that were in fact sometimes conflicting, even outright contradictory, to the all-encompassing vision of a peace-loving Asia in Okakura's original pronouncements.

It is of course impossible to speculate what Okakura might have thought of the Fifteen Years' War had he lived longer. Yet the case of Noguchi Yonejirō (1875–1947) speaks quite dramatically of how one so devoted to Okakura's Pan-Asian vision could become convinced of the legitimacy of Japan's expansionist course after the Manchurian Incident of 1931 and later the China War in 1937.

Noguchi, a Japanese poet, who fathered the sculptor Isamu Noguchi with an American woman, was first critically recognized in a New York literary circle. Besides teaching English Literature at Keiō Gijuku, he made extensive lecture trips around the world, which established him as one of the very few interpreters of the outside world for Japan, and *vice versa*. Noguchi was profoundly affected by Rabindranath Tagore's teaching since their first meeting in Tokyo in 1916, and like Ōkawa, remained one of the most ardent publicists of Tagore in Japan. In a public lecture delivered in Tokyo in 1936, Noguchi recalled the excitement of visiting Tagore during a recent speaking tour he had made at the invitation of Indian state universities. He stated:

> The party that Tagore held in my honor amid a forest of mango trees was one of the most memorable events of my life. . . . Tagore spoke in that pleasing voice, and welcomed me with kindly words. A poem selected from the Vedas entitled "Welcoming a Poet" was recited in Sanskrit, which Tagore himself translated for me into English. . . . Nothing was as pleasing, encouraging, and thought-provoking as

Tagore's welcome, because it clearly indicated to me how I should, as a man of letters, nay, as a poet, proceed on my called path from then on.[32]

As it turned out, the nature of Noguchi's "called path" had something to do with the pursuit of a blend of Pan-Asianism and Japanese nationalism. He described how he was moved by the ritual singing of a school song carried out by Tagore's students while taking an early morning round of a walk at Santiniketan, echoing the call of "Awaken India, Awaken India."[33] On another occasion, at a welcome reception held by a Hindu association, he was again moved to tears by a speech given in his honor that called for a "necessity to forge a cultural union between Japan and India," leading him to conclude that "any thinking Indian expects a great deal from Japanese."[34] Noguchi elaborated:

> A state is not a state, not a respectful nation, if it is merely being supported by other nations, unable to support others. Therefore, I always think and wish that Japan could support other nations, be that India or China. . . . [E]ver since I arrived in Calcutta, I witnessed numerous impoverished people and beggars, which led me to realize how fortunate a Japanese life was. . . . Also, I have confirmed my belief that, even from the viewpoint of international relations, there is nothing shameful about being a Japanese.

Having traveled in overpriced India, Noguchi pondered that a country could be called "civilized" only after every individual, including the poor, could benefit from the conveniences and comforts of modern life, such as being literate and being able to buy newspapers cheaply every day. Ultimately, it is the British colonial policies in Noguchi's mind that were at the heart of the Indian—and implicitly, all the colonized Asian—predicament.[35] For Noguchi, Japan's increasing material strength meant that there was now a genuine chance for him personally to reconcile his "life-long question of how to come to terms with my Japanese and international identities."[36] Now that Japan itself was a recognized international player and a legitimate "civilized" country, Noguchi believed that Japan should heroically liberate the rest of Asia. Such a grossly sentimental but apparently heartfelt conviction was to propel him in his enthusiastic support of Japan's China War, resulting in a fallout with his long-time idol Tagore.

* * *

In the actual application of political ideology, the law of reverse logic often reigns as an easy answer to the very problem that produced that ideology in the first place, creating a circular argument that defeats the existing meaning of the ideology itself. Pan-Asianism was no exception. With the increasing gap to be filled between theory and practice, the following logic would emerge predominantly in Japan's Pan-Asianist thinking of the Fifteen Years' War: irrespective of the beauty of the peace-loving character of the Teaist view of Pan-Asianism, the very lack of recognition from the West remained a mournful result of Asia's overwhelming material weakness, which in turn made it impossible for Asia to assert itself in spheres other than artistic and cultural. Therefore Japan, the strongest and arguably the best equipped Asian power, had to undertake the building of a stronger Asia by making the rest of Asia more like Japan. Such an extended reasoning in effect refuted the important premise of the Teaist rendition of Pan-Asianism that tried to supersede Asia's material weakness by emphasizing its spiritual dimension.

As the power configurations of the world oscillated and Japan became increasingly entrapped by its own paradoxically "anti-imperialist imperialist" rhetoric, this reverse logic became indispensable. Also, the temptation to see a panacea for all national, international, and indeed Asian problems in the imagined Pan-Asian utopia became almost impossible to resist, even among the most enlightened Japanese. Yet the sheer appeal of Pan-Asianism tends to be downplayed.

By saying that Pan-Asianism called for deeper and wider reaching roots than is generally assumed, the present and the previous chapters have attempted to counter the seemingly convincing but in fact misleading assumption that Japan's Pan-Asianism was simply a convenient excuse for Japan's solely self-interested nationalism. It is critical to remember that while "Asia" may feel like a natural condition in our own time, major aspects of what was meant by "Asia" or what it meant to be an "Asian" did not crystallize until such categories began to be projected upon and internalized by "Asians" themselves. In this sense, Pan-Asianism in its embryonic form was primarily a theoretical exercise. It tried to make sense of the broader historical process of incorporating the world into a single society of nation-states that dictated international relations. Facing the forceful waves of this expansion, Pan-Asianism in its most nonmaterialist embodiment rendered by Okakura aspired to a grand expression of identity and group solidarity based on that immense—though never clearly delineated—spatial and psychological divide between "East" and "West," even transcending smaller Asian nationalisms within.

Precisely such an all-inclusive and transnational character explains the peculiarities of Pan-Asianism specifically and of pan-nationalisms broadly. The evaluation of Japan's Pan-Asianism during the Fifteen Years' War is difficult because of the ease with which the analyst is tempted to dismiss *any* Pan-Asianist claims as a guise for Japan's self-serving, state-centric nationalism. The other side of the same coin tells us that some fall into the converse danger of taking *all* of Japan's wartime Pan-Asianist pronouncements for an expression of its genuine and unselfish motives to the celebration of Japan's "just war." Both views are flawed, for the former puts Pan-Asianism entirely in the shadow of Japan's national interest, while the latter presents the exact mirror image, that is, Japan's interest being unconditionally synonymous with grander Pan-Asianist aspirations. When superimposed, it is true that aspects of Japan's wartime Pan-Asianism overlapped with Japan's nationalism; Pan-Asianism was, on many occasions, made to accommodate and correspond to Japan's more "selfish" and exclusively Japanese interests.

More critically, however, there also existed a place where Pan-Asianism was not completely overshadowed by Japan's nationalism. It may have been small, but it was still a critical margin that should not be ignored. This problem of analysis then raises some pertinent issues to be considered throughout the rest of this study. Nationalism, as such observers as Madame de Staël and Elie Kedourie have insisted, may well be a doctrine based on egoism and selfishness of a nation.[37] To what extent, then, was Japan's Pan-Asianism "unselfish" to the point of sacrificing its more "selfish" interests? As a nationalist movement, could Pan-Asianism, too, be considered a "selfish" doctrine?

On a related but more general point, pan-movements—as they existed in twentieth-century international politics—were solidarity movements of paradoxical, even oxymoronic "transnational nationalist" ambitions. Here lies the essence of a dilemma for all pan-nationalist movements. While quasi-universal, romantic, and fraternal aspects of pan-nationalism appear attractive in theory, many a pan-nationalism has failed in its practical application precisely because of such a grand—and often grandiose—universal aspiration. Another imperative question thus emerges: How is one to reconcile existing nationalisms and political arrangements within the broader scope of a pan-national union? A reconciliation of this sort is extremely difficult; the record of the past—in Pan-Slavism, Pan-Germanism, Pan-Americanism, Pan-Arabism, Pan-Islamism, and Pan-Africanism—speaks for itself. However, reconciliation, if and when somehow achieved, is not without its rewards and inspirations, as the case of Pan-Europeanism and some other instances of economic and cultural regionalism on a limited scale continue to remind us. Taken together, perhaps one is obliged at first to accept the profound gap that more often than not separates the theoretical and the practical in pan-nationalisms. The grander the ambitions, the more difficult their implementations, naturally.

In the end, it would be premature to regard Pan-Asianism simply as a manifestation of Japanese nationalism with anti-Western or anti-imperialist twists. To be sure, such a reactionary and ambivalent relationship with Western imperialism was a built-in, though not sufficient component of Pan-Asianism. Hence a critical distinction can be made between "anti" and "counter" movements here. While "anti" forces only result in spontaneous resistance, "counter" forces call for organized programs of collective action in the hope of bringing about decisive social change. If Japan had used Pan-Asianism in a war that was simply meant to preserve its entirely selfish interest, it would not have bothered to imagine and invent other Asian nations in the involved and comprehensive fashion that it did during the Fifteen Years' War. In other words, Pan-Asianism was an ideology of "counter" rather than "anti" forces, precisely because it provided a concrete exegesis for Japan's mission in conceiving the rest of Asia in its own self-image, as shown in the implementation of extensive wartime "re-education" programs with all types of social, economic, and cultural ramifications that were meant to, in their misguided ways, save Asia.

As an ideology forming the basis of Japanese expansionism, and, in the minds of many, a conceptual partner to Japanese ultranationalism, Pan-Asianism in the 1930s became further "ideologized" with the added specifications of its ultimate goals of disseminating Imperial Japanese values to the rest of Asia. The subsequent Japanese renditions and interpretations of Pan-Asianism during the war were, at the very least, not a purposeful manipulation to fit Japan's premeditated expansionist designs but rather an ideological glue that gave purpose and cohesion to an otherwise divided and uncoordinated wartime policymaking body. For a Japan that was catapulted onto the prime stage of international politics, while still lacking its own philosophical framework of foreign policy, the Pan-Asianist call for the liberation and independence of Asia became a beguiling concept upon which many were willing to take a chance.

3
From Internationalism to Pan-Asianism

The Japanese Kwantung Army's takeover of China's northeastern provinces in September 1931 is conventionally regarded as the starting point of the Fifteen Years' War. In light of Manchuria's association with the subsequent rise of its militarism, then, the odd thing about Japan's foreign policy in its immediate wake was not that it was so very different from that of the previous decade, but that it was so very similar: Japan after the Manchurian Incident did not undergo a decisive regime change from "democracy" to "fascism." Equally in foreign policy, it would be a mistake to think that Japan abandoned its regard for liberal internationalism of the 1920s entirely in pursuit of national interest under the convenient guise of Pan-Asianism. Focusing on the initial phase of the Fifteen Years' War, roughly from 1931 to 1934 when the impact of Japan's action in Manchuria remained unabsorbed both internally and externally, this chapter shows that Japan's official policy underwent neither a violent nor a decisive break in its overall ideological outlook.

As the previous discussion has shown, Pan-Asianism and its multiple threads had long been in existence before 1931. This simple fact dispels the notion that Pan-Asianism suddenly emerged as a justification for the Manchurian Incident. While it is true that Japan increasingly came to rely on Pan-Asianist vocabulary to explain its position in Manchuria, it did so in an attempt to reconcile its position within the existing international arrangement rather than to advance its interests, be they of "self," "national," or indeed a "Pan-Asianist" kind, in outright confrontation with larger currents of international politics. Reference to and dependence on Pan-Asianist language became a vital necessity for Japan's diplomatic elites, as they faced the task of defending its appropriation of Manchuria to the outside world. In such a process, Pan-Asianist aspects of the Manchurian *fait accompli* proved an acceptable, arguably even attractive, ground upon which to explain Japan's case. Thus the legitimization of Japan's post-Manchuria foreign policy along Pan-Asianist lines did not conceal a set of preconceived designs. Rather, Pan-Asianism provided a loose but overarching sense of cohesion for an otherwise confused and uncoordinated policymaking body.

While the Manchurian Incident itself was very much a direct result of action-oriented, Meishuron-inspired Pan-Asianism, the Japanese government portrayed the *fait accompli* in terms of a less confrontational and more *status quo*-oriented brand of Pan-Asianism. But the line demarcating the two types of Pan-Asianism would become ever so fine, as Japan's liberal internationalists, too, began to subscribe to the argument that the Manchurian takeover constituted Japan's legitimate crusade in Asia. Accordingly, Japan's official stance came to revolve around the explanation of why it was entitled to some sort of a regional leadership, while still trying to stick to the emerging internationalist norms that had so markedly shaped its foreign policy of the previous decade. Arguments could be made that Tokyo merely resorted to such a blend of internationalist and Pan-Asianist language simply because it had to. But a closer inspection of Japan's major internationalist figures shows that even those individuals who had ostensibly been beholden to the idea of liberal internationalism willingly asserted Japan's case, perhaps because they, too, had accepted the basic Pan-Asianist motives behind the Manchurian venture and, moreover, were even excited about the prospect of Japan's leadership role in Asia.

That there was no unambiguous departure of Japan's foreign policy orientation from internationalism to Pan-Asianism, however, does not diminish the overall importance of the Manchurian Incident as a turning point for Japan's Pan-Asianism, or indeed as a starting point of its Fifteen Years' War. Instigated by the charismatic field officer and devoted Pan-Asianist Colonel Ishiwara Kanji, the Incident looms spectacularly not only as a prelude to the militarist turn of the central power structure at home but also as the first significant and practical application of Pan-Asianism to Japan's official policy. Thus another crucial task here is to understand the precise combination of forces and factors that molded Ishiwara's conception for Japan's invasion of Manchuria in the first place.

The role of Pan-Asianism considered in this episode of the Fifteen Years' War becomes twofold. The first function of Pan-Asianism was to provide a guide to action that culminated in the Incident. The second function was to provide a foreign policy framework convincing enough even for Japan's liberal internationalist elites, enabling them to defend the military insubordination in terms of a grander ideological vision to the outside world. With those two specific manifestations of Pan-Asianism unique to this period in mind, the present chapter will provide a discussion of the historical context surrounding Japan's foreign policymaking. It will then be followed by an examination of Pan-Asianism in the thought and action of Ishiwara Kanji as well as of Japan's liberal internationalists who gradually but surely came to accept the Pan-Asianist tenets of the Ishiwara's field initiative as Japan's official position.

I. Elements of Japan's Foreign Policy

Liberal Internationalism of the 1920s

In a broad sense, the Manchurian Incident stands out in interwar international history because of its link with the failure of internationalism, and more specifically, with the principle of collective security.[1] Therefore, one must be clear about what exactly one means by the term "internationalism." The term is often carelessly and uncritically used as an antonym for "Pan-Asianism" in the narrative history of Japanese expansionism.

Here, "internationalism" refers to post–World War I ideas, movements, and institutions that sought to reformulate the nature of relations among nation-states (and their aspirants), as most boldly realized in Woodrow Wilson's conception of cooperation and interchange *via* the founding of the intergovernmental organization, the League of Nations. Given its obvious failure to prevent the coming of World War II, numerous analysts and historians have pointed out that the League suffered from both intrinsic and circumstantial flaws. One such flaw was its overly optimistic assumption that Lockean principles applied to international politics. By presuming that man—and the state—would be guided by what was "good," the League did not clarify when and how members were expected to take actions. In effect, the League left the workability question of collective security unanswered, failing to define what constituted "aggression" and how the burden of preserving security was to be shared among the concerned parties. Moreover, successful enforcement of the League law assumed as an absolute prerequisite that an aggressor state remain in the League and play an active role within its deliberation processes. As the cases of the Japanese, Italian, and ultimately German withdrawals from the League showed, the revisionist powers did not care to remain in the machinery of conciliatory deliberation past a certain point, leaving the League virtually ineffectual in times of real and heightened crises.

Its obvious shortcomings notwithstanding, however, the League did try to transform the rules and conduct of international relations. It made threat and use of force by one state against another a matter of international concern, with the possibility of international condemnation acting as a restraint on further aggressions. Although in imperfect and uneven ways, the League introduced smaller states into an arena in which they became a part of a larger international system. In light of this development, "internationalists" in this chapter should be understood as those who accepted the validity, or at the very least utility, of such institutionalized norms embodied by the League and its partner institutions. Those "internationalists" similarly engaged in the reciprocal process, beyond finer political motivations and differences, of legitimizing their foreign policy objectives in terms of those internationalist concepts, and so conferred credence to those very principles by the act of paying attention to them.

Also outside the League framework, the Washington Conference (1921–22) introduced a new multilateral treaty regime that took international politics beyond the traditional diplomatic arrangements based solely on the politics of balance of power, sphere of influence, and right of conquest. The signatories of the Washington treaties were to reconcile their competing interests by pledging themselves to naval disarmament and international cooperation, especially where they concerned the future of China.[2] Such an emerging spirit of internationalism and multilateralism came to be called the Versailles-Washington system. It had paradoxical implications for Japan's Pan-Asianism, for it was this system that had enabled Japan to become a full-fledged member of the club of the great powers. At the same time, however, the country's struggle in the 1930s emerged directly out of its dissatisfactions with the Versailles-Washington system, the very institution that could have further secured its rising status.

There were external as well as internal sources of Japan's ambivalent international position at the start of the 1930s. For one, the external environment within which Japan operated was itself far from stable. The great powers, too, fluctuated between their embrace of internationalist norms and more traditional conceptions of international relations, leading some

Japanese to question how firm the powers' commitment to internationalism really was. Adding to such uncertainties were Japan's domestic problems in the second half of the 1920s. Indeed on the domestic front, the Fifteen Years' War began a year prior to the Manchurian Incident, making it a full fifteen years to Japan's defeat in 1945.

Japan's Budding Liberalism and the Death of the Lion

On November 14, 1930, at Tokyo Station, an ultranationalist gunman, named Sagōya Tomeo, shot Prime Minister Hamaguchi Osachi of the Rikken Minseitō (Constitutional Democratic Party, or Minseitō for short). Hamaguchi survived this attempt on his life, at least for the time being. Aptly nicknamed "Raion Saishō" (Lion Premier) for his dignified looks and principled behavior, the popular premier even continued to attend a series of grueling Diet sessions. But his resilience gave way eventually, and he resigned his post in April 1931. On August 26, he died from complications of his unhealed wounds.

In the wake of Hamaguchi's ordeal, the opposition Rikken Seiyōkai (Friends of Constitutional Government Party, a.k.a. Seiyōkai), in an effort to topple its rival increased its reliance on nonparliamentary methods, disrupting sessions and even resorting to physical assaults. Helped by the ineffectiveness of the *pro tem* prime minister Shidehara Kijōrō, who was not a party member and woefully lacked the parliamentary skills and personal charisma that were an integral part of Hamaguchi's leadership, the Minseitō quickly disintegrated. The decline of party politics, in turn, compounded a crisis of values that had been plaguing Japan for quite some time. At the center, the depression shook the tightly interlocked power base of *zaibatsu* capitalists and party politicians. The most obvious power contenders to replace party politicians were military officers, along with other unimaginative bureaucrats devoted to narrow interests of their respective specialties.

As far as the actual policymaking was concerned, the Meiji Constitution of 1889 stipulated that the emperor had the formal right (though hardly exercised in practice) to formulate and implement foreign policy with the assistance of his advisers. But the affairs of the military were excluded from the Constitution's definition of "foreign policy," distinguishing military advisers from the emperor's civilian advisers. This arrangement, commonly called *tōsuiken no dokuritsu* (the Autonomy of the Supreme Command), thus permitted Japan's armed forces to assert their influence more directly on the making of its external policy. Already by the 1910s

Japan *de facto* had two governments, one military and the other civilian.[3] Such a system did function insofar as the *ex machina* authority of the *genrō*, or the elder statesmen, acted as mediators of conflicting views. But the inevitable power vacuum left by the deaths of most of the elders, aggravated by social and economic hardships of the 1920s, was to be increasingly replaced by conservatives in the government and right-wingers in the armed services. The relevance of this change in the power dynamic for Pan-Asianism was enormous, as young officers indoctrinated from an early age in the mystical majesty of Japan's imperial institution came to seek an answer in radical reform and called for revolutionary programs at home and abroad.

Indeed, it was precisely "the Autonomy of the Supreme Command" that those who opposed Hamaguchi's signing of the London treaties claimed to safeguard.[4] Through the conservative Privy Council, the Navy attacked Hamaguchi as blasphemously interfering with military affairs formulated to serve the best interest of the Empire. But the prime minister turned out to be even more defiant, threatening, for the first time in history, the constitutional removal of the councilors. The Lion Premier's defiance ultimately cost him his life, as it was directly on the account of the successful ratification of the London treaties that his assassin gunned him down. Coupled with the "the Autonomy of the Supreme Command" argument, in the late 1930s, the provision that the Army and Navy ministers had to be actively serving generals and admirals, would often act against forming a uniform foreign policy, allowing the services the power to veto and to force a cabinet resignation by refusing to provide a substitute minister.

It bears repeating, however, that the military, neither then nor since, took complete control of the government. Nor was the military itself united or motivated by any unflagging pursuit of a tangible goal. For instance, most, though not all, high-ranking officials of the Army known as the "Control Faction" (*tōseiha*) were opposed to assassinations as a means of achieving control and preferred maneuvering within the limits of existing political organs. The young cadets who carried out the murderous tactics and called for radical change largely belonged to the so-called "Imperial Way Faction"(*kōdōha*). But those officers were not without powerful backers in high circles either. General Araki Sadao (1877–1966), who served as Army Minister in Inukai's and Saitō Makoto's cabinets, was at one point deemed the leader of the Imperial Way Faction. Not surprisingly, Araki lent strong support to the instigators of the Manchurian Incident.

Starting from Hamaguchi's predicament, Japan would witness a series of assassination plots that ended many of the lives of liberal-minded and moderate politicians, including his closest colleague, Finance Minister Inoue Junnosuke, who was brutally murdered in February 1932, not long after Hamaguchi's death by an ultranationalist gunman inspired by apocalyptic Nichiren Buddhism under the motto of "One Believer, One Killing." While Japan would not become a total military dictatorship or a fascist state, there would be more and more reasons for Japan's leaders to concede to various bureaucratic and military pressures. In order to prevent another coup attempt, leaders of lesser courage and principles, including the emperor, more concerned about their own survival, would be prompted to confer authority to the armed forces, which had bred the climate of terror in the first place, each time giving in to military demands a little more than the last time, until it was too late to reverse the pattern. Although enough to prevent a successful coup, this tactic in the end amounted to a spiral of ineffective appeasement.

There appears to be more to this self-destructive path, however. The appeasers preferred to look for a common ground with the ultranationalists and to legitimize their decisions in a grander ideological scheme of things rather than to indict the coercive and forceful methods of which they did not approve. Since Pan-Asianism, at the very basis, provided a morally unobjectionable ideological glue for people of all political persuasions. It is not difficult to see why it would achieve the elevated status of Japan's war aim just as the center of decision making became more and more fragmented. Japan's first decisive turn toward this road was the Manchurian Incident that began in September 1931.

Two Schools of Foreign Policy: An Elusive Distinction

The increasing influence of the armed forces tempts us to conclude that with its ascent came the more ultranationalist, regionalist policy (aspects of which can be equated to Pan-Asianist policy), in turn signifying a total loss of control of foreign policy by the Foreign Ministry and moreover, the death of Japan's liberal internationalism. The truth was more complicated than this. It is true that there existed two foreign policy orientations by the time of the Manchurian Incident that could be broadly termed "internationalist" and "Pan-Asianist." It is also true that the Foreign Ministry was a representative institution advocating the former, while certain factions of the military strongly advocated expansionist ideas steeped in the Meishuron line of Pan-Asianist thinking. However, the two orientations were far from mutually exclusive.

Traditionally, Japan's "internationalism" had been associated with those who denounced outright confrontation with the great powers as a means of enhancing Japan's international position. The seasoned diplomat and the last *genrō* Prince Saionji Kinmochi (1849–1940) remarked, on the occasion of the London Conference, that "[t]he Eastern questions should resolve themselves through the cooperation with the Anglo-American powers alone."[5] Such a statement encapsulated this school's philosophy.

Saionji himself had been exposed from a young age to the nineteenth-century European liberal tradition, having been personally influenced by his fellow lodger Georges Clemenceau during his stay in Paris under the Commune, as well as by the noted liberal thinkers of early modern Japan, Nakae Chōmin and Matsuda Masahisa (1847–1914), who studied with him in France and became his lifelong friends. The liberal internationalist principle of "*Où règne la justice, les armes sont inutiles*" meant that Japan would abide by the emerging norms of the Versailles-Washington system, and thereby concentrate on maximizing its position in China by way of free market competition, rather than military expansion. The conventional wisdom identifies the key players of this group as Shidehara Kijōrō, financiers Inoue Junnosuke and Takahashi Korekiyo, and Minseitō politicians such as Prime Minister Hamaguchi Osachi.

On the other end of the spectrum stood a group that saw in continental expansion an answer to solving the very same question of how best to improve Japan's international position. This group, more problematically (for reasons that will be explained later), is often regarded as "Pan-Asianist." With the ultimate goal of achieving an autarchy under Japan's leadership, its advocates aspired to a reversal, or at least a readjustment of the *status quo* of the international system. Their agenda thus presupposed Japan's Asian alliance leadership in transforming the system dominated by Britain and the United States. Such a view was most loudly asserted by the Japanese Imperial Army, the right-wing, ultranationalist organizations of the Genyōsha-Kokuryōkai ilk, as well as jingoistic party politicians, more often from the Seiyōkai—those who espoused the radicalized version of Meishuron Pan-Asianist thinking with specific reformist as well as expansionist designs. As the historian Eguchi Keiichi explains, "the latter [Pan-Asianists] rose because the *status quo* preferences of the former [internationalists] were dealt a body blow. . . . [T]he *status quo* itself was changing, as proven by the great powers' decision to retreat into economic blocs following the Great Depression of 1929."[6]

On careful reflection, however, it is precisely such an easily made distinction of ideological allegiances between internationalism and Pan-Asianism that obfuscates a proper understanding of Pan-Asianism in Japan's war. While Eguchi's broad distinction of the internationalist/Pan-Asianist divide is a widely accepted one across varying historiographical interpretations, it is a misleading dichotomy nonetheless. There were many trans-group agents who operated across the two camps, seeing legitimacy in the arguments—or at least some aspects of arguments—of both groups. The relatively value-free definition of Pan-Asianism, as an ideology that sought to achieve self-awareness and external recognition of Asia, was indeed in accordance with the policy preferences of most policymakers. For instance, the liberal internationalist diplomat Yoshizawa Kenkichi, who remained vocal in his criticisms of the Army's China policy throughout the war, acted as Foreign Minister for the pioneering Pan-Asianist and Seiyōkai premier Inukai Tsuyoshi, who also happened to be his father-in-law.[7]

The reality was that in the immediate wake of the Manchurian Incident, there were no obvious disagreements between the internationalists and the so-called Pan-Asianists over the legitimacy of Japanese presence in Manchuria *per se*. Rather, disagreements emerged from the niceties of the means to be employed, timing to be had, and the degree of maintaining or maximizing Japan's Manchurian possessions to be pursued. Recognizing Japan's long-term interests in Manchuria, the two groups did not in the least represent polar opposite foreign policy viewpoints. The two camps shared enough common grievances and anxieties about Japan's international position and, by natural extension, the weakness of Asia and especially China, which were concerns of both a strategic and an ideological nature.

Matsuoka Yōsuke as an Internationalist

Perhaps, the most potent example of individuals holding overlapping allegiances to internationalism and Pan-Asianism is the Seiyōkai member Matsuoka Yōsuke (1880–1946). In early 1931, before the outbreak of the Manchurian Incident, he famously criticized Shidehara for his China policy, on the basis of the liberal foreign minister's "absolute no-action, standing-by principle,"[8] and his lack of recognition of "Manchuria-Mongolia as the country's lifeline" (*Manmō wa waga kuni no seimeisen*). Matsuoka is often regarded as a foe of Japan's internationalism, having led the dramatic walkout of the Japanese delegation from the League of Nations Assembly (even though this was not a formal withdrawal), and having single-handedly concluded alliances with Adolf Hitler and Joseph Stalin on the eve of the Pacific phase of the Fifteen Years' War. But in some important respects, Matsuoka, especially in his earlier incarnation, was one of the foremost internationalists in Japan, particularly in the way he attempted to use international organizations and conferences as a legitimate forum in which to negotiate Japan's position, and this was at a time when international conferences were still rare.

Because of his prominent role in articulating Japan's international position both in and outside Japan, Matsuoka's ideological composition is worth examining. From the impressionable age of thirteen, he lived in the United States, where he suffered great financial difficulties and possibly racial discrimination.[9] After much struggle, he was trained to be a lawyer at the University of Oregon, followed by some diplomatic postings and an appointment to the board of the South Manchurian Railroad. Such a singular background might explain the delicate blend of realism and idealism that colored his view on diplomacy. He was, in his conduct as a foreign minister, a self-professed believer in classical power politics of a Bismarckian persuasion. On the eve of his signing of the nonaggression pact with Stalin in 1941 and in a state of cheerful drunkenness, he proudly declared to Saionji Kinkazu (1906–93), a young Foreign Ministry adviser and a grandson of the last *genrō* who accompanied Matsuoka on his trip, "Diplomacy is power. The Axis diplomacy is a leverage used to gain power. The Tripartite Pact is not about an alliance made to wage war."[10]

At the same time, Matsuoka was also enough of an idealistic "internationalist," certainly for a good part of his active career, to engage rigorously in the politics of international and intergovernmental organizations. That he took the business of those organizations seriously is important in itself. By not making light of the liberal internationalist norms, he helped to legitimize the efficacy of such organizations in return, qualifying him as an internationalist.

As a testimony to Matsuoka's dedication, Japan's renowned journalist Matsumoto Shigeharu (1899–1989) recalled in his memoirs his first experience of attending an international conference. At the third Biennial Conference of the Institute of Pacific Relations held in Kyoto at the end of 1929, Matsuoka participated in a series of intense debates with Chinese delegates over Manchuria.[11] Matsuoka impressed the young journalist with his oratory, backed by substantial knowledge of international affairs and international law. Furthermore, Matsumoto was doubly impressed when he later saw Matsuoka amicably having lunch with those very Chinese delegates with whom he had been, only minutes earlier, exchanging fire in the debating chamber, leading him to conclude that Matsuoka understood the art of both the onstage and backstage politics of international organizations exceptionally well.

An English pamphlet circulated by the Sino-Japanese Association of Manchuria, published during Matsuoka's tenure as the vice-president of the South Manchurian Railroad, confirms Matsumoto's impressions. Matsuoka elaborated on the nature of the changing international system in terms of emerging liberal internationalist principles, stating:

> The old conception of the state, as an independent entity exclusively concerned with the pursuit of selfish national interest, is no longer accepted as satisfactory by a world in which the interdependence of peoples is increasingly more obvious; . . . We no longer apply a twisted Darwinism to the life of nations and see international politics as a perpetual struggle for survival. . . . The world's statesmen, who since the Great War had been seeking means by which lasting peace may be established, agree on certain fundamentals . . . that every race should be protected in its right to existence: that every race has a right to equal opportunity for its enjoyment of civilization; and that co-operation among the nations is the best road to this desirable end.[12]

He then proceeded to link Japan's economic interests in Manchuria, whose existence he never denied, to the idea of interdependence and mutual benefit.

> The development of Manchuria and Mongolia is and should be, first and last, for the benefit of these countries themselves. We know at the same time that no consideration in the interest of these countries is necessarily incompatible with the question of relieving the situation of Japan as regards her national life. On the contrary, a wealthier and better developed Manchuria, we know, will mean greater prosperity to Japan and her people. Increase in Japan's demand for Manchurian products will not only have the effect of stimulating development of Manchuria and Mongolia, but will also impress China with the importance of such development. The correlation thus existing between Japan and China is bound, from the very nature of the thing, to work for the good of one as well as the other, ultimately serving the international life of the whole world.[13]

What one sees here are some serious efforts made to articulate Japan's economic expansionism in liberal internationalist language. At the same time, his overall vision for Japan's role in Asia portends Japan's Meishuron-inspired "Greater East Asia Co-Prosperity Sphere" ideology of the later years of the Fifteen Years' War, the naming of which is generally attributed to Matsuoka. This suggests that ideological themes of internationalism and the Meishuron thread of Pan-Asianism had been tightly interlocked even before the outbreak of the Fifteen Years' War, making it difficult to assert that there was a clear break between Japan's internationalist and Pan-Asianist thinking. If the distinction could be made between those two groups of foreign policymakers at all, it was not over the internationalist or Pan-Asianist principles, or, as the following will demonstrate, even over the acceptance of the Manchurian *fait accompli*. Rather, differences arose over the question of whether further expansion would provide a feasible and legitimate means of upholding Manchuria as Japan's—and by Pan-Asianist extension, Asia's—lifeline.

II. The Manchurian Incident, Ishiwara Kanji, and the Internationalists

Recounting the Manchurian Incident

The Manchurian Incident, though varying interpretations exist as to its exact significance, can be roughly summarized as follows. On the night of September 18, 1931, the Kwantung Army (Kantōgun in Japanese), a faction of the Japanese Imperial Army stationed in Manchuria since the Russo-Japanese War, planted a small bomb on the South Manchurian Railroad. Claiming that anti-Japanese Chinese elements were responsible, and that retaliation was in order, the Japanese started a full-scale assault on Chinese troops in Mukden (Shenyang) and Changchun.

The makers of this operation were Colonels Ishiwara Kanji and Itagaki Seishirō. In Tokyo, Prime Minister Wakatsuki Reijirō and Foreign Minister Shidehara, among others, protested against the field army's further northward advance. Immediately following the development of September 18–19, the cabinet pressed for containing hostilities, to which the Army Minister Minami Jirō agreed. However, neither the civil nor military instructions stopped the young officers in the field, leading them to seize Jilin on September 21.

In the meantime, Japanese public opinion emphatically supported the insubordination, as the uncritical media added fuel to the patriotic fire by feeding the public with reports commending the courage of the Kwantung Army. This eventually led the Wakatsuki cabinet to approve the seizure of Jilin by September 24. The pattern of field insubordination followed by a reluctant government acceptance continued, as the Kwantung Army took over Jinzhou, southeast of Mukden, and Qiqihar in the far north. Along with this development emerged the Kwantung Army proposal to establish a republic governed by pro-Japanese Chinese leaders. In December, a frustrated Wakatsuki cabinet resigned, finally unleashing the Kwantung Army's northern operation in full force. Inukai's cabinet initially hoped for a peaceful settlement, but the new Army Minister Araki Sadao encouraged rapid field advance, with the forces securing their hold on Harbin on February 5, 1932.

This brought all three Manchurian provinces of Liaoning, Heilongjiang, and Jilin, in addition to Jehol province in Inner Mongolia under the Kwantung Army's control. Soon after the Lytton Commission, a team of international investigators, arrived to take stock and write a critical report of Japanese actions, declaring them to be invasion of China in contravention of the Nine-Power Pact and the Pact of Paris, the establishment of the republic of Manchukuo was proclaimed on March 1 under the regency of Henry Pu Yi (1906–67), the last Qing emperor of Manchu descent, on March 9, 1932. Inukai's assassination on May 15, 1932 (the so-called 5-15 Incident), eventually led to the official recognition, four months later, by the Japanese government of Manchukuo as a sovereign state. This was followed by international opprobrium, which resulted in Japan's announcement of its intention to withdraw from the League one year later in March 1933 and the formation of a Manchurian empire under Emperor Pu Yi two years later in March 1934.

Evident even in this parsimonious account of the Incident was the absence of a unitary policy voice within the Japanese government, which added to a general sense of hesitancy and confusion about how best to respond to the field initiatives. Reasons for this, in addition to the structural impediments noted above, were many. For a start, the country's domestic scene was marked by an atmosphere of terror and insubordination, as demonstrated by the murders of the former Finance Minister Inoue and the Mitsui chairman Baron Dan Takuma in early 1932, followed by the assassination of Inukai. Precisely because of the absence of any coordinated response at the very center, it seems only natural that there are wide-ranging interpretations about the nature of Japan's military conduct in Manchuria.

In search of clearer causal factors, some of the most important historical accounts on the origins of the Manchurian Incident have focused primarily on the accountability question of who made the decision for military action. The resounding question that emerges across the board in most classical accounts is whether the Incident was an act of insubordination or instigated directly from Tokyo. Because of the fundamental and lasting split in the historiographical view that colors one's perception of the meaning of this event, it is useful at least to outline the strengths and shortcomings in the contrasting interpretations of the Manchurian Incident, before venturing into an analysis of the role Pan-Asianism played within it.

On the one hand of this spectrum of classical interpretations stands a "realist" account presented by James Crowley.[14] Arguing for a continuity of intentions, Crowley has argued that Japan's foreign policy in the early 1930s was a combined effort of military and civilian leaders concerned about the uncertain prospects of Japan's national security. Japan's policymakers thought that the country's survival could only be assured by undermining Kuomintang China and securing sufficient resources to permit the country to confront the Soviet Union, or possibly the United States, and thus clinching Japan's hegemony in East Asia.

However, Crowley's take on Japan's peculiar imperialism of "defense through expansion" presupposes only one of myriad possible conceptions of Japan's "national interest" in Manchuria, as they were perceived by different Japanese leaders of the time. An alternative explanation, I would contend, is that the eventual acceptance of the Manchurian Incident as a done deed came about not because the Japanese government held a uniform perception of Japan's exclusive national interest, but more because Japan became entrapped by the dynamic of its own highly ideological rhetoric of both a realist *and* Pan-Asianist nature. In this alternative picture, "realism," too, becomes an ideology of sorts and not an unequivocal "reality" in its own right.

As with any historians concerned with revising existing interpretations, Crowley highlights the notion that the Manchurian Incident was a "rational" action taken in order to maximize, or at the very least, preserve Japan's national interest. Thus his view sits in stark contrast to an earlier monograph by Ogata Sadako, who is herself one of the most famed internationalists of the post–World War II world.[15] This great-granddaughter of "Pan-Asianist" Inukai Tsuyoshi and granddaughter of "internationalist" Yoshizawa Kenkichi argues that the Manchurian Incident was essentially an independent action of the Kwantung Army, not necessarily in agreement with the views held by the headquarters. On careful inspection, her thesis does not belittle the responsibility of Tokyo in the least, contrary to what might be suggested by the title of her book, *Defiance in Manchuria*. She nonetheless emphasizes elements of field-led initiatives in this episode, paying utmost attention to the authority-defying actions, statements, and programs of the field officers.

In assessing the validity of the two disparate viewpoints put forward by Crowley and Ogata, the latter's account proves more convincing in its deep-rooted understanding of Japanese belief in its national destiny as a *meishu* of Asia. Ogata accepts that Japan's commitment to racial harmony was qualified. But she does not categorically deny that nonmaterial factors provided formative elements in its strategic thinking. She argues that the prevailing sentiment of the Japanese Army in Manchuria left room for the fraternal aspect of Pan-Asianism and thus signified genuine belief in the professed principle of racial, cultural, and geographical propinquity.[16] In that sense, she accepts, albeit implicitly, the important role played by Pan-Asianism in the Manchurian Incident as an ideology that precariously elevated the role of Japan in Asia in Japanese self-image.

Ogata's analysis, however, falls short of making a specific case for the force of Pan-Asianism as an engine behind policy development. The most critical question becomes not so much one of identifying the more responsible party between Manchuria and Tokyo, if there was indeed such a clear split to start with. Rather, it is one of understanding how Pan-Asianist components of the Incident, as initially conceived by the instigators of the Incident, eventually cohered with the government's official policy orientation in its aftermath. In order to arrive at this synthesis, we must first consider the ideology of Colonel Ishiwara Kanji (1889–1949), whose role as the mastermind of the Manchurian Incident is beyond dispute in almost any interpretation of this important historical episode. Although Colonel Itagaki Seishirō also played an instrumental part in it, his function was more one of a field strategist, planning general tactics in accordance with the overall goals set by Ishiwara, thus qualifying Ishiwara as the undisputed ideological mastermind behind the operation.

Ishiwara Kanji, the Pan-Asianist

Indeed, to study Ishiwara is to study the immediate ideological genesis of the Fifteen Years' War at large. Ishiwara, sometimes dubbed the "Japanese T. E. Lawrence" for his conception of a Pan-Asianist utopia as a parallel to

Lawrence's Pan-Arabist conception of building a "Dream Palace of the Arabs," was at the same time a military historian, staff officer, strategist, theorist, plotter, and above all Pan-Asianist. He was the central figure in devising the strategic goals of the Manchurian operation, based on his apocalyptic dialectic of "Final War" (*saishō sensō*), to be fought between Japan and the United States.[17]

Prior to 1931, Ishiwara had long believed Japan's security depended on Manchuria. This concern was backed by his equally obsessive attachment to the idea of Asian unity. He was also taken to sophisticated military analysis, in part derived from his exposure to the German total war doctrines of Carl von Clausewitz and Helmuth von Moltke, picked up in the three years of his sojourn in early 1920s Berlin. This body of knowledge in advanced strategic studies was coupled with his faith in the mystical wisdom of fundamentalist Nichiren Buddhism, which he shared with many other ultranationalists of his time.[18]

Ishiwara's theory of "Final War," perfected during his lectureship at the elite Army Staff College in the mid-1920s, revolved around the subsequent points: (1) An apocalyptic struggle between Eastern civilization, represented by Japan, and Western civilization, represented by the United States (but also possibly the Soviet Union), is imminent; (2) What comes out of this titanic clash is an age of global unity and universal peace, followed by a synthesis of the best of East and West, whose exact character will be dictated by the victor of the war; (3) Thus Japan has a sacred mission to perfect its institutions and arm itself, so that the "righteous way of the East" would prevail; and (4) To achieve the said long-term objectives, the most immediate goal for the Japanese armed forces in this struggle is to concentrate on the "Manchurian Problem" by annexing the area, securing its continental resources, and paving ways for the subsequent Japanese mission to save the rest of Asia and the rest of the world.[19]

Ishiwara's Pan-Asianist thinking was further clarified in his formulation of a multinational Asian utopia. His argument went that racial harmony and equality among Asian "races" was possible, granted that Japan fulfilled the sacred mission of leading that endeavor as the leader of the Eastern union, making his brand of Pan-Asianism most directly relevant to the Meishuron tradition. His May 1931 article, "Personal View on the Manchurian-Mongolian Problem," which specifically outlined his invasion and occupation plans, claimed that decisive military actions alone would bring a settlement to the so-called "Manchurian Problem." A similar missionary conviction was shared not only by those young officers in the field, who carried out the actual operation, but also by some high-ranking officers in the General Staff Headquarters in Tokyo.

Because of the popularity of Ishiwara's theory within the Army, the degree of Tokyo's involvement in the making of the Manchurian Incident has been such a contested point. With that in mind, this much can safely be said of Tokyo's responsibility for the Incident, as well as its responsiveness to its ideological claims. Since the operation was carried out, either ostensibly or actually, in defiance of the policymakers in Tokyo, Ishiwara was prepared to resign from the Army. However, what awaited him upon his return to Japan in 1933 was not court-martial, but a medal in recognition for his "accomplishments" in Manchuria. The Army, by rewarding rather than punishing such military insubordination, which in ordinary circumstances could have amounted to a death sentence, and the government, by not protesting the Army's decision, in effect endorsed the conviction with which Ishiwara carried out his bold initiative.

The Road Not Taken

The Army's recognition of Ishiwara's action aside, the question of why other segments of the Japanese government did not categorically denounce the Kwantung Army remains. One conceivable explanation is that civilian leaders simply gave in to military pressures. But it seems premature to accept such a thesis of this watershed event when there were other conceivable options available to the government. For instance, the cabinet could have resigned in protest long before the Incident became a *fait accompli*. Moreover, the emperor himself held the ultimate authority of putting a decisive end to the matter, as he did in prompting the resignation of General Tanaka Giichi's cabinet in June 1929, when the prime minister failed to explain the murder of Chang Tso-lin, carried out by Kwantung Army officers. In his postwar memoirs, the Japanese Consul General in Mukden at the time of the Manchurian Incident, Hayashi Kyūjirō, reflected:

> Had the government resigned within a few days of the Incident . . . had the government issued a statement of protest and treated the matter with the same spirit . . . all—including the dignity of the government, Japan's international position, her economy, and her party politics—could have been salvaged.[20]

Hayashi's assessment of the Wakatsuki cabinet is especially damning. He regarded the cabinet's "irresoluteness for almost three months even though they knew very well that the situation [in Manchuria] was deteriorating minute by minute" as largely responsible for "exacerbating the unprecedented national emergencies."[21] They were "unable to let go of power and kept on engaging in petty internal power game."[22]

It is of course impossible to know what the Lion Premier Hamaguchi would have done had he lived just a little bit longer to see the outbreak of the Manchurian Incident. The strength of his principles evident in his leadership, especially when institutional pressures placed upon him were at their greatest, suggest that he probably would have taken one decisive action or another to display his rejection of military insubordination. Hamaguchi's strength was in his readiness, literally, to risk his own life for what he believed to be a righteous goal. The irony of his courage, however, was that once dead, someone else with equal courage and determination would have to carry on the task. There were such, but not nearly enough.

As Hayashi pointed out, the desire of the successor Wakatsuki cabinet to remain in power must have been part of the explanation for its wavering response to the Incident. In pondering why a more decisive course was never pursued, however, another compelling hypothesis emerges: that military and nonmilitary leaders, the so-called "internationalists" and "Pan-Asianists" alike, came to accept the Incident precisely because they saw sufficient legitimacy in what Ishiwara sought to achieve. Even Hayashi himself acknowledged as much that although Inukai's foreign minister, Yoshizawa, was in principle opposed to the establishment of Manchukuo, his opinion was that of a small minority. Hayashi further explained that "[w]ithin the ministry [of Foreign Affairs], the majority wanted to go along with the mainstream opinion, recognizing the independence of Manchukuo as a *fait accompli* and get it over with once and for all."[23]

At the very least, it is not difficult to recognize that policymakers were all uncertain about the future of internationalism, owing to several developments on the Asian mainland that provoked Japan's more deep-seated Hobbesian worldview and exaggerated the degree of the Manchurian Problem. First, there was a problem for Japan of increasingly more assertive Chinese nationalism under the leadership of Chiang Kai-shek. Chiang, having established his power base in southern China by the mid-1920s, launched the Kuomintang's third Northern Expedition (1926–28) together with the Communists in an attempt to extend his sphere of influence into Beijing and Nanjing. He eventually parted ways with the Communists and the left-wing of the Kuomintang, establishing a government in Nanjing. Though interrupted by the tasks of containing opposition and the Communists, he was able to recommence his northward advance in April 1928. Despite clashing with Japanese forces, his army successfully drove out the warlord Chang Tso-lin from Beijing, completing his mission.

Thus between 1928 and 1931, the Kuomintang's political control under Chiang Kai-shek came to be consolidated. This prompted the Western powers to recognize and back Chiang and his bourgeois industrialist supporters. This shift in some Japanese minds represented a betrayal of the spirit of "cooperation" among the great powers, and further endangered Japan's concessionary rights on the continent. Moreover, by the end of the 1920s, the Soviet Union's Far Eastern military presence began to threaten Japan's position in Manchuria. Taken together, Pan-Asianism became the preferred organizing principle around which to articulate Japan's foreign policy in the wake of the Manchurian Incident.

Internationalist Response to Pan-Asianism

One could effectively explore the validity of the above proposition by examining the response of Japan's diplomats dedicated to the liberal internationalist principles, who presumably would have deplored the coercive ways in which the Kwantung Army invaded Manchuria and prevailed over Tokyo. The overall politics surrounding the Anglo-American nonrecognition of Manchukuo, as well as the Lytton Commission's report that eventually led to the Japanese withdrawal from the League of Nations, are all well-documented. However, it is still worth remembering that despite the seemingly decisive character of its rhetoric in condemning Japanese action as an unlawful violation of Chinese sovereignty, Lytton's report embraced many ambiguities so as to accommodate existing realities of imperialism, such as concessionary rights and extraterritoriality, which the great powers, too, enjoyed in China and elsewhere. Most importantly, the report *de facto* recognized Japanese interests in Manchuria by recommending for Manchuria a large measure of autonomy even while emphasizing the importance of Manchuria as *de jure* belonging to China.

These ambiguities allowed for various historical and legal claims to be made by Japanese and Chinese diplomats as well as legal scholars over

Manchuria.[24] The Japanese claim usually stressed the backwardness and chaos of China, which made China unequipped to take on the development of Manchuria. In any event, Manchuria should be considered independent of China because of its historical, geographical, and even ethnographical detachment from the Han Chinese. As the Japanese Chargé d'Affaires to the United States declared:

> In contrast to the disorderly conditions in China proper, Manchuria has for the past quarter of a century enjoyed peace and order, progress and prosperity, having accomplished great strides in its commercial and industrial development. That has been admittedly the result of Japanese influences. . . . She would be satisfied if Manchuria were a dependable bulwark against the possible onrush of outside aggressions. She would be quite content if the resources and the markets of Manchuria were legitimately open for Japanese enterprise.[25]

The Chinese interpretation on the other hand stressed the historical and cultural ties of China and Manchuria through centuries of migration and acculturation, as well as the external sovereignty accorded to China, including its northeastern provinces, under international law. While they differed in emphases, both Japanese and Chinese interpretations derived their main theses from internationalist vocabulary of progress, mercantile liberalism, national self-determination, and sovereignty, presenting their disputes as a matter of international political concern rather than simply between two countries.

The discursive aspects of the politics of Japanese withdrawal therefore built upon, rather than marked a departure from, Japan's continuing attempt to legitimize its takeover of China's northeastern provinces. Matsuoka's infamous "withdrawal" speech, delivered in Geneva on February 24, 1933, pointed to those familiar themes of China's backwardness and chaos with an appalling condition of "internecine warfare, tyranny, banditry, famine and flood," which prompted Japan, "a great civilizing nation" and "the mainstay of peace," to "assist Manchukuo to her feet."[26] At least superficially, however, we can see that by leaving the League, Japan "left Europe and entered Asia," in the exact reversal of Fukuzawa Yukichi's proposition almost half a century earlier. At the declaratory level of Japan's foreign policy, it is beyond dispute that Japan's policy aims and justifications began to be couched more in Pan-Asianist than internationalist language. In a perhaps more illuminating constructivist neologism, an "uptake," or a process whereby certain concepts are adopted by policymakers, commenced some time after the Manchurian Incident, gradually but surely.

The Asiatic Monroe Doctrine

On February 23, 1934, Foreign Minister Hirota Kōki informed the Diet that "the Empire, as the only cornerstone (*ishizue*) for the edifice of peace in East Asia, bears the entire burden of its responsibilities."[27] This same idea of Japan, as Asia's leader, was reflected in Japan's enunciation of the "Asiatic Monroe Doctrine" that surfaced dramatically in the form of the "Amō Statement" shortly after Hirota's official pronouncement. In the unofficial comment made by the Foreign Ministry Information Division Chief Amō Eiji on April 17, 1934, Japan's diplomatic objectives were identified as the sustenance and improvement of friendly relations with the great powers, while concomitantly pursuing an independent East Asian policy. The statement read:

> Last March, Japan was compelled to announce its withdrawal from the League of Nations. . . . That resulted from the gap in understanding between Japan and the League of some fundamental principles concerning the sustenance of peace in East Asia. . . . As regards East Asia, Japan's position might not necessarily coincide with that of the powers. Japan should share the responsibility of sustaining the region's peace and order with other East Asian nations. . . . Although such a stance should explain itself in Japan's previous policy course, it does not seem futile to state Japan's position clearly now that various powers in recent times have indicated their active advancement plan into China under the name of mutual cooperation.[28]

By no means was the idea of the "Asiatic Monroe Doctrine" new in Japan's policy discourse. Already in 1898, Konoe Atsumaro, in a meeting with Kang You-wei (1858–1927), addressed his Chinese friend as a colleague facing the shared challenge and responsibilities of "exercising the Asiatic Monroe Doctrine in the East" because, after all, "Asia is for Asians."[29] Kang was a Qing reformer who led opposition against Japan in protest against the Treaty of Shimonoseki in 1895 but later attempted to find an answer for the future of the dynasty in a drastic internal reform modeled on Japan's modernization. Konoe's use of the concept of "Asiatic Monroe Doctrine" as highlighting mutual responsibilities for the future of Asia was gradually lost on the Japanese, however, as the Doctrine became popularized in the wake of the Russo-Japanese War, for example, by its most vocal advocate Tokutomi Sohō, as a policy propping up Japan's regional hegemony.

The evolving interpretations and claims of the Asiatic Monroe Doctrine reflected two important power-political realities. One was the rising self-consciousness and confidence of Japan as a regional power. The other was the conceptual vagueness and the subsequent development of the original Monroe Doctrine (1823) itself. The original doctrine was a unilateral declaration of hemispheric hegemony intended to fend off European intervention in its neighboring countries. While pledging that the United States would not interfere in the affairs of "the existing colonies or dependencies of any European power," it declared that if the European powers were to intervene in independent countries, the United States "could not view any interposition . . . in any other light than as the manifestation of an unfriendly disposition toward the United States."[30]

Needless to say, this is a very open-ended statement, without clear specifications as to the actual commitment on the part of the United States. The basic assumption behind it was that the United States would interpret and clarify the Monroe Doctrine as events and situations necessitated. It was not until the emergence of the Olney Corollary (1895) and, even more importantly, the Roosevelt Corollary to the Monroe Doctrine (1906) that the Doctrine became associated with U.S. self-interest and commercial imperialism.[31] The emerging reinterpretation of the Monroe Doctrine, heralding the advent of Big Stick diplomacy, was especially critical, as it transformed the original doctrine from one of fending off intervention by European powers to one of sanctioning intervention by the United States in the spirit of Pan-Americanism. Such a new understanding, nonexistent at the time of Konoe Atsumaro's statement, mirrored and reinforced the evolving Japanese conception of the Asiatic Monroe Doctrine as a doctrine authorizing Japanese presence on the Asian mainland in the wake of the Russo-Japanese War.

As far as the post–Manchurian Incident diplomacy was concerned, Amō's statement became infamously associated with Japan's sinister attempt to check interventions by the treaty powers, provoking strong reactions and media coverage from Britain and the United States. Despite the external condemnations of the statement, interpreted as a declaration of Japan's further expansionist ambitions in East Asia, the incorporation of the "Asiatic Monroe Doctrine" as the crux of Japan's venture in Manchuria continued and was probably complete by December 1936. At that time, a study of the original Monroe Doctrine by the eminent scholar of public international law Tachi Sakutarō (1874–1943) was published as part of a Foreign Ministry monograph series.[32] Tachi accused the United States of hypocrisy in blaming Japan for "following the very spirit of the Monroe Doctrine pronounced by the United States itself. . . . It is against its own principle to blame Japan for acting on behalf of the principles of 'Asia for Asiatics,' especially since Asia is all within Japan's rightful sphere of influence."[33] He continued:

> Professor Whitton, a Princeton professor of international law, claims that . . . it would be against the spirit of the Monroe Doctrine, or at the very least, the United States' own logic, not to allow the principle of reciprocity between the United States and Asia. . . . Coolidge, who taught at Harvard, asserted that Asia would provide an ideal ground on which to apply the Monroe Doctrine. He insisted that if Americans were to prohibit Asians from intervening in the affairs of the Western hemisphere, they must in turn accept their reliance on the European argument of reciprocity. . . . He asked to consider how threatening it must be for Japan to have the United States occupying the Philippines. It is, indeed like Japan occupying Ecuador.[34]

In addition to Tachi's preoccupation with formulating a convincing international legalistic argument around the concept of reciprocity, the fact that he took pains to substantiate his points by referring to the works of legal scholars in the Ivy League universities suggests that he regarded established Anglo-American institutions as the ultimate arbiter of international jurisprudence after all. This irony highlights that even as late as the end of 1936, some influential Japanese tried to legitimize the Pan-Asianist turn in the country's foreign policy in terms of liberal internationalist conceptions of public international law, indicating that there remained a merger of internationalism and Pan-Asianism in the general character of Japan's Asia policy.

Saitō Hiroshi and Nitobe Inazō: The Limits of Liberal Internationalism

Hence at the very basic level of justifying the Manchurian Incident and what followed, there was a perceptible increase of Pan-Asianist overtones in Japan's policy articulation. However, this realization does not quite show us the extent to which Japan's individual internationalist elites subscribed to this ideological shift. The prevalent postwar explanation is that the Foreign Ministry in the 1930s simply did not have the strength to fight and was no longer able to influence the course of Japan's external policy in any meaningful way. But such an assumption distorts a proper perspective on Pan-Asianism's far-reaching appeal as well as the role of those elites. While it is impossible to attempt a comprehensive study of how individual internationalists reacted to the Manchurian Incident, the case of Saitō Hiroshi (1886–1939) presents a powerful case of a Japanese internationalist's reconciliation with and seeming embrace of Pan-Asianism as a guiding principle of Japanese foreign policy in the post-Manchurian Incident period.

Saitō, who was consistently at the forefront of Japan's internationalist diplomacy throughout his entire professional career, was one of the most internationalist Japanese diplomats at the time of the Manchurian Incident. At the Paris Peace Conference, he acted as a press officer, the post he shared with Matsuoka Yōsuke, followed by various critical appointments in the United States and Europe, eventually becoming the Japanese Ambassador to the United States in 1933. His final appointment at the exceptionally young age of forty-seven reflected Japan's eagerness to salvage its reputation after the Manchurian Incident. In the words of Foreign Minister Hirota, "I dare to appoint Saitō, because now is the time that demands young talent at any cost."[35] Saitō was Konoe Fumimaro's first choice as foreign minister in the summer of 1938, but his ill health, which led to his untimely death in early 1939, prevented him from taking up the post. In spite of deteriorating U.S.–Japan relations at the time of his death, he had won the hearts and minds of his American counterparts to such a degree that Franklin D. Roosevelt made the extraordinary gesture of sending his ashes home aboard the *USS Astoria*.

Because of the singularly important, yet curiously forgotten place he occupied in Japan's diplomacy of the 1930s, Saitō's views on the Manchurian Problem are worth noting. His diplomatic objectives were encapsulated in the government's decision reached at the Five-Minister Conference in October, 1933, entailing "the development of Manchukuo," "the realization of an alliance among the three countries of Japan, Manchuria, and China" under Japanese guidance, and "the achievement of sufficient mutual understandings" concerning the matters of naval arms limitations and Manchuria.[36] In short, Saitō's mission in Washington was one of renewing U.S.–Japan relations of the pre-Manchuria days. His task was made difficult precisely because he had to rebuild those relations on the entirely new basis of the Manchurian *fait accompli* that had already resulted in Japan's establishment of Manchukuo.

Accordingly, he devoted substantial time and energy to giving lectures and speeches, painstakingly pointing out the importance of the triple alliance of sovereignties of Japan, Manchukuo, and China and enlightening Western audiences to Japan's unique position as a Pan-Asianist leader.[37]

More revealing of Saitō's ideological commitment than these official diplomatic speeches, however, were the opinion pieces he wrote for general Japanese audiences in popular magazines and journals; for here, a sound argument can be made that he expressed his thoughts not in the obligatory, official capacity of a diplomat providing explanations for the existing situations to outsiders but as a Japanese citizen attempting to convey to fellow Japanese what he regarded as a preferable future course for the country's foreign policy. He conceded that the method by which the Kwantung Army pursued its goal might have been naïve. However, he was more than enthusiastic about the future of Manchukuo. Declaring that Manchukuo was "indeed an interesting event for mankind as well as an experiment," he saw it as "the world's only meaningful political body in the making" that "integrated the development of humanity with a Japanese spirit."[38] His reference to the propagation of "Japanese spirit" as a positive basis for the building of Manchukuo indicates that his commitment to Pan-Asianism in fact went beyond the *status quo*–inclined Sinic Pan-Asianist contention, employed to explain Japan's international position that made sense to his Western audiences. In fact, his line of reasoning for Japanese readers is an argument more in line with Meishuron Pan-Asianism.

Still, much like the legal scholar Tachi, who used the examples of U.S. authorities to authenticate his points, Saitō referred to already established Western examples to substantiate his views. In accepting and propounding that the Manchukuo "experiment" was a grand cultural mission led by Japan, Saitō drew a parallel to the nineteenth-century British case, stating that "Britain actually contributed to the progress of the human race, despite the fact that the method of cultural expansion it employed was rather questionable."[39]

The sense of historical inevitability of Japan's leadership in Asia, the consequentialist defense for its military conquest already committed in Manchuria, and, most notably, the importance of Manchukuo as a cultural experiment in light of unstoppable and broader trends of world history characterized his optimistic vision of Asia's future. Certainly, these were to be familiar themes sounded by policymakers and intellectuals alike in the later phases of the Fifteen Years' War, especially after Japan's launching of war against the Allied forces. But the active display of enthusiasm and optimism coming from such a public internationalist as Saitō at this point is noteworthy; for his case signifies that the very obviously Meishuron-inclined argument was an element, picked up by Saitō, presumably not only to justify, but also to endorse Japan's policy in the aftermath of the Manchurian Incident.

Another similar and equally compelling example was Nitobe Inazō (1862–1933), the most well-known figure whom the Japanese today regard as an embodiment of Japan's interwar internationalism. In order to explain Japan's position to his Western colleagues, he embarked on a lecture trip to the United States and Canada from which he was never to return, as he died in Victoria. His espousal of internationalism, along with his Christian faith and his Japanese nationalism represented a particular, but by no means unique, blend of allegiances held by Japan's foreign policy elites of this period.

Born to a high-ranking samurai family on the eve of Japan's birth as a modern nation-state, Nitobe was greatly influenced by the Christianity he encountered at the national Agricultural School in Sapporo. His subsequent studies in the United States introduced him to Quakerism, a Christian sect he regarded as the least constrained by racial prejudices, and he eventually married a Quaker from Philadelphia.

Nitobe had various roles in his life, first as a colonial administrator in Taiwan, and later an educator at various elite schools including Kyoto Imperial University, the First Higher School—where he was a formative influence on the young Konoe Fumimaro—and Tokyo Women's College. Above all, he is today most known for his role as an interlocutor of Japanese values for Western audiences.

The international success of his book *Bushido, The Soul of Japan* (published in 1900) in the wake of the Russo-Japanese War distinguished him as an exemplary internationalist, who still retained his traditional Japanese identity. His appointment to the position of undersecretary-general of the League of Nations in Geneva (1926–33) and of Japanese chairman of the Institute of Pacific Relations (1929–33), where he was a close associate of Matsuoka Yōsuke further solidified his high reputation.

Nitobe's role as the primary Japanese internationalist and public servant also meant that in his capacity, he would always be the first to defend Japan's policy to his great power counterparts. Calls of duty aside, his views religiously mirrored the general climate of mainstream internationalist opinion. For instance, following the brutal suppression of the *Samil* Independence Movement in Korea in March 1919, he stated that he was himself "among the best and truest friends of Koreans."[40] He noted: "I like them. I think they are a capable people, who can be trained to a large measure of self-government, for which the present is a period of tutelage," and Japan's enlightened stewardship had already brought Korea numerous success in "[m]ining, fishery, and manufacturing."[41] Here, he seems to be merely echoing the sentiments shared by many colonialists-*cum*-internationalists of the time about the notion of mandate and protectorate as a developmental stage before a complete nation-statehood. And such was a view he had held for quite some time, as he noted, in an English-language book entitled *The Japanese Nation* in 1912:

> You read now and then in the newspapers of arrests in Korea, and forthwith Japan is charged with being a cruel master. Let the world remember that a change of masters is rarely made without friction. It takes some time for a people to know that a jural state means enforcement of justice, and that this does not imply encroachment upon personal liberty, which under the old regime Korean countries identified with royal favor.[42]

Nitobe's Japanese exceptionalism was even more apparent in his *Bushido* thesis, in which he explained why Japan, unlike other Asian countries, was able to progress as an international power because of its traditional samurai values that were comparable in their moral sophistication to the best of Western traditions. While paralleling Okakura's evocative language full of civilizational allusions, Nitobe portrayed Japan as quite intrinsically and temperamentally different from the rest of Asia. In comparison, Okakura was at pains to see Japan as part of Asia, despite his claims of Japanese superiority as a synthesizer of different influences. In Nitobe's view, Japan, with its special concoction of Confucianism, Shintoism, Buddhism, and other moral guidelines that shaped the specifically Japanese way of the chivalrous warrior, knew how and when to use force, citing: "When Mahomet proclaimed that 'The sword is the key of Heaven and of Hell,' he only echoed a Japanese sentiment."[43] Extolling uniquely Japanese character, he took Japan out of Asia and placed it alongside Europe. He continued:

> While in India and even in China men seem to differ chiefly in degree of energy or intelligence, in Japan they differ by originality of character as well. Now, individuality is the sign of superior races and of civilizations

already developed. If we make use of an expression dear to Nietzsche, we might say that in Asia, to speak of humanity is to speak of its plains; in Japan as in Europe, one represents it above all by its mountains.[44]

No wonder Theodore Roosevelt, greatly admiring this book, allegedly regarded Japanese as an "honorary white race."

While exercising a simplistic and linear view of "Asians" that exempted his beloved Japanese nation, Nitobe himself was sensitive to any suggestions of Western racial prejudices toward Japanese. His exposure in his student days to American Christians, who appeared far from being free of racial prejudice, and the opposition he faced in marrying a white woman, dismayed him. The feeling that Christianity as exercised in the West did not sufficiently deliver to the needs of non-Westerners was shared by his old school friend from Sapporo, Uchimura Kanzō (1861–1930), who established the Mukyōkaiha (Nonchurch) evangelical Christian church that influenced generations of Japanese intellectuals, including Yanaihara Tadao (1893–1961), a scholar of colonial policy at Tokyo Imperial University. When the U.S. Congress adopted a series of anti-immigration laws that culminated in the Immigration Act of 1924, Nitobe swore never to return to the United States so long as such exclusionary laws remained. He kept his vow until his final journey.

Nitobe believed in Japanese superiority and distinctiveness all the while still espousing egalitarian values of Christianity. It seems like hypocrisy, but perhaps it would be premature to indict him of double standards. In trying to reconcile his Christian faith and its apparent contradictions reflected in the realities of everyday life as well as international relations, such as imperialism and colonialism, one might say that Nitobe almost had to believe that progress and enlightenment would bring resolution to the problems of inequalities among nation-states, eventually. With that conviction, Nitobe, rather uncritically, thought Japan to be far ahead of other Asians. Although difficult to indict him of hypocrisies, however, his lasting high reputation either as a "liberal" or "internationalist" is quite misleading if taken out of such a specific context of interwar liberal internationalism, as defined previously.

The Myth of Japanese Uniqueness

Another remarkable aspect of the internationalist embrace of Japanese exceptionalism, as articulated in Nitobe's *Bushido* and as confirmed in concrete policy terms in the wake of the Manchurian Incident, is its link to Japan's increasingly convoluted and uneasy relationships with "race," "ethnicity," and "nation." From the late nineteenth century on, Japanese scholars have approached the problem of identifying with and distinguishing themselves from Asia from multiple disciplinary perspectives of Japanese history, Oriental studies, anthropology, ethnology, linguistics, economics, and other natural and social sciences, the development of which discourse has been effectively studied.[45]

Of particular interest here is Oguma Eiji's historical sociology on the discourse of ethnic identities of the Japanese nation.[46] In his exhaustive study of theories of Japan's origins from the Meiji period onward, he challenges the seemingly age-old Japanese belief in the racial purity and homogeneity of their race (or ethnic nation). It is a powerful indictment of the short-memoried tendencies of the Japanese, especially those who espouse the jingoistic *Nihonjinron* line of argument popular since the 1970s and 1980s that uncritically assumes the homogenous origins of the nation. He exposes the myth as a rather recent product rooted in the racialist discourse of the period roughly covering the Fifteen Years' War.

Before the 1930s, in fact, there existed varying views on the origins of the Japanese nation, the most influential of which concerned the Ural-Altaic thesis of Pan-Turanism mentioned previously and, on a related theme, the common origins of the Korean and Japanese nations, which proved a powerful argument in advancing Japan's official and unofficial alliances with Korea. In fact, even Nitobe in 1912 said as much that compared to Formosans (Taiwanese), he expected the Japanization process "will be found easier in Korea, for the reason that the Korean race is very much allied to our own."[47] In spite of such variance in views, and in spite of the prewar willingness by some Japanese to endorse multiple origins of the Japanese nation, however, the wartime racial discourse eventually became dominated by the homogeneity thesis, advanced by such figures as the historian Tsuda Sōkichi (1873–1961) and the philosopher Watsuji Tetsurō (1889–1960). Even the renowned ethnologist/anthropologist Yanagita Kunio (1875–1962), who had earlier advanced a multiple origins thesis based on his own extensive empirical research, came to hold a view more in line with the homogeneity thesis during the war. The mythic notion of Japan as a chosen race began to predominate in the political discourse of the final phases of the Fifteen Years' War, leading for instance to the July 1943 Ministry of Health and Welfare's proposal that the Yamato (Japanese) race should form a nucleus of Asiatic autarchy.[48]

In the end, however, such an oscillation between the claims of uniqueness and inclusiveness of Japan's roots signified the two sides of the same
coin. So long as Japan could legitimize its superiority, either by claiming
the successful synthesis of multiple Asian roots, or by claiming the
inborn uniqueness of the Japanese race within Asia, Japan could in the
end justify its preponderant position in what it regarded as its rightful
sphere of influence. Moreover, internationalists who were engaged in the
art and craft of advancing and securing Japan's position could be found at
the forefront of such discourse formulation, publicly and externally giving credence to the supremacy of the Japanese nation-state in diplomatic
capacity, just as anthropologists, historians, linguists, and the like strove
to do the same from within their respective fields.

* * *

However loosely, the idea that Japan had a unique role to play in
Manchuria managed to unite Japan's divided government in the wake of
the Manchurian Incident and carry it through the country's foreign policy shift from internationalism to Pan-Asianism in an uncoordinated and
confused, but on reflection less puzzling and more continuous fashion
than is generally believed. By recognizing the establishment of an "independent" state under a precarious combination of internationalist as well
as Pan-Asianist banners, the ideological orientation of Japan's foreign
policy at the onset of the Fifteen Years' War could be characterized by
both of these seemingly irreconcilable yet actually related principles. We
have examined that confluence of internationalist and Pan-Asianist
tenets within Japan's foreign policy pronouncements and observed how
such a nuanced shift in relative ideological weight took place.

In the final analysis, the Manchurian Incident did not signify a blatant
or abrupt departure on the part of Japan's foreign policy course from liberal
internationalism to Pan-Asianism, or even to Japanese ultranationalism or
"fascism." Rather, the very gradual yet sure shift in its outlook revealed the
uncontested and even sympathetic acceptance of the Manchurian *fait
accompli* by Japan's elites, including those who espoused a very strong
internationalist proclivity in their personal and professional lives.

This is not to say that Japan's internationalists accepted the ascent of
the military uncritically. Nor is it suggested that they approved of Japan's
further military expansion past the borders of Manchukuo. The subtle
shift in foreign policy discourse, seen both at the declaratory level of

diplomacy and at the individual level, never marked an explicit turning point in Japan's policy articulation. Its leaders still believed in diplomatic negotiations and maneuvers, hoping for an eventual acceptance of Japanese claims and making sure that the country would not be entirely isolated. They tried to sustain the existing diplomatic ties, wishing for the international opinion, which were by no means completely hostile to Japan's position in any case, to tilt in their favor.[49] For example, two months before his death, at the opening of the Institute of Pacific Relations Conference held at Banff, Canada, Nitobe spoke "on the dangers of intolerance," and as "a son of Japan," pleaded for more understanding for Japan's position, stressing that even though "Japan notified the League of Nations of its intention to withdraw from it," Japan's true intention was "to cooperate with the world" as it had always done, and that Japan was "proud to think that she is still an inseparable part of the great world."[50]

However confusing and confused Japan's internationalist response to the Manchurian field initiative might have been, it illuminates a larger truth about the sheer magnetism of Pan-Asianism beyond its utility as a motive behind and/or justification for military insubordination. Even with a fair deal of vestiges remaining of Japanese internationalism, the positive understanding with which Japan's noted internationalists looked to Manchukuo as a meaningful civilizational experiment led by Japan cannot be explained without acknowledging some deep appreciation of Pan-Asianist tenets on their part.

To present another example, Fujisawa Chikao (1893–1962) was a devoted Esperantist, international law scholar, and a League of Nations official in the 1920s. He also embraced Manchukuo and Pan-Asianism. According to Fujisawa, who was now a professor of Great Eastern Cultural College of Tokyo (Daitō Bunka Daigaku), the internationalism of the 1920s had been derived from Western liberalism, which then was imposed on the rest of the world.[51] Taking the program of propagating Japanese culture in Manchukuo seriously, he harked back to the Teaist thesis of universal Asian heritage in pointing out the high morality of Asian civilization.

In a special lecture delivered at Tokyo Imperial University in the summer of 1932, Fujisawa drew from Okakura's cultural and spiritualist emphasis for "Asian One-ness," calling for the revival of spirituality over materialism, and action over words, stating, "We are now as weary of the empty words of sentimental pacifists, as we are indignant about the inhuman exploitation of the weaker peoples by an international *coterie* of imperialistic capitalists."[52] Despite the claim to the universality of Asian culture his ultimate proposition was one of accepting and endorsing Japan's hegemonic position over the rest of Asia, placing his conclusion more in line with Meishuron Pan-Asianism. He argued that Japan had to establish the material as well as psychological foundation for a more "just" pattern of international relations, built on the principles of harmony and trust, by carrying out its cultural reform programs throughout Asia.

Certainly, material and strategic considerations did profoundly affect Japan's domestic life, which in turn was marked by various pressing concerns, including its weak economy, declining party politics, and ascending yet internally split armed forces. All the same, even after having considered various factors that contributed to Japan's crisis of values, one is compelled to conclude that the Manchurian Incident would probably not have come about, and moreover, would not have gained the level of legitimacy from the Japanese government that it ultimately did, had it not been for its association with Pan-Asianism.

Merely pointing out the rise of Pan-Asianism in Japan's external policy pronouncements is not a sufficient measure of its true impact on the course of the Fifteen Years' War. The recognition alone that ideology interacts with and sometimes reinforces more immediate material considerations in foreign policymaking would not tell us much about how and why ideology should have been all that important. Therefore, the critical question to ask next is to what extent and how exactly such Pan-Asianist language translated into the actual implementation of Japan's policies within and beyond Manchuria.

4
Manchukuo and the Dream of Pan-Asia

Owing to a burgeoning body of sophisticated historical works, it has become almost a cliché to say that Manchukuo was an imperialist creation of a unique brand. By addressing the relevance and particularity of Manchukuo in various fields of imperialism as well as transnational and sovereignty studies that transcend the simple nation-state matrix, the authors of some of the most important works on Manchukuo have enhanced our understanding of this nation- and state-building (*kenkoku*) enterprise. To draw attention to only the illustrative few, Louise Young has put forward her seminal thesis of a "total empire" to explain the comprehensive manner of Japanese mobilization for Manchukuo. In her study, as a methodology and a description of a phenomenon in itself, the term "total empire" is proposed as a parallel term to "total war."[1] Like total war, total empire was made on the home front, entailing multidimensional mobilization of the Japanese nation in all cultural, military, political, and economic endeavors. In her view, Manchukuo signifies not only a military conquest, but also a vast socio-politico-cultural project that represented Japan's modern efficiency expressed in the forms of Manchukuo's cosmopolitan cities and agricultural settlements.

Huge Japanese material and psychological stakes in Manchukuo notwithstanding, such a total mobilization involved rather complex networks of dependence and interdependence among Japanese leaders and Japanese settlers as well as non-Japanese citizens of Manchukuo. That intricate power dynamic resisted the classic ruler and ruled dichotomy of colonial relationships. On this point, Rana Mitter has deftly probed into the "myth" surrounding Chinese resistance to the Japanese takeover of Manchuria from 1931 to 1933.[2] In debunking that myth, he demonstrates, for instance, the methodical efforts made by relatively few activists and nationalists to ingrain on the popular psyche the image of heroism of Chinese resistance. He also reveals the localized and uneven character of the rise of Chinese national consciousness under the Japanese occupation, the fact that enabled the Japanese occupiers to utilize the existing social structures to sustain their power-hold initially.

Likewise, Prasenjit Duara's nuanced analysis of Manchukuo has brought our attention to many other interpretive layers, both theoretical and empirical, that accompany the study of Manchukuo. In his presentation of Manchukuo as a product of regional mediation of modernity, which he calls "East Asian modern," he cogently demonstrates how a "state" derives its authenticity from a "nation." In the case of Manchukuo, such an authenticating process began with the Japanese insistence on the independence of Manchukuo and its sovereignty, followed by the formation of "Manchukuoan" national identities by creating the discourse of Asian civilization. This in turn produced social and political projects that channeled the participation of Manchukuo's men and women into such tangible organizations as redemptive societies, as well as the establishment of more abstract discourses of spatial and ethnological propinquity of Asian peoples.

In light of such emerging understanding, however, one also becomes aware that the cliché of Manchukuo is not really a cliché at all but merely provides a starting point for a new set of analytical challenges. The task of firmly embedding the Manchukuo experience within broader disciplines, such as comparative imperialism and postcolonial critique, as well as within the narrative of longer historical episodes, remains. With that challenge in mind, this chapter does not seek to supersede the excellent works already done on Manchukuo but rather attempts to disassemble our present understanding, identify and polish the relevant parts, and reassemble them as integral components of the history of Pan-Asianism in the Fifteen Years' War.

The following discussion will be divided into two parts. The first part aims to examine the character of Japanese imperialism in Manchukuo on the proposition that its founding marked a significant departure from Japan's imperialism of the earlier period. The Manchurian Incident and the building of Manchukuo are critical. They demonstrate that Japan, as a matter of state policy, began to practice Pan-Asianism (and not just "anti-imperialist imperialism" marked by sporadic and unorganized expressions of Pan-Asianist sympathies) as a call for collective and concerted actions to bring about a power-political change in the wider context of international relations.

The previous chapter has shown how Pan-Asianism, albeit gradually, became an organizing principle of Japan's official policy after the Manchurian Incident. The present chapter looks at Pan-Asianism as a guide to Japan's imperialist project to build Manchukuo. Although differing interpretations exist as to the idiosyncratic nature of this *kenkoku* enterprise, I would contend that Japan's attempt at constructing a Manchukuo nation and nationalism should be regarded as yet another form of imperialism: a pan-nationalist imperialism, so to speak. This is because asymmetry of power was Manchukuo's characteristic feature, and it was effectively intertwined with, despite Japan's grander claims of salvaging Asian civilization, the act of legitimizing the Japanese Empire as a central institution behind its national identity.

The second part of the chapter more explicitly examines the role of such Pan-Asianist imperialism exercised in Manchukuo. It takes issues with the Sinic Pan-Asianist concept of the "Kingly Way," which was variously interpreted in practice, but still provided a basic common ground for the nation-building mobilization for Manchukuo. In particular, the discussion centers on how Sinic Pan-Asianism complemented the egalitarian preferences of Japan's left. In Manchukuo, Sinic Pan-Asianism existed in tandem with more chauvinistic, Meishuron manifestations of Pan-Asianism advanced by the Kwantung Army, and both played an instrumental role in Japan's *kenkoku* project.

Despite the earnestness with which some of the Japanese reformers attempted to fashion the "East Asian modern" in the vast lands of Manchuria, Manchukuo's modernity was ultimately built on the system of unilateral exploitation, coercion, and cruelty that changed and cost the lives of an unknown magnitude, making a Pan-Asianist utopia a hollow promise in reality. In fact, Manchukuo became more a dystopia in which anything—ranging from exploitation of local populations as cheap labor to biological experiments on alleged anti-Japanese elements by the infamous Unit 731—became justified in terms of the Pan-Asianist slogan of the "Kingly Way."

I. Japanese Imperialism and Manchukuo

An Overview

Time and again, Manchukuo has eluded an attempt at straightforward characterization. Established on March 1, 1932, by the Kwantung Army under the mottos of "harmony of the five races" (*gozoku kyōwa*, usually implying the five "racial" groupings of Chinese, Manchurians, Mongolians, Koreans, and Japanese) and "the Kingly Way in paradise" (*ōdō rakudo*), Manchukuo could be regarded neither as Japan's formal colony, nor as a traditional sphere of influence, but as a pseudo-autonomous empire within an empire. Tokyo's initial reaction to the founding of Manchukuo, especially among the civilian leaders, was one of astonishment. Even more extraordinary, however, was the ensuing zeal with which certain segments of the Japanese nation—notably its progressive, educated middle class—took part in the country's Manchukuo-building venture once the military *fait accompli* came to be accepted. What exactly made that degree of Japan's endorsement of Manchukuo possible?

From its inception, Manchukuo was a Pan-Asianist creation in the sense that its birth cannot possibly be explained without reference to Ishiwara Kanji's Pan-Asianist worldview. But even past that initial departure point, Japan's Pan-Asianism continued to manifest itself in Manchukuo in various incarnations of its *kenkoku* projects. This is not to assert that Pan-Asianism was the only ingredient that inspired and propelled Manchukuo's creation. There are other familiar and powerful reasons for its emergence, ranging from the orthodox argument about Japan's "national interest," the peculiar structural factors surrounding the *tōsuiken* problem as discussed earlier, the indoctrination and politico-socialization of the bulk of the generations involved in the cult of Emperor Worship, to most simply, adventurism and recklessness. But Pan-Asianism was undoubtedly one of the more salient factors and an independent variable in the making and building of Manchukuo.

Japanese mobilization for Manchukuo from 1932 to 1945 was remarkable, not necessarily because it was carried out *under* war conditions, but because it was carried out *in spite of* them. From a purely strategic vantage point of attempting to win the war in a material sense, Japan conceivably could have made more effective and logical resource allocations—and that, especially after the outbreak of wars with China in 1937 and with the Soviet-Mongolian troops in Nomonhan in 1939—to better preserve its national interest. Indeed, the continuing Japanese preoccupations with its wartime *mission civilisatrice* of the rest of Asia, with the building of

Manchukuo as the first and foremost expression, is an aspect of the Fifteen Years' War that cannot be understood without considering the broader appeal of Pan-Asianism. Such galvanizing power of the ideology has to be examined independent of the moral and normative judgment that necessarily follows the dystopian consequences of Japan's Pan-Asianist programs.

By 1931, Japan had long ceased to be a novice in the world of imperialism. In fact, it had itself come to exercise some sort of imperialism in both formal and informal senses, owing to its successive victories in the Sino-Japanese War and the Russo-Japanese War.[3] In the 1920s and into the 1930s, many could still vividly recall, either through actual experience or through education, the memory of sacrifices that Japan had made in order to win those wars. It was popularly repeated that "100,000 Japanese soldiers died and 2 billion yen in national reserves spent" in protecting Japanese interests in Manchuria, compounding the common perception that Manchuria was the resource-strapped Empire's "lifeline" (the term allegedly coined by Matsuoka Yōsuke) and that the region almost constituted a part of Japan to be defended at any cost. And so, the idea that Japan somehow possessed Manchuria at the time of the Manchurian Incident was not lost even on a fifth-grader, who complained: "How callous of them, those bad Chinese soldiers who are trying to drive Japanese out of Manchuria! Please, dear soldiers . . . please do protect our precious land of Manchuria."[4] Similar letters of moral support were featured frequently in newspapers and magazines.

Officially, such Japanese sentiments were expressed in the more restrained language of the protocol signed between Manchukuo and Japan in September 1932. It brought to the fore Japan's public and formal recognition of Manchukuo, indicating that "the Japanese government and the government of Manchukuo shall maintain the existing friendly relationship for eternity, respecting each other's territorial rights and striving to secure Asia's peace."[5] What lay at the basis of this declaration, couched in deferential and international legalistic vocabulary, were the legacies of old diplomacy and power politics. Tak Matsusaka aptly points out that the independence of Manchukuo was almost a fictional construct whose territory was managed as a Japanese possession, enjoying no more sovereignty than the formal colonies of Taiwan or Korea.[6] Yet another critical fact looms large on second reflection: the founders of Manchukuo actually did bother to create such a fiction, thereby setting Manchukuo apart from the earlier examples of Taiwan and Korea.

Moreover, as Duara has noted, the making of a sovereign state (be it a nation-state, multinational state, or pan-national state) was an enterprise that Japanese rulers would continue to take seriously, long after the country's withdrawal from the League of Nations. In theory, the withdrawal would have made it unnecessary for Japan to perpetuate that fiction of sovereignty. This suggests that perhaps the *kenkoku* venture had serious ideological components for Japan that superseded the reasons and logic of power politics.

By the end of 1931, Ishiwara Kanji, the mastermind behind the Manchurian Incident, had become convinced of the viability of making an explicitly independent state of Manchukuo as a Pan-Asian utopia with a republican structure, for which he was said to have been even willing to forsake his own Japanese citizenship. Ishiwara publicly acknowledged that the local land-owning leader Yu Chonghan was the person who rendered most services to the building of Manchukuo because he came up with the Kingly Way platform as the basis of independent Manchukuo's national identity.[7] Pan-Asianist ambitions on the part of its ideological progenitors did not reach their fullest potential, however, leading most historical verdicts to conclude that Manchukuo was a part of Japan's "colonial" or "wartime" empire. But the overall failure of Manchukuo as a Pan-Asian utopia should not imply that Pan-Asianism as a *kenkoku* ideology did not have any bearings on the reality of Japan's actual nation-building efforts.

To be sure, any imperialism is unique in that it is necessarily attached to a certain location and history of that particular empire. But because of Japan's own unique position as an Asian imperialist in Asia, and its emotional, economic, and historical association with Manchuria, defining its imperialism in Manchukuo becomes even more challenging. The argument here is that Japan's imperialism after the Manchurian Incident changed from its previous reactionary "anti-imperialist imperialism" to something more decidedly ideologically driven. It became more overtly Pan-Asianist, and more explicitly action-oriented in character, making it a type of pan-nationalist imperialism. Pan-nationalist imperialism is a doctrine that purports to overcome the existing imperialist order in a more systematic and organized manner by proposing an alternative form of social and international existence, backed by a certain ideological program that promises the coming of a more just pattern of social order on a transnational scale. In other words, Pan-Asianist imperialism signified a step beyond Japan's anti-imperialist imperialism that had sporadically resisted but paradoxically and generally followed the existing models of Western imperialism.

In pan-nationalist imperialism, the presence of a hegemonic nation is justified in terms of the consequential and overarching common good it would purportedly bring to the greater pan-union. Other instances of pan-nationalist imperialism include Soviet Russia's Pan-Slavic overtures to its Slavic satellites during the Cold War and Nasserite Egypt's insistence on its Pan-Arabist and Non-Alignment leadership in the Arab Middle East and its United Arab Republic union with Syria specifically, albeit to a much lesser extent. Neither Soviet Russia's Pan-Slavism, nor Nasser's Pan-Arabism, nor Japan's Meishuron Pan-Asianism of the Fifteen Years' War suddenly emerged as expedients to disguise their hegemonic rules, but rather, their hegemonic rules were seen to be essential by the hegemons themselves in completing their incomplete pan-nations. (Note, too, the mid-eighteenth-century origins of František Palacký's Pan-Slavism within the Hapsburg Empire and the dual monarchy; Pan-Arabism of the first decade of the twentieth century in resisting the Ottoman Turkish rule; and Teaist and Sinic Pan-Asianism of the late nineteenth century.) But the asymmetry of power and the uninvited and unilateral imposition of one social and ideological order on the rest make this type of pan-national arrangement yet another form of imperialism.

Initially, Japan's venture in China was characterized by its more informal character. Following its victory over Russia, Japan had first acquired a sphere of influence in the northeastern provinces of China, where it quickly transformed the former Russian railway network into the powerful quasi-official joint-stock corporation, the South Manchurian Railroad (Mantetsu or the SMR).[8] The so-called "quadripartite governance" (*yontō seiji*) characterized by the sectionalism of four Japanese administrative organs in Manchuria emerged between 1905 and 1931 under this "railway imperialism."

The four basic building blocks from which the Japanese later assembled Manchukuo's administrative system were the Mantetsu, established in 1906; the Kwantung Army stationed around the Railroad concessions to protect the Mantetsu-related interests; the Foreign Ministry with its extensive network of consulates acting under the terms of extraterritoriality with the Consul General based in Mukden; and finally, the government of the Kwantung Leased Territory (Kantōchō), a civilian agency responsible to the Colonial Ministry in Tokyo situated on the Liaotung Peninsula.[9] The inherited structures could help the smooth running of

Manchukuo up to a point. Within the couple of years of the Manchurian Incident, it became increasingly clear that the Kwantung Army was there to reign. With its ascent, Pan-Asianism of progressively Meishuron inclination began to occupy a central place in the formation of a national identity for Manchukuo.

Theorizing Manchukuo

Revealing of the peculiar character of Japan's imperialism in Manchukuo, then, was its exaggerated preoccupation with the idea of a special, Pan-Asian leadership. Japan's claim to leadership was always expressed in terms of its active pursuit of a hegemonial role in simultaneously protecting Japanese *and* Asian strategic and cultural interests, of a modern *as well as* ancient character, and that for the sake of a greater Asian civilization, and even possibly for the whole of humanity. Such a self-perception on Japan's world role gave rise to the most immediate question of how to reconcile its bid for an Asian leadership with the rise of modern Chinese nationalism.

Japan's concerns were made clear already in 1929, at the Institute of Pacific Relations conference in Kyoto, when the future Foreign Minister Matsuoka responded to Chinese criticism that Japan had already benefited enough from its presence in Manchuria, and that the time was ripe to return it to China. Matsuoka retaliated:

> I hardly need point out, as you all know well, that the South Manchuria Railway and other things that came into our possession upon conclusion of the [Russo-Japanese] War, we got *from Russia, not from China*, and even these things would not have meant very much to us but for the investments that followed after the War. You could certainly not run a railway, for instance, without money to run it. (laughter) Japan has been making, down to this day, a huge investment (one billion six hundred million yen) in Manchuria, and this has largely enabled us to keep up our works in Manchuria. . . . Has China contributed to this huge investment of Japan, which has been and is being expended for the development of Manchuria and Eastern Inner Mongolia? Not a cent! Whatever Japan is getting, she is getting not from China, but is being earned through her own investment and by her own efforts.[10]

Matsuoka then continued to point out Japan's lone effort in preparing for a possible Soviet advance in terms of a clash between the two great pan-nations of Pan-Slav and Pan-Asia, stating:

The reaching out for ice-free seas is one of the blind forces of the Slav race. This may impel that race to strike out in other directions, but at least one direction points to the Far East. . . . Against this comeback or onslaught of the Slavs, are our Chinese friends prepared to come forward with a reasonable measure of assurance that China will successfully guard her northern frontiers . . . ? History repeats itself, and we Japanese entertain a very grave apprehension on this point. . . . What concrete and satisfactory consideration are you ready, my Chinese friends, to accord to us Japanese for the sacrifices of the past in blood and treasure? And then, are you prepared to extend us a guarantee . . . in the serious question of national security? In short, unless and until some satisfactory answers are offered to these fundamentals, I am afraid we cannot get very far in any attempt to solve the so-called Manchurian Questions.[11]

The above reasoning shows that Japan's historical and emotional attachments to Manchuria had ramifications of a continental scale. While on the surface operating under the indirect mechanism of a puppet state, Japanese leaders in Manchukuo built on that existing foundation to achieve a farther-reaching goal and deeper involvement than any other traditional concepts of informal imperialism could have envisaged. As such, broad categories of imperialism fall short of explaining the all-encompassing fashion in which a critical segment of educated, middle-class Japanese—including leftist intellectuals, some of whom were strongly beholden to anti-imperialist ideas—mobilized for the construction of Manchukuo's new sovereignty and national identity. In this light, Louise Young's thesis of "total empire" seems valid in its ability to convey why Manchukuo appealed to the Japanese imagination to such an extraordinary degree. For instance, heralding the birth of Manchukuo, the metropolitan daily *Osaka Asahi Shimbun* reported that it was not only the *zaibatsu* conglomerates "but small and medium businesses that were at the bottom of despair" who were "rushing into the midst of the storm-like Manchurian fever, to the new land of promise."[12]

Despite the haunting echoes of the "total empire," there are, however, reasonable counterarguments to be made both from contemporaneous observers and historians about the extent of "total-ness" with which Japan took to the Manchukuo *kenkoku* venture.[13] Such interpretational differences are important. Still, the apparent peculiarity of Manchukuo, from the perspective of Pan-Asianism, was not its ability to mobilize Japanese society at large. Its peculiarity rested in its ability to appeal successfully, in a total and all-consuming fashion, to a critical segment and critical mass of the Japanese population, who were willing enough to take a chance on Manchukuo.

Pan-Asianism as a *Kenkoku* Ideology

That Pan-Asianism inspired those Japanese nation-builders is clear, for instance, in Manchukuo's architecture. The architectural planning of the capital city Xinjing was influenced greatly by the Tokyo Imperial University professor Sano Toshitaka (1880–1956) and his disciples. All ministry buildings as well as other official state structures, such as railway stations, followed a particular stylistic pattern that came to be called Asianist (*Ajiashugi yōshiki*), or the "Asian-revival" or "Founding of Asia" school (*Kōashiki*). The most commonly identifiable features of this style were their stark but imposing modernist bodies made of reinforced concrete, topped with Chinese or Japanese-inspired ornamental roofs, adorned by other classically inspired and Asian-influenced decorations. Such artificial efforts to celebrate Pan-Asianism as Manchukuo's state ideology were, in the words of the head of Manchukuo's Architecture Unit, "most difficult, because we had to come up with proper designs that encapsulated the ideals of the infant state, in such a short time at that too."[14]

The results were more often than not a curious hodgepodge of the austere and the ornate oriental kitsch likely to be found in present-day amusement parks. Manchukuo's Pan-Asianist architecture became a target of derision and harsh criticism by architects back in Japan; however, no one could dispute its singularity. Thus at the very minimum, Pan-Asianist architecture can be said to have created a specifically "Manchukuo" style, which would remain a permanent fixture in the cityscape of present-day Changchun.[15]

Admittedly, the architecture was one of the more salient manifestations of Pan-Asianism in Manchukuo. In other areas, the contention that there was a major Pan-Asianist ideological stake in the Manchukuo-building project becomes more difficult to substantiate. This is so because Pan-Asianism was not the only *kenkoku* ideology. And here, Yamamuro Shin'ichi's description of Manchukuo as the tripartite Greek mythological creature Chimera, with the head of a lion, the body of a sheep, and a tail of a dragon, is helpful.[16] He identifies the head of the Chimera as the Kwantung Army, the body as the Japanese imperial institution, and the tail as old, as well as newly emerging China. It is difficult to deny, even only by looking at its architectural policy, that the Kwantung Army's conception of Manchukuo had a deep ideological root in Pan-Asianism, even as such an idea in reality presumed Japan's imperial institution to be at the center of the Pan-Asian union, thus relegating both the Manchukuo emperor of the old China and the nationalism of the new, to the position of mere appendages. The end result, as the name Chimera accurately suggests, was a genetically warped monster of destructive capability. While all the three parts were important, even necessary constitutive ingredients to the conception of this monster, none proved as tempting for many educated Japanese as the Pan-Asian ideology, appropriately found in the lion's head. However misconceived or uninvited, Manchukuo was Japan's first, foremost, and most probably, final "Pan-Asianist empire."

II. Pan-Asianism and the Building of Manchukuo

The Kingly Way in Manchukuo

Harping on the slogans of "harmony of the five races" and "the Kingly Way in paradise," Japanese leaders claimed that the ideological basis of Manchukuo could be found in their conception of multiethnic, Pan-Asian utopia, which drew its strength from the venerable Eastern civilization. That civilization was both modern and ancient in its collective spirit. The broad theme of the predominant slogans was anchored in Teaist Pan-Asianism, which dramatically pitted Eastern spirituality against Western materialism. At the same time, they also had conceptual roots in Sinic Pan-Asianism, which stressed the common East Asian bond shaped by centuries of Sinic and Confucian cultural influences. Japan's increasing suspicions of modern Chinese nationalism by this time sat in stark contrast to its historical embrace of it.

In fact, both Japanese and Chinese supporters of Sun Yat-sen had earlier referred to the Confucian concept of the "Kingly Way" (*ōdō* in Japanese/*wangdao* in Chinese) as a specifically Asian phenomenon. They stressed that unlike the Western notion of the "Forceful Way" (*hadō/ badao*) in which materialistic interest prevailed over the weak, the Kingly Way was grounded in a higher moral ground of enlightened benevolence of the ruler to benefit all under his leadership. But despite Japan's admiration for the old China, the Japanese claim, especially that of the Kwantung Army leaders in Manchukuo, increasingly and overtly reflected Meishuron Pan-Asianism. This brand of Pan-Asianism directly linked the future of East Asia with Japan's hegemonic leadership, and specifically Japanese spirit and Japanese culture—which had in their minds managed to create the only successful synthesis of modernity without sacrificing the ancient Asian heritage—as the foundation of Eastern civilization.

As is usually the case with political slogans, however, a discrepancy between theory and practice was bound to emerge. Or, to be more precise, theory would come to be interpreted in varying and inconsistent ways so as to completely discredit the original theory in reality. Precisely how the Kingly Way slogan panned out in reality is illuminating on this point.

Broadly, there were three ways in which the Kingly Way came to be interpreted and practiced (or not practiced) by Manchukuo's Japanese "kings." First, there were those who approached the idea of the Kingly Way with realism and caution, arguing that the idea amounted to a pipe dream. Second, there were those who saw the Kingly Way through the lens of revolutionary romanticism, convinced that it provided a firm basis for a singularly Manchukuo identity. The third interpretation was the mainstream understanding of the Kwantung Army that legitimized Japan's preponderance.

There is little space here for the first line of interpretation, as that sort of realism was not heeded in any meaningful way as to prevent "the Kingly Way in paradise" platform from becoming Manchukuo's official slogan. It is still worth remembering, however, that not all Japanese interpreted the idea of the Kingly Way uncritically. For example, Naitō Konan, who headed a Japan-Manchukuo cultural research institute at Kyoto Imperial University and whose impact on Sinology has been studied by Joshua Fogel, sounded a warning in 1933.[17] To him, the Kingly Way was "impeccable in theory, allowing no one to object to them," but their realization, "depending on who carries out that task, sometimes creates the exact opposite results of those ideals, judging from frequent examples in history."[18] He elaborated further:

> This "Kingly Way" slogan is being repeated, and being celebrated as the nation-building ideal [for Manchukuo], . . . but could anyone please explain what that really means? Nay, that would be difficult. In fact, even in the birthplace of the term itself, in China, the Kingly Way has almost never existed as a reality in its history. It has always been, since ancient times, not much more than a proverbial ideal.[19]

Naitō's misgivings about the "reality" of the Manchukuo project were shared by Yanaihara Tadao, who would be forced out of his post at Tokyo

Imperial University as the head of colonial studies following the publication of his articles criticizing Japan's military expansion in China in 1937.[20] In an opinion piece, written shortly after the inspection trip he made to Manchuria in August 1932, he summarily concluded that the notion that many Japanese entertained that "economic boom is arriving from Manchuria" was "a false propaganda."[21] According to Yanaihara, "even motel owners and prostitutes, who are said to be prospering have not been faring too well due to the decline in the number of tourists owing to increasing banditry."[22] It was indeed on the account of abundant expectations that the Japanese nation was excited about the Manchurian Incident. To him, huge Japanese industrial investments—for instance, in the aluminum industry—made very little economic sense on the account of realities.

The second interpretation of the Kingly Way, which assigned Japan the mission of prompting a decisive social change in Manchukuo, reflected a heightened desire among young nation-builders for radicalism and egalitarianism that could probably be best described as a form of revolutionary romanticism. They regarded the Kingly Way as a pithy slogan that conveyed their egalitarian, progressive, and pioneering outlook befitting of their peculiar understanding of Manchukuo's self-rule. To that end, the members of the Manchurian Youth League, established in 1929, were instrumental in presenting and circulating the Kingly Way as a partner concept to another foundational concept of Manchukuo "harmony of the five races." The league's key players including Ozawa Kaisaku (who named his would-be world-famous conductor son Seiji after the two instigators of the Manchurian Incident, Itagaki SEI-shirō and Ishiwara Kan-JI), Yamaguchi Shigetsugu (Jūji), and Kohiyama Naoto, along with several Chinese colleagues who studied at Japan's elite educational institutions, tended to be highly idealistic.[23] Their group motto of "Concordia of Various Nations" (*shominzoku no kyōwa*) was originally proposed as a defensive keyword for protecting minority Japanese interests from heightened anti-Japanese sentiments in the late 1920s. The motto implied that Japanese presence could be validated through the formation and promotion of a harmonious, multiethnic society.

At around the same time, the Daiyūhōkai (Great Mountain Peak Society) was formed by younger members of the Mantetsu, such as Nakano Koitsu and Kasagi Yoshiaki. They were taken by the idea of "founding Asia." Then, their *kōa* (founding Asia) philosophy was most energetically advanced by Ōkawa Shūmei in the ultranationalist organizations he helped found, such as Kōchisha (Action on Earth Society) and

Yūzonsha (Endure and Remain Society). Joined by the Manchurian Youth League, the Daiyūhōkai formed the Guidance Group for Self-Rule, headed by the local leader Yu Chonghan, who played an instrumental role in maintaining order and securing local support for the Japanese as the Manchurian Incident unfolded. After the founding of Manchukuo, the Guidance Group developed into the state-administered organization specifically geared toward the dissemination of Manchukuo values, called the Concordia Society (Kyōwakai) in July 1932.

The Concordia Society held the realization of the Kingly Way, the revival of agricultural reforms, and the development of harmony of various races and mutual respect as its organizational ideals. Its more practical function was to assist the Kwantung Army's governance by organizing, protecting, and accommodating different requirements of multiple nationalities and communities by granting them due representation in the new state apparatus. It was the only political organization sanctioned by the state of Manchukuo, which rejected parliamentary democracy and party politics as products of corrupt Western liberalism.

In the minds of those looking to effect a sweeping social change, for example, in Manchukuo's urban planning, the Kingly Way was the keyword that signified Japanese leadership in bringing about a uniquely Manchukuoan way of life. Here, both the "future" and "Japanese leadership" were taken seriously. Japan's technical knowledge, often couched in the language of modernity as rendered by the only modern Asian power, claimed to fashion Manchukuo into a vision of a future that was yet to be found in Japan itself. The planning was carried out by young educated Japanese, emerging middle-class professionals, and urban planners, more than a few of whom could be clearly regarded as leftist or at least left-leaning progressives rather than ultranationalists. Manchukuo proudly boasted of its express train, named *Ajiagō* (*Asia Express*) and its capital's spacious boulevards, with the main street 100 meters wide with 18 traffic lanes. In addition to the Pan-Asianist architecture, these features were all meant to symbolize an era of Asian superiority guided by those innovative and ambitious Japanese nation-builders. We will come back to this question of progressive fascination with Pan-Asianism shortly.

The third interpretation concerned the Kingly Way as a concept directly legitimizing the Japanese imperial institution and Emperor Worship in Manchukuo. As a garrison force of the Japanese Imperial Army protecting the interests of the Empire, the Kwantung Army regarded itself as the primary emissary of the imperial will, whose *de facto* military occupation of Manchukuo was then justified by its claim of exercising the

Kingly Way for the better future of Asia as a whole. In this interpretation, the Japanese emperor, as the King of Kings, became the *idealtypus* for all Asian rulers, including even the Manchukuoan emperor. In a farewell speech made on his departure from Tokyo by General Mutō Nobuyoshi, who was simultaneously appointed the Commander of the Kwantung Army, Director General of the Kantōchō, and ambassador plenipotentiary to Manchukuo in August 1932, he summarized the Kwantung Army reading of the Kingly Way as follows:

> I suspect that the resolution of the Manchurian-Mongolian Problem is earnestly hoped for by the whole of Manchukuo, including both the upper and lower segments of its society. . . . [I]n order to ensure the future survival of our compatriots, it is the preordained mission of our Yamato [Japanese] nation to resolve that problem. Moreover, the Kingly Way, the concept which ought to be propagated throughout Manchukuo, is an extension of our Empire's unique Imperial Way, therefore, [the building of Manchukuo] is a great work destined to contribute spiritually to world culture. . . . I believe that not only could the co-prosperity of Japan and Manchukuo be realized, but also the pure development of world culture to be possible.[24]

In suggesting that there existed "upper and lower segments" within the Manchukuo society, Mutō was alluding to some sort of a *sui generis* and incontrovertible social hierarchy within that newly founded state. From his subsequent remark about the preordained nature of the Yamato nation's mission, moreover, it appears that in his view, Japanese citizens belonged to a category *par excellence* that reigned over both of those "upper and lower segments" of Manchukuo. As such, the position of Manchukuo's emperor was innately secondary to that of the Japanese Emperor. The resultant hierarchy was set in stone in the Concordia Society guidelines:

> The Emperor of Manchukuo was installed as emperor according to the heavenly will, the wish of the Heavenly Sovereign [the Emperor of Japan], thus the very existence of the [Manchukuo] throne depends upon its occupier's willingness to serve the Heavenly Sovereign who is at the heart of the federation of the Imperial Way.[25]

Just as the Kingly Way concept operated alongside the blurred and shifting lines of interpretation, so too did the notion of "harmony of the five races." In practice, "racial" or "national" categories showed a great deal of conflict and inconsistency of classification. As deftly argued by Mariko Asano Tamanoi, the very claim of the five races as consisting Manchukuo's population was determined by differing assumptions about racial categories, with different Japanese proposing varying combinations of groupings of the Manchurian population and with overlapping and contradictory claims being made about who exactly constituted the Manchus (i.e., are the Manchus a distinct ethnic nation, different from Han Chinese, or even from Mongols?).[26] Even the most fundamental question of what constituted the Japanese nation itself was to be left untouched (i.e., where do Koreans, Taiwanese, and descendents of Japanese immigrants outside of Japan fit into this mythic notion of the homogenous Yamato nation?).

The blurred and overlapping racial categories notwithstanding, as far as the Kwantung Army was concerned, there were no misgivings about the Japanese emperor's unrivalled position as the King of Manchukuo. This in effect meant that the Army stood at the pinnacle of that Japanese racial category. The great irony of Manchukuo was that the Kwantung Army, the *soi-disant* purveyor of the uniquely superior Japanese imperial values as the purest expression of the benevolent and enlightened Kingly Way, depended upon a great deal of support and participation coming from its unlikely allies—"dangerous" leftist elements and "corrupt" conglomerate capitalists—in the actual building of Manchukuo, especially from the mid-1930s to the early 1940s.

As far as economic "planning" of Manchukuo was concerned, the Kwantung Army owed much to its leftist, technocratic colleagues who saw in the anti-capitalist, Soviet-inspired centralized economy a way to transcend old-style imperialism. The economic "doing," on the other hand, required a flow of capital channeled through newly emerging business conglomerates, efforts most notably led by Ayukawa Yoshisuke (1880–1967), founder of the Nissan conglomerate, who headed the Manchurian Development Corporation for Heavy Industries from 1937.

Together with Matsuoka Yōsuke, who returned to Manchuria as the Mantetsu president from August 1935 to February 1939, and the postwar prime minister Kishi Nobusuke (1896–1987), who, as a vice minister of Manchukuo's industrial department implemented many of its bold development initiatives, Ayukawa was called one of the "Three Suke's of Manchuria." All were related by marriage, and all came from Yamaguchi prefecture, and their combined determination was thought to be instrumental in transforming Manchukuo into a huge industrial machine in a relatively short time in the second half of the 1930s. The first decade of Manchukuo's existence also witnessed a rapid growth of Japanese population in urban areas. For example in Fengtian, the population almost quadrupled from 45,567 to 163,591 over the course of 1931 to 1941. For the same period, Harbin witnessed a dramatic increase of its population from 4,151 to 53,295, while the capital Xinjing also experienced an impressive increase from 17,464 to 128,582.[27]

The consistent flow of Japanese into urban areas, however, belied the critical absence of agricultural settlers in this *kenkoku* endeavor. In spite of the Kwantung Army's concerted efforts to recruit farmers to build agricultural defensive fortifications along Manchukuo's northern border, rural settlers amounted to less than 15 percent of Japanese migrants in Manchuria in 1945. This proves the predominantly urban appeal of Japan's Manchukuo project, as an agency for disseminating culture and constructing the vision of the East Asia modern.[28] As such, Manchukuo remained a city, rather than country, phenomenon, which produced a marriage of convenience between the anti-capitalist progressives and anti-Marxist capitalists, with the benediction of the Kwantung Army. It is relatively easy to fathom the reasons why fledgling *zaibatsu* leaders such as Ayukawa at least initially saw enormous business potential in Manchukuo's natural resources and bountiful cheap labor flowing in from other parts of China. More puzzling yet is why Japan's progressives, many of whom were Marxists or Marxist-inspired leftists, and sometimes even anti-imperialists, came to see enough convenience in this marriage, to which specific question we now turn.

Egalitarianism and Pan-Asianism

The interpretation of the Kingly Way as a concept signaling the arrival of a new and morally accountable *modus vivendi* is important, as it provided a ground upon which Manchukuo's progressive nation-builders could develop a working relationship with Japanese leaders of otherwise disparate persuasions. The egalitarian interpretation explains many of Manchukuo's singular features, be they manifested in the spheres of its urban and industrial planning, agricultural programs, or cultural activities. The South Manchurian Railroad played a central role in advancing that version of the Kingly Way.

Of special importance within the Mantetsu was its Research Unit, founded already in 1907. The Railroad's first president Gotō Shinpei had ensured its reputation as an extensive information-gathering network with research records ranging in topics from politics, to economics, and to anthropology. Having undergone several internal reforms and expansions by 1932, the Research Unit was handpicked by the Kwantung Army to work out the economic planning of the new state. The group's close associations with the authority continued, and by 1939, it had developed into a think tank employing more than 2,000 researchers.

To the extent that any ideological characterization of a vast institution is possible, the Research Unit had strong Marxist tendencies, though to say that the members had to be Marxist would certainly be an exaggeration. Those planners, who played the precarious power game with their ideological foes to make Manchukuo into a vision of an egalitarian, multiethnic society, were mostly the products of middle-class upbringing. They came of age when Marxian categories of analysis were immensely popular in modern institutions of higher education. In addition to suffering from a record-level rate of unemployment at home, many of them also endured state persecution of leftists, especially after the large-scale roundup of March 1928.

The "First Economic Construction Plan for Manchukuo" of March 1933 was marked by such ideological preferences, and brought to the fore the ultimate goal of constructing a viable East Asian economic bloc.[29] It also outlined the four accompanying goals of "first preventing any one particular class from monopolizing benefits of industrial developments, but rather ensuring their even distributions among all Manchukuo citizens," "second making ways for state control to realize an efficient development of existing resources," "third remaining open to investments coming from the outside world in the spirit of equal opportunities, employing existing and cutting-edge modern knowledge where appropriate," and "finally, in that spirit of international cooperation, ensuring first and foremost that Manchukuo develop a close cooperative economic relationship with Japan, in order to create one efficient East Asian economy."[30]

Indeed, the conception of the East Asian Cooperative Body (*Tōa Kyōdōtai*), which some Japanese Marxists would come to see as a localized and specifically Asian expression of transnational egalitarianism and a viable Asian alternative to Marxist-Leninist development of a just society in the late 1930s is already detected in this plan. Thanks in large part to the work of the Shōwa Research Association, a brain trust for Prime Minister Konoe, whose members overlapped the members of the Mantetsu Research Unit, the idea that a collectivized Asian economy provided a step toward a more "just" social order would find its policy application in Japan's war with China in the late 1930s. Such thinking eventually metamorphosed into Japan's official policies of constructing a "New East Asian Order" and the "Greater East Asia Co-Prosperity Sphere," more of which will be said in the following chapters.

By the mid-1930s, the Mantetsu had turned into wide-ranging subsidiary ventures in business, educational institutions, and film studios. This coincided with the heyday of the Mantetsu Research Unit. The 1936 Five-Year Plan, commissioned by Ishiwara Kanji and perfected by Miyazaki Masayoshi (1893–1954), boldly advanced the need to create a defensive state based on heavy industry, concentrating on the production of steel, coal, electricity, automobiles, weapons, and airplanes.[31] The plan provided the basis for the Manchurian Development Corporation for Heavy Industries led by Ayukawa in 1937. Miyazaki, who as a student in St. Petersburg witnessed the Russian Revolution witnessed firsthand, was clearly inspired by the Soviet model to make Manchukuo an efficient building block of Japan's war economy and Japan's war economy eventually part of a larger Asian economic bloc.

Partly pushed by the escalation of the China War, a whopping 5.2 billion yen was invested in the Corporation, at a time when the Japanese government's annual expenditures were appropriated at a mere 2.7 billion in 1937 and 3.2 billion in 1938.[32] In some areas, most notably in the production of pig iron and coal, the Plan proved successful. However, the Five-Year Plan's ultimate success depended almost entirely on local as well as migrant labor being exploited in appalling working conditions. In the Fushun coal mine alone, approximately 40,000 miners were working at any given time, and it is thought that about 25,000 of that number had to be replaced yearly, owing to a high rate of deaths, escapes, and executions presumably following failed attempts at resistance and escapes.[33]

In this way, the Manchukuo project was theoretically driven by the left and pragmatically implemented by industrialists and bureaucrats. This power dynamic also had its clear limits, however. The Research Unit's pursuit of efficient wartime resource allocations began to alarm the military as the China War dragged on, and the war in the Pacific loomed. The idea of maximum wartime efficiency, such as the ratcheting up of productivity in certain industries and the elimination of intermediaries in agricultural productions made enough sense even to the conservative elements within the Kwantung Army, leading them to concede to the socialist-inspired economic planning. But in the face of the escalating war, whose prolongation made little strategic sense to begin with, the logical argument for efficiency, such as finding accommodation with Chinese nationalism, withdrawing troops from China, and abandoning industries that had already proven inefficient, increasingly came to be seen by military hard-liners as unpatriotic, un-Japanese, subversive, and tantamount to defeat.

A similar intolerance with reasoned criticism of the self-destructive war, coupled with the longstanding fear of communism, paralleled developments within Japan, where police roundups of the left culminated in the Economic Planning Board Incident (1939–41) and the Ozaki-Sorge Incident (1941). The rising suspicion of the left eventually led to the demise of the Mantetsu Research Unit, ending in the so-called Mantetsu Research Unit Incident of 1942 and 1943, in which 44 researchers were arrested by the military police. As many of them held important positions in Manchukuo's state planning, the military police was ordered to handle them with care, meaning they were not tortured. Four of them died in prison due to bad conditions nevertheless, and the roundup effectively put an end to the most animated period of Manchukuo state-planning by the Research Unit.

Tachibana Shiraki's "Change in Direction"

Like those Research Unit planners, Tachibana Shiraki (1881–1945) was inspired by Marxism in his interpretation of the Kingly Way. Specifically, he regarded agrarianism-based cooperativism as a sure road to Manchukuo's eventual self-rule. Tachibana, a resident of China since 1906, was a Sinologist and a journalist of some renown, who allegedly prompted the great Chinese novelist Lu Xun to say, "That man knows infinitely more about China than us." While many of his Japanese contemporaries saw China as lacking in order and incapable of fostering its own modern nationalism, Tachibana had remained an outspoken believer in modern Chinese nationalism, and repeatedly warned Japan to adopt a more prudent approach in its policy in his monthly *Gekkan Shina Kenkyū* (China Studies Monthly) over the course of the 1920s. When the Manchurian Incident broke out, he expectedly took a position harshly critical of the Kwantung Army.

Shortly afterwards, however, Tachibana went on to make a dramatic turn in his view. He became a passionate advocate for Manchukuo. In the 1934 confessional-style article "My Change in Direction," published in the pro-Manchukuo magazine *Manshū Hyōron* (Manchuria Review), of which he was the chief staff writer, Tachibana elaborated on the reasons for his active support of Manchukuo. He described his meeting with Ishiwara and Itagaki, the two masterminds behind the Incident, in early October 1931. Tachibana claimed that he came out of the meeting convinced that the instigators genuinely believed in creating an independent Pan-Asianist state, leading him to say that previously, he failed to

> understand that the direct goal of this action [the Manchurian Incident] was the creation of an independent state with the four northeastern provinces resting as the cornerstone of Asian liberation, . . . that Japan should place unconditional trust in this state and moreover, actively support it in all possible ways. At the same time, [the instigators aspired to] the more indirect goal aimed at a reform of the home country [Japan], so that it would be able to procure enough force to lead Asia's liberation and the establishment of an ideal state by freeing the proletarian masses from the autocracy of capitalist political parties. . . . I was once a liberal. At the same time, I was always inclined to reject capitalism, which formed the basis of liberalism. Thus I was never entirely at ease with liberal philosophy. . . . [A]s a result of self-reflection, I bade farewell to liberalism and capitalist democracy, and came to take a deep interest in proletarian democracy, especially of agrarian democracy, with the goal of building Manchukuo. This differs from the present directions of the [Kwantung Army] officers; nonetheless, I value their new leadership because they are dependable partners traveling down the same path, up to a point.[34]

Tachibana's logic depended upon an appreciation of Pan-Asianist ambitions on the part of the Kwantung Army officers, which he regarded as essential in liberating the oppressed peasantry and fostering indigenous Chinese nationalism. This change in his direction, in his words, constituted "a step forward in my philosophical outlook, and at the same time, a stabilizer on my view on society."[35] Like the Communist Ozaki Hotsumi, another influential China expert, Tachibana seemed to reconcile his Marxian inclinations with the official Pan-Asian ideology of Manchukuo without much difficulty. Having published on the topic of the Kingly Way and self-rule from as early as 1925, he was delighted and eager to find an opportunity for practical application of his philosophy in Manchukuo. He insisted that

> [t]he Kingly Way governance should not be seen as some glorious historical legacy from ancient days, but should rather be seen as a guide

to bringing happiness to the future political life . . . suggesting an alternative and providing a stimulus to the Western civilization which has come to a standstill.[36]

More specifically, for Manchukuo's majority agricultural (up to 95 percent) and majority Han Chinese population, Tachibana found it vital that the planners of Manchukuo pay special attention to reviving the existing local structures embedded in Chinese culture rather than to try to alter them. In his eyes, Japanese lagged far behind the West *and* China in developing its own system of local self-rule, and Tachibana believed that they had no business telling Chinese peasants how they should rule themselves.[37] To that end, he advocated the "establishment of security," "abolition of unreasonable taxation," and "the development of agricultural cooperatives" in Manchukuo.[38] His Kingly Way, differing greatly from the Meishuron interpretation in its rejection of the innate superiority of the Japanese Imperial Way, was most clearly expressed in the Manchukuo state program for autonomous cooperative farms, which he advanced with Noda Ranzō. It was carried out by his ideological inheritors in the Research Unit, such as Satō Daishirō and Ōgami Suehiro in the form of the Cooperative Movement. But the movement was crushed in November 1941, with more than fifty being arrested on the account of engaging in communist activities. Satō perished in prison. And the leaking of names eventually led to the Research Unit Incident of 1942 and 1943.

Transnational Institutions and Agents: Kendai Experience

The gap between the egalitarianism-inspired interpretation of Pan-Asianism and Meishuron Pan-Asianism perceptibly began to widen, especially after the intensification of Japan's war in China around 1940. That year, the Kwantung Army built the Nation-Building Shrine (*Kenkoku Shinbyō*) inside the garden of Pu Yi's palace. In July, at the ceremony commemorating the completion of this structure, Pu Yi declared Shintoism to be the spiritual basis of Manchukuo. This followed the comment allegedly made by Lieutenant-General of the Kwantung Army Yoshioka Yasunao: "Your Majesty, . . . You seem to believe in the higher power of Buddha, but don't you know there is a proper god celebrated by Shintoism in Japan? Why can't you believe in that instead?"[39] According to his brother Pu Chieh, Pu Yi was a committed Buddhist who often meditated and chanted in times of emotional difficulties. To be forced to worship the Japanese ancestral god was one of the most painful experiences he ever had to face during his Manchukuo years.

Outside of Manchukuo, the intensification of Meishuron Pan-Asianism in Japan's external policy around this period meant that the homogenization of Asia after the Japanese model was more than ever justified as providing a way for Asia's liberation, leading, for instance, to the Japanese coercion of Koreans to adopt Japanese surnames. In contrast, so long as Manchukuo was predicated on the multiracial tenet of "harmony of the five races" (with Russian and Jewish minorities also occasionally contributing to the mix), overt assimilation of the kind seen in the formal Japanese territories such as Korea and Taiwan could not take place. But the Meishuron assumption was felt in every aspect of life in Manchukuo. While purporting to be a Pan-Asian utopia in which different races peacefully cohabited, such peaceful cohabitation depended on Japan's ability to create and sustain a utopia in the image, or arguably in a more puritanical and grander image, of the imperial metropole.

Efforts were made at squaring the egalitarian principles with the hegemonial impulses of the Meishuron brand of Pan-Asianism. One of the most explicit attempts came in the form of Kenkoku Daigaku (Nation-Building University, or more commonly, Kendai), opened in Xinjing in the midst of the China War. It was established under the leadership of General Tsuji Masanobu, the foremost ideological inheritor of Ishiwara Kanji, aimed at producing "pioneering leaders in the establishment of a moral world."[40] In 1938, the first class matriculated 141 students, of which 70 were Japanese, 46 Manchurians, 3 Taiwanese, 10 Koreans, 7 Mongolians, and 5 Russian Caucasians.[41] Striving for egalitarianism in all aspects of university life, Japanese students insisted that all students have meals of equal quality, and this was publicized in the newspapers.[42] Still, the fact that this was deemed newsworthy confirms that equal treatment of different "races" was an anomaly rather than the norm in everyday life of Manchukuo.

Indeed, Manchukuo had by then developed into a highly stratified society, with Japanese enjoying various social and economic privileges. For example, the income ratio of Korean and Chinese female factory workers to their Japanese counterparts in Japanese-owned businesses in Manchukuo in August 1939 averaged at 41.8 and 29.1, respectively. For male workers, the figures were 40.2 and 28.8.[43] Such was the reality upholding the "harmony" of Asian races.

That even the self-consciously egalitarian Kendai was unable to live up to its declared creed revealed the limitations of Manchukuo's Pan-Asianism, precisely because the egalitarian claim and Japan's paternalism competed with, rather than complemented, one another. In fact, not even all Kendai students accepted the "Japanization" of the rest of Asia as the first step toward Asian salvation. On August 17, 1945, after Japan's surrender, Korean and Chinese students came to Assistant Professor Nishimoto Sōsuke to bid their old teacher farewell. A Korean student told him that only with very few exceptions, his fellow students at the university belonged to a secret society working for Korean independence, declaring that "only when Korea freed itself from Japanese servitude . . . would a Japanese-Korean alliance be realized."[44] A Chinese student, too, confessed that each time they were made to take part in the ritual morning worship of the Japanese emperor, he and other Chinese students prayed silently that "imperialist Japan would be defeated." While they claimed that they had guilty consciences doing so because they felt that at heart all their Japanese teachers "had good intentions," they concluded that "Manchukuo was regrettably a puppet state of Japanese imperialism in actual substance."[45]

A sense of disillusionment was also felt by Kendai's Japanese students as well. Morisaki Minato (1924–45), whose youthful idealism prompted him to come to Manchukuo rather than finish his studies in Japan, was one of them. His diary has been studied by Matsumoto Ken'ichi and Mariko Asano Tamanoi, providing a glimpse into what might have gone through the minds of an impressionable and vulnerable young man.[46] Unable to overcome the sense of disillusionment he felt with the university's Pan-Asianist claim and the reality of its divided student body, Morisaki concluded that the Kendai project was a sham, leading him to leave without a degree and to enlist in the Navy. On September 2, 1942, less than a year before he left Kendai, he noted:

> If one really thinks about it, one has to admit that the Chinese who are fighting on behalf of [Chiang Kai-shek's Nationalist] Chunking or [the Communist] Yanan are worthy of admiration. In their ways, they are noble and committed fighters. They are aware of their own missions and are dedicating their lives to their goals. . . . The Soviets too are striving for the realization of their own version of the slogan "Eight corners of the world under one roof." . . . The Soviet new order, well, that's rather admirable on its own terms. Compared to the Anglo-American imperial order, the Soviets are more noble for sure. . . . I suppose we

should not consider Manchuria's Han Chinese and the Chinese of China proper as separate peoples. Manchukuoans are also Chinese, and moreover, the more patriotic one is, the more one tends to think of himself as a "Chinese" rather than "Manchukuoan." Sadly, those human resources who should be welcome as worthy colleagues by our camp, who could really work for the good of Asia and our ideals, are working for the opposing camps. Their anti-Japanese and counter-Japanese movement too should be admired accordingly.[47]

Forever idealistic, and forever desiring to believe in the cause higher and more noble than life itself, Morisaki eventually committed suicide once the war was over.

Stars, Spies, and Princesses

Kendai, at least in principle, was an institution aimed at the production of cross-cultural, Pan-Asianist agents, in which women had little visible part. In fact, Manchukuo's military-dominated public life afforded little room for women to hold positions of substantial political power. Nevertheless, the mobilization of women, Japanese or non-Japanese, was certainly an integral and important part of Manchukuo's everyday nation-building effort.[48] Especially in the fields of primary school education and agriculture, women participated in enacting and disseminating Manchukuo values that claimed to be at once pioneering and traditional.[49] Shifting our perspective, nonetheless, I would like to draw attention to the extraordinary cases of two women, whose lives became inextricably intertwined with the fate of Manchukuo and its identity. Though their stories were not in any way representative of Manchukuo's everyday struggle, their cases do illustrate how certain women became its most public and conspicuous cross-cultural agents meant to serve as the epitome of Manchukuo's identity.

The first woman of note is the Manchurian-born Japanese actress Yamaguchi Yoshiko (1920–), who appeared in propaganda films produced by the Mantetsu-run Manchurian Film Association (Man'ei) under her Chinese name, Li Xianglan (pronounced Ri Kōran in Japanese). Born to a father who taught Chinese to Mantetsu staff and having studied as a Chinese under the guardianship of her Chinese godfather in Beijing, Yamaguchi grew up to be thoroughly bilingual and bicultural. With what many Japanese at the time considered to be striking and exotic looks and with her voice rigorously trained from a young age by a Russian-Italian émigré opera singer, she became hugely popular in Japan in the late 1930s as a pro-Japanese Chinese actress. Curiously, Yamaguchi's feigning of Chinese identity was done in the exact mirror image of her namesake and the legendary spy Kawashima Yoshiko (1907–48), better known as "the beauty in man's clothes" as she preferred to wear the Kwantung Army military uniform, who was in reality a Japanese-educated Aisin Gioro princess, a Manchurian royal.

Yamaguchi's postwar career was just as dramatic as her wartime role as Manchukuo's top film star. The numerous twists and turns of her extraordinarily turbulent and public life are difficult to convey in this space. Having barely escaped execution by the Kuomintang Army as a Chinese spy at the end of the war, she recommenced her singing and acting career in Japan and even in Hollywood. In the United States, she found a soulmate in another cross-cultural product who suffered as a result of Japan's war—the half-Japanese, half-American sculptor and son of the poet Noguchi Yonejirō, Isamu Noguchi, to whom she was married for a few years. Later, in her more overtly political incarnation, she served as a television talk-show hostess in Japan. In that capacity, she reported from Vietnam and the Middle East, adopting the Palestinian cause somewhere on the way, and eventually served as the member of the Upper House of the Japanese Diet from 1974 until her semiretirement in 1992.

Throughout the Manchukuo phase of her career, Yamaguchi's Japanese identity was not revealed even to her colleagues at the film studio, which was led, from 1939, by the notorious Military Police Captain Amakasu Masahiko (1891–1945), the alleged instigator of the 1923 assassination of the anarchist Ōsugi Sakae and his associates. Her Chinese colleagues suspected that something was different with her because the Japanese treated her as one of their own, allowing her to live in a hotel room rather than in a communal dormitory, being served white rice as opposed to inferior sorghum, and being paid more than her Chinese colleagues (ten times more), leading them to conclude that she must be at least half-Japanese.[50] Even though both her parents were Japanese, reconciling with such a state of in-betweenness became her lifelong challenge, in real life as well as on film. On her first trip ever to Japan, upon entering her "home" country at the Port of Shimonoseki in 1941, an immigration officer rebuked her for acting like a Chinese, speaking Chinese, and wearing a Chinese dress despite carrying a Japanese passport. He said "Don't you know that we Japanese are a superior people? Aren't you ashamed of wearing thirdrate Chink clothes and speaking their language as you do?"[51]

Yamaguchi was caught by a similar dilemma on-screen as well. In the film *The Chinese Nights* (*Shina no Yoru*), which was a huge hit in Japan but flopped in Manchukuo, she played a Chinese who was saved by a Japanese sailor. Her character has lost her parents amid a struggle against the Japanese, and for that reason, she abhors any Japanese, even though the sailor saved her from destitution. She stubbornly rejects the sailor. Though sympathetic to her plight in the beginning, the sailor finally loses his cool and admonishes her by slapping her face, telling her to snap out of it. Somehow touched by his display of attention on her, she falls in love with him, repenting her earlier recalcitrance and rejection of Japanese commitment to putting her and her compatriots on the right path.

The film's plot infuriated the Chinese audience. Yamaguchi herself, in her 1987 recollection, attributed the severe Chinese reaction to cultural differences. The finer nuances of affection, such as in the case of parents disciplining children, or of military superiors slapping lower-ranking soldiers as a rite of passage, were completely lost in translation. From the Chinese perspective, it simply told a story of a Chinese woman being slapped by a barbaric Japanese. And as if that were not enough, the Chinese woman fell in love with the man who slapped her, making this film an exercise in "dual humiliation."[52] As such, Yamaguchi's part in this film led to the Kuomintang indictment of her as a Chinese traitor, from which she narrowly escaped by proving her genuine Japanese identity.

Various contradictions and ambivalence in Yamaguchi's life as the star of Manchuria mirrored Japan's artificial and narcissistic effort in the making of Manchukuo's identity. The idea that Japanese were the superior nation leading other Asian nations in the construction of a Pan-Asian state, in an area where chaos, corruption, and disorder had earlier prevailed, provided higher moral grounds for many Japanese involved, starting from very young children to well-educated adults. For example, a female sixth-grader in a Japanese primary school in Jiamusi in the Jilin province in 1940 noted in a school essay, with a mixture of affection and condescension:

[Manchu women] love wearing bright clothes, and they have a taste for lavishness. Our former babysitter powdered her face, and moreover, wore lipstick, and didn't bother to go to school, loafing around all day and somehow amusing herself. . . . The other day, on the way to the photographer's studio, I bumped into her on the street. As I was wearing a beautiful dress [especially for that occasion], she noticed it and walked towards me while munching peanuts. As she touched my dress, I could not help but notice that her finger nails had been painted bright red. Sensing that I had noticed them, she quickly recoiled and hid her hands. . . . But the Manchus, I must say, are artless and lovable people indeed.[53]

The *idée fixe* communicated in this little composition—that a Japanese girl of eleven or twelve could think of herself as a more prudent and virtuous disciplinarian—is illuminating. The air of superiority and pride, mixed with a not insincere fondness and concern for her older Chinese or "Manchurian" babysitter is something that was directly translatable to the top diplomat Saitō Hiroshi's reading of the Manchukuo situation. In a speech given at the American Academy of Political and Social Science in November 1934, he summarized his impressions of his recent two-week visit to Manchukuo and North China. He was "agreeably surprised to find that the situation there was very much better than I could have imagined in distant parts of the world."[54] This was so largely because of Japan's modernizing efforts that would "[i]n a few years' time" transform the Manchukuo capital into "a model city of the Far East, even excelling Tokyo and Osaka in many respects."[55]

For genuinely transcultural agents whose lives were molded by Manchukuo's multinational platform, things were not as rosy as Saitō's depictions would have us believe. Another extraordinary woman rivaling Yamaguchi in her thoroughgoing involvement with the making of Manchukuo was Saga Hiro (1914–87), a daughter of a Japanese marquis who married Aisin Gioro Pu Chieh (1907–94), a younger brother of the Last Emperor Pu Yi. Though it was orchestrated by the Kwantung Army and was consummated at the worst possible time—only three months before the outbreak of the China War—their union proved to be a lasting and successful meeting of minds that endured many an obstacle, starting from Pu Yi's lifelong suspicions of Hiro as a Japanese spy, the Kwantung Army's constant meddling and pressures on her to produce a male heir (which she never did), Hiro's postwar transcontinental escapes, Pu Chieh's imprisonment by the Communists, the murder of one of their two daughters, the sixteen-year separation that was ended only by Chou Enlai's diplomatic dexterity in 1961, and finally, attacks on them by the Red Guards during the Great Cultural Revolution. In their respective memoirs, both the wife and the husband claim love at first sight, and in her action and words, Hiro gave her utmost to become a member of the Manchu dynasty.[56]

Like the 1920 marriage between Princess Nashimotonomiya Masako (1901–89), also known by her Korean name Lee Bang-ja, and the so-called Korean Last Emperor Lee Eun (1897–1970), this marriage between a Japanese aristocrat and the Manchukuoan emperor's brother was claimed to signify genuine Japanese commitment to Pan-Asianism.[57] The earlier

Korean-Japanese imperial marriage was portrayed as the ultimate symbol of uniformity of Korean and Japanese peoples, encapsulated in the catch-phrases *naisen ittai* and *nissen yūwa*, both suggesting complete assimilation of Korea into Japanese sphere of influence. The Manchukuo-Japanese union, however, had a less blatant claim of assimilation and uniformity, most likely in order to accommodate the multinational Pan-Asianist claims of Manchukuo.

Unlike Nashimotonomiya Masako, who was after all a top bridal candidate for Emperor Hirohito himself and was a full-fledged member of Japan's imperial family before and after the marriage (precisely because the Japanese made the point of regarding Lee as one of their own also), Saga Hiro was related to, but never a member of the Japanese imperial family, making her more vulnerable to abuses by the Kwantung Army. In Hiro's memoirs, Lieutenant-General Yoshioka, one of Yamaguchi Yoshiko's primary supporters, is portrayed as a callous, despicable, and opportunistic officer who could not give a damn "to a lesser being who was married to Manchukuo's imperial brother," because "despite the 'harmony of the five races' slogan, Japanese were first-class citizens, and among them, the Kwantung Army had the absolute authority over others. If you are not in the Kwantung Army, one did not exist in their eyes."[58] Again unlike Masako, who produced two male heirs (the elder of whom was allegedly assassinated by opponents within the Korean imperial court as an infant), Hiro only produced two daughters to the great dismay of Yoshioka, who had presumably aspired to interlock Japanese interests in Manchukuo by creating a half-Japanese Manchukuoan emperor.

Young, romantic, and idealistic, Hiro in her first year of her life in Manchukuo was hopeful about the role she could play in building a bridge between Manchukuo and Japan. But she was forced to reassess her views shortly after the birth of their first daughter. By regularly strolling with the baby in the park in Manchukuo's capital city, she gradually made friends with local children, who became her reliable source of information about what ordinary life was like. Uninhibited, the children would tell her how life had suddenly changed for the worse after the Japanese arrival. In listening to various specific episodes ranging from how the price of eggs had gone up tenfold, to how Japanese police officers and soldiers refused to pay bills at Chinese-run restaurants, she was "shattered, as all those stories were beyond my wildest imagination. And as I began to learn the realities of Manchukuo, I feared for the future of 'harmony of the five races.'"[59]

* * *

What makes a study of Japan's Pan-Asianism in Manchukuo so complex are the contradictory aspirations that shaped it. In the end, generalizations about Japanese selfishness and Japanese self-sacrifice in Manchukuo were equally true. The country's selfishness was made abundantly clear, not only in its "simple" nationalistic desires to secure material gains from its imperial holdings, but also in its "simplistic" assumptions that its leadership would benefit those whom it aspired to lead. At the same time, Japan's Pan-Asianist ambitions embraced certain elements of self-sacrifice as well. To be sure, the largely unilateral and uninvited character of Japan's self-sacrifice, especially in light of its horrific consequences in terms of local human lives and livelihood, makes it hard to appreciate such a claim. Nonetheless, sustaining a leadership position involved an enormous dedication of its resources to projects that were not of direct relevance to the changing and pressing situations of war. And in that qualified sense at least, the use of the term "self-sacrifice" makes sense.

From a Japan-centric perspective of "world history," Manchukuo from the outset represented an overdetermined cultural mission of sorts. Japan's determination to influence, if not totally to recompose, the educational, intellectual, and cultural landscape of Manchuria was reflected in Manchukuo's hypercultivated urban planning and educational institutions. However ineffective and even counterproductive these programs proved to be in reality, the fact remains that many Japanese saw reforming implications in what they were doing. They were dedicated to the cultural goals of Japan's wartime expansion, carried out under the most comprehensive banner of Asian awakening. Why else would the Japanese have bothered to talk of grand ideals *and* engage in rigorous programs of "re-education" at all, especially at a time when they were involved in a costly and bloody war?

Hence the case of Manchukuo escapes the readily available categories offered in the study of imperialism and empires. The ideological zeal with which Japan's *kenkoku* efforts were carried out also created many practical uncertainties about how best to realize those proclaimed Pan-Asianist ideals. A conceptual realignment of Louise Young's "total empire" thesis is thus called for: Manchukuo was the type of empire that was total, not so much in its broad-based mobilization, as in its Pan-Asianist delusions, making it a type of pan-nationalist imperialism exercised by a revisionist power with an ambition for leading a new world order and playing a world role.

Such a total delusion, nevertheless, is not at all unique in modern history.[60] A compelling analogue to Manchukuo can be found in the Soviet Union of the Cold War era, for example. The Soviet satellite states created in Eastern Europe after World War II can be seen as an extension of the idea of pre-Soviet Pan-Slavism, as a variant expression that closely overlapped more exclusive and narrow Russian nationalism. Like Japan's Pan-Asianism of the Meishuron strand, Soviet expansion in the region was a crusading force that claimed to oust old-style imperialism. Unhappily for both Japanese and Soviet reformers, not to mention the people under their subjugation, such imposition of social and political orders proved, in effect, a regurgitated form of imperialism. Indeed, this may have taken on an even more oppressive form than traditional imperialism and thus proved utterly incapable of attracting the broad-based support from those who were supposedly being liberated. The lack of appeal to other Asians notwithstanding, Manchukuo became a linchpin, or in the widely invoked metaphor of the time, the "cornerstone" of Japan's Pan-Asianist struggle for many Japanese.

In a strictly strategic sense, it has been argued quite persuasively that Manchukuo did not necessarily make the later wars with China and the Allied powers "inevitable." All the same, this does not negate the fact that the social and cultural mobilization that accompanied the building of Manchukuo made the maintenance of its control through those later wars *appear* absolutely necessary to those who were called to mobilize for it. In that sense, Japan's wartime venture is a classic case of "imperial overstretch" in which the benefit of the metropole's commitment to the periphery does not justify the actual material costs of sustaining the Empire. On this point, Ishibashi Tanzan, the chief columnist of *Tōyō Keizai Shinpō* (New Eastern Economic Review) and prime minister after the war, rightly pointed out the various disadvantages of maintaining Japanese presence in Manchuria and warned precisely of the danger of such overextension. His was one of the only conspicuous oppositional media voices fighting a lonely battle, however.

In this Manchukuo mobilization, which had immense historical and emotional implications but which made little material sense, Japan's educated middle class of the left played a significant part. Because many of them embraced progressive social ideals and dreamt of far-reaching changes on a transnational scale, they willingly took part in Japan's empire-building efforts under the Pan-Asianist banner, hoping that the empire they were creating would bring a better future for all involved. And here, some normative evaluations of the Manchukuo project are finally called for.

Needless to say, the most tragic aspect of Japan's Manchurian venture was the gap between its intentions and practice. Most profoundly affected by such a gap were those who were conquered, as the lingering debates about Japan's war crimes that accompanied its "civilizing mission" of areas under Japanese occupation would prove. Issues at stake here, for example, are the Rape of Nanking (Nanjing), and other atrocities perpetrated by the Japanese Army, as well as more systemic programs of exploitation, including forced labor, forced prostitution, and the bacteriological experiments done on living human beings by the infamous Unit 731 stationed near Harbin.

Also, the Japanese agricultural settlers, who came to Manchukuo misled by the propaganda vision of modern farm machinery and egalitarian communities as late as only one month before Japan's unconditional surrender in 1945, suffered tremendously. As noted earlier, farm settlers only accounted for less than 15 percent of the Japanese in Manchukuo. That same group, however, made up almost half of the Japanese civilian casualties after August 1945.[61] Abandoned by the retreating Japanese Army in the face of Chinese vengeance and advancing Soviet troops, many infants were killed by their desperate parents in their hiding places so that their crying would not be heard. Still many other parents either sold or entrusted their children to sympathetic Chinese families, hoping that this way the children might at least survive. The problem of dislocated identity continues to haunt those left-behind children, who speak no Japanese, yet visit their homeland *en masse* in an increasingly vain search for relatives, roots, and perhaps a better life.[62]

Equally, the few survivors who made it back to Japan suffered from survivor's guilt, as repeatedly articulated by such popular postwar writers as Itsuki Hiroyuki, Yamazaki Toyoko, Miyao Tomiko, and Nakanishi Rei. In general terms, Louise Young's assertion that Manchukuo "has receded into the recesses" of present-day Japanese memory might be true on one level.[63] However, so long as the individual and indeed national reconciliation with the consequences of Japan's Pan-Asianist venture—enabled not only by the command of the military but the participation of well-meaning but dangerously naïve progressive elements—remains unacknowledged, Manchukuo could not and should not be regarded as "a dusty relic of a rather sordid past."[64] For this reason, Manchukuo and other Japanese Pan-Asianist programs carried out during the Fifteen Years' War, with the full awareness of their high aspirations, as well as their disastrous failure, beg to be explained and understood.

Following this realization, the next important question emerges: How and why did Japan fall prey to the idea of further expansion, even when such a course almost certainly promised self-destruction? Moving our analytical focus from the field of Manchuria to Tokyo, the next chapter traces the evolution of Pan-Asianism into the Japanese government's official ideology of a "New East Asian Order." In the light of the intensifying China War, Pan-Asianism came to assume an ever more critical and central role both in building an official consensus and galvanizing domestic attention to its war aims for the ever overextending and overextended empire.

5

The China War and
Its Pan-Asian Rescue

Let us imagine being an intelligent, inquisitive, and creative person in wartime Japan. What could one do to remain intellectually free? One might, for example, try to keep a low profile and guard one's inner thoughts like gold and hope that it would all be over soon. More courageous people might speak up against the regime at the risk of imprisonment or even death. Yet the reality was slightly more nuanced, as many intelligent, sensitive, and well-meaning individuals opted to support Japan's war.

In the summer of 1937, Japan's hostilities with China began without any clear strategy. As in the immediate aftermath of the Manchurian Incident, Japan was again faced with a challenge of reorienting its foreign policy in a coherent framework. Eventually, with the help of some key intellectuals participating in think tanks and policy advisory institutions, the most significant of which was a prime ministerial brain trust known as the Shōwa Research Association (SRA), the Japanese government under the premiership of Konoe Fumimaro came to advance the construction of a "New East Asian Order" as the country's objective in China by the end of 1938. It regarded the establishment of an East Asian regional bloc and cooperation as dependent upon Japan's assumption of leadership. This in effect meant that Japan-centric, Meishuron Pan-Asianism was to be the basis of Konoe's *dakaisaku*, or a policy, literally of "hitting and opening" the deadlock for the Japanese government vis-à-vis China.

Shifting our analytical focus from Manchuria to Tokyo, the present chapter will deal with the ideas behind the escalation of Japan's *de facto* war with China from 1937 to 1940. The period in question is especially important as it marked the process of heavy intellectualization—and Pan-Asianization—of Japan's high politics. Although the government's identification of its external policy with Pan-Asianism had already commenced in the first five years of the Fifteen Years' War, in its post-Manchurian diplomacy as well as in its Manchukuo policies, the Pan-Asianist overtone in politics became even more pronounced and more entrenched in Japan's policymaking in the late 1930s. By claiming that the China War was being fought for a more moral and just world, they effectively drove Japan deeper into the quagmire. Moreover, in this episode of the Fifteen Years' War, select intellectuals, not unlike the neoconservatives in the twenty-first-century United States, played a critical role in rendering a further ideological dimension to Japan's policy.

Certainly, the part played by those Japanese intellectuals was not exactly analogous to the case of the U.S. neoconservatives in masterminding a democratic revolution in Iraq in the period leading up to the U.S. invasion of 2003. After all, the Japanese intellectuals did not have to convince the government to start the China War. Yet those Japanese were not entirely dissimilar to the neocons of our time in that they presented themselves as able agents bringing about a radical change and a new vision for the future, not only for their own country, but for the outside world. When their "vision" for the rest of Asia proved much bloodier and more difficult to realize than anticipated, the failure was attributed to military incompetence, lack of determination, and strategic miscalculation of enemy strength without calling into question the practicability of their lofty ideals and convictions. For the moral goal of establishing a "New East Asian Order," they insisted from their offices in central Tokyo that "even with enormous sacrifices, one had to keep on fighting with dogged perseverance."[1]

In fact, however, the Japanese were not of one mind when it came to ideas of the most desirable world, and they drew their ideas from both the right and the left of the political spectrum. On a different scale, we have already seen a convergence of military and Marxist interests in the planning of Manchukuo. Such a rapprochement between Japan's right and left was made possible, as Tachibana Shiraki put it, because they were "partners traveling down the same path, up to a point."[2] Some might have envisioned a Pan-Asian utopia presided over by "the Kingly Way" of the Japanese emperor. Others might have dreamt of a communist world government and saw Japan as lending a helping hand to other Asian nations in realizing their own revolutions along the way. Either way,

Meishuron Pan-Asianism could present itself as a progressive body of thought aimed at creating an improved human condition.

Owing in no small part to William Miles Fletcher's seminal work, this period of rising intellectual influence is often associated with "Japanese fascism."[3] My own interpretation of the SRA, as well as those on its periphery, draws from Fletcher's argument that they pushed Konoe's policy toward more "fascistic" directions, especially since Konoe himself had already been predisposed to such ideas before the crisis in China. However, even though certain fascistic features of the regime explain much of the development of the late 1930s, the role of intellectuals was felt not simply in the increasingly fascistic character of the Japanese society, but also in the elevation of Pan-Asianism as an officially sanctioned state ideology to explain what had turned out to be an unexpectedly difficult war. In that process, SRA intellectuals were neither the only nor the primary agents of power pushing for Meishuron Pan-Asianism. By according particular brands of specialist language and theoretical credibility to their Pan-Asianist policy recommendations, they nonetheless did help elevate the government's pronouncements to a new height of moral righteousness and conceptual respectability. As a result, any retreat from China came to be regarded as not merely a sign of military weakness, but also an unacceptable moral concession.

The first part of this chapter will be devoted to explaining domestic and international events as they concern the ascendancy of Pan-Asianism under Konoe's premiership. At the same time, it will pay attention to other political ideas and forces prominent in this period—particularly, Emperor Worship and Japan's "fascism"—that gave an added dimension to Pan-Asianism of the Konoe years. Most importantly, it will look at Prime Minister Konoe himself, who was arguably the primary example of an intellectual affecting politics. The second part of the chapter will then look at the re-intellectualization of Pan-Asianism by the SRA specifically and attempt to assess the overall impact of the brain trust on the period concerned and beyond.

Part I. Konoe and the China War

Impending Doom

The collaborative effort of the Konoe government and certain intellectuals that transformed Pan-Asianism into the country's official war aim emerged amid increasing political unrest at home and abroad. At home,

intramilitary divisions were apparent in the continuing plots and assassinations orchestrated by the armed forces' radicalized elements. The first
notable incident of this kind in the second half of the 1930s occurred on
August 12, 1935. Major General Nagata Tetsuzan, Chief of the Bureau of
Military Affairs, who had launched a reorganization of the Army, was
slain in his office by Lieutenant Colonel Aizawa Saburō. Nagata's assassination became a bloody testimony to the mounting factionalism
between the so-called Control Faction (*tōseiha*) and the Imperial Way
Faction (*kōdōha*), particularly divided over the trend, led by the former, of
the Western-style professionalization of the armed services, which the
latter, with its nativist fervor, resented greatly.[4]

Out of such an intense atmosphere was born an event even bloodier
than the one before, the Young Officers Revolt on February 26, 1936 (the
2-26 Incident). In this nearly successful coup, Imperial Way Faction officers assassinated several key figures of the government, including the
Finance Minister Takahashi Korekiyo. Emperor Hirohito displayed
uncharacteristic determination when he issued a direct order for the
rebels to surrender, bringing an anticlimactic end to a three-day stand-off
in snow-covered Tokyo. While it failed to accomplish its specific objective
of replacing the government, the 2-26 Incident did not entirely discredit
the Army's general preferences for more governmental control. Indeed,
the Incident encapsulated Japan's imperial paradox: while the emperor
demonstrated enough power of office to quell the rebellion, which was
waged in his very name, his action also stimulated a further yearning
among officer classes for a military takeover of the government under the
patriotic banner of selfless devotion to the Emperor, who had to be pro-
tected from his corrupt, often Westernized, liberal advisors.

The ambiguous position of the throne provides some clues to why
Hirohito did not use his direct access to the militarists as commander-in-
chief of the armed forces. According to the historian Tanaka Sōgorō, such
a demonstration of imperial reluctance was also witnessed in Konoe
Fumimaro, a scion of the second noblest family, next to the imperial family itself, making this discussion all the more relevant here.[5]

Sewn in the heart of every Japanese since childhood was the awe and grat-
itude-inspiring figure of the Emperor-God presiding over the pyramidal
structure of the family state. A remarkable attempt at crystallizing this
"modern myth" was the indoctrination textbook *Kokutai no Hongi* (Cardinal
Principles of the National Polity), issued by the Bureau of Thought Control
of the Ministry of Education in March 1937.[6] It illustrated Japan's moral

and martial superiority by drawing attention to ancient deities, mythic heroes, court records, and rituals, all geared toward the further sacralization of the Japanese polity. These were critical components of the state-led ultranationalist movement called *Kokutai Meichō Undō* (Illumination of the Body Politic Movement), which followed the 1935 persecution of the legal scholar and House of Peers Parliamentarian Minobe Tatsukichi, who argued that even the Emperor was an organ of the constitutional government not entirely immune to the judgments of law.[7] The emperor-first ideology presented in the textbook cohered around and fed the arguments for a Pan-Asianist policy of the Meishuron variety, which was equally self-indulgent in its assumption of Japanese superiority over other Asians. This marriage, in turn, dramatically narrowed the scope for Japan's official understanding of Pan-Asianism.

On a related note, the curious contrast of awe-inspiring power of the Emperor on the one hand and the absence of a clear political authority on the other makes the interpretation of Japan's ultranationalism as "fascism" problematic. One has only to look at Japan's policymaking process in the late 1930s to see this point. After the military command composed of the Army and the Navy agreed upon a new policy, they would convoke a General Headquarters Liaison Conference. At the Liaison Conference, the military and the cabinet would unify various opinions over a range of policy matters. When it came to a matter of special importance, another conference had to be convened. This was the Imperial Conference held in the presence of the Emperor. It was customary for the emperor to only listen to the debate, as there was a general uniformity of opinion by the time this conference was held; the decision approved by the Emperor was deemed conclusive and inviolable, thus carrying the stamp of supreme legitimacy. Thus neither Hirohito, nor the unimaginative and bureaucratic Prime Minister Tōjō Hideki, who worshipped and sought to protect the Emperor until the end of his life, can easily be compared to the fascist leaders of Europe.

Insofar as Hirohito's more personal role is concerned, what seems beyond dispute is that his general passivity during the war in his awe-inspiring position effectively appeased the armed services acting under the Autonomy of the Supreme Command, and certainly concealed whatever private objections or approval he might have had at his disposal. By the same token, his decision to equate his survival to the whole of the Japanese nation and to remain in the imperial position even after he ceased to be a god needs to be scrutinized and debated. Without a general awareness of these questions, one cannot appreciate what exactly constituted the Meishuron thread of Pan-Asianism, as it based its argument of Japanese superiority upon the cult of Emperor Worship.

Either for fear of more political assassinations, or for his lack of authority, or for his ability to adapt to changing situations, or most likely for all these reasons, Hirohito became what he was—a benevolent father figure, an inspiring and thoroughly modern military leader in a Western uniform on a white horse, a priest king and a guardian of age-old ancient rites, a living God—all in one. Various qualities of both a modern and an ancient nature represented by Hirohito provided an answer to the key challenge that a modern Pan-Asianist of any persuasion necessarily had to face: How does one reconcile the overwhelming forces of secular modernity born by "Western" civilization with the claims of ancient greatness of "Eastern" civilization? The answer for the proponents of Meishuron Pan-Asianism was to remake the rest of Asia in the image of Japan, where modernity and spirituality somehow found a way of cohabiting successfully, albeit in reality rather uneasily. In their view, the success of Japan's rise as a modern power was credited to the emperor, who acted as a spiritual linchpin for the whole nation. This meant that the subsequent proponents of the "Japanization" programs of occupied Asian territories could just as easily invoke their reformist visions in the images of modernity as they could in the incomparable and mythical majesty of the Japanese emperor.

The Apostates and the Imperial Nation

Such a convergence of the modern and the ancient, purportedly embodied in the Japanese imperial institution, was celebrated and driven farther afield as a matter of Japan's policy under the banner of Pan-Asianism. But those who pushed it were not necessarily always from the political right. Most critically, some erstwhile Japanese Communists found an alternative in another transnational, anti-Western, and anti-*status quo* ideology of Meishuron Pan-Asianism. The June 1933 declaration by the leading Communists Sano Manabu and Nabeyama Sadachika, commonly known as "The Apostasy Declaration" (*Tenkō Seimeibun*) in which they criticized the Comintern and liberal democracies of Western "Christiandoms" is a powerful example.[8]

In the statement, which prompted a large-scale recantation of communist beliefs among Japanese Communists, they declared that they were renouncing the Comintern and Soviet-led Communism. Referring to the lessons of "the world historical facts, including the [failure of] socialist movements in the Western Christiandoms," they decided that it was futile to attempt to reach the goal of world revolution at the expense of really existing nationalisms, because they were now "awakened to various excellent conditions particular to Japan."[9] They acknowledged that they had been "fundamentally mistaken in advocating the abolition of the [Japanese] imperial institution" because Japan's imperial household was indeed "a rare example in the world" that provided "a national core" and a long historical continuity unbeknownst to the rest of the world.[10] Thus

> [Japan's] war with Chinese Nationalists, objectively speaking, has a very progressive meaning. Also, under today's international conditions, if Japanese were to fight the United States, that war could turn from both countries' war of imperialism into Japan's war of national liberation. Furthermore, a world war fought in the Pacific could turn into a war of liberation for the proletariats of underdeveloped Asian nations from the oppression of Western capitalism.[11]

It was as if they had scripted Japan's foreign policy course for the following decade already in 1933. In that sense, the second half of the Fifteen Years' War was a case of self-fulfilling prophecy made real by those who yearned for a decisive and radical change on a world scale.[12] Ultimately, the invigorated *kokutai* argument of the period that consolidated the imperial institution as the spiritual backbone of Japanese ultranationalism easily meshed with Meishuron Pan-Asianism. As was the case in Japan's Manchukuo project, this combination proved compelling enough, not just for Japan's ultranationalists, but also for its persecuted left, presumably owing much to its professed humanistic, revolutionary, and egalitarian goals. This odd marriage begot a wave of conversions and mass defection of Communist Party members. Threats and coercion employed by the police notwithstanding, the more fundamental reason for this trend stemmed from the altered understanding of communism on the part of Japan's left. In that alternative interpretation, Meishuron Pan-Asianism was seen as the solution for what the far left perceived as deep-seated social and economic problems of Western imperialism in Asia.

Without abandoning their Marxian worldview, many erstwhile believers came to recognize that the class struggle thesis was more useful in explaining international relations than Japan's domestic condition. The evidence of Europe's New Imperialism seemed to indicate that Japan, as a kind of proletarian nation among the society of nations, was the victim of exploitation by Western—especially Anglo-American—capitalists. By concluding that Japanese domination of Korea, Taiwan, Manchuria, and what seemed increasingly likely, Southeast Asia, too, represented a transitional and inevitable stage in the liberation of Asian nations suffering even more under the exploitative West, Japan's left reasoned that Japanese expansionism was an acceptable, and moreover, inevitable mission that was preordained by the tides of world history.

This line of thinking seemed to validate a set of "have-not" claims made also by the political right, often articulated by none other than Konoe Fumimaro, about Japan's difficult position of having unjustly suffered from its historical lateness in the international power-political game, its lack of natural resources, and what was most humiliating, the racial prejudice inflicted on Asia by the West. As an extension of the same argument, it was also claimed that only Japan as Asia's preordained leader was equipped to conduct the awesome task of salvaging Asia from Western avarice. Thus it is not surprising, despite the demise of Japanese Communism as a political movement, that Marxist analysis served an important function in the formulation of Japan's increasingly Meishuron-inspired Pan-Asianist policy of the late 1930s.

Still, not every Japanese Communist followed such an ideological trajectory. Ozaki Hotsumi (1901–44), who was a prominent China expert and a spy who passed on vital intelligence to the German-born Soviet agent Richard Sorge in the years leading to Pearl Harbor, was a notable exception. Ozaki made use of the accurate information gained from Prime Minister Konoe's closest aides, with whom he was linked by concerns about the future of Asia, especially in regard to China and Japan. As a boy growing up in colonial Taiwan and later as a reporter for the metropolitan daily *Asahi Shimbun* in Shanghai, he observed at close range the turmoil of China, torn apart by warlord factionalism, the rise of modern Chinese nationalism, and Japan's expansionism. Seeing China's chaos firsthand deepened his sympathy for Chinese Communism, as a way of awakening a sense of national identity. This conviction led him to seek contact with Chinese Communists, a Communist student group of the Tōa Dōbun Shoin (East Asian Same Letters Academy), and Shanghai's cosmopolitan residents with like sympathies, such as Agnes Smedley, an American writer, and Richard Sorge.

Until the end, Ozaki held on to his view of the Soviet Union as the proponent of principles that would help to strengthen nationalism in the countries under Western imperialism. Still, like Sano and Nabeyama who left Soviet-led Communism, Ozaki was also a Japanese nationalist. Upon his return from China in 1932, he felt an overwhelming sense of national crisis in Japan's rising terrorism. Such pressing political developments at home made a "conceptual and formulaic theorist" like him face the problems of contemporary Japanese politics head-on.[13] He recalled in his prison cell, where he awaited execution:

> I myself remained an internationalist and a Communist. Nonetheless, my specific understandings of Japan, its politics, or its nation grew more practical. . . . My writings mainly dealt with the issues of national policy, critiques written from Japanese standpoints, the China problem as well as the reorganization of the nation. . . . [M]y enthusiasm for these problems was after all a reflection of my second side [as an analyst of Japanese politics and as a nationalist] and never a camouflage for my other side [as a Communist], nor a convenient means to earn money for my writing. . . . Certainly in recent years, I have been an internationalist as well as a Japanese nationalist. . . . [T]he two did not seem to contradict one another.[14]

In Ozaki's mind, communism was not diametrically opposed to nationalism. As the history of the twentieth century suggests, there are in fact very few examples of active nonnationalist communists. Like Mao Zedong, Ho Chi Minh, and Josef Tito among numerous and nameless others, Ozaki inclined toward communism not because he thought nationalism and other variants of nationalist ideology, such as Pan-Asianism, did not exist or were unimportant. Rather, he was attracted to communism precisely because he believed it could reconcile at least some aspects of emerging and clashing "national" and "state" interests, upon which the existing international order, however deplorable and unjust it might be, was predicated. And he hoped that such a reconciliation could be reached within a broader-than-nation-state, Pan-Asian framework, based on the cooperation of his two homes, China and Japan.

To this end, therefore, there was no inconsistency in being a Japanese nationalist as well as a communist. Ozaki's concern for Japan's crisis was epitomized in his "Plan for National Reorganization" (*Kokumin Saisoshiki no tame no Kōsō*), whose outline he devised while he was an aide for the first Konoe cabinet. His ideas for reform complemented those of his fellow researcher in the Shōwa Research Association, Miki Kiyoshi, in their emphasis on the need for internal reform to improve the future of Asia. Miki's idea about historical progress based on a cooperative federation of Asian countries led to a call for the "East Asian Cooperative Body" (*Tōa*

Kyōdōtai). Just as the skeleton of Miki's proposal was picked up by the Konoe cabinet, Ozaki's outline provided a foundation for Konoe's Imperial Rule Assistance Association (Taisei Yokusankai, or IRAA), established in October 1940. From the outset, however, the IRAA was a product of compromise rather than a true agent of reform, suffering from Konoe's chronic conciliatory tendency to appoint representatives of conflicting viewpoints.[15] In any event, unlike Miki whose concerns for Japan's internal situations were coupled with the goal of Japan's securing the Asian *meishu* position, Ozaki's vision was truly more communistic and egalitarian, aspiring to cooperativism in a very literal sense.

Because Ozaki was "not a simple Communist,"[16] his view of internationalism, too, was far from simple. He decisively rejected Wilsonian liberal internationalism, the Versailles-Washington system, and even the utopian internationalism of the Comintern. Rather, his internationalism always revolved around the pressing questions of what Japan should do, at home and in Asia, and especially China. Because Ozaki recognized the force of nationalism in China and its ramifications for Japan's position, he was reluctant to embrace those optimistic brands of internationalism wholeheartedly. He stated that "the 'world' only exists conceptually and abstractly. Realistically and specifically, there are only 'international' relations as consisting of various nation-states," citing the dissolution of the Comintern as clear evidence of how state interest usually overrides universalistic claims.[17]

Crises Abroad

What then was the state of such realistic and specific "international" relations that the Japanese government faced in the second half of the 1930s? By around 1936, Japan had in fact come to prefer a cautious and more even-handed policy vis-à-vis China. That feeling was mutual. Preoccupied with consolidating his own power, Chiang Kai-shek opted to dodge the question of Manchukuo recognition, in effect demilitarizing Beijing after the T'ang-ku Truce of May 31, 1933. This signified his virtual acquiescence to the Japanese control of northeastern China. But the truce rested on a very shaky foundation, and in the end, it proved ephemeral.

The situation deteriorated quickly over the course of 1936 for several reasons. As far as Japan's Army was concerned, the failure of the young officers in achieving their domestic reform objectives consolidated their determination to seek more military-driven policymaking in the post–2-26 period. True, the Imperial Way Faction's fixation on a preventive strike against the Soviet Union was checked. But its demise gave way to the rival Control Faction's preference for all-round military preparedness abroad. Correspondingly, the Hirota cabinet, convinced by the argument that Japan's position on the Asian mainland was too insecure, began to pronounce the view that Japan no longer felt obliged to fulfill the Versailles-Washington treaties.

Such a hard-nosed stance in foreign policy, no doubt shaped by the rising military demand for the preservation of national interest, was clearly expressed in "Fundamental Principles of Natiuonal Policy" of August 1936. It called for more military preparedness on the Asian continent in order to, among other things, "enable the Empire to become a stabilizing force in East Asia," "to attain peace in East Asia," "to contribute to the peaceful welfare of mankind," and "to eliminate the hegemonic way of the great powers in East Asia."[18] This was significant as it amounted to an official governmental call, as opposed to an exclusively military call, for a general build-up in preparation for an all-out war with China, with the Soviet Union, as well as with the Atlantic powers, all the while gearing up for the country's advance into Southeast Asia. In fact, its all-inclusive approach revealed that the plan lacked any real strategic details required for fighting any of those powers. For the time being, nonetheless, it satisfied both the Army and the Navy, who were often at loggerheads with one another when it came to deciding who exactly Japan's actual enemies were.

Diplomatically, Japan's gradual drift away from the liberal internationalist, multilateral treaty regime was formalized in its Anti-Comintern Pact with Germany, reached in November 1936 and joined by another revisionist power Italy one year later. Around the same time, equally dramatic events unfolded in North China, where tensions had been building up ever since the Kwantung Army divulged its intentions of establishing another puppet regime. In December 1936, the son of the Japanese-assassinated warlord Chang Tso-lin, Chang Hsüeh-liang, popularly known as the "Young Marshal," orchestrated a kidnap of Chiang Kai-shek with the help of Chinese Communist leaders, which resulted in the three parties' agreement to form a United Front against Japan. Against this background, when the Konoe cabinet had been in office for just one month, a skirmish transpired on the night of July 7, 1937, when a minor clash between Japanese and Kuomintang soldiers broke out at the Marco Polo Bridge just north of Beijing.

It did not take two months for this small-scale clash to turn into high-level hostilities. The Kuomintang launched aerial bombardment on

Japanese naval installations at Shanghai on August 14, prompting Japan to retaliate with an all-out, though undeclared war with China. Neither side made a formal declaration of war, to avoid embargoes on supplies under various neutrality agreements. Then followed the Rape of Nanking (Nanjing) and a full-blown Japanese war with both the Kuomintang and the Communists.[19] It is essential to recognize that there was undoubtedly an underlying tendency in the Japanese forces, in various places at various times and not just in Nanjing, to regard the occupied populations as less than human, even though they were the very Asian brothers and sisters the Japanese were claiming to liberate.

To illustrate this point, in his May 1936 interview with Tanaka Ryūkichi, a Kwantung Army Staff Officer, who later spoke against his former colleagues on the witness stand of the International Military Tribunal in Tokyo, the journalist Matsumoto Shigeharu, then working for the Dōmei News Agency in Shanghai, quoted Tanaka: "To be perfectly frank, the ways you [Matsumoto] and I look at the Chinese are fundamentally different. You seem to think of them as human, but I see them as pigs."[20]

Matsumoto, a child of enormous privilege and a product of Western education who prided himself on being Japan's pioneering international journalist, was astonished:

> [Tanaka's] frankness notwithstanding, I had never before encountered such callous thoughts or manner of speech from Japanese military men. That such a terrible fellow was behind the Kwantung Army strategies not only appalled me, but also made me grieve for Japan.[21]

That anyone in high office should unabashedly vocalize such a view to a journalist of some renown might have been politically imprudent, but the thinking itself might have been not as rare or confounding as Matsumoto's reaction shows. It is not difficult to imagine how the prevalence of such a dehumanizing attitude among officers, in a state of heightened excitement of war, could lead to mass murder, rape, and various other atrocities. The institution of sex slavery in the name of "military comfort women" from early 1938 onward may have been a desperate attempt at controlling the sexual urges of soldiers in the field to prevent another Rape of Nanking. However, such an attempt to create a semblance of order was made possible at the sacrifice of a steady, though not as conspicuous, exploitation of powerless women, many of whom were Koreans, and other Asians, confirming that there were apparent hypocrisies in the Japanese claim of Pan-Asianist liberation.

In facing the immediate war situation, another prevalent Japanese perception was that China would easily surrender after one decisive blow
delivered from the Imperial Japanese Army. This proved to be a vast
underestimation of the economic and military capabilities of the
Kuomintang under Chiang Kai-shek's leadership, which had been growing dramatically over the previous decade. Among the Japanese on the
front, there appears to have been a feeling of genuine surprise over the
unexpected resilience of the Chinese forces. Such a sense of disbelief was
related by Sugiyama Heisuke (1895–1946), who started his career as a
columnist of a liberal persuasion. He reported from China as an embedded journalist, an experience that made him turn gradually toward the
right of the political spectrum. In December 1938, upon his return from
Shanghai, he painstakingly described how, after having witnessed the real
battle, he was convinced of Japanese forces' superiority.[22]

In this piece, in which he repeatedly quotes from Friedrich Nietzsche
and refers himself to be a typical "intellectual" or a member of the "intel-
ligentsia," Sugiyama recounts how the Chinese forces turned out to be
stronger than anticipated. In the midst of the battle, he confesses to have
yearned for greatness in death, saying: "Even though I was glad to come
home alive. . . . [S]omewhere in my mind, it is true that I regret that I have
survived this experience alive."[23] His death wish can be understood as his
romantic yearning for heroism and also a reflection of his desire to escape
a deeper ethical dilemma. He says as much: "Whenever I saw the Chinese
masses' miserable sufferings, I could not suppress my feeling of somehow
wanting to perish in this war."[24] Despite the sensibilities and emotional
struggle that are evident in his writing, however, he is never specific
about what those "miserable sufferings" of the Chinese people he witnessed were, and his conclusion is unequivocal: the Chinese forces,
despite what one might say about their unexpected performance, are
inferior to the Japanese, and Japan should finish off the job that it had
already started once and for all.

In likening the Chinese forces to an uncoordinated sumo wrestler, who
is huge and strong, but does not know quite how to apply his strength in
a real match effectively, Sugiyama declares:

[M]y conviction that the Chinese forces are weak never wavered. This
is not meant to belittle the danger faced and efforts undertaken by the
Japanese forces at all. Those are two fundamentally different problems.
Even though the Chinese forces are weak, if they were to come in ten,
twenty-fold numbers, it is evident that the Japanese would have to

fight a tough battle. But equally true is that the Chinese forces are still weak. . . . It is foolish to give them the satisfaction of being told that they are strong and to add to their conceit.[25]

To him, Japan's victory is imminent. More alarming for Japan, he claims, is the danger of being too used to fighting a weak foe. Furthermore, in his mind, the tougher and real battle to come is Japan's war with the West.[26]

How much of a typical "intellectual" view this really was in Japan is difficult to tell. In the late 1930s, many thinking men and women were still troubled by Japan's protracted military engagement in China and were skeptical that Japan's war with its Asian neighbors amounted to a holy Pan-Asianist war.[27] But there were also those who enthusiastically adopted the Meishuron brand of Pan-Asianism and presented its argument to the outside world. The most prominent example was the poet Noguchi Yonejirō, the erstwhile follower and vocal advocate of the Teaist rendition of Pan-Asianism. He responded to external criticisms in an acrimonious exchange with his former idol Rabindranath Tagore, expressing the view, not unlike Sugiyama, that Japan was battling not China, but simply the corrupt, Western-backed government of Chiang Kai-shek. He maintained that Japan's mission was thoroughly noble and that the Japanese were "ready to exhaust our resources of money and blood."[28]

To Tagore, the consequentialist argument (that the value of an action is determined by the value of its ultimate consequences, rather than its processes) applied to Japan's special role in leading Asia's liberation was morally unacceptable in any event. The essential contention of Teaist Pan-Asianism he and Okakura had advanced was that Asia needed to assert itself in nonmaterial terms, not necessarily because of its weakness, but because of its deliberate choice in favor of a higher moral claim, and that, *in spite of* its material weakness. Recognizing that unbridgeable gap in their basic assumptions, Tagore firmly responded:

> You claim that Japan's situation was unique, forgetting that military situations are always unique. . . . [Y]ou are ascribing to humanity a way of life which is not even inevitable among the animals and would certainly not apply to the East, in spite of her occasional aberrations. You are building your conception of an Asia which would be raised on a tower of skulls. I have, as you rightly point out, believed in the message of Asia, but . . . [t]he doctrine of "Asia for Asia" which you enunciate in

your letter, as an instrument of political blackmail, has all the virtues of the lesser Europe which I repudiate and nothing of the larger humanity that makes us one across the barriers of political labels and divisions.[29]

Tagore confessed that he was perplexed to have read Tokyo's statement that the recent alliance of Japan with Italy and Germany was made for "highly spiritual and moral reasons" and "had no materialistic considerations behind them."[30] Coming from a politician, he thought this was still understandable. "What is not amusing" in his mind was "that artists and thinkers should echo such remarkable sentiments that translate military swagger into spiritual bravado," pointing out that in the West "even in the critical days of war-madness," there was never any scarcity of artistic and thinking spirits who raised their voice to defy their own war-mongers in the name of humanity.[31]

In his determination to see positive meanings in Japan's Asian hegemony, Noguchi seems to have felt very little internal conflict between Japan's pronouncedly ultranationalist rendition of Pan-Asianism, as well as the militaristic modes that went with it, and the idea of tea-drinking, peace-loving Asian civilization. What probably accounts for his ideological shift is a mixture of genuine faith in lofty ideals of Asian brotherhood, a proud nationalist belief in Japan's role as a transformative agent for the rest of Asia, and a degree of intellectual gullibility as well as conceit, that led to the overestimation of one's own ability to interpret, and sometimes even to influence, matters of politics. Such a dangerous brew, made doubly intoxicating by elements of flattery and power, seems to be the recipe to which even more serious intellectuals succumbed in this period.

The realities in the field looked quite grim for the Japanese forces. The enemy was not just the corrupt, Western-backed Chinese Nationalists as Noguchi claimed. Japan was increasingly expending its resources on a series of brief yet extremely draining and seemingly illogical battles with Soviet troops, as Japan encroached on the Soviet Union's Pacific-Mongolian frontier. The battle grounds thus included the Amur River in 1937, Changkufeng (Lake Khasan) in the summer of 1938, and Khalkhin Gol (Nomonhan) in 1939, adding to the sense of being bogged down deeper in a continental quagmire.[32] Furthermore, the Marco Polo Bridge Incident and what followed was a blow not to Chiang Kai-shek, but rather to Japan, as it pushed the limits of Tokyo's barely emerging consensus on sustaining, not expanding, Japan's presence in North China.

The Konoe Puzzle

How was such a situation of internal divisions and external challenges to be approached? That was the question Konoe Fumimaro (1891–1945) faced throughout his tenure as prime minister.[33] At the time of his appointment, he enjoyed immense popularity, as the Depression-worn nation expected him to lead the country out of its economic and political plight. In spite of his high public profile as a scion of one of Japan's most aristocratic families, however, the private side of Konoe remains a mystery to this day, leading the historian Marius Jansen to conclude that "[m]odern Japanese history has not known a more enigmatic man."[34]

Impeccably groomed and flamboyant in public, the young premier was deeply melancholic and contemplative in private. He was also at once a pampered prince, a serious student of philosophy trained at Imperial University of Kyoto in Nishida Kitarō's neo-Kantian idealism and Kawakami Hajime's Marxism, and an ambitious politician, with contacts with men of many stripes. However, his own ideas, even while residing over Japan's highest political office, were rarely made explicit, thus earning him the reputation of being a listener more than a talker.[35] He himself succinctly described his vague political position: "I have neither obvious enemies nor allies. Even if one had five enemies, one could manage to do politics with five true allies. But ten allies [of the kind I have] could very well become ten enemies at any given time."[36] Such a position certainly predisposed him to make a series of compromises with his opponents. Such skills might have been a valued political asset in the short run, especially within the limited confines of domestic politics. They proved too costly for the country in the long run, however, when so much was at stake in a prolonged state of *de facto* war on the Asian mainland.

While Konoe's complex character remains little understood, there is still an unmistakable element of consistency in his beliefs, going back to as early as the immediate wake of World War I. He believed that Japan needed a clear foreign policy framework if it were to achieve any sort of a great power status. His worldview was one infused in Social Darwinism and a racialist understanding of international relations, which was amply demonstrated on the eve of the Paris Peace Conference, when he published his previously noted article "Reject the Anglo-American Peace."

Less known is a booklet he penned in 1920 at the age of twenty-six, upon his return from his trip to Europe and the United States, on which he partly accompanied his political mentor Prince Saionji Kinmochi to the Peace Conference. It reveals how his travels confirmed his view of the Anglo-American powers as the only true arbiters of the rule of international politics. In describing the rising anti-Japanese sentiments in the United States, Konoe states:

> The causes of the anti-Japanese movement are various, but racial prejudice is one of them. That the white people—and the Anglo-Saxon race in particular—generally abhor colored peoples is an apparent fact, so blatantly observable in the U.S. treatment of its black population. I for one felt a sort of racial oppression more in London than in Paris, and furthermore, that sense was heightened upon my arrival in New York.[37]

Konoe probably had a legitimate case, up to a point. It would be hard to reject the possibility that he could indeed have witnessed or encountered racial discrimination on his journey, but his argument becomes more twisted when he discusses China. Following from the above reasoning, one would have thought that Konoe would see Chinese as a fellow colored people, as brothers-in-arms, suffering under the oppressive yoke of the Anglo-American powers. But not quite so. In a curious mixture of admiration and frustration, Konoe regards China only as a competitor that might outdo Japan in the race for recognition by the Anglo-Americans, the very powers whose dominance he polemically called out to reject. In explaining to his readers why U.S. intellectuals see Japan in an antagonistic light, he summarily attributes the phenomena to the failure of Japanese public relations and the triumph of Chinese propaganda in the United States.

> They [educated Americans] are intoxicated by the glibness of Chinese propaganda, the one that paints a simplistic picture of Japan as a self-interested military expansionist. . . . Furthermore, the exaggerated propaganda from the Chinese side tremendously benefits from the emptiness of American knowledge about Japan, and for that, the Japanese residing in the United States have to take their share of the blame [for not engaging in effective intellectual exchange with Americans outside of business contacts].[38]

To him, Chinese students studying in the United States are far superior to their Japanese counterparts, managing to enlighten their American peers about their country and helping them develop sympathetic views of China. Examined in this light, it makes perfect sense that Konoe's long-term project of grooming his eldest son Fumitaka for a career in politics meant sending him to Lawrenceville, an exclusive preparatory school, and Princeton, so that he would be trained to be an effective publicist of Japanese interest vis-à-vis U.S. elites. (Fumitaka, though he excelled in golf and even became a captain of the varsity team, was never much of an intellectual, unlike his father. He was expelled from Princeton in 1938, and became a soldier and died in the Soviet POW camp in Siberia in 1956.)

Konoe's admiration for those Chinese students notwithstanding, he insists that they are engaged in "propaganda," though he is too intelligent not to recognize that it might be "propaganda" for a reason. He elaborates:

> The reason why the Americans misperceive Japan as a nation of invaders or thieves is undoubtedly a result of Chinese propaganda that exaggerated our past foreign policy, and yet, there is no smoke without fire. On this point too, I believe that our people must take a step back and reflect on ourselves. But this does not mean that I praise the so-called soft diplomacy approach.[39]

Konoe urges that Japanese should not let the United States coax them into doing whatever it tells them to do. But it would also not do to blindly "carry out war policy in today's [internationalist] world, as some militarists have been trying to do," as evidenced by Japan's reckless and futile Siberian Expedition that started in 1919.[40] His prescription for Japan's foreign policy then was to be confident enough to be able to assert its position in the Anglo-American-dominated world and to have the dominant powers engage in listening to Japan's position. In other words, he is speaking for a "Japan that can say 'No,'" well before the populist politician Ishihara Shintarō popularized such a phrase seven decades later.[41]

Being able to say "No" means that Japan has its own unwavering foreign policy philosophy, and without it, it could never dream of standing at a par with the great powers, especially Britain and the United States. Worse, he fears that China might even outdo Japan in that department, even though Japan has had a decent head start. To make matter more twisted, his obsessions and fears seem to come from his heartfelt recognition of Chinese excellence, which was the crux of his father Atsumaro's Sinic

Pan-Asianist programs. However much Konoe points to the "oppression of colored peoples," he sounds more like xenophobic nationalists, especially like other discontented and paranoid leaders of "have-not" revisionist powers, such as Italy and Germany.

Indeed, one of the most important facets of Konoe is his penchant for fascistic ideas comparable to the leaders of those countries. Sometimes with seemingly genuine convictions, sometimes with aristocratic guile, but perhaps more often with an awe-inspiring air of *ex machina* authority that was evocative of none other than Emperor Hirohito himself, Konoe was brilliant at garnering enough political support from the civilian and military leaders alike. Despite his elusiveness, nonetheless, it seems beyond dispute that he was drawn to fascistic philosophy as a basis of both his domestic and foreign policy reforms that he had so craved for Japan since his twenties. With that in mind, what many regard as an innocuous and frivolous anecdote might suggest his deeper political sympathies. Shortly before he became prime minister, at the rehearsal banquet on the eve of his second daughter's wedding in April 1937, Konoe appeared proudly disguised as Adolf Hitler, sporting a Nazi uniform and a small moustache. An aristocratic diversion, one might say perhaps, but the news of the event was enough to infuriate Prince Saionji, with whom Konoe had had a strained relationship for some time. Since then, Konoe might have been more reluctant to profess his admiration for Hitler openly, but his political programs seem to suggest that he was drawn to some major aspects of fascist ideology, especially its idea of a "New European Order," celebrated by both Benito Mussolini and Adolf Hitler.

In the eyes of a contemporary observer, Kenneth Colegrove, a Northwestern political scientist, the part of Konoe's premiership in at the very least propelling the China War was a simple and undisputed fact. He observed in November 1941:

> For many years, Prince Fumimaro Konoye [*sic*], a protégé of the *genrō*, Prince Saionji, had been looked upon as a liberal. Nevertheless, in his first cabinet the combination of militarists, bureaucrats, and capitalists which had won control of the government following the invasion of Manchuria in 1931, was firmly entrenched. Prince Konoye's ministry supported the army in China, dispatched re-enforcements of almost a million men to the continent, guided the General Mobilization Law through the Imperial Diet, and converted the *junsenji keizai* or semi-war

economy into the *senji keizai* or war economy which carried Japan a long way on the road to totalitarian statehood. [42]

And so, the question that often fails to be asked, in large part due to general sympathies generated by his dramatic suicide to defy the U.S. indictment of him as a Class-A war criminal, is the nature of Konoe's role in government before 1945, especially in the late 1930s. Did he not allow the war, which he apparently tried to end after it had long escalated, to escalate in the first place? Did his letting the Japanese forces occupy southern Indochina in July 1941 during his third tenure as prime minister not prompt U.S. oil embargo the following month? More specifically, did his acceptance of the "Essentials for Carrying Out the Empire's Policies" of September 6, 1941, not dramatically eliminate other "no-war" options available? Did it not unnecessarily place a self-imposed deadline on negotiations with the United States, effectively propelling Japan to go to war with the West? And finally, did he not abandon his cabinet when pressures of facing up to that deadline became unbearable?

The answers to all of these questions appear to be an affirmative. Konoe's fixed and hostile view of the outside world as being dominated by the Anglo-American powers, whom he wanted to reject and from whom he craved recognition at the same time, determined the overall outline of his foregin policy. He more often than not sought answers for Japan's problems in fascistic thoughts, interlaced in the anti-*status-quo*, morally unobjectionable, and dangerously romantic vision of Pan-Asianist ideology. The resultant foreign policy was to push Japan onto an even more destructive as well as self-destructive path.

Japan's "Fascism" and the "*Aite to sezu*" Statement

As noted earlier, Japan's "fascism" has long been an interesting point of contention.[43] While the question of whether the Japanese wartime regime was "fascist" is fascinating in and of itself, I take as a given that Japan, though never a fascist state, had fascistic elements. Furthermore, these elements provided an ideological link between Japan's domestic life and its Pan-Asianist programs abroad, especially at this juncture. For the sake of clarity, nonetheless, I would delineate certain features of fascism that I presume to have been prevalent for the period concerned. The most reasonable place to start is the definition of the concept itself.

As employed in twentieth-century politics, fascism connotes a philosophy, movement, or regime that is characterized by the exercise of state control over most aspects of society under an authoritarian leader. Fascism is once and at the same time authoritarian, anti-Bolshevist, and ultranationalist, as was the case with Italy under the leadership of Benito Mussolini (1922–45), Spain under Francisco Franco (1939–75), or Germany under Adolf Hitler (1933–45). As a political philosophy advancing an anti-materialist and organic view of the world, fascism opposed scientific Marxism.

In advancing Meishuron Pan-Asianism, Japan became captive to and actively employed many aspects of fascism. Still the Japanese state never centralized their institutions to the point of becoming a fascist regime. Even on the sheer conceptual level, the transnational and trans-state claims of Pan-Asianism (as opposed to, say, those of monoethnic and monolingual Pan-Germanism) undermined the exacting fascist standards of ethnic purity seen in the orthodox types of fascism. But it would be difficult to deny the existence of fascistic inspirations in Japan's policy. Violent tactics and the resort to force exercised by the far right initially, and then by the military government, were but one manifestation of fascist-inspired politics. More symbolically, the evocation of ancient glories in the form of the emperor cult, the glorification of a collective past in the form of the family state principle, the vehement anti-Anglo-American, anti-capitalist stance shared with revolutionary Marxists, as well as the high degree of state control over industries and media increasingly marked Japan's public life.

In reorienting Japan's foreign policy along those partly fascist-inspired lines, Konoe's government actively attributed Pan-Asianist significance to what was initially meant to be a desperate attempt to contain new hostilities in China. In purporting to construct a "New East Asian Order," his government referred to the slogan of *"Hakkō Ichiu"* (Eight Corners of the World under one Imperial Roof),[44] coined by the leader of an apocalyptic and politicized rendition of Nichiren Buddhism, Tanaka Chigaku, earlier in the century. By reviving what was once a uniquely Japanese take on the organic view of the state, and taking it outside the context of Japan by turning it into a Pan-Asianist slogan, Konoe's policy in effect linked Japan's "fascism"—that is, a combination of fascistic models with certain strands of ultranationalism, socialism, and Marxism—to the broader arena of international politics. This, needless to say, required intellectual acrobatics. His government did have a measure of success in pushing this course.

A decisive moment in his foreign policy came in mid-January 1938, when Konoe pledged to eradicate Chiang's government in the infamously arrogant statement that proclaimed Japan's intention "no longer to deal with the Kuomintang government" (*Kokuminseifu wo Aite to sezu*). This statement, commonly known as the "*Aite to sezu*" declaration, was the first and the most perplexing of a series of foreign policy pronouncements the prime minister would make over the course of 1938. It read:

> The government of the Empire, even after the siege of Nanjing, to this day, has accorded the Kuomintang government a final opportunity to repent. Yet it did not appreciate the Empire's true intention, and kept on fighting us, not considering the toll on civilians inside China or reflecting on the peace and the tranquility of the whole of East Asia. Therefore, the Imperial government would no longer deal with the Kuomintang government and instead anticipates the establishment of a new Chinese government worthy of true cooperative relations with the Empire.[45]

The statement was confounding, to say the least, in the very light of Japan's continuing engagement in an effective war with that very party with whom the Empire had declared it would not deal. Its harsh tone was meant to intimidate the Kuomintang into suing for peace. It certainly surprised, and then alienated Chiang Kai-shek, especially as it came after Japan's earlier proposals—and Konoe's personal involvement—in bringing him to the negotiating table.

The possibility of a direct talk with Chiang Kai-shek had been pursued by a number of different routes. An attempt to contact Chiang in which Konoe seems to have invested a great deal was the secret mission that involved the grandson of Prince Saionji, Saionji Kinkazu. Immediately following the Marco Polo Bridge Incident, Konoe dispatched the young Saionji to Shanghai to meet with T. V. Soong, the powerful brother-in-law of the Generalissimo. Though initially skeptical, Soong eventually agreed to arrange a meeting between Chiang and Konoe to seek ways for a truce. Upon his return to Japan, however, Saionji learned to his astonishment that Konoe's cabinet had just approved an Army request to send three additional divisions to North China, effectively putting an end to his secret mission, leading him to say: "I was made a clown in a project, for which I had risked my life."[46]

In light of his seemingly half-hearted commitment to pursuing peaceful options, then, it becomes difficult to separate Konoe's "*Aite to sezu*" statement from his stronger conviction about Japan's desirable international position. The idea that Japan should not appear weak to the rest of the world, and especially to China, is perfectly consistent with his rhetoric from 1920. Thus this statement should not be regarded as an anomaly. It made little sense and proved enormously damaging in foreign policy terms, as it virtually snuffed out any hope of a diplomatic settlement with Chiang Kai-shek. Such a show of defiance made an effective populist politician on the domestic front, but damaged his credibility as an international leader.

The remarkable correspondence of his views between 1920 and 1938 should warn us to avoid any simplistic reading of Konoe as either a villain or a martyr. It would be difficult to imagine that Konoe was unwillingly forced by the military to utter those words calling for "Japan that can say 'No'" back in 1920, when he was merely a novice politician penning his impressions from his first travels abroad and making known to the world his political philosophy. Rather, despite his complex personality and varying intellectual interests, Konoe was from his early public career an ambitious politician with a very fixed worldview about Japan's position vis-à-vis the rest of the world, especially with the United States, and also with China.

The elder Saionji, who was, in spite of his advanced age, more intellectually flexible and thoroughly versed in the world of diplomacy, was uneasy with his one-time protégé's increasingly public pronouncements of his ideas of foreign policy. The *genrō's* veiled, yet damning criticism simply went like this:

> It is indispensable to make him [Chiang Kai-shek] into a legitimate negotiating partner. . . . The Chinese negotiator for the settlement of the Sino-Japanese War [of 1894–95] Li Hongzhang too had a terrible reputation in Japan. But then, there was only him to be dealt with in China. So one makes do with what one has got. There is nothing else to do other than to identify who is at the top, and then negotiate with that person.[47]

Despite his best senses and judgment telling him that the escalation of the conflict would not be advisable, it appears that Konoe's impatience about negotiating partners who would not immediately respond to his princely condescension, coupled with his rigid idea about how Japan should assert itself when challenged, made him temperamentally more in sync with those who wanted and believed Japan to be able to defeat the Chinese in one clean blow.

In the end, Konoe's "*Aite to sezu*" statement revolved around the two ideological pillars now familiar to us: first, the conviction of the superiority of the Japanese Imperial Nation and, second, Pan-Asianism, reflected in the Empire's stated dedication to East Asia's peace. They certainly complemented one another, and possibly made Japanese expansionism harder to resist for those inside, and impossible to comprehend for those outside of Japan. At the same time, it is also important to recognize that Emperorism was not the only political force that interacted with Pan-Asianism in this period. In their worthy renditions of an East Asian union, various thinkers operating in different capacities, possessing different political temperaments and sympathies ranging from fascism on the right to Marxism on the left, sought to locate a moral and grand meaning to Japan's China War. Especially in light of the rise of SRA intellectuals from mid-1938 on, more intriguing questions emerge: What were those intellectuals challenging? Why were they drawn to Pan-Asianism? Was there something about Pan-Asianism that attracted intellectuals more than others?

Part II. The Shōwa Research Association and the New East Asian Order

Why the SRA?

The period following the "*Aite to sezu*" statement represented the height of intellectual influence on the making of Japan's foreign policy, evidenced by the burgeoning body of research organizations and policy-advisory institutions. The critic Yamaura Kan'ichi contemporaneously observed that all these institutes eagerly vied to influence Konoe's policy preferences. What surprised him was that those who advised Konoe almost always did so voluntarily, without any remuneration. This prompted him to muse that:

> [I]t is doubtful that all of those around him are sacrificing their egos to devote themselves to Konoe. At least, it is assumed that Konoe's bureaucratic followers are lobbying for secretarial posts, and the political ones for ministerial positions. Therefore, if their loyalty is not returned in kind, dissatisfaction would surface. . . . [H]ere lies a danger for Konoe.[48]

Among those countless contenders for the position of influence, none was as prominent as the Shōwa Research Association (SRA).[49] It enjoyed the membership of more than one hundred experts in major academic disciplines, including politics, economics, sociology, and philosophy, represented by such renowned figures as Rōyama Masamichi, Tōhata Seiichi, Yabe Teiji, Sassa Hiroo, Ryū Shintarō, Miki Kiyoshi, Takahashi Kamekichi, Ozaki Hotsumi, and Arisawa Hiromi, as well as many other reform-minded journalists, businessmen, and bureaucrats. While there are divergent characterizations of the SRA's political inclinations, because of the participation of both left- and right-leaning intellectuals (as well as of intellectuals with both left- and right-leanings within), it is difficult to deny that the membership embraced a generation of generally recognized *crème de la crème* of Japan's educated elites. Again, in Yamaura's somewhat cynical assessment, the SRA was "spending quite a lot of money— although I have no idea on what—and acting in any case as a factory in charge of manufacturing Konoe's intellectual vitamins."[50]

Irrespective of their political orientations, those intellectuals' personal quests for influence as well as their Pan-Asianism, propelled by the general belief that Japan was positioned for some kind of a historic leadership role, appeared to keep them in overall harmony. Founded originally on an informal basis in 1933 in the wake of the 5-15 Incident, when Prime Minister Inukai was assassinated by a young naval officer, the SRA incorporated various self-contained specialist groups.[51] But it was the expansion of Japan's war zone from North to Central China that prompted the association to reorganize. More specifically, the desire to reverse the ineffectiveness, or rather, the adverse effects of Konoe's January 1938 "*Aite to sezu*" statement propelled some key members of the SRA to come up with a corrective policy.

The SRA's enormous challenge was recalled by one of the founding members, Rōyama Masamichi, forty years later:

> Konoe himself knew that the China policy meant a confrontation with the United States. The problem for the cabinet was that while desiring to avoid war with the United States, the cabinet aimed . . . to consolidate Japan's foothold on the continent. . . . This was the gist of the problem that I wanted to address in the SRA.[52]

In other words, at least in the assessment of Rōyama, who was the primary figure of the SRA by this time, the government's aim was not simply to end the war with China, but to end it without a loss of face, either militarily or diplomatically. Konoe wanted to do this on terms favorable to Japan while avoiding confrontations with the United States, and moreover, consolidating Japanese interests on the mainland. As such, the policy the SRA would come up with had to be necessarily groundbreaking.

New East Asian Order

The pronouncement of the construction of a "New East Asian Order" as a primary aim of Japan's foreign policy marked the pinnacle of the SRA's influence on Konoe's leadership. The premier's radio broadcast on November 3 proclaimed that the ultimate objective of Japan's military engagement in China was the following:

> Already, the Kuomintang government amounts to no more than a local political authority. Nonetheless, so long as that government maintains its anti-Japan/Communist-tolerant policy, the Empire cannot put her sword down until she sees the end of that government. What the Empire craves is the construction of a new order to secure the perpetual stability of East Asia. . . . The Empire wishes the responsibilities for the construction of this East Asian Order to be shared. The Empire expects the Chinese nation to understand our true intentions fully and to respond to the Empire's support.[53]

The key figure in the philosophical formulation of this statement, commonly termed the *Tōa Shinchitsujo Seimei* (New East Asian Order Declaration), is thought to be Miki Kiyoshi (1897–1945), a former student of Martin Heidegger. He headed the SRA's Cultural Research Group, created by the summer of 1938. In an attempt to reconcile Pan-Asianist claims with the principle of national self-determination, the statement assured that Japan harbored "no designs on Chinese territory," "no desire to curb China's autonomy," nor "any hostility towards the Chinese people."[54] Those were in many respects commonplace Pan-Asianist themes sounded earlier in Manchuria. The statement was nonetheless novel in its suggestion of a more systematic approach to creating trans-nation-state political and economic arrangements, which might in turn prompt a reorientation of the existing international order entirely. As such, it was filled with more ambitious and all-encompassing claims than any other previous statements issued by the Japanese government since 1931.

This is exactly when and where Pan-Asianism, in the garb of the "New East Asian Order" and "East Asian cooperativism," became a clear link between "fascism" at home and expansionism abroad. Miki elaborated his argument in December 1938:

The philosophy of an East Asian Cooperative Body—which I shall simply call East Asian Philosophy (*Tōa Shisō*)—must be argued from the perspective of world history. If the East Asian Philosophy were to be born as a result of the abandonment of certain unifying principles (*tōitsuteki rinen*) of world history, that would only have a reactionary meaning. . . . True, East Asia points to a region, and in fact, today, it means Japan, Manchukuo, and China. . . . Since the outbreak of the China Incident, on many occasions, I have reiterated that the Incident provided us with an opportunity to overcome narrow-minded nationalisms. And now, with the emergence of the ideology of an East Asia Cooperative Body, it appears that my claim has been vindicated. Needless to say, the East Asian Cooperative Body implies a certain [greater] whole transcending [smaller] nations. Nevertheless, I am not ready to reject the significance of nationalisms in the present stages of world history. . . . [N]o matters of world historical significance are carried out objectively or universally. Rather, that task is always spearheaded by a certain nation. In that sense, in other words, any world historical events begin as an action of a certain nation.[55]

Having found accommodation with a Marxian understanding of world history with Japanese chauvinism, Miki further declared: "The only way for this [China] Incident to achieve world historical significance is for Japan to stand up to the task [of creating the cooperative body] along those unifying principles."[56]

While careful not to deny the role of modern Chinese nationalism, Miki still regarded Japan's leadership as instrumental in the making of that historical cooperative body. He asserted:

Unifying the ideals of the East goes with the task of breaking out of the so-called Europeanist (*yōroppashugi*) perspective of world history, which equates the history of white people to the history of the world. . . . At the same time, the ideals of the East must not simply be viewed from a Japan-only perspective. If the unification of the East were to provide the basis for the true unification of the world, the unification of China should also be the basis of the unification of the East, and if it were so, Chinese nationalism is significant from the viewpoint of the East Asian Cooperative Body. Nonetheless, the question of how the nationally unified China must be governed, in terms of its new political structure, must be considered from the new perspective of the East Asian Cooperative Body as a whole.[57]

For Miki, *dakaisaku* meant that Japan should break the material deadlock of actual field conflict in a decisive manner by mobilizing the nation in a concerted, determined fashion. To do so, Japan had to be more self-aware about its broader mission of breaking the immaterial, historical deadlock of Eurocentricism in respect to world history. Much though Miki tried to give credence to his uniquely "Eastern" argumentation for the future of world history, he clearly relied on Western sociological/philosophical concepts to substantiate his claim. Employing the then fashionable distinction used by the German sociologist Ferdinand Tönnies, but also implicitly accepting Japanese agrarian revivalist ideas, embraced by the likes of Tachibana Kōzaburō and Ōkawa Shūmei, Miki argued that his rendition of cooperativism differed from the Western emphasis on *Gesellschaft*, that is, an organization marked by rational and contractual relationships. Rather, Japanese and other Asian societies were more like a *Gemeinschaft*, dominated by close linkages of kinship reminiscent of a traditional agrarian (or in Marxian terms, "primitive communist") community. However, such a community still needed to be qualified, as Japan had to represent innovation as well as tradition in its modern, great power incarnation. He distinguished his view of the Japanese-led East Asian *Gemeinschaft* from a historical agrarian notion as follows:

> One must be aware that the view of the East Asian Cooperative Body as *Gemeinschaft* might precariously refer to feudalism. . . . In abstract terms, *Gesellschaft* carries the image of openness, while *Gemeinschaft* always connotes something closed in its entirety. But the new cooperative body must not be as closed as the feudalistic *Gemeinschaft*. I have already mentioned that the modernization of China is the prerequisite to the formation of the East Asian Cooperative Body. Thus while it is clear that the East's ideals must ensure the continuation of Eastern cultural traditions, it should not inhibit such modernization efforts.[58]

However, even this theory of a purportedly more spiritual and organic Pan-Asian nation was not unique, but one that resonated a great deal with the National Socialist claims of an ideally and organically structured Pan-German nation, and by extension, their idea of a New Order in Europe led by Germany. It is clear that Pan-Germanism under the Nazi dictatorship relied heavily on their hatred of "Western" (i.e., Anglo-American) hegemony, the shorthand for which, increasingly, was "Americanism." And

Miki and his colleagues' understanding of Pan-Asianism drew from a similar kind of hostility, and in expressing it, borrowed rather shamelessly from those ideas.

Indeed, the foremost and original enemies of democracy were early twentieth-century German intellectuals, such as the brothers Ernst (1895–1998) and Friedrich Georg Jünger (1898–1977), Arthur Moeller van den Bruck (1876–1925), and Houston Stewart Chamberlain (1855–1927), the younger brother of the renowned Japanologist Basil Hall Chamberlain. Most of them celebrated, in their different but equally obsessive ways, the superiority and heroism of the super German race and pit its racial glory against the corrupt and corrupting images of the West. When this kind of thinking was fully developed, their enemies became degenerate, impure, rootless, and above all, less than human, thereby justifying their indiscriminate and murderous impulse.

Those German chauvinists in the 1920s and 1930s built upon the earlier Romantic ideals that inspired blood-and-soil nationalism of the counter-Enlightenment. They argued that rationalism, individual freedom, and peace—all features of the liberal democratic West in their eyes—would potentially undermine the grandeur of a nation. While looking upon the Old World (primarily Britain and France) as degenerate and effete, they regarded the New World as an increasing threat, as the United States, with its cold-hearted individualism, fierce competition, blatant commercialism, rampant consumerism, and inane mass culture signified rootlessness and frivolity. In such a place, intellectuals tended to be driven to the margins of society. Instead of philosophy and literature, so the argument went, mass culture reigned in an Americanized society.

Such intellectual fears and prejudices seem to be what drove a group of German, and almost simultaneously Japanese intellectuals too, to launch their "spirit-versus-material" argument against the West, and the United States and "Americanism" in particular.[59] Pan-Germanism was born of and reinforced the intense version of ethnic German nationalism that provided the basis for National Socialism. Its claims were also appealing to non-Western intellectuals—such as Pan-Arabists or the early Baathists, or Pan-Asianists in this period of Japanese history—precisely because they made such an emotive case against Western imperialism. Such an anti-Western imperialist and transnational stance was shared by Marxism and communism in its many different manifestations, making it relatively easier for a left-leaning intellectual such as Miki to accept the argument about the uniqueness of a nation (Japanese ultranationalism) and its special role in remaking and reordering the rest of Asia according to Japanese blueprints (Meishuron Pan-Asianism).

This, Miki and his SRA colleagues asserted, would not only be a "theory" for Asia *per se*, but for an entirely new principle of reorganizing the rest of the world. While highlighting and arguing for the superior character and features of Asian culture over the West, however, they almost uniformly expressed their ideas in predominantly imported academic parlance. In this endeavor, none of the most prominent figures in the SRA, such as the political scientist Rōyama, the philosopher Miki, and the economist Ryū, was an intellectual pioneer.[60] Rather, they helped devise foreign policy out of a hodgepodge of existing ideas coming from Germany and especially Berlin, where so many of the primary figures of the SRA lived and studied previously.

Indeed, one tends to overlook how much of a direct influence interwar Germany provided Japanese elites in ways of new political ideas and vocabulary. From the wake of the Great Kantō Earthquake (1923) until the early 1930s when the currency exchange rate was vastly favorable for Japanese living in inflation-hit Germany, Japan's Ministry of Education stepped up its effort to expand its state-sponsored study-abroad programs. Remarkably, more than 80 percent of those studying outside of Japan were to be found living in, or at the very least, visiting Germany over the course of this period.

For example, Ishiwara Kanji was a student in Berlin and was greatly inspired by the Clausewitzian theory of total war. The pro-Nazi philosopher and a visiting professor in Berlin, the totalitarian thinker Kanokogi Kazunobu, too, claimed that Japan's war was a holy war to save the rest of Asia from Anglo-Saxon encroachments.[61] Also in Berlin was the SRA leader Rōyama. He was instrumental in founding a local reading group in 1926, which became a precursor body to the so-called "Berlin Anti-Imperialist Group" (Berurin Hantei Gurūpu).[62] This group of Japanese students, which included scholars of various natural and social sciences, dedicated themselves to the discussion of Marxist literature in their regular meetings. The SRA member Arisawa Hiromi (1896–1988), who ghost-wrote many of the Association's economic policy recommendations, as well as Kunisaki Teidō (1894–1937), who defected to the Soviet Union where he was executed during the Stalinist purge, were also active members of this group.

In this light, it is a curiously understudied fact that the primary SRA figures' association went back to their German experiences. True, many of them had gone to the same elite schools back home to begin with. But the fact that this generation of intellectuals, mostly in their forties at the time of the China War, had spent their formative years in a country that was itself a battlefield of competing radical ideologies should not be overlooked. Where more provincial Japanese nationalists might have referred exclusively to the Confucian formulations of "the Kingly Way" and other classical Chinese and Japanese texts for an inspiration to reinterpret Pan-Asianism, this group of intellectuals had presumably groundbreaking theories of social sciences under their belt.

Rōyama's article "Theory of an East Asian Cooperative Body," which preceded Konoe's "New Order" radio broadcast, emphasized the importance of such social scientific "theories." In his words, the idea of a "regional body with a common destiny" should be expressed in a "theoretical format" because such a theory would "serve as an ideological weapon for [Japan's] proud nationalism [and its challenge] in overcoming the tragedy of the East."[63]

Despite the repetition of the word "theory," in the end, however, Rōyama was unable to provide a concrete proof behind his own "theory," and concluded:

> [B]ut such a theoretical characteristic [of the East Asian regional body] has to be developed hand in hand with actual experiences of the peoples of the East. Often, theory does not first emerge from natural scientific observations or rational explanations. Rather, . . . a theory has to be sought by the intuitions of a poet and an artist. . . . The combination of the fact of the Eastern peoples' persecution by the world—the West—and the national tragedies that characterize that fact is precisely the present destiny of the vast land and millions of peoples of the East.[64]

Rōyama insisted, that his theory emanated foremost from the East's "spirit and soul," in other words "its nations' mentality of regional destiny (*das Raumsschicksal* [sic])."[65] Most likely, he was stuck in this circular argument about the true theoretical rigor of his "innovative" theory because there was none to work upon to start with. For him, this theory of a regional body with a common Eastern destiny was one of meta-theoretical belief, just as many of Germany's National Socialists' claims about German national destiny were often based on dubious scientific theories.

Likewise, other erstwhile Marxist sympathizers, such as Miki and Ryū, grew to admire and support the idea of a state-controlled economy modeled after the Italian cooperative system and Nazi Germany's effective heavy industrial mobilization for war economy. The combination of their leftist inclinations and their increasing fascination with certain aspects of fascist ideologies, with a specific reference to Meishuron Pan-Asianism, indeed formed Konoe's "New East Asian Order" statement.

The SRA's Impact

One should of course be careful not to either under- or overestimate the SRA's influence. Any "direct" influence of an individual or a group on policymaking is hard to demonstrate, unless perhaps the regime is a dictatorship. However, one can still usefully point out common characteristics within a certain political discourse and assess the impact of individuals and ideas in terms of policy vocabulary and language.

The primary role of the SRA intellectuals in my mind is the elevation of Meishuron Pan-Asianism to the height, not only of academic respectability, but also of seemingly unassailable moral righteousness in Japan's high politics. Konoe's brain trusters did much to embellish Meishuron Pan-Asianism in the language in which any suggestion of retreat from China became difficult to accept, and the eventual war with the West, built on past sacrifices in China and elsewhere, grew to "appear" the only righteous path to follow for the Japanese government in the final phases of the Fifteen Years' War. No matter how earnest these intellectuals may have been, or how brief their place in the sun, the re-intellectualization of Pan-Asianist thinking along revolutionary doctrines of both right and left drew Japan's foreign policy closer to its eventual War with the West.

By attributing philosophical and social-scientific legitimacy to the interpretation of practical problems plaguing Japan's war with China, the key SRA intellectuals in effect provided the government with an impetus as well as invaluable exegeses for the wider conflict to come. They claimed desperately to want to end the China conflict, and by implication, to restrain the military running its independent policies. They were probably sincere in their wishes. But their identification of Japan's Pan-Asianist mission against the Western-backed Chinese Nationalists as its war aim in fact made more practical concessions to Chiang Kai-shek and withdrawals of troops, which could possibly have led to face-saving measures on both sides, unimaginable. In this instance, those intellectuals concerned were active agents of politics and war, having been beguiled by the great ideological temptation of the Meishuron strand of Pan-Asianism and the misplaced self-importance and overconfidence in their ability to bring about a radical policy shift.

Later, following up on the "New Order" scheme, Konoe's supporters helped create a regime in Nanjing allied to Japan, which eventually came into being in March 1940. Wang Jingwei (1883–1944), an idealistic disciple of Sun Yat-sen, fled the Kuomintang government, by then based in Chongqing (Chungking). Konoe's closest allies and certain factions of the Army resorted to various covert operations to boost the power of Wang's government.[66] However, Wang was to be repeatedly discouraged by the weakness and indecisiveness of Konoe at critical moments. Konoe's tendency to be overwhelmed by the ever increasing resistance to troops withdrawals from hard-liners within his own government effectively discredited what he himself had hoped would be "a new Chinese government worthy of true cooperative relations with the Empire."[67]

It was as if Konoe were in the habit of sincerely desiring and fathering a child in the hope of letting a fresh breeze into a bad marriage, only to lose interest in raising it, even with the help of many overeager nannies, as soon as he realized that the child did not fundamentally change the marriage itself. His various policies and political programs, which more often than not conflicted with one another, were his brain-children. He never quite raised any of them properly and always succumbed to abandoning them at the moment they became unruly.

Ultimately, Konoe's own frustrations with his inability to steer Japan out of the China quagmire compelled him to resign in January 1939. Although he would return to premiership six months later with a renewed hope, he was never able to break free of his ineffectual leadership style. But while the Konoe administrations failed in realizing their goals, the imprint of this complex leader and his intellectual associates on Japan's foreign policy was to prove much more lasting than they themselves were probably ever aware. Konoe's foreign policy, and by association the SRA's shaping of it, legitimized Japan's imperial overextension by appealing to grander Pan-Asianist ideals couched in the highly obfuscating jargon of social sciences. While the SRA dissolved itself after the establishment of the Imperial Rule Assistance Association in late 1940, the Pan-Asian concepts reformulated by the SRA intellectuals would continue to dominate Japan's wartime vocabulary.

Once the conceptual underpinnings were set in place, the government's task of making the case for national mobilization became a relatively clear-cut affair. In large part, what legitimated the eventual suicidal tactics of *kamikaze* pilots and human torpedoes toward the end of the Fifteen Years' War was precisely the belief in heroism and self-sacrifice of the Japanese nation articulated in the language of SRA intellectuals. As Emiko Ohnuki-Tierney has skillfully demonstrated, the young pilots, who tended to be idealistic students of humanistic disciplines from top universities, believed that their deaths would bring a better and more just world, despite the impending Japanese defeat.[68] The suicide attacks thus stemmed from "modern" nationalism, and not from ancient warrior codes, poverty, or backwardness that might often be associated with such drastic tactics. They represented a physical expression of the earlier SRA claim that Japan's war represented an innovative turn in world history, one so very different from "ordinary international wars that are driven by material reasons," but one built upon "enormous sacrifices" of the Japanese nation "beyond the calculation of territorial, material, or market acquisition."[69]

* * *

The significance of Pan-Asianism in Japan's policy response to the escalation and prolongation of the China War and the intellectual climate under Konoe's leadership that allowed for such a development were the main concerns of this chapter. At the general level of policy pronouncement, Meishuron Pan-Asianism began to assume increased legitimacy as a state ideology, as the SRA intellectuals began to regard it as an answer to not only solving the China War question, but also more ambitiously, to altering the conduct of international relations. In that endeavor, Meishuron Pan-Asianism became an even more critical instrument of first ill-prepared, and later ill-conceived expansion.

Beyond its importance as providing a direct ideological link to the Pacific phase of the Fifteen Years' War, the development of this period has enormous contemporary relevance and implications for a broader ideational analysis in foreign policymaking. A case in point is June 2006, Washington, DC. In a debate over troops withdrawal from Iraq, the U.S. Senate became sharply divided along partisan lines. The Democrats argued that the war had cost the United States too much already to justify the presence of U.S. troops any longer, while the Republican administration insisted that any kind of withdrawal would be tantamount to conceding defeat. The most impassioned claims were made about the importance of "the courage of our convictions" in fighting on, so that the deaths of more than 2,500 troops would not be in vain.[70]

The most confounding aspect of such reasoning was that it flatly ignored the basic question of whether the decision to enter the war was the right one to justify the 2,500 deaths already incurred to start with, and whether the same *casus belli* still stood three years later to justify the presence of U.S. troops, and even more deaths to come. It appears that insofar as one genuinely believes that seemingly dubious choices are made for just ideals, such as ousting imperialism, toppling dictators, and spreading democracy, it becomes less arduous for one to make peace with even the most mistaken of policy decisions. So, too, are the choices that are made based primarily on material considerations. Again, so long as the advancement of such material interests could be justified in terms of grander ideals, an individual, or a government would not have to face a moral or ethical dilemma. Such overarching policy goals might give a semblance of uniformity and consistency to one's policymaking. At the same time, they could easily lead a government to make wrong choices, without necessitating those involved to reflect on their "smaller" mistakes that might eventually add up to an adverse outcome in any number of ways.

This was exactly the case with the wartime Japanese government. The grand mission of establishing a new order was loudly sounded, and a similar inversion technique in debate was employed by those who were reluctant to accept more immediate realities and misplaced strategic decisions, in order to divert valid criticisms. With the outbreak of new hostilities with China, and later with Japan's war against the West, that argument would be pushed to an absurd extent. Future sacrifices and even the destruction of the entire nation would be reasoned, without any apparent internal conflict, in terms of grander—even revolutionary— ideals, such as the establishment of peace and tranquility in Asia for the sake of a more peaceful world, so that the countless deaths that came before would not be in vain. Disturbingly, more and more people seemed to share that sort of "courage of conviction." One would have to keep on fighting for a higher purpose that is heavier than life, indeed, for "courage of their conviction."

The emergence of the "New East Asian Order" concept under Konoe completed the full circle of Japanese intellectuals' courtship with Pan-Asianism.

What started out as an intellectual backlash against wholesale Western-ization around the turn of the century drifted farther afield as Japan became engrossed in its imperialist program in an utterly disorderly fash-ion—in both formal and informal senses—on the Asian mainland. With the SRA endorsement of Meishuron Pan-Asianism, it came back into the hands of intellectuals once again with the pressing need for Japan to break free of its military deadlock in China. What resulted was not the "hitting and opening" of that situation, but rather, further entanglement and expansion. Because of Japan's mounting need to procure resources beyond the boundaries of the Sino-Japanese union envisaged before, it did not take long for the "New Order" concept to evolve into an even more ambitious notion of a "Greater East Asia Co-Prosperity Sphere," which was to become the official aim for Japan's war with the West in Asia and the Pacific. As such, the SRA's Pan-Asianist vision, intended to offer a *dakaisaku*, ended up creating even more deadlocks that needed somehow to be smashed and broken. This was the beginning of a New East Asian Dis-Order.

6
The War of "World Historical Significance"

Paradox, like accident, is one of the main engines that drive history. The divergence of interests and perceptions that catapulted Japan into the "Pacific War" phase of the Fifteen Years' War is a clear case in point. The Imperial Navy's surprise attack on the U.S. Pacific Fleet at Pearl Harbor and its opening of hostilities with the West point to some of the most poignant and profound paradoxes to be found in the studies of war origins. Especially confounding are the seeming inconsistencies between Japan's decision to enter the war to ensure its national survival when Tokyo was sufficiently informed of the self-destructive implications of such a war in material terms.

Outside the immediate policymaking arena, Japan's attack on Pearl Harbor was followed by a conspicuous movement of intellectuals, on an ever larger scale, propounding the ideological significance of the country's military expansion, ultimately leading many to declare the war's "world historical significance" and its Pan-Asianist objectives. It is true that such views predated the Pacific phase of the war, as the preceding chapter has already demonstrated. But the degree of enthusiasm, euphoria, and even intoxication felt by Japan's public figures after the success of Pearl Harbor sheds a great deal more light on the question of why Pan-Asianism held such an attraction for the Japanese nation at large. Having captured the hearts and minds of even those who had hitherto opposed Japan's military engagement in China, Japan's Pan-Asianist war was now gaining a new momentum. Now that Japan was truly fighting a war with the West, the legitimacy of Meishuron Pan-Asianism seemed beyond doubt for many, which accounted for the eruption of broad-based endorsement that followed the success of the Pacific operation.

We now face the following two questions. How could Japan have entered such an apparently self-destructive war by rejecting other available options? How could such a ruinous war have been welcome by its public? Or, to reduce those questions to the core, what constituted the policymakers' "realities"? And what compelled those who had been against Japan's military engagement up to that point, suddenly to start proclaiming the "world historical significance" of Japan's war? The answers to both of these questions can be found in Pan-Asianism.

Still, the main aim of this chapter is not to assess the actual impact of Pan-Asianism on Japan's wartime programs and its declared goal of constructing the "Co-Prosperity Sphere," to which the next chapter is devoted. Rather, by pointing out the ideological continuity of Japan's war with the West from the previous episodes, the following pages aim to provide a conceptual bridge between the pre– and post–Pearl Harbor phases of the Fifteen Years' War, in hope of better understanding two paradoxes. The first paradox concerns Japan's decision to enter a self-destructive war with the West, and the second concerns the pervasive support, led by its public figures, of such a disastrous decision.

My first argument is that Pan-Asianism played an instrumental and practical role in Japan's war entry as a tool of consensus-building—in terms both of cementing divided opinions and of moving policy along—by creating a larger common goal that managed to override finer differences in strategic perspectives. Meishuron Pan-Asianism, on rapid ascendancy within the policymaking circles since the China War, provided Japan's decision makers with an invaluable and morally unobjectionable ground upon which to create a uniform foreign policy voice, eventually leading them, albeit in a highly elusive and individually unaccountable manner, to proclaim the construction of the "Greater East Asia Co-Prosperity Sphere" as the overarching goal of the Empire's war with the West. This was true, remarkably, in the face of severe and chronic disagreements within the highest government circles concerning the necessity and feasibility of such a war.

Although it is difficult to see why anyone would have wanted, in principle, to contest such a morally righteous goal as Pan-Asianism, the first part of the discussion accepts neither that all the policymakers whole-heartedly believed in Pan-Asianism, nor that the considerations of more immediate, strategic importance did not take precedence over Pan-Asianism in their minds. Those types of arguments are difficult to sustain simply on the basis of textual analyses of policy records and the circumstantial evidence that they provide. This is especially true of Japan on the eve of Pearl Harbor. It was often what was left unsaid that fed the internally driven dynamic of Japan's policy formulation. Instead, I would stress that the notion of Japan's "national interest" by this time had become deeply enmeshed with Pan-Asianist considerations. Pan-Asianism was hardly negligible in what the policymakers perceived as the Empire's "national interest" in a strategic sense. Also, the fact that the war was declared under a Pan-Asianist banner speaks, at the very least, for the notion that the ideology was an implicit yet decisive element, on a functional level, that pushed and pulled other policy preferences in favor of Japan's ultimate decision to go to war with the West.

Taking the argument beyond the confines of policy analysis, the second part of this chapter will consider why Meishuron Pan-Asianism should have been so appealing, or at least, so uncontested, to the point of being turned into the country's official war aim. This will be done mainly through an observation of Japan's leading people of letters, who, more than any other societal agents, effectively echoed, articulated, and reinforced the Pan-Asianist sentiments that underpinned Japan's war aims.

Ultimately, the role of Pan-Asianism in policymaking has to be examined primarily in its instrumental capacity because of the very limitations of foreign policy analysis. But Pan-Asianism's real galvanizing power, and hence the importance of such a policy decision, could be more appropriately appreciated by looking at the ready endorsement of Japan's self-appointed *meishu* role accorded by its opinion-makers, who in turn shaped and led public attitudes toward the war. In this sense, Pearl Harbor marked a critical turning point for the history of Pan-Asianism, as the ideology would not remain merely a "state" ideology, but also a "national" ideology with a popular mandate, propelling the entire nation toward the paradoxically and maximally destructive, as well as self-destructive goal of achieving peace and tranquility in the "Co-Prosperity Sphere."

I. Pan-Asianism and the Making of Japan's War with the West

Pearl Harbor: Some Theoretical Considerations and Constraints

The Pacific War phase of the Fifteen Years' War was marked by a decisive beginning, because of Japan's attack on Pearl Harbor and the United States' declaration of war shortly thereafter. This formal sense of a beginning was lacking at any other juncture of the previous decade, such as the

Manchurian Incident, the Marco Polo Bridge Incident, and the battle of Nomonhan, all of which were *de facto* part of Japan's Fifteen Years' War, but none of which *de jure* constituted an official war by itself. Along with this sense of formality we come to the question that has long confounded and fascinated international relations theorists: Why did Japan consciously enter a war that seemed destined, even in the eyes of some of its highest ranking policymakers, to be self-destructive?

It is beyond doubt that economics played a vital role in Japan's strategic thinking, thus prompting the neorealists to argue that an attack signified the only "rational" action to maximize Japan's chance of safeguarding its "national interest" and to ensure its survival. In this explanation, ideology, such as Emperor Worship or Pan-Asianism, had no part to play in the actual decision to go to war. On closer inspection, however, the neorealist explanation proves a case of self-fulfilling prophecy. Conceivably, "national interest" could have been at once a justification for either why Japan refrained from war, or why it preempted a disastrous war with the West. In each instance, Japan could be said to have made a "rational" decision to uphold its "national interest," *ex post facto*. Such a tautological view is flawed, merely providing a snapshot of the longer and larger policymaking process. Beyond that frozen moment in time, a hard power-driven description explains nothing more of the processes in which often "irrational" and "unrealistic" factors come to inform an individual and collective perception of "national interest."

A slightly modified version of the above explanation is that the perception and misperception of the parties involved influenced Japan's war entry. The proponents of this school would still organize their arguments around the considerations of material capabilities, stressing that Japan depended heavily on imported resources and on export goods—especially textiles—which began to be limited by quotas, as the world economic depression deepened in the 1930s. Japan's acute awareness of its dependence on external resources led the country to seek an ambitious program of expansion in order to establish a self-sufficient economic and security bloc, in turn prompting Western democratic states to respond to Japan's advance with the imposition of severe sanctions. Thus according to this school, Pearl Harbor was an outgrowth of resultant Japanese misperceptions that the United States' naval presence could be effectively ousted from the Pacific. Equally, the Western—and especially the U.S.—miscalculation that the war with Japan could be avoided by gradually and progressively squeezing the Japanese economy, in fact solidified Japan's determination to seek war resources in Southeast Asia.

The above-line of interpretation certainly illuminates Japan's own awareness of its weak international position, measured principally in terms of material capabilities. It explains nothing more, however, about the kind of self-perception that prompted Japan's decision to pre-empt an enemy, whose known war-making capacity was far superior to its own.[1] Besides, even though there appeared to be a provisional and vague consensus by the beginning of autumn 1941 that the war with the United States could not now be avoided was likely, the perceptions of threat felt by Japan's leaders were far from uniform. The most basic neorealist assumptions that foreign policy is made on the basis of rational calculations of material advantages and disadvantages, and that policymakers act in unison toward a single goal could therefore be discounted.

What then unified the opinions of Japan's policymakers at last? Furthermore, once their opinions were unified, what drove the country onto a collision course with the West, and into a catastrophic war?

Pan-Asianism as Japan's Official War Aims

Rather than providing a cloak for Japan's "national interest," Pan-Asianism became a cloak for the Japanese government's deeper hesitations, uncertainties, and disagreements about the necessity of fighting a war with the United States.[2] Considering the range of divided opinions within the government, Japan's attack on Pearl Harbor provides one of the most dramatic instances of ideology pulling a policy outcome in different directions from those which reasonable, although never absolute, considerations of material advantages would have dictated. Why should a country opt for such an apparently ill-fated policy? At least part of the answer lies in the theory of "coalition politics," explained by Jack Snyder.[3]

This theory, as applied to the examination of expansionist foreign policy, posits that a state organ is not taken over by any single group, such as "capitalists," "militarists," or "bureaucrats." Rather, foreign policy is more often a result of coalition-building and log-rolling processes among multiple players, who hold differing perspectives of "national interest," but who nonetheless share some common ground in their most basic ideological commitment. When a certain group develops aggressive programs to serve its short-term strategic agenda but manages to justify it in terms of a longer-term goal on the basis of that broader, overlapping ideological consensus, that aspect of commonality becomes dominant in the government's policymaking discourse. The ideology could, in due course, acquire an inherent dynamic to hold the otherwise divided government together and moreover to roll policy in certain directions pushed by a particular faction. This makes even the most obviously problematic strategic decisions irreversible in the face of a more general, overriding consensus that permeates through policy negotiations and bargaining over a period of time.

In what Japan's policymakers on the eve of Pearl Harbor saw as an increasingly narrowing funnel of options, Pan-Asianism played exactly that critical role. The ultimate policy outcome, after all, became one of fighting a "Greater East Asia War" (*Daitōa Sensō*), aiming to build the "Greater East Asia Co-Prosperity Sphere" (*Daitōa Kyōeiken*). In the face of "finer" strategic disagreements, the "grander" ideology of Pan-Asianism, as expressed in terms of the "Sphere" ideology, enabled those who were eager for an immediate preemption to justify their views. Moreover, once Pan-Asianism became a glue strong enough to hold conflicting strategies, it swayed the policy pendulum in the direction of war with the West. By this reasoning, Pearl Harbor was a consequence of, and not a precondition for, the rise of Pan-Asianism as is often assumed. Again, to cite a more contemporary example, not unlike the Japanese case, the neoconservatives in the United States effectively appealed to democratic ideals as well as the evils of transnational terrorism and weapons of mass destruction in an effort to cement U.S. government policy toward toppling Saddam Hussein's regime in 2003.

The crystallization of Meishuron Pan-Asianism as Japan's grand war aim in the Pacific in a remarkably short span of time strongly suggests that the ideology performed just those instrumental functions. Despite disagreements over finer strategic and diplomatic methods, the military hard-liners prevailed in the end precisely because they were able to couch their argument in terms of Japan's larger and nobler struggle; that Japan was being strangled by the hostile encirclement of the ABCD (standing for American, British, Chinese, and Dutch) powers, thus forcing Japan to procure war materials from Southeast Asia. In such a survival- and security-focused argument, Pan-Asianist factors are admittedly implicit rather than explicit. It is true that there was not much direct discussion of Pan-Asianism in the policy debate immediately leading to the war. Indeed, the examination of policy development before Pearl Harbor amply demonstrates the divisiveness of the government over different strategies, but it does not tell how exactly Pan-Asianism built a coalition and log-rolled Japan's policy toward war.

However, the simplest reading of events can be misleading in this instance. The self-consciousness of Japan as the preordained leader of Asia had by this time been firmly established within the collective perception of "national interest." This was because Japan had gradually but surely committed and overextended enough of its resources, both in material and nonmaterial senses, to its Pan-Asianist imperialist venture. With this awareness of continuity, it can be sustained that Pan-Asianism was considered perhaps beyond contestation, acting almost as furniture of the mind, so as not to merit explicit scrutiny. This was all the more so when there loomed other more pressing issues of a tactical nature, which was why the main disagreements in the government on the eve of Pearl Harbor were primarily over materials rather than ideologies.[4]

The immediate situation leading to Pearl Harbor was as follows: on July 16, 1941, the Konoe cabinet resigned for the second time. The third Konoe cabinet, formed on July 18, saw little change in the composition of its members, save for the critical replacement of Foreign Minister Matsuoka by the Navy Admiral Toyoda Teijirō. Matsuoka had been reduced to being a *persona non grata* because of his unaccomodating approach with the United States and his rift with Konoe. His exit meant that there was now much less chance of Japan ever going to war with the Soviet Union. It also meant that its advance into southern Indochina became highly likely.

By the end of that month, Japan had managed to take over southern Indochinese interests from Vichy France, allied to Germany. Konoe's compromise with military hard-liners on September 6, 1941 begot the original "Essentials for Carrying out the Empire's Policies." It still left the option of continuing talks with the United States, while making it clear on a separate attachment that Japan would immediately go to war if talks did not bear fruit before the October deadline. Unable to face the deadline to which he himself had earlier agreed and feeling defeated by a series of failed approaches to the United States as well as to the Japanese Army, Konoe opted to dissolve the cabinet and resign once and for all. The emperor ordered the new premier Tōjō to reconsider the war entry plans from scratch, with an extended deadline.

The following awkward exchange between Prime Minister Tōjō, who felt that the war with the United States, and Emperor Hirohito took place after such a "reconsideration." On November 2, 1941, the former presented a report on the Imperial Headquarters Liaison Conference held the previous day. Hirohito asked, "What do you regard as Japan's grand war aims?" to which the premier answered: "We are still in the process of examination. . . . We shall report to Your Majesty on that point at a later date."[5]

Still, by the November 5 Imperial Conference, more overtly ideological dimensions of *casus belli* emerged as major bones of contention in policy conference proceedings.[6] The President of the Privy Council Hara Yoshimichi was concerned with the effects of what he saw as the potentially dangerous and inherently "racial" character of the impending war. Specifically, he was worried that Hitler, who had "called Japanese a second-class race," might opt for an alliance with the United States and Britain.[7] He speculated that the minute Japan declared war on the United States, Germany would join forces with the United States and Britain, united by "the common hatred of the yellow race."[8] He advised those attending the meeting to "consider thoroughly the state of race relations and to guard against the possibility of Japan being encircled by the Aryan race, . . . making sure to strengthen more than ever our relations with Germany and Italy."[9]

Tōjō, too, agreed with Hara, stating that "we shall make sure that it will not end up becoming a racial war."[10] But Japan's subsequent wartime attitude toward the Allied countries proved in fact to overplay rather than underplay aspects of a racial struggle. That anyone in the highest policymaking circles should point out "the common hatred of the yellow race" by the rather erroneous understanding of Western powers as together constituting a single "Aryan race" in and of itself indicates that there were such innate, though often tacit, preoccupations—if not paranoia—about the question of race, and more critically, that those racial considerations might even overrule formal political alliances to Japan's disadvantage.

Pan-Asianism Rising

Morally compelling and conceptually ambiguous enough to supersede immediate disagreements within the chronically divided government, Pan-Asianism, in the end, proved powerful enough to rise to the status of Japan's official war aim in its war against the West with precipitous speed. One could clearly see the increased emphasis given to the point of ideological convergence by the time of the November 5 Imperial Conference. In fact, already at the previous November 1 Liaison Conference, one could sense Pan-Asianism rising. At the meeting, which famously lasted for seventeen hours and during which the military and Foreign Minister Tōgō (not to be confused with Prime Minister Tōjō) hotly debated possible scenarios over diplomatic settlements, a compromise was finally reached. That plan was to become the revised "Essentials for Carrying Out the Empire's Policies" with a new deadline.[11] While still hoping for diplomatic settlements, the anti-war foreign minister seemed already to have accepted, with even a sense of self-conscious fatalism of a fallen hero, that the war was more likely than not. When he later presented his case to the emperor on November 5, Tōgōcouched his argument in terms of the overriding importance of the establishment of the "Greater East Asia Co-Prosperity Sphere." He explained:

> Basically, the conclusion of the China War and the establishment of the Greater East Asia Co-Prosperity Sphere signify as a prerequisite the Empire's own survival, while acting as a cornerstone of East Asia's stability. Therefore, the Empire must eliminate, at all costs, any obstacles that might come in her way of achieving those aims.[12]

By pledging his commitment to the grand ideology, he appeared to be at once justifying his compromise with the military hard-liners and preparing himself for the eventuality of Japan's war entry in the increasingly hopeless prospect—especially given the deadline to which the government had already agreed—of reaching diplomatic solutions with the United States.

By the fateful day of December 8, 1941, the Empire's war aim had become unambiguous. "The Imperial Proclamation of War," dramatically broadcast that noon to inform the country of the Imperial Japanese Navy's attack on Pearl Harbor, highlighted the Empire's need to fight for its own survival and defense as well as the "establishment of eternal peace in East Asia."[13] Further, at the General Headquarters Conference on December 10, 1941, the war that Japan had entered against the United States and the British Empire, as well as the war that Japan had unofficially been fighting in China, were officially named the "Greater East Asia War."[14] And on December 13, 1941, it was publicly announced that the goal of this war was "to construct a new order and prosperity for the Greater East Asia, inviting the great moral and cultural revival of the East."[15] The Japanese government proclaimed the establishment of the "Greater East Asia Co-Prosperity Sphere" as its ultimate aim, promising the achievement of "order for co-prosperity, mutual respect for sovereign independence among Asian nations, while calling for the elimination of racial discrimination" and "full freedom for Asiatics."[16]

As for the idea of the "Sphere" itself, the coining of the term is attributed to Matsuoka Yōsuke, who, upon becoming Foreign Minister in the second Konoe cabinet in the summer of 1940, had clarified Japan's foreign policy orientation as one of

> establishing the Greater East Asia Co-Prosperity Sphere, with the Greater East Asia Co-Prosperity Sphere signifying the same thing as what has hitherto been termed the New East Asian Order or East Asian Stability Bloc, and encompassing broadly the southern regions of the Dutch East Indies and French Indochina, with Japan, Manchukuo, and China constituting part of that sphere.[17]

Apparently building upon the SRA-inspired Konoe policies vis-à-vis China, the statement emphasized the ideological continuity upholding Japan's advance into Southeast Asia, where colonial possessions appeared to lay open for the Japanese due to the war in Europe's colonial metropoles. It signified that the government was now intent on expanding its geographic scope of "Asia" beyond the old Sinic cultural sphere into more diverse realms of Southeast Asia, where there were natural resources that would enable Japan to continue fighting with China, and possibly with the Soviet Union, or the United States.

That the Japanese government should pronounce this "Co-Prosperity Sphere" ideology as its official war aim only confirms that Pan-Asianism grew to be a point upon which various interests could, however tenuously, converge. The prospect for diplomatic settlements that Tōgō wished for proved elusive because of the government's interpretation of the Hull Note of November 26 as an effective ultimatum, as a direct result of a specific deadline of Japan's own making. Even at this final stage, however, there was no true consensus. Imperial Adviser Wakatsuki, along with Yonai Mitsumasa and Okada Keisuke, was openly skeptical and so voiced his concern, in front of the emperor on November 28. Another opposition came from Admiral Yamamoto Isoroku, the tactical planner of the Pearl Harbor operation. Thus even though there existed no firm consensus about the war's absolute inevitability, Pan-Asianism became a reason for war. This is not to assert categorically, without being able to demonstrate a cause-and-effect mechanism, that Japan's leaders in fact believed in Pan-Asianism. The catch-all appeal of Pan-Asianism makes it vulnerable to the criticism that it merely became an all-embracing umbrella for everyone, something meaning all things—and nothing—to all people. There is some merit in the criticism that it might have been simply convenient for those who tried to maximize their strategic perspectives to pay homage to Pan-Asianism, without truly subscribing to it. Still, even those limitations do not diminish the actual and functional importance of Pan-Asianism in Japan's declaration of war on the West.

In order to grasp the true meaning of Japan's war aims, however, one must look further into how Pan-Asianism adapted to actual circumstances. To that end, the discussion will now turn to the second paradox introduced at the beginning—namely, that Japan's war with the West was welcomed by those who had thus far been skeptical of Japan's continuing military engagement on the Asian continent. The examination of a positive, broad-based response to Pearl Harbor, spearheaded by Japan's literati, becomes ever more important, as it demonstrates how Pan-Asianism managed to gain a firm grip on the warring country's collective imagination, leading the Empire to fight its Pan-Asianist crusade with a heroic, albeit false, sense of conviction and self-sacrifice.

II. The War of "World Historical Significance"

The Referents and the Changing Environment

We have already seen that a certain group and generation of scholars, mostly social scientists, played a prominent role in the formulation of Japan's foreign policy in the years preceding Pearl Harbor, in their privileged function as policy advisers to Konoe. The present discussion requires us to stretch our frame of reference. Those discussed here include unlikely supporters of war, whom Tagore had earlier identified as "artistic and thinking spirits,"[18] people previously thought to have been genuinely beholden to humanistic values, who would presumably have been most inclined to embrace the peace-loving, anti-militarist Teaist vision of Pan-Asianism.

Why then were so many people of letters, including those who had been unconvinced of the legitimacy of Japan's war in China, able to welcome Japan's entry into an even more colossal battle? Before dealing with that question, however, I must specifically mention the role of certain intellectuals in promoting Japan's Pan-Asianist war aims. Those who participated in a series of famous roundtable discussions held between

November 1941 and November 1942, proudly reiterated Japan's war in terms of "world history." They were all Kyoto Imperial University-trained disciples of Nishida Kitarō—namely, Kōsaka Masaaki, Suzuki Naritaka, Takayama Iwao, and Nishitani Keiji. It is probably true that they played an important part in setting the general tone of post–Pearl Harbor philosophical discourse. In a prologue to the March 1942 compilation volume of their roundtable discussions for the journal *Chūō Kōron* (Central Forum), they claimed:

> The outbreak of the Greater East Asia War coincided with the final stages of the editing process [of the first roundtable discussion article]. We were moved and became determined beyond words, as our speculations began to be validated by the awesome realizations of world history.[19]

In suggesting the "world historical significance" of Japan's war with the West, however, those scholars were not asserting the most inventive thesis. Rather, the concepts they often employed, such as Japan's "world historical position" in international politics, and the "moral energy" behind Japan's ability to counter the West, can be traced back to the writings of the SRA participants already examined earlier, most notably those of Miki Kiyoshi, another philosopher often identified with the so-called Kyoto School of philosophers under Nishida's influence.[20] Unlike Miki, working out a *dakaisaku* of a deadlock situation was not at all the roundtable philosophers' goal. Those scholars, and others who proclaimed Japan's prominent role in altering the course of world history after Pearl Harbor, merely echoed and repeated the already pervasive excitement shared by most Japanese. The intellectual endorsement not only gave credibility to Japan's proclaimed war aims but rendered a clear shape to the public euphoria following the spectacular success of Japan's naval operation.

In this sense, those philosophers, or similarly, the jingoistic *Romanha* (Romantic School) writers such as Kamei Katsuichirō, Yasuda Yojūrō, and Asami Akira, who publicized Okakura's "Asia is One" dictum at the height of the Pacific War, should not be regarded as the most influential agents in Japan's Pan-Asianist discourse. By this point of the game, they merely helped create a fertile ground in which ensuing war mobilization and support could readily take root. Thus the question of the role played by intellectuals is fundamentally and qualitatively different from their role in the previous years.

The overwhelming support of Japan's war with the West among literati, even including those humanists and artists who had previously held anti-war dispositions, was immediately palpable in the wake of the successful Pacific operation. Japan's glowing military record against the United States and its allies seemed to prove that Meishuron was not merely a hypothesis, but a proven fact. Of course, Japan was now fighting a very different enemy. The slippery justifications for its military conflict in China rested in the self-contradictory nature of fighting a Pan-Asianist war against fellow Asians. The consequentialist strand of moral philosophy, with which the Japanese government explained its involvement in China as justifiable in light of the war's intended positive consequences—for example, the salvation of Asia from Western imperialism and the installation of Japan as a *meishu* for the creation of a new Asian order—had innate contradictions. But that was all different now. The Fifteen Years' War had finally been turned into a "just" and "holy" war, precisely because Japan had directly attacked a Western power.

To reverse the argument, it took an event of Pearl Harbor's magnitude for Meishuron Pan-Asianism to become Japan's wartime ideology with a proper national mandate. As soon as it gained the seal of approval from the erstwhile skeptics and critics of Japan's war, the ideology held the most cogent case for Japan's further military engagement. And the mandate would prove strong enough to sustain a disadvantageous war for an additional four years in spite of the Empire's precipitous strategic decline that soon followed its initial combat successes.

The Philosophy of December 8

The pervasive sense of national celebration over Japan's victory at Pearl Harbor gave rise to a body of ideas that came to be known as the Philosophy of December 8 (*Jūnigatsu Yōka no Shisō*: 8, rather than 7, accounting for the time difference with the United States) in Japanese intellectual history. The term encapsulates the extraordinarily all-consuming and affirmative alteration of intellectual attitudes toward Japan's war after that date. Almost overnight, a crisis of confidence that had plagued Japan's political, social, and economic life for so many years was replaced by an outburst of confidence and enthusiasm. One of the most, if not the most, celebrated *tanka* poets of the twentieth century, Saitō Mokichi (1882–1953), tersely expressed the essence of the Philosophy of December 8 in a serial verse written shortly after hearing the Imperial Proclamation of War. It read:

The voice that told us that the war began was at
  once a roar of victory.
This nation, which endured the raging and engulfing
  fire with patience and perseverance,
Now cannot be kept from doing battle. So watch
  those selfish and smug nations.
By whatever means possible, the conceited, great,
  senile nations shall be shot down.
Like whirling, rough waves and a shooting fireball,
  the battle advances.
Oh, the fire portending the inevitable rise of new history,
With freshness, the emotional dregs at the bottom of
  my heart have been eliminated completely.
In a fleeting moment, the battle met with a victorious
  cry, shaking the earth's foundation.
"The Greater East Asia Way." Pay attention and feel
  the sound of these Japanese words!
In facing such a momentous occasion, I am
  overwhelmed with tears and filled with high spirits.[21]

The poet then went on to record in his diary: "The red blood of my old age is now bursting with life" because "the formidable imperial forces spectacularly attacked Hawai'i!!"[22] On the night of December 9, Saitō continued with his excited tone in an article for his highly respected literary coterie magazine *Araragi*. His assessment of the situation now included the divine spirit of the Japanese nation and more explicit remarks, indicative of his view of the war as a racial struggle. It read:

[The opening of war] was a natural course of events, an act carried out under the protection of an omnipotent god. How on earth can they have the audacity to demand the retreat of the whole of the Imperial Army, to refuse to recognize the Nationalist [Wang Jingwei] government in Nanjing, and to order us to abandon the Triple Alliance with Germany and Italy? Such extremely ill-mannered, impudent behavior against this Imperial Nation governed by the Emperor-God should not be taken lightly. . . . Stop saying such decadent, self-indulgent things as "Love thy enemy." . . . [W]e must destroy those animal-like, red-headed, blue-eyed, spineless nations.[23]

In many respects, Saitō's outpouring of emotions was a faithful reflection of the vindicated national pride of a Japanese, and an Asian, demonstrating that the Philosophy of December 8 signified a momentous occasion in which Japan became positively convinced of its *meishu* role. Saitō had been a devotee of the imperial institution before December 8, 1941. Racism encountered in his medical student days in late nineteenth-century Austria and Germany and during his travels in Europe as a young man may have reconfirmed his stubborn Japanese chauvinism long before the start of the Fifteen Years' War. In that sense, Saitō's excitement indeed appears to have been a "natural course."

Another symbolic victory against another enemy, the fall of what the British had called the "impregnable fortress" of Singapore, added to that already pervasive sense of excitement. The novelist Hino Ashihei (1907–60) wrote of the event on February 16, 1942: "Like dispersing debris, with an ear-splitting roar, we heard the old nation of Britain collapse. From the invading nation once proud of its never-setting sun, we have reclaimed the sun. The sky of East Asia has been cleared once and for all."[24] Hino had earlier provided stimuli to Japan's war mobilization with a series of award-winning and best-selling novels based on his combat experiences in China, which still retained a remarkable degree of his multifaceted humanist perspectives, and put forward a nuanced indictment of the cruelty of war.

In this instance, the powerful observation made by Richard Rorty that it is often literature, not philosophy, which helps a society navigate historical contingencies by appealing to the notion of human solidarity, still rings true.[25] Intellectual support for the official war aims of the Empire, from such popular literary figures as Saitō and Hino, did more to touch the emotional chord of the nation and to make people pay attention to the official Pan-Asianist slogans than any governmental proclamations or roundtable discussions of the Kyoto School philosophers, could have done.

Like Hino, many of the intellectuals associated with the Philosophy of December 8 immediately voiced their optimistic conviction that Japan would be the guiding light and leading force in Asia's salvation, which would open a new chapter of world history. The *Shirakabaha* (White Birch Group) writers, whose association with the literary journal *Shirakaba* was synonymous with aristocratic privilege and youthful idealism, proved no exception to this rule. Writers such as Mushanokōji Saneatsu (1885–1976) and Shiga Naoya (1883–1971), whose aristocratic backgrounds and elite education had much in common with those of Konoe's social circle, genuinely lamented Japan's military presence in China. Like Inukai Ken, a *Shirakabaha* writer and Konoe's aide, who deplored Japan's China War and actively sought to end it, Nagayo Yoshirō (1888–1961) had been dismayed about the development of Japan's expansionist program previously. But he proudly spoke of his renewed sense of commitment to Japan's war after the event of December 8. He wrote:

> I had never been able to conceive of our welcoming such a happy, thrilling, and delightful day. The doldrums that have been hanging over our heads for the past few months, nay, for the past twelve years, have been dispersed like clouds and disappeared like mist by the Imperial Proclamation of December 8.[26]

On the question of such a dramatic turn and the unqualified embrace of Pan-Asianism by many of Japan's liberal-minded literary figures, Yoshimoto Takaaki (1924–2012), whose renown as one of the most provocative postwar thinkers preceded that of being the father of the Generation-X author Yoshimoto Banana, was confronted in a 1999 interview by the journalist Tajika Nobukazu. Tajika found it extremely difficult to grasp that the Japanese nation at large, including its leftists, could believe in the military government's grandiose Pan-Asianist proclamations. Yoshimoto responded:

> At that time, many Japanese, myself included, believed in them at face value. In retrospect, such [Pan-Asianist] slogans are looked upon with disdain and people would say it was mad to have thought that the rest of the world would understand. . . . But as ideals, in principle, the "construction of the Greater East Asia Co-Prosperity Sphere" and "the liberation of East Asia" were not inherently evil notions.[27]

Japan's Pan-Asianist war aims, as resonated in the writings of the Philosophy of December 8, managed to transcend generations, classes, and political affiliations. Almost instantaneously, the commencement of Japan's Pacific operation transformed a narrow and limited claim of Japan's Pan-Asianist mission in China into a nation-wide euphoria and a willing endorsement of the "Co-Prosperity Sphere" ideology. December 8 enabled such a devoted patriot as Saitō Mokichi to reconfirm his allegiance to Japan's cause, while a humanist such as Hino Ashihei, a sophisticated liberal like Nagayo Yoshirō, not to mention an impressionable and extremely intelligent university student like Yoshimoto Takaaki—all of whom were sensitive men and articulate thinkers—became convinced of the legitimacy of Japan's preemptive war against the West.

However, none of the post–December 8 transformations was as dramatic, from an ideological standpoint, as the one that came to a China expert, who had been a harsh critic of Japan's China War. Indeed, the case of Takeuchi Yoshimi (1910–77) provides a powerful example of someone who claimed to be so vehemently opposed to Japan's military engagements in China becoming entranced by Japan's war entry. In the January 1942 issue of the journal *Chūgoku Bungaku* (Chinese Literature), the thirty-one-year-old scholar of Chinese explained his psychological transformation in an article entitled "The Greater East Asia War and our Determination—Commitment Statement." The declaration read:

History was made. The world was changed in one night.
We saw it with our own eyes.
Trembling with deep emotions, we watched intently
  where one ray of light had led.
We felt a sudden fit of something that cannot quite be
  named springing up in our heart.
On December 8, on the day when the great imperial
  proclamation of the war's start took place, the Japanese
  nation was ignited by one determination. . . .
Who would have imagined that things would turn out
  the way they did?
"War should be avoided." Until the very last minute, we believed so.
"War is miserable." This was the only thing that came to our mind.
But it was this kind of reasoning that turned out to be miserable. . . .
To be honest, we were somewhat reluctant to accept the China
  Incident. Suspicions tormented us.
We loved China, and in turn, loving China
  gave meaning to our lives.
China grew, and we grew too. And surely
  we had faith in that growth.
But with the China Incident happening, this
  conviction was shattered and torn into pieces . . . we ignored the
  purpose of a holy war.
We doubted that Japan, hiding behind the beautiful name of
  "Founding of East Asia," would bully the weak, until this very
  moment.
Our Japan was not afraid of the strong after all. The act
  of this frosty autumn proves that . . .
It is now our determination to labor, without stint, for the true goal
  of creating a new order in East Asia and of liberating all nations.

> In order to liberate East Asia to the new world order, from today on, we must in our own capacities do our best. We shall study China, cooperate with the just liberators of China, and enlighten the Japanese nation about the true China.[28]

In no time, Takeuchi came to relish the term "overcoming modernity" (*Kindai no Chōkoku*) as a variation on the thesis of Meishuron Pan-Asianism.[29] In his understanding, the definition of modernity heavily depended on the adversarial position of the West, and especially the United States, whose way of life Takeuchi and his colleagues often pejoratively termed "Americanism" (*Amerikanizumu*).[30] By virtue of fighting the very country that embodied the essence of modernity, the converts of December 8 could easily maintain Japan's alliance with other more purportedly "spiritual" revisionist powers such as Germany and Italy. To be sure, as in the case of the privy councilor Hara, there was a sense of mistrust of any "white" nation in certain quarters. This, in turn, buttressed Japan's claim to the superiority of its national spirit and the *meishu* prerogative to present the rest of Asia with the right developmental model in "overcoming modernity." Japan was to be the *ideal-typus*, so to speak, for all other Asian nations to aspire to. For this reason, the Japanese way should prevail in Asia, even with force if necessary.

Hence December 8 released even those who had been most skeptical of Japan's policy from their doubts. Moreover, this release pushed them energetically in the opposite direction, turning them from critics into willing servants of power. Capturing the *Zeitgeist* of December 8, the literary critic of Anglo-American literature Honda Akira conveyed his overwhelming sense of relief in the following:

> The proclamation of war against the United States and Britain has cleared up my mind. Thanks to it, the meaning of a "holy war" has become clear, with the war aims simplified and clarified; there is a renewed sense of courage to go about carrying out all the business smoothly.[31]

In light of such an outburst of support, expressed after December 8, 1941, one is tempted to accept the controversial "clash of civilizations" thesis, albeit in a very qualified sense.[32] The emotive vocabulary that accompanied the terrorist act of September 11, 2001, bears some striking similarities with the Philosophy of December 8. The obvious differences between the two cases notwithstanding, the two events exhibit the same qualities of universal ambitions and skewed senses of world history. Japan's Pan-Asianist ambition by late 1941 was to create an Asian economic and cultural bloc led by Japan. The Pan-Islamist claim of the al-Qaeda terrorists parallels Japan's ambition to lead Asian prosperity. The Pan-Islamists see themselves as the *meishu* in the elusive, transnational, trans-state Islamic union, irrespective of the actual wishes of the parties to be included in such a union. In addition, they are both ideologies, bred by a sense of humiliation and exclusion, pitting their traditional ways, real or imagined, against the hateful images of the West, even though their own methods of countering the West primarily depend on Western technologies.

But no matter how hard they try to legitimize their lopsided battles with the United States, or the West, or with Americanism, neither the Pan-Asianist nor the Pan-Islamist agenda manages to deliver convincing justifications for those looking at it from the outside. Precisely on this point, Yoshimoto Takaaki, an untiring interpreter of intellectual responsibility during the war, suggested in the previously noted interview that it was "mad" to think that the "the rest of the world would understand" Japan's wartime Pan-Asianist claims.[33] For those who have not fallen under the spell of those ideologies, or for those devastated by the actions taken in the name of such ideologies, madness indeed seems the only description. While noble in their essential claims of aspiring to a greater union to correct what they see as deplorable injustices of the world, they are both ideologies whose quasi-religious implications are enormously destructive. The proponents of the ideologies destroy the enemy, the self, and even those whom they purport to salvage. They are at once an expression of political failure and a sense of social, cultural, and economic exclusion.

* * *

Pan-Asianism after December 8, 1941, in the minds of many public intellectuals that encompassed a wide spectrum of creative minds, seemed to open up a new opportunity for Japan to fulfill its ambition for a world role at long last. However small, or indeed misguided, it was an opportunity all the same to complete the incomplete nation, to become Asia's liberator, and to preside over the future course of world history. It was thus the ambition and temptation of Pan-Asianism—rather than material considerations, which were at the very heart of the Japanese state's immediate grievances—that made the government's official war aims acceptable and appealing to many and shaped a sense of national solidarity.

A commonplace but reasonable conclusion to be drawn from this important moment in the Fifteen Years' War is that it was utterly short-sighted of those who believed in the "world historical" position of Japan to think of history as malleable. This verdict rings true for both the policymakers and the December 8 literati. In stark contrast to the majority euphoria and optimism, the scholar of ancient Greek philosophy Tanaka Michitarō (1902–85) issued a quiet warning that set him apart from the rest of his colleagues in both the explicitness and perspicacity of his sense of history.[34] He contended, in November 1942, when Takeuchi and others were loudly declaring the importance of "overcoming modernity," that it was foolish to claim to locate "world historical realities" within the "mere context of the past year or two," and to proclaim their opinions as one of "world historical observation."[35] Such an exaggerated sense of self-importance would, Tanaka opined, surely be overturned by "world history itself."[36]

All the same, to feel frustrated with the uneven perspective of "world history," as it existed at that time, was not entirely groundless. The philosopher Watsuji Tetsurō (1889–1960), for instance, who expressed his fundamentally pessimistic view of Japan's possible war with the West in the summer of 1941, still complained that Westerners often "casually use such a phrase as 'the *discovery* of the Pacific' without giving it much thought."[37] In a secret meeting, convoked by Lieutenant-Captain Takagi Sōkichi (1893–1979) a few months prior to Pearl Harbor, under the heading of *Shisō Kondankai* (Philosophical Discussion Group), Watsuji concluded that "Japan must write a history of the world from a Japanese standpoint. Only we the Japanese people have the rare ability to view history from the opposite side of whites."[38]

Reinterpreting the original phrase slightly, the war with the West in which many intelligent people succumbed to the irresistible idea of Japan's countering larger historical tides can be said to be of "world historical significance" indeed. This was so not because Japan was actually able to alter the course of world history. Japan's war with the West was of world historical significance precisely because it showed that even those who attempt to write history cannot be detached from the historical context in which they operate.

It is certainly dangerous to overemphasize the degree to which the Japanese nation became captivated by the slogans of the Pan-Asianist venture, or, to assume that those who formulated the actual policy in the military government truly embraced Pan-Asianism in abstract terms. But it does seem difficult to imagine otherwise because of the moral high ground of the ideology. That Asia needed to be liberated and recognized were, as Yoshimoto has put it, "not inherently evil notions."[39] By the same token, one should not presume that there were no examples of people who refused to embrace the so-called Philosophy of December 8, although, again, such examples appear to be very few.

One of those rare cases was the writer Dazai Osamu (1909–48), who on the day of Pearl Harbor wrote a short story entitled *"Jūnigatsu Yōka"* (December 8).[40] The story takes the form of a diary of a novelist's wife, starting with the passage: "I shall write today's diary with special care. I shall record what sort of a day a housewife of a poor Japanese household passed on December 8, 1941."[41] The housewife's December 8 was filled with what she regarded as more pressing tasks of cooking and taking care of children, regardless of the day's being December 8, 1941. But Dazai's quiet protestations—or perhaps more accurately, indifference—expressed in the character of this housewife, constituted a minority voice in the months after Pearl Harbor.

7
Pan-Asianism in the Co-Prosperity Sphere

Japan's occupation of the "Co-Prosperity Sphere" began on a strategically auspicious note. The speed at which the Japanese Empire grew in the initial stage of its war with the Allied forces was astonishing. Equally impressive was the geographical extent of this rapidly expanding empire. By March 1942, Japan had extended its war theatre 8,100 by 6,250 miles while bringing about 500 million people under its rule.[1] Within a few months of the opening of hostilities, the Empire stretched eastward to the Solomon Islands, westward to Burma, and southward to Timor. This meant that Southeast Asia could now provide Japan with immediate war resources in raw materials and Pacific islands, a cluster of unsinkable aircraft carriers with oil stocks, and military facilities.[2]

From an ideological perspective, Meishuron Pan-Asianism, now palpable in the "Greater East Asia Co-Prosperity Sphere" construct, acted as a catalyst for Japan's comprehensive mobilization. Even those who had hitherto disapproved of Japan's expansionist course could not restrain their enthusiasm in the face of Japan's initial military successes, leading many to participate in the effort to win what they perceived as a titanic struggle, claiming that they were waging a "Greater East Asia War" to liberate Asia from Western domination. At the onset, such a claim appeared well justified as Southeast Asia was suddenly rid of a Western colonial presence that had seemed like a permanent regional fixture only a short time ago. Yet constructing and administering a "sphere of mutual respect and prosperity" quickly proved a task far beyond Japan's capacity. Over the course of the Japanese occupation of Southeast Asia, it became painfully clear that there was a wide gap to be filled between Japan's *meishu* ambition and the realities of its rule.

The nature, extent, and impact of Japan's rule that followed the dramatic beginning differed considerably from place to place, time to time, and group to group.[3] Nonetheless, the most pressing objective for Japan in the newly added territories of the Sphere remained resource acquisition until the very end of the war, barely enabling Japan to continue fighting its lopsided battle. This urgent and persistent strategic impetus behind Japan's Pacific operation leads some to conclude that its wartime Pan-Asianist pronouncements were simply disingenuous rhetoric employed to justify its material motives, which only resulted in economic, physical, and emotional hardships for the local populations. For example, Grant Goodman characterizes Japan's Southeast Asian venture as not only an imitation, but also an aggravation of Western-style colonialism, stating that the Japanese "'out-colonialed' the colonials from whom they were supposedly freeing the colonized."[4]

Certainly, such an observation is useful insofar as it draws attention to the actual consequences of Japanese conceit, arrogance, ill-preparedness, and cruelty, which were all undeniably part of their administration. Stories of Japanese atrocities and recklessness abound. The Bataan Death March of April 1942 and the Thai-Burma Railway immediately come to mind. The former was a forced days-long march in which American and Filipino POWs were led by ill-equipped Japanese to the internment camps. The staggering number of deaths, said to be around more than one in ten of the 76,000 captured, was caused by violence, starvation, sickness, and exhaustion. The construction of the Thai-Burma Railway resulted in half of the 200,000 conscripted Asian laborers and nearly one-third of the Allied POWs perishing. It would be very wrong indeed to overlook the brutal and immoral side of Japanese programs.

Even so, to compare Japan's wartime occupation to Western colonialism, which lasted so much longer, by the standard of who was more "colonial," as if it were a competition in exploitation, seems to miss the point. Such a sweeping statement also presents a danger of oversimplifying a rather powerful nonmaterial drive that existed behind Japan's war that made its administration of the "Co-Prosperity Sphere" markedly different—though neither more nor less "colonial"—from earlier European examples. Japan's embrace of Meishuron Pan-Asianism was what made the final stages of the Fifteen Years' War so uniquely and utterly hypocritical, confusing, devastating, and destructive, for both the rulers and the ruled precisely because of its seeming potential and promises. As Japan sought to

"Japanize" the population it ruled, the self-proclaimed *meishu* of Asia turned Okakura's earlier "Asia is One" dictum into "Asia is Japan," giving rise to problems of much greater social, cultural, and historical implications than that which mere wartime or colonial exploitation of resources would have presented.

That said, Japan's occupation of Southeast Asia cannot be generalized, and it is impossible to provide a comprehensive and comparative account of those different experiences in this space. However, an important argument must be made that there existed a certain ideological consistency in Japan's Co-Prosperity Sphere. The pervasive conviction that Japan served as the preordained leader of Pan-Asian union and that it could remake the societies in the likeness of Japan lay at the very basis of many of its policies. Much like the case of Manchukuo mobilization, albeit on a more extensive scale, Japan's Pan-Asianism was not a vacuous ideology claiming to provide an *ex post facto* explanation for its expansionism, but rather an integral part of the very active force behind its expansionism. That is why Japan's expeditious acquisition of territories had resonance and consequences well beyond material or strategic considerations.

To be sure, the assumptions of Meishuron were heavily racial, and even racist in character, as it presupposed Japanese superiority over other Asians. And the problem of analysis is bound to occur when one tries to distinguish Japanese behavior, conceivably based on idealism, from pure racism. For instance, even the common Japanese practice of slapping the occupied peoples, depending on who does it for what reason, can be regarded as an act either of gratuitous favor (with reformative implications that "they too could be like us, so we need to treat them like any other junior or lower-ranking Japanese") or of contemptuous disregard (with the assumption that "they would never be like us, and they will continue to get slapped"). There are also well-reported instances of Western POWs being physically abused in front of other Asians to demonstrate the impotence of former colonial masters. Likewise, Chinese in Southeast Asia were often treated with special brutality, partly because they resisted Japanese domination, but also because Japanese feelings toward the Chinese included inferiority complexes fundamentally rooted in their awe of Sinic civilization, which did not exist vis-à-vis Southeast Asians. In sum, the slapping of subject peoples tended to be seen as part of Japanization, whatever the real personal motives. The only way of overcoming such blurring of the line demarcating the behavior of

Pan-Asianist idealists and nonidealists is by delving into the motives of individuals behind certain actions.

With that pitfall in mind, the bulk of this chapter will revolve around Japan's cultural policies in what now constitutes Southeast Asia, and especially Singapore and Malaya, where many literati recruits were based and where the most rigorous Japanization programs were carried out in the name of Pan-Asianism. This focus is not meant in any way to belittle the impact of Japanese military administration on other areas of the "Co-Prosperity Sphere," including Taiwan, Korea, Manchuria, and the Pacific islands. It is hoped that the range of examples drawn in this chapter will point to some larger truths about the recurrent symptoms and failings of Japan's Pan-Asianism as translated into practice.

I. Cultural Policies in Southeast Asia

Basic Features of Japan's Military Administration

In anticipation of Japan's conquest of Southeast Asia, the Liaison Conference of November 20, 1941 outlined Japan's occupation goals in "The Outlines of the Administration of Southern Occupation."[5] It set forth three basic objectives for a Japanese move into Southeast Asia. They were the "restoration and maintenance of law and order," "acquisition of resources vital to Japan's war effort," and "establishment of self-sufficiency of the needs of the occupied territories and the area armies."[6] Those were all pressing and practical goals without any mention of more ideological aspects of Japan's endeavor.

On top of securing resources, there was another logistical difficulty to be overcome: when it came to dividing up the region for military administration, the old tensions of Army-Navy rivalry emerged. "The Central Army/Navy Agreement on the Execution of the Military Administration of the Occupied Territories," issued on November 26, 1941, managed to clarify the boundaries of jurisdiction between the two authorities, however.[7] Accordingly, the Army became responsible for administering the Philippines, Malaya, Sumatra, Java, British Borneo, Burma, and Hong Kong while the Navy took over the Celebes, the Moluccas, the Lesser Sunda Islands, New Guinea, the Bismarck Islands, Guam, and Dutch Borneo.

Having established the basis of military administration and completed the acquisition of Southeast Asian territories, Japan now took to devising the longer-term task of establishing the "Co-Prosperity Sphere." Independently but similarly, the Army and the Navy formulated their plans.[8] Inherent in both Army and Navy schemes was the notion that the most important goals for Japan rested on procurement of resources, such as oil, in the short run, while ultimately constructing a self-sufficient economic bloc of the "Greater East Asia Co-Prosperity Sphere" in the long run. In Tokyo, on January 21, 1942, Prime Minister Tōjō made a statement that reflected such importance of Southeast Asia, declaring that "the establishment of the Greater East Asia Co-Prosperity Sphere originates in the great spirit of nation-building, with every nation and every race of Greater East Asia in its respective place and with moral principles of the Empire resting at the core."[9]

In February 1942, Tokyo founded the "Greater East Asia Department" (Dai Tōakyoku), which later became the "Greater East Asia Ministry" (Dai Tōashō), in order to coordinate Japan's relations within the Sphere. In practice, the Imperial General Headquarters or Staff Officers in the occupation governments in the field conceived policies on an improvisational basis.[10] Thus the Japanese military itself operated neither as a monolithic policymaking organ, nor as an effective practitioner of Pan-Asianist programs.[11] Nonetheless, the founding of the Ministry solely dedicated to the affairs of Greater East Asia did suggest Japan's desire to follow through with a large-scale reorganization of the occupied countries.

Critically, the former Ambassador to the United States, Viscount Ishii Kikujirō, and Foreign Minister Tōgō, among others, opposed the establishment of such a ministry on grounds that the diplomatic rights of the Foreign Ministry would be compromised. The fact that the military prevailed showed that the Japanese government no longer saw a place for diplomacy in any ordinary or traditional sense within the "Co-Prosperity Sphere." That kind of insistence, reinforced by the more pervasive belief in Japan's leadership role, directly translated into what the government hoped would be programs of radical reform to create a shared political culture after the Japanese model that would render old-style diplomacy superfluous.

Japan's Cultural Policies

One of the most unusual features of Japan's cultural programs in Southeast Asia was the scale of their literati (*bunkajin*) participation. Immediately following the outbreak of the war in the Pacific, the leftist critic Nakajima Kenzō started recruiting intellectuals for the Army's Propaganda Unit.[12] About 150 were enlisted, going on to serve in the

Twenty-fifth Army in Malaya, Singapore, and some other parts of the Indonesian archipelago. The recruits included prominent writers, poets, painters, photographers, filmmakers, actors, and the like for the implementation of cultural policies throughout the Sphere. Among them were the most illustrious *bunkajin* of the time, such as the writers Ibuse Masuji, Takami Jun, Ozaki Shirō, the critic Ōya Sōichi, the painter Miyamoto Saburō, and the cartoonist Yokoyama Ryūichi.

Many different types of cultural programs were carried out in different areas. Nonetheless, the ultimate objective set forth for those recruits was a uniform one of disseminating the following basic ideas: (1) that Japan had been compelled to start the war for the establishment of peace and order in East Asia; (2) that Japan's leadership in this new order would benefit all the occupied societies in the Sphere; and (3) that Japan's enemies did not even try to understand Japan's true intentions and continued to harass it.[13]

Originally, Tokyo announced that "the occupation governments should carefully devise their cultural policy so as not to interfere with indigenous religions and customs of the South Seas."[14] More often than not, however, many field governments opted to pursue the policy of Japanization of the region through an indoctrination program known as *Kōminka Kyōiku* (Education for Transforming Non-Japanese into Japan's Imperial Subjects) at the expense of indigenous cultures and budding local nationalisms. This program to make the occupied peoples more Japanese was especially pronounced in Singapore and Malaya, where the Japanese rulers deemed indigenous cultures to be made up of primordial, tribal kinships, or else of transient populations dedicated to commercial activities developed under British colonial rule, without any sign of national consciousness or awareness of either a "Singaporean" or "Malayan" national identity.

Since such people under colonial rule had been incapacitated by Western exploitation and lacked a respectable culture of their own, so the Japanization logic went, they needed to be taught Japanese moral principles or *seishin* (spirit). By homogenizing the differences of the locals, the Japanization project would eliminate any basis for conflicts among different Asian groups to start with. Homogenization in turn meant infusing all Asian citizens of the Sphere with the values and culture of the Japanese Empire, making its occupation, in the eyes of their proponents, fundamentally different from and superior to the colonialism of Western empires.

One of the key objectives that accompanied this bold education scheme was the establishment of the Japanese language as the *lingua franca* of the Sphere. The Twenty-fifth Army in Singapore and Malaya repeatedly stressed, in its monthly journal *Senji Geppō* (Wartime Monthly), that "[t]he total dissemination of the Japanese language and the elimination of the national languages of the enemies (*tekisei kokugo*) . . . are declared to be the most important policies for the occupied regions."[15] The importance of carrying out such cultural programs, concomitantly with military operations, was a sentiment embraced not exclusively by Japan's military leaders, but also by some intellectuals who actually devised those policies. The use of the Japanese language was deemed critical, since many, embracing the Herderian notion of language in nationalism, believed that understanding of Japanese culture could become complete only once the language of the superior nation had been mastered.

One of the most important figures of twentieth-century Japanese literature, the novelist Ibuse Masuji (1898–1993), was a primary advocate for the Twenty-fifth Army's language policy. Writing under the Indian pseudonym of Prakas in English, he reiterated in his *Syonan Times* columns that if one learned to speak Japanese, one would start thinking like the Japanese. Following this line of reasoning, an editorial in *The Syonan Times* announced:

> One of the first considerations in the construction of mutual well being [*sic*] and prosperity in Asia is that of introducing a common language. The suggestion therefore that the language of Nippon becomes the *lingua franca* of Malaya while startling at first becomes an obvious necessity. . . . The substitution of Nipponese for English as the lingua franca in Malaya is but the natural recognition of a nation which has stood up for things Asia [*sic*] and which is now in the process of saving Asians from continuing to be the victims of the British strategy to squeeze the wealth and culture of Asians. . . . As a preliminary step it is suggested that shop signs and street names be substituted by Nipponese signs and names as a material indication that Malaya is included in the new order of things.[16]

Cynics would hold that Ibuse was simply going along with the official line of policy in articulating the virtue of the imperial institution and Japanese culture. However, his distaste of the military and qualms about having to cooperate with the occupation government, expressed in such novels as *Hana no Machi* (Town of Flowers), written in 1943, were well-known and unwavering throughout the war.[17] Also in his postwar auto-biographical essay, he reminisced how he frequented the office of Shinozaki Mamoru, a sympathetic city government official, "to complain how much I hated to be in military service."[18] His feelings about the Japanization program were, however, something else. He was in fact unapologetic about his commitment to the promotion of Japanization, leading him to say that the experience of giving lectures on Japanese history to Malay students made his "life worth living."[19]

In practical terms, Ibuse made use of his creative energy in devising slogans, commemorating the opening of Japanese language schools for adults and children in Singapore. The Ibuse-coined slogan of *"Manabe! T[s]ukae! Nippon-go"* (Learn! Use! Japanese) appeared in the newspapers every day of the "Japanese Week" in June 1942. The starting letters of the following, longer version of the catch phrases roughly correspond to the shorter version, revealing his painstaking efforts:

Manabe Tukae Nippon-go [Learn, Use, Japanese]
All you who live in Syonan-to [Singapore]
Now you will see in every page
Are words in this language
Beautiful, graceful, refined.
The words so near at hand
Unfold the beauties of the island
Kind spirit of Nippon!
A culture that must win
Enshrined in heart of Nippon-zin [Japanese people]
Now power will give to you
Instruction in our Nippon-go
Portal to a higher mind
Obey the call, I ask once more
Nippon-go o tukaimashyo [Let's use Japanese]!
Go study then and persevere
Onto the goal which is so near.[20]

In addition, the military administration ordered the Propaganda Unit to issue more than 500,000 leaflets and posters with the slogan printed in English, Chinese, and Malay and distributed them all over Singapore and Malaya.[21] Similar efforts followed in Burma and Indonesia.

On April 29, 1942, in Singapore, where many prominent recruits of the Twenty-fifth Army assembled, the Imperial Birthday was celebrated. Although schools had reopened only recently, local teachers under the guidance of the Propaganda Unit made thousands of schoolchildren march to the city center, carrying Japanese national flags of the rising sun and wishing the longevity of Emperor Hirohito.[22] This ceremonial expression of allegiance to the Empire moved Lieutenant-General Yamashita, the Tiger of Malaya, to tears, as he is said to have observed to his secretary: "They are just like Japanese children! Yes, they are the same. Really the same."[23]

There was nothing spontaneous about the celebration, however. Yamashita's unit had made painstaking preparations for the smooth proceeding of this ceremony, providing the military officers and Japanese civilians alike with meticulously drafted manuals replete with references to Meishuron Pan-Asianism and the glory of the Japanese emperor. For instance, the manual stated that until the day before the actual birthday, "the importance of the construction of East Asia, along with the importance of the Emperor's birthday, shall be propagated through newspapers, loudspeakers, and various other available media."[24] The actual ceremony, in addition to those marches made by the school children, included a worship ritual in the direction of the Imperial Palace in Tokyo, "a moment of silence to commit oneself to the construction of the East Asian Co-Prosperity Sphere," followed by the "distribution of free meals to the poor," and the "showing of films informing the local populations of Japanese position."[25]

In the end, such an all-out effort, carried out with a curious blend of arrogance and self-consciousness as the guardian of social welfare, proved ineffective. As far as the Japanese language program was concerned, it was an utter failure. The newspaper *Syonan Times* remained the most important medium of communication for the Japanese military administration in Singapore and Malaya until the very end of the occupation. Even though it was renamed *Syonan Shinbun*, it continued to be written in English, the language of the enemy banned with a vengeance in Japan itself. Although the Japanese rulers sporadically intimated their intention of banning the use of English altogether, a voice of protest raised by officials on the grounds of impracticability was always enough to abandon such a drastic measure. Enrollment in Japanese language courses declined after initial enthusiasm waned.

Ōmori Matsuyo, one of the two personal secretaries for Marquis Tokugawa Yoshichika, whose role as a special adviser to the Twenty-fifth Army will be examined later, spoke of the lack of interest in the Japanese language among the local population. In her postwar recollection, she regarded her Singapore years as *"kūhaku no jidai"* or an "era of utter emptiness," represented by the monotony of having to translate British colonial policy documents, with nothing else worth remembering.[26] She nonetheless vividly remembered the embarrassment of having to lecture to only a handful of Malay students taking Japanese.

Largely, the lack of enthusiasm for learning Japanese was thought to be the result of the difficulty of the language itself and the lack of preparation for teaching it effectively. The need to revise language textbooks was recurrently addressed as an urgent matter for the administration in the *Senji Geppō* articles, and the problem remained a sore point until the end. Similar problems surfaced across the occupied territories. In Indonesia, Japanese and Bahasa Indonesia replaced Dutch and English in elementary school curricula. But the ineffectiveness of the language program led the administration to acknowledge its failure and to revise the textbook entirely in 1944. The more remarkable legacy of Japan's language program was seen not in the propagation of Japanese but in the proliferation of Bahasa Indonesia, which eventually became the common language and the powerful unifying force behind the independence movement of multilingual, multiethnic Indonesia.

In addition to the technical difficulties of teaching Japanese and of the language itself, the Japanese style of teaching struck the local students as extremely spartan. Japanese instructors emphasized that Japanization would transform the local population into good citizens, who would then be able to "comprehend the supernatural will of the Japanese Emperor."[27] Accordingly, face-slapping was employed to discipline the students as part of character-building efforts. But corporal punishment only shocked and antagonized the locals. Like the effort to spread Japanese, Emperor Worship, which was the ultimate goal of the *Kōminka Kyōiku* program predicated upon the tenets of Meishuron Pan-Asianism, carried insufficient appeal to take root in the Sphere. Most locals did not believe in the mythology of Amaterasu, the Sun Goddess who was regarded as the ancestress of the Japanese imperial house or in the divinity of the emperor.

In a series of important interviews conducted by the historian Akashi Yōji in the mid-1970s, the local elite youth, such as graduates of Japanese-run military training schools, who were the supposed beneficiaries of Japanese cultural programs, explained their uneasy attitudes toward Emperorism. One graduate, who had also received a British education at Raffles College before the war, contemptuously dismissed Japanese instructors as people who simply "did not seem to understand that many cadets were degree holders of such higher institutions of learning as Raffles and King Edward VII Medical College, the highest educational establishments in British Malaya."[28] A similarly skeptical view was voiced by another graduate, who stated flatly that it was quite fine by him that the Japanese worshipped the emperor as the divine *pater familias* of all, but that it was "their business and not mine."[29]

Training Programs

While the military administration's ambition of establishing Japanese as the *lingua franca* of the Sphere had very little overall success, there were notable and critical exceptions. For a more intensive and effective Japanization of Southeast Asian youths, the Japanese occupiers established training schools for the select few. The objective of those training schools was to educate superior intellect in order to "produce future leaders of various peoples of the Eastern Hemisphere."[30]

On May 15, 1942, the Kōa Kunrenjo (Founding of Asia Training School) opened in Singapore. It started with an enrollment of 49 Malays, 19 Chinese, 15 Indians, 2 Eurasians, and 1 Italian, totaling in a class of 86.[31] These students lived together with Japanese instructors to receive a rigid guidance in physical as well as moral discipline. They took intensive courses in Japanese culture and language, specifically designed by Ibuse and his *bunkajin* colleagues to develop their spiritual outlook as citizens of the Japanese Empire. The strict program was modeled on the curriculum of the first-year recruits in the Japanese military system. The morning routine, for instance, included flag-raising ceremonies, a deep bow in the direction of the Imperial Palace in Tokyo, and then Swedish-inspired calisthenics known as *rajio taisō* (radio exercise), broadcast on public radio and television and still performed all over Japan as part of a national health-enhancing scheme.

Strange and difficult though such training must have been for the cadets, it seems reasonable to say that this indoctrination program left a considerable imprint on impressionable minds. In some cases, it worked just as the instructors had wanted. One graduate interviewed by Akashi declared that, after one year of training, all his old habits and ways of thinking had changed and that he learned "never to give up on anything no matter how difficult."[32] Another graduate commented that the training school taught him to be "confident, resilient, and unafraid to take on responsibilities, and especially not to consider the white man as a superior race," making him "proud" to be "an Asian."[33]

The Nantokusei Program

Training in the Japanese spiritual outlook and Asian consciousness were taken one step further in Japan's study abroad program. The Southern Special Students (*Nanpō Tokubetsu Ryūgakusei*, or *Nantokusei* for short) program was a unique achievement, especially in contrast to wartime Japan's many other miscarried cultural efforts. It was Japan's first international educational policy that systematically invited a large number of scholarship students from the occupied areas of the Sphere. Not unlike the U.S. Fulbright Scholarships, the program aspired to foster goodwill toward Japan in future leaders of the Sphere countries. The idea was first proposed by the Greater East Asia Ministry, and executed by International Scholar Friends Association (ISFA), a fringe organization of the Foreign Ministry.[34] The Propaganda Unit explained that the objective of the program was to train capable young men who would think and behave like Japanese, renouncing their blind adoration of the Anglo-American way of life in order to construct a Greater East Asia.[35]

Under the guidelines specified at the Liaison Conference, the respective authority of various regions began the selection process of the program participants in early 1943. According to the recollection of the ISFA Guidance Director Kanazawa Tsutomu, the program upon its conception was called "Education Scheme of the Special Leaders for the Cultural Engineering of the South."[36] But such a blatant-sounding title was soon dropped in favor of the simpler "Southern Special Students." The term "special" was an apt description for the high caliber of this group of young students, who, had it not been for the war, would probably have studied abroad anyway, most likely in the United States or Europe. The first group of 104 came to Japan in 1943 and the second group of 101 in 1944. The students were chosen from various social strata. They included former POWs as well as sons of local notables, such as Mariano Laurel, a son of the renowned politician Jose Laurel of the Philippines.

The majority of those who studied in Japan later became influential figures in postwar Southeast Asia. Like the Kunrenjo graduates, one of the students recalled that he was taught the invaluable *"ganbari seishin"* (never-give-up spirit) while in Japan. When asked by his teacher how much he studied, the student answered, somewhat proudly, that he worked until midnight every day. But the teacher was unimpressed with the answer, retorting that "[i]n order to catch up with the United States, Japan had to stride a few extra steps every time the United States took one . . . you too have to make an extra effort to catch up with the West."[37]

Many former *Nantokusei* attribute their postwar career successes in government and businesses to this *ganbari seishin*. In the case of Tungku Abdullah from Malaya, he summarized the impact of the *Nantokusei* program on his character in the following points: (1) sense of discipline; (2) *ganbari seishin*; (3) dedication to work; (4) respect for the elderly; (5) punctuality; (6) politeness and understanding of others' feelings; (7) love for nation; and (8) an orderly lifestyle.[38] Likewise, Ungku Aziz, a Kōa Training School graduate and the former vice-chancellor of the University of Malaya/Singapore commented on the general impact of the Japanese programs on the postwar careers of the training school graduates and the scholarship students:

> Many Malayans who received the Japanese training at the Kunrenjo and in Japan are very successful. There are hardly any leaders in Malaysia today who were not trained at the Kunrenjo and in Japan and hardly any of those trained by Japanese at the Kunrenjo and in Japan who did not become leaders.[39]

On top of embracing the seemingly exaggerated virtue of self-discipline advocated in Japan's Meishuron Pan-Asianism, the former students also spoke fondly of their everyday life in Japan, recalling a genuine sense of welcome they felt from their Japanese hosts in spite of the pressing war situation. Remarkably, the Filipino Leocadio Diasis, a former prisoner-of-war who fought on the side of the United States and was tortured by the Japanese in a detention camp in the Philippines, was one of the students sent to Japan in 1943. He recalled that it had never occurred to him that he, who experienced the hellish concentration camp, should end up studying in Japan one day.[40] To him, it was indeed an ironic twist of fate. While he maintained conflicting feelings about Japan's war, he made enough friends in Japan to say that "[o]nce I arrived, I came to see an entirely different side of the Japanese from those barbaric Japanese soldiers."[41] Furthermore, at the reception celebrating the signing of an alliance between Japan and Laurel's Philippines on April 22, 1944, Prime Minister Tōjō approached a group of Filipino *Nantokusei* and gave them words of encouragement, leading Diasis to say: "It was a thrilling experience that a man of such great stature should care to speak in so friendly a manner to us, mere students."[42]

II. Politics of the Co-Prosperity Sphere

Outlines of Japan's Sphere Policy

It bears repeating that the relative success of the *Nantokusei* program in cultivating pro-Japanese sentiments was an obvious exception rather than the rule. Neither could such a limited success exonerate Japan's war policy at large. In Malaya, there had already been an indication of strong anti-Japanese sentiments among the Chinese community, as reflected in a large-scale boycott of Japanese goods, long before the Fall of Singapore. Japan's purge of suspected anti-Japanese Chinese elements at the outset of the Singaporean occupation, in which some estimate the casualties to have numbered around 50,000, further intensified Chinese hatred. Over time, the military leaders began to repress even Malay youth groups that had supported Japan, fearing their increasing desire for independence. Also, anti-Japanese sentiments were rampant in the Philippines. Even in Indochina, where hopes for Vietnamese independence were firmly rooted in the long history of Japan's association with Prince Cuong De (1882–1953), who was exiled in Japan, the occupation administration remained ever cautious. The Japanese kept the Vichy French authorities and put them in charge of maintaining civil control, rather than to grant Vietnamese nationalists immediate independence.[43]

In order to ameliorate Japan's precarious position, the Tōjō cabinet decided on "The Outlines for Greater East Asian Policy" at the Imperial Conference on May 31, 1943.[44] The announcement confirmed the need for various nations of Greater East Asia to cooperate toward the goal of winning the war. This in specific terms meant revising Japan's relations with the Wang Jingwei government and granting independence to Burma and the Philippines. In contrast, Malaya, Sumatra, Java, Borneo, and Celebes were officially "designated as the Empire's territories."[45] At the same time, Japan acknowledged the necessity of making "the utmost effort to grasp the popular minds" in those territories.[46] And while "Japan's military occupation would be carried on for the time being," it would allow for "political participation of the locals" depending on the "national level" of sophistication.[47] In order to demonstrate and confirm this renewed Japanese commitment to the construction of the Sphere, the cabinet announced that it would convoke the Greater East Asia Conference in Tokyo.

Between that announcement and the November 1943 Conference in Tokyo, there were some notable changes, at least nominally, in Japan's Pan-Asianist diplomacy. On August 1 and October 14, respectively, Ba Maw's Burma and Jose Laurel's Republic of the Philippines were granted independence. For both countries, this "independence" was a limited concept accorded as a member of the Sphere community, with organizational and military command still very much resting in Japanese hands. Then on October 21, Japan helped Subhas Chandra Bose, a Bengali revolutionary and former president of the Indian National Congress, proclaim the establishment of a Free India government in Singapore.[48] There is some evidence that Bose was concerned about the level of Japanese commitment to his temporary government. One Japanese Foreign Ministry memorandum stated that "Bose advised that if Japan were to take an unclear stance" toward his government, as warranted by Japan's past dealings with Wang's government in China, "the enemy propaganda would exploit it as an indication of Japan's lack of ideological commitment" and also "Indians would become suspicious" of Japan's intentions.[49]

In spite of Bose's worries over their loss of nerve, Japan's leaders were in fact mostly excited about the cause of Indian independence. The anti-British stance of Indian nationalism could further glorify the Japanese victory over what Britain had once regarded as an "impregnable fortress." Moreover, India's aspirations for independence paid homage to Okakura's and Tagore's idea of Eastern spirituality, which formed the basis of Teaist Pan-Asianism, confirming in their minds the elevated status of Indian nationalists over other Asian groups. One proof of a clear Japanese commitment to the Indian nationalist movement was the formation of an intelligence unit known as "F Kikan" (F Agency).[50] The unit was founded shortly before the outbreak of the war in the Pacific under Major Fujiwara Iwaichi, as part of the Twenty-fifth Army, to carry out liaison duties among Indian troops stationed in Malaya.[51]

By collaborating with Sikh nationalists in Bangkok, the F Kikan hoped to bridge the Japanese military and Southeast Asia's Indian population.[52] In December 1941, an Indian National Army (INA) was formed under the leadership of Captain Mohan Singh, with the approval of Lieutenant-General Yamashita, on condition that the INA was to be considered an allied force of Japan. After the Japanese had occupied the island of

Singapore, Fujiwara and Singh gathered about 55,000 Indian soldiers, who had fought on the side of the British, at Farrer Park.[53] They encouraged the soldiers to join the INA. The majority (approximately 40,000) who refused to join were interned in prisons, and some of them were presumably executed.[54] With the arrival of Bose, the patriotic fervor among Indian nationalists reached its peak. However, the INA in the end lacked a direct correspondence to the movement back home. Like the Wang Jingwei regime, the INA was regarded as a tool of Japan's propaganda by those who opted not to collaborate.

In terms of political participation promised in Tōjō's declaration, some efforts to include locals in Japan's military administration took place in Java. As an advisory committee, representative bodies such as a house of councilors, a prefectural assembly, and a special city council, were established on October 16, 1943, with Ahmed Sukarno presiding over them. At the same time, Japan's military administrations in Sumatra, Northern Borneo, and Malaya encouraged local populations to take part in their own defense. Young males were urged to enlist in the Volunteer Force (Giyūgun), Volunteer Corps (Giyūtai), or Auxiliary Service (Heiho), all of which had paramilitary functions. But again, both kinds of political and military participation were carried out under Japan's uncontested leadership, falling utterly short of nationalist cravings for true independence and sovereign rights.

The Greater East Asia Conference and the Joint Declaration

Japan's amplified efforts to strengthen its ties with the Sphere communities culminated in the Greater East Asia Conference held on November 5 and 6, 1943, in Tokyo. Representatives such as Wang Jingwei, Jose Laurel, Ba Maw, and Subhas Chandra Bose attended this event, which Tōjō informally and proudly called a "Greater East Asia Family Conference."[55] There, the "Greater East Asian Joint Declaration" was promulgated. It sounded the by-now familiar and impressionistic themes of co-existence and co-prosperity as well as the elevation of Greater East Asian cultures as the joint goals of the Sphere.

Still, there was something remarkable about this statement. It specified the rescue mission of Asia not only as the sole and exclusive cause but also the very aim of Japan's war. Moreover, it self-consciously pitted Japan's claims against those put forth by the Allies in the Atlantic Charter, the joint statement issued on August 14, 1941, by U.S. President Franklin D. Roosevelt and British Prime Minister Winston

Churchill that delineated the common principles for the reconstruction of postwar international community. The Greater East Asia Joint Declaration read:

> To begin with, the fundamental principle for the establishment of world peace lies in the realization that nations recognize their own places in the world to come together and cooperate in the joy of co-prosperity of all countries. Nonetheless, the United States and Britain have oppressed other nation-states and nations, and they have endlessly exploited Greater East Asia in order to fulfill their ambition of enslaving it, ultimately overturning the stability of Greater East Asia. These are the origins of the Greater East Asia War. Every Greater East Asian nation must cooperate [with Japan] and fight the war till the end, liberate Greater East Asia from the yoke of the United States and Britain, complete its survival and self-defense . . . thereby contributing to the establishment of world peace.[56]

Acutely aware of the Atlantic Charter proposed by the Anglo-American leaders, the Joint Declaration highlighted the hypocrisies at the base of Allied war aims couched in the language of "certain common principles in the national policies of their respective countries on which they base their hopes for a better future for the world."[57] The Foreign Minister Shigemitsu Mamoru, the mastermind behind this statement, had to at least match the Allies' claim that they "respect the right of all peoples to choose the form of government under which they will live; and they wish to see sovereign rights and self government restored to those who have been forcibly deprived of them."[58]

Curiously, after the war, those who most earnestly believed in Japan's wartime Pan-Asianist crusade advanced the interpretation that the Joint Declaration was merely a shallow rhetorical device used to serve Japan's exclusive material interest. Again, the critic Yoshimoto Takaaki reflected that it always struck him as sad that those with a good conscience tended to be the biggest believers in the legitimacy of Japan's Pan-Asianist war, thereby ending up suffering the most, because of a guilty conscience for having supported the war so enthusiastically.[59] The Sinologist Takeuchi Yoshimi, who in the wake of Pearl Harbor proclaimed that Japan was "overcoming modernity," was a perfect example. Writing in 1963, Takeuchi evaluates the relationship between Pan-Asianism—which he simply calls "Asianism" (*Ajiashugi*)—and Japan's "Co-Prosperity Sphere" policy as follows:

The ideology of the "Greater East Asia Co-Prosperity Sphere" was, in one sense, an end point for Asianism, but in another sense, it was a departure or a deviation from Asianism. If Asianism were a substantial, historically developed ideology, it might have produced the Sphere ideology, which ceased to be an "ideology" with Japan's defeat. . . . [T]he Sphere ideology was a pseudo-ideology resulting from suppression of all other ideologies, including Asianism. Ideology would not be an ideology if it were not productive. But this "Co-Prosperity" ideology did not produce anything . . . propagandists merely spread an expansive cloak of Sphere ideology in order to suppress all other ideologies. They convened the Greater East Asia Conference and promulgated the "Greater East Asia Joint Declaration," but they entirely lacked substance. . . . [I]t can be understood that the Sphere ideology was the extreme limit of Asianism's de-ideologization.[60]

Takeuchi's categorical rejection of the viability of the "Greater East Asian Co-Prosperity Sphere" as a Pan-Asianist ideology, although understandable in light of its profound shortcomings, is flawed. He fails to explain his definition of ideology in the first place and merely states that ideology is supposed to be a "productive" force. Even more problematic is his denunciation of the ideology on the basis of its historical outcome rather than its historical substance. If ideology were to be understood away from its historical context, as he claims it should, what remains of "other ideologies," such as the original Teaist strand of Pan-Asianism, which he seems to regard so highly? Could ideologies that are detached from history really "produce" anything in social terms? If he truly thinks the "productivity" of ideology is the utmost criterion for a definition of ideology, he should at least attempt to assess the "productive" implications that the Meishuron strand of Pan-Asianism had on Japan's wartime program in Southeast Asia. Moral questions surrounding Japan's actions in the Sphere aside, it seems difficult to deny that Japan's Pan-Asianism did "produce" something in the Sphere in actuality. If so, what exactly did Japan's Pan-Asianism produce?

The Meaning of the "Greater East Asia Co-Prosperity Sphere"

Japan's occupation of Southeast Asia produced some palpable and important legacies. Only those on the extreme right in Japan, who wholeheartedly believe in today's historical "revisionism," could seriously claim that the country's occupation of Southeast Asia brought only positive impact to the region. The Japanese atrocities, including forced labor, sex slavery, rape, biological experiments, and executions of perceived anti-Japanese elements, and more generally, the Sphere's unwanted involvement in the war itself, make it impossible to sustain such an argument. Certainly, the Japanese insistence on their superiority over and racist attitudes toward the conquered populations marked both the cultural and military administrations of the occupied territories. By the same token, to dismiss entirely the aspirations of many Japanese at the time, expressed in the Joint Declaration, would be equally presumptuous, since they were the result of real anger at Western colonialism in Asia.

Most importantly, the Japanese occupation in general gave Southeast Asia a historical uniformity and geographical coherence. Before the war, even the term "Southeast Asia" was not in common usage. The region had been referred to simply as the "South Seas." In addition, fragmented by colonial boundaries, the whole area of what constitutes modern Southeast Asia lacked a sense of historical contiguity. But the collective memory that the Japanese occupation brought to the region accorded "Southeast Asia" an independent and specific identification in international political discourse, as was already predictable in the establishment of Admiral Lord Louis Mountbatten's "South-East Asia Command" in 1943 as a response to the Japanese occupation. Ultimately, the institutionalization of the term "Southeast Asia" suggested that the region should now be regarded as a legitimate "Asian" entity in its own right, with a history of its own, rather than as the "appendages" or "colonies" of greater powers, be they European or Asian (such as India, China, and Japan).

While the impact of the Japanese occupation of Southeast Asia was far from uniform, the occupation did provide the region with a platform from which local leaders could articulate their position to their Western rulers in the process of decolonization. Shortly before the Fall of Singapore, the ambivalent and prophetic Dutch Prime Minister in exile, Pieter Gerbrandy, spoke to Churchill and other Allied leaders:

> Our Eastern peoples were, for the greater part, still subject to racial instincts and inferiority complexes. The Japanese slogan "Asia for the Asiatics," might easily destroy the carefully constructed basis of our cultural synthesis. . . . Though a lengthy Japanese occupation of important parts of the Pacific Territories might not necessarily turn the final victory of the Western powers into virtual defeat, it would at least prove a formidable obstacle to a real peace in the Far East. Japanese

injuries and insults to the White population—and these were already being perpetrated by the detestable Asiatic Huns—would irreparably damage white prestige unless severely punished within a short time.[61]

As prophesied above, Southeast Asia embarked on the process of redefining and renewing its identity during the war. There were, however, regional variations in that redefinition and renewal (as well as new inventions). After the Japanese surrender in August 1945, the Philippines—offered complete self-rule by the United States already before the war—witnessed relative continuity before and after the war under U.S. rule. Singapore and Malaya experienced neither a smooth readjustment nor a coherent resistance movement to the returning British. Indonesia on the other hand launched a war of independence against the returning Dutch "invaders," who tried to restore their colonial supremacy, and the Vietnamese engaged in a prolonged war with France and later with the United States. In the end, the Philippines was decolonized in 1946, Burma in 1948, Indonesia in 1953, Cambodia in 1953, and Brunei in 1984. Malaysia was born in 1963 out of the merger of the former British Malaya (independent in 1957) and Singapore, which together formed West Malaysia, while Sabah and Sarawak in north Borneo constituted East Malaysia. Singapore seceded from this union in 1965.

All in all, however, "Southeast Asia" stood at the point of no return after the Japanese occupation. Certainly, the restoration of the colonial governments evoked a sense of temporary relief in some parts of the region. But the political awakening and the search for a new communal identity had already begun in the minds of some. For example, two decades after the Japanese arrival, Lee Kuan Yew, who was then Singapore's Prime Minister stated:

> My colleagues and I are of the generation of young men who went through the Second World War and the Japanese Occupation and emerged determined that no one—neither the Japanese nor the British—had the right to push and kick us around. We are determined that we could govern ourselves and bring up children in a country where we can be proud to be self-representing people. When the war came to an end in 1945, there was never a chance of the old type of British colonial system ever being re-created. The scales had fallen from our eyes and we saw for ourselves that the local people could run the country.[62]

While not in the manner that Japan's cultural policies and training programs had originally intended, Japan's programs then ingrained in the region the awareness of belonging to "Asia". That fundamental realization was ultimately and directly relevant to the very irreducible essence of Pan-Asian ideology, that Asia as a cohesive whole existed and that Asia needed to be recognized by their former colonizers.

Dilemmas of the Japanese Rulers

While devising policies based on their imperative to win the war, as well as on their often misguided presuppositions about the people they ruled, Japanese rulers rigorously sought to incorporate the population into the life of their Empire. As unwanted as this attention was, the Japanese policies ended up introducing the population of Southeast Asia to a new *modus vivendi* outside the past colonial context: their world now belonged to Southeast Asian, Asian, and indeed international contexts.

Although they claimed to have ousted Western influence from the region, the Japanese themselves in Southeast Asia were never free of the overwhelming presence of the West throughout the period of their occupation. On the contrary, Japan's cultural recruits, who were more often than not Western-educated, were continually faced with the question of how to overcome the limits set by the Western discourse of modernity, which legitimized their own social status.

Deeply influenced by the idea of modernity, many *bunkajin* recruits attempted to claim the spiritualism of Asia to be superior to the materialism of the West. At the same time, many also believed that Japan was superior to other Asians, precisely because it had singularly succeeded in modernizing and in part "Westernizing." That is why Japan's wartime cultural policies often ended up being predicated upon the paradoxical notion that Japan should lead Asia in the pursuit of Pan-Asianist ideals, because Japan was the most modernized, Westernized, and thus the most successful Asian country recognized by the West, with the emperor presiding at the top of their nation as the paragon of ancient as well as modern wisdom.

Such an ambivalent position was well exemplified by Marquis Tokugawa Yoshichika (1886–1976), the heir to the regional Owari clan of the shogunal family that ruled Japan between 1603 and 1867. His pioneering efforts in education for the deaf as well as his patronage of Suzuki Shin'ichi, the founder of the Suzuki violin method, are little remembered today. However, Tokugawa was far more than a generous philanthropist or a quiet scholar with a love of art. He was implicated as a financier in the failed March 1931 coup by the Army officers, in addition to taking part in the founding of Japan's Socialist Party. All in all, he seemed to embrace radicalism and adventurism as his life philosophy. First enthralled by the excitement of tiger-hunting, to which he was introduced by the Sultan of Johor in 1921, he became interested in Malay culture. His interest in the region and connections in its high society eventually led him to the position of Special Adviser to the Twenty-fifth Army.

During the war, as a biologist and an avid student of history, Tokugawa devoted himself to joint scientific projects with a team of Japanese and Allied European scientists, such as the Cambridge biologist E. J. H. Corner. Their projects included the preservation of botanical and zoological collections as well as research on light-emitting organisms to be used as a secret means of communication in warfare. These scientists lived with their Japanese colleagues and in some cases developed life-long friendships.[63]

For example, Corner, after the death of Tokugawa, wrote a book in his memory, extensively recalling his experience during the Japanese occupation. In the prologue, he expressed his great respect for the Japanese with whom he worked:

> Upon hearing that Singapore might fall, the British scholars and scientists neglected their scholarly duties and rushed off to their homeland. Those who saved the invaluable cultural legacies of Singapore from the chaos of war were a group of admirable Japanese led by the Marquis. They were profound scholars.[64]

What Corner does not say, perhaps as a diplomatic gesture to his exclusively Japanese audience, is that the Japanese forces themselves caused that chaos of war in the first place. Nevertheless, his recollection is interesting as it proves that Tokugawa's academic interests were deeply rooted in the Enlightenment tradition of amassing, analyzing, displaying, and preserving a collection of local *objets d'art* by protecting British cultural legacies in Singapore.

Yet Tokugawa was also clearly a Japanese nationalist who advocated the Japanese language program, as well as a committed Pan-Asianist, who loved Malay culture and insisted on speaking Malay to his museum staff. Perhaps, most educated idealists who participated in the Sphere policy held such contradictory values. They were at once nationalistic and Pan-Asianist, with a genuine but often sentimental and naïve yearning for a radical change of which they saw themselves as key agents. Tokugawa said as much in his postwar memoirs:

Japanese are strange people. . . . [W]e annexed Korea but never tried to learn Korean. Most never even bothered to learn the tradition or the history of Korea. When we occupied the south in the Greater East Asia War, we never learned the local languages and insisted on using Japanese. But then strangely enough, we ourselves worship English and belittle Japanese. . . . Once after the war, I received an invitation to the coronation ceremony of a Malay sultan . . . which read . . . "Please come dressed in your nation's traditional attire." Thinking that a Western-style frockcoat was their formal national attire, the Japanese consulate people attended the ceremony in tailed tuxedoes.[65]

In the end, the *bunkajin* recruits had very limited success probably because they themselves had not reconciled those dilemmas in their own minds. At the very least, their misplaced and often narcissistic efforts examined in the preceding pages show that Pan-Asianism mattered to the Japanese enormously. The ideology prompted them to engage in endeavors that were, from a purely materialistic perspective, neither necessary nor relevant nor useful in the more immediate and practical administration of the occupied territories, especially in the midst of a losing war. Rather than concentrating only on material mobilization for the war and sending recruits to the frontline, the wartime government took a chance on the longer-term and fantastic project of building the Co-Prosperity Sphere.

* * *

By trying to impose the Japanese mode of existence on the Sphere, the Japanese rulers' attitude, to an extent, paralleled the European colonial assumption of cultural and racial superiority. And yet, there were more fundamental differences than similarities in both Pan-Asianism and European colonialism. Such differences were aptly observed by a contemporaneous analyst, Sir Frederick Whyte (1883–1970), a former political adviser to the Kuomintang (1929–32), and one of the founders of the Pan-Europeanist New Europe party. He explained his reading of Japan's motives for its expansion in a sixty-page policy advisory paper circulated in November 1941. Although primarily meant as a strategic studies piece, he devoted more than one-third of his paper to an explanation of the role of Pan-Asianism behind Japan's war mobilization. He defined the Sphere ideology as "a Japanese version of Hitler's 'New Order.' . . . [I]t means that Japan should be the paramount Power . . . and that all political control by the white men should be removed from that area."[66]

Whyte was nonetheless reluctant to dismiss Pan-Asianism as a mere justification for Japan's solely self-interested expansionist agenda. Although clearly unwilling to sympathize with the Japanese, he was intellectually intrigued enough to want to grasp the nature of the zeal behind Meishuron Pan-Asianism in some detail, going on to discuss the cultural and historical roots of Japan's sense of its own uniqueness. He concluded:

> Not only do [the Japanese] seek to reserve it for their particular brand of totalitarianism, but they contend that its peoples have a mystical destiny wholly different from that of Western nations. They wish to protect the spiritual essence of Asia from corruption by the "material" civilization of Europe and America. And though they are far astray from the truth in branding the West as "material," they pursue their own mystical mission with fervor, believing so strongly in its necessity that no estimate of Japanese expansion would be complete or true without an appraisal of what the Japanese would claim as its spiritual motive.[67]

One might say that such Japanese fervor, expressed in the Empire's attempt at propagating its values throughout the Sphere, in effect provided the inhabitants of the region with a common experience of disruption, dislocation, and oppression that ultimately led to the awakening of their political consciousness. Ironically for Japan, therefore, Meishuron Pan-Asianism, put to practice in the Co-Prosperity Sphere, inadvertently ended up fulfilling one of the most fundamental Pan-Asianist objectives, that is the self-awareness to become one's own. For those who were newly awakened to their political identity, the image of European invincibility and superiority grew more and more tarnished. The memory of undernourished white soldiers engaged in forced labor for the Japanese, for instance, left a deep impression on the local population. Furthermore, remembering that the colonial masters were unable to defend them, the local populations questioned the colonialists' right to return and restore their rule. In many areas of Southeast Asia after the war, Western-educated elites, who either made the use of leadership opportunities that the Japanese had granted them, or became politically awakened as a result of Japanese rule, replaced the Japanese in inflicting what in Gerbrandy's words constituted "injuries and insults to the White population." Notable examples for the former type include Sukarno and Hatta in Indonesia and the latter Aung San in Burma.

In the end, Pan-Asianism never quite captured the hearts and the minds of the conquered to the degree that the Japanese had anticipated, except for some local nationalist activists who received moral as well as material assistance from the Japanese military. But this does not mean that Pan-Asianism was not a "productive" force without real political and historical consequences or that it was merely a rhetorical tool. Until the end of the Fifteen Years' War, the Pan-Asianist doctrine never disappeared, even when the Japanese defeat became increasingly imminent and even when the desperate acts of *kamikaze* pilots failed to reverse the verdict already sealed by the utter imbalance of power in military technology and war matériel.

Perhaps this was because Japan's leaders and those who mobilized for the war had been conditioned, and conditioned themselves, to believe that the war that they had been fighting for so long, and were now losing, held a grander purpose even more important than their defeat or their lives. Even if they were to be defeated, they could comfort themselves with the conviction that the war had been fought for Japan's single-handed and heroic mission of liberating Asia until the very last gasp of the Empire.

On August 21, 1945, six days after Emperor Hirohito's announcement of the Japanese surrender, *The Syonan Shinbun* officially declared the Japanese defeat. The editorial nevertheless added: "[B]y imperial command the Dai Tōa Sensō is coming to an end, but our ideas for the existence of Nippon and the stabilization of Greater East Asia will never die."[68]

Conclusion:
From Tea to Co-Prosperity

On August 15, 1945, the "Greater East Asia War" ended with the imperial radio broadcast that devastated the already shattered nation. Emperor Hirohito somberly announced:

> We declared war on America and Britain out of Our sincere desire to secure Japan's self-preservation and the stabilization of Asia, it being far from Our thought either to infringe upon the sovereignty of other nations or to embark upon territorial aggrandizement. . . . We cannot but express the sense of deepest regret to our Allied nations of East Asia, who have consistently cooperated with the Empire towards the emancipation of East Asia. . . . The hardships and suffering to which Our nation is to be subjected hereafter will be certainly great. . . . However it is according to the dictate of time and fate that We have resolved to pave the way for a grand peace for all the generations to come by enduring the unendurable and suffering what is insufferable.[1]

This announcement was succeeded by the dissolution of the short-lived Suzuki Kantarōcabinet, followed by the immediate appointment of Prince Higashikuni to the premiership and the signing of the surrender treaty on the *USS Missouri* on September 2.

For those "Allied nations of East Asia" on the Co-Prosperity front, a close of the war came on September 12, 1945, when a team of Japanese delegates accompanied by the British Military Police marched to the Municipal Building at Singapore's city center. They were greeted by the Supreme Commander of South-East Asia Command Admiral Lord Louis Mountbatten, who presented the Japanese with the surrender treaty to sign. Crowds greeted the defeated party with a Japanese curse *"Bakayaro"* (bastards). As one eyewitness recalls the scene: "The *'Bakaro'* [*sic*] of thousands of throats expressed the pent-up hatred of the Nip, a hatred generated by the excesses of the Nip at his coming and deepened during the three and a half years of his occupation."[2] This was one symbolic conclusion to the Fifteen Years' War that began on September 18, 1931, in Mukden.

In spite of such formal conclusions of the war, however, there still remain fundamental questions. Did the Japanese surrender also mark the end of Pan-Asianism? Or, had this already died earlier, at other turning points in the history of the Fifteen Years' War? Conversely, has the ideology endured as a viable concept even to this day?

In a now classic article entitled "The End of Pan-Arabism," Fouad Ajami once identified the Six-Day War as the "Waterloo of pan-Arabism."[3] In a like manner, if one were to identify the Waterloo of Pan-Asianism, what would that be? And more generally, does the legacy of Pan-Asianism hold some relevance to contemporary international politics? I have argued in this book that Japanese Pan-Asianist thinking of the war period had been rooted in the intellectual atmosphere already palpable before the Manchurian Incident of 1931. Just as its continuity from the prewar period has been duly considered, it seems worthwhile, in conclusion, to reflect on the impact and the implications of Pan-Asianism into the postwar period.

The Death of Pan-Asianism?

In examining the making of Japan's expansionism, this book recounted how Pan-Asianism came to assume a prominent place in Japan's foreign policy—as declared on paper and put to practice—over the course of the Fifteen Years' War. The expression "prominent place" should be savored in its fullest meaning. The possibilities and prospect of a bright future that Pan-Asianism seemed to intimate for many Japanese became harder and harder to resist as the Empire stretched its territorial as well as ideological limits. For Japan's wartime leaders, Pan-Asianism often functioned as a consensus-building tool for an otherwise divided government, whose foreign policymaking tended to be stifled by service rivalries and diverging opinions about Japan's national interest of a more immediate and material nature. For many intellectuals, Pan-Asianism at once provided a chance to reconcile their Western knowledge with Japanese—and by extension, Asian—values and produce changes that might realign what they perceived as an unjustly West-centric perspective of world history and international relations. Finally and most importantly, Pan-Asianism provided a sense of purpose for those who mobilized for Japan's imperialist mission.

At the same time, Japan's insistence on the superiority of its values along the Meishuron line and the coercive methods by which Japan attempted to disseminate such values increasingly became palpable. The salient characteristics of Teaist and Meishuron Pan-Asianism—the all-encompassing view of Asia and the missionary zeal of Japan, respectively—proved to be conflicting, even incompatible. This was because the Meishuron argument, in practice, became a futile reverse argument that tried to substantiate the spiritual strength of Asia by forceful means—the very "Western" method of asserting power that the Teaist Pan-Asianists such as Okakura and Tagore had earlier tried to transcend. The middle-of-the-road perspective, offered by Sinic Pan-Asianism, with its limited claim to Japan's leadership role and more regard for the already existing international order, might have allowed Japan some leeway to turn Pan-Asianism into a viable foreign policy framework. However, the temptation of the more domineering ideology coupled with increasing material considerations in the end proved too strong for Japan to rest.

In understanding how Japan as a nation and a state became entrapped by its own Pan-Asianist rhetoric, it is useful to recall the two questions that were posed at the start of this book: "What was the role of ideology in Japan's foreign policy in the 1930s?" and "What does Japan's case tell us about the role of ideology in foreign policy in general?" With reference to the former, the examination of the history of Pan-Asian ideology has shown that the role of Pan-Asianism was a changing but critical one, subject to successive reinterpretations as political events at home and abroad unfolded and intensified. Nonetheless, the emotive tenets of Pan-Asianism remained remarkably consistent in their basic yearnings for self-awareness and external recognition. Japan's policy was often pulled in directions that do not support the arguments of those who claim that material concerns are the exclusive determinant in the formulation of a country's foreign policy, especially in war.

The objective of this study is not, however, just to trace the evolution of Pan-Asianism *per se*. The chronicling of facts, important as it is, does not take us beyond the nineteenth-century Rankean notion of history as showing "simply how it was" (*wie es eigentlich gewesen*), an endeavor, by the way, which is neither "simple" nor perhaps even possible. Rather, I have attempted not only to demonstrate, but also to evaluate the character of Japan's expansionist policy and its intimate relationship with Pan-Asianism in its broader and longer historical context.

Put differently, ideology is not an independent animal with a mind of its own. Ideology is born of interactions with its environment, consistently shaping the thinking of those who embrace it and take part in its actualization. What emerges clearly here is the theme of continuity. Japan's expansionism was part of the country's continuing struggle with the wider world and search for a role within that world ever since its door was forced open by U.S. gunboat diplomacy in the second half of the nineteenth century.

The binary view of early Pan-Asianism, dividing the world into East and West, provided a robust incentive for Indians, Chinese, Koreans, Japanese, and other Asians to wake up to the resilience and beauty of their shared legacies and the eventual goal of liberation and recognition of Asia by the West. Such theoretical elasticity to accommodate interests of other nationalisms stands in contrast to Pan-Arabism. At the height of its power, Pan-Arabism rendered smaller nation-state divides irrelevant under the banner of "the one Arab nation with an immortal mission."

Precisely, the goal of refuting the post-Ottoman settlements gave Pan-Arab movement its sense of purpose. Thus Pan-Arabism was most influential at a time when there were still misgivings about the legitimacy of those physical boundaries. For those propagators of the notion of Pan-Arabia, the distinctions among Arabs seemed negligible, if not altogether nonexistent. This uninational aspect of Pan-Arabism was unlike any early Pan-Asianist movements, which assumed from the onset the existence of different national traditions and missions among Asians. In a sense, "Asia" as an existential unit did not encounter the modern discourse of nation-state nationalism entirely as a *tabula rasa*. In contrast, Pan-Arabism, given the collective Ottoman memory, the common language, and the relative lack of indigenous divisions within (with the notable exception of Egypt), had far more exacting standards for the uniformity of a group.

However, the gap between Pan-Asianism and Pan-Arabism may not be as great as all that. Just as Pan-Asianism was formulated by Western-educated intellectuals, Pan-Arab nationalism was conceived and spread by intellectuals, many of whom were in exile in Europe. Both pan-movements started out as abstract theorizing by intellectuals who were keen to see their cultures claim credit for their own historical heritage when pitted against the West. At the same time, however, both pan-movements were acutely aware of their material weakness in the face of Western dominance.

Perhaps one could only rely on hindsight to make sense of their ambivalent grievances. The "West" as spoken for by those early Pan-Asianists and Pan-Arabists alike did not quite correspond to realities. Just as "Asia" or "Arabia" did not exist in enduring and fixed forms at any given time, the boundaries of the West, too, were often shifting. Moreover, the "West" itself, faced with the new challenges of having to accommodate the "Rest," was going through drastic transformations in its normative and philosophical outlook on its conduct of international politics.

It was indeed in a complex world that the East emerged as a counter-point to the West. It was a world of empires managed by the powerful, with an arms race still going on, but also a world that was quickly becoming more international and pacific in its aspired outlook.[4] Thus the Pan-Asianists' "West" could not have had much to do with the organic and rapidly changing West, however thorough their exposure to the Western *modus vivendi* may have been. The premise that Asia needed to be liberated from the West or, as was later declared, that Japan should lead Asia in its quest for freedom, was formulated on the basis of a combination of *idées fixes* about both East and West. In this regard, Pan-Asianism was based on a less substantive and a more fictional premise, necessitated by an over-whelming emotional, rather than practical need, from the very start.

A fiction can often take on a real life in politics, however. Even the late nineteenth-century Sinic Pan-Asianists of "the same letter, the same race" movement, such as Konoe Atsumaro, who were profoundly enamored of classical Chinese culture, assumed that Japan was to lead Asia's ascent in the new century. The original Meishuron Pan-Asianist, Tōyama Mitsuru, himself a lifelong friend of Sun Yat-sen and patron of modern Chinese nationalism, also rejected Sun's interpretation of "Great Asianism" in which Japan and China were to be perfect equals. Indeed, with the Japanese victories in the Sino-Japanese War and Russo-Japanese War, the notion that the process of liberation and recognition of Asia had been put in motion by Japan, albeit in an indirect manner, appeared to hold some legitimacy. The demise of Pan-Asianism came when, and only when, Japan became excessively self-conscious about its own role and began actively to engage in that role-playing. Such a decisive moment arrived with Ishiwara Kanji's initiative to create a Pan-Asian utopia in Manchuria.

Therefore, the most fateful phase of Japan's pursuit of Pan-Asian leadership began in 1931, heralding the fifteen years' period in which Pan-Asianism came to occupy a central place in Japan's foreign policy formulation. In Ishiwara, a brilliant but erratic student of war who staged the Manchurian Incident, Japan's Pan-Asianist crusade found its catalyst. Over the course of the 1930s, Japan muddled through terrorism and economic uncertainty at home, while on the Asian mainland it often overreacted to Chinese nationalism and the Soviet threat with increased militarism.

Nonetheless, Japan's shift from internationalism to Pan-Asianism—and effectively, expansionism—was neither an abrupt nor a clear-cut episode. The very pretence of Manchukuo's sovereignty and various attempts to justify this pretense in the legalese of liberal internationalism that accompanied the invention of Manchukuo showed that Japan continued to care enormously about the climate of international opinion. To make the situation even more nuanced, those who took part in the actual project of building Manchukuo were neither obvious nor direct agents of imperialism. In fact, quite a few of them, in sentiment and in principle, or sometimes even in practice, opposed Japanese imperialism. It was often upon the account of Pan-Asianism that Japan's nation-builders of the progressive left joined with the military and the capitalists in the building of a Pan-Asianist empire.

The Marco Polo Bridge Incident and its escalation into a military conflict with the United Front of China in 1937 were followed by Prime Minister Konoe's declaration of the establishment of a new order in East Asia to "create a new culture and realize close economic unity throughout East Asia."[5] "Culture" by this time had acquired a decidedly narrower, more Meishuron than Sinic or Teaist meaning, making the ideology no longer a concept that suggested the sharing of common values and aspirations based on "love for the Ultimate and Universal," which was "the common thought-inheritance of every Asiatic race."[6] Thus began the Leviathanic *bellum omnium contra omnes* for the legitimization of Japan as Asia's sovereign on the anarchic mainland, or that is at least how many Japanese perceived and portrayed it.

The promulgation of the "Greater East Asia Co-Prosperity Sphere" ideology tracked this restricted interpretation of culture by overtly trying to exclude Western powers from the Sphere. The verdict does not reflect well on the intellectuals, at least for those who, with varying degrees, regarded Japan's war as an Asian struggle against Western imperialism. To be sure, such an admission of intellectual responsibility does not in the least exonerate Japan's leaders in the actual adoption of Meishuron Pan-Asianism as a matter of official policy. Without facing up to more critical disagreements about the feasibility of tactics to fight the West in the first place, they agreed to go to war, loosely united under the vague and grandiose aim of launching a Pan-Asianist crusade.

While the confrontational style of U.S. diplomacy did not help and while there were genuine and legitimate historical reasons for Japan to feel humiliated and threatened, the responsibility for deciding to go to war rested entirely on the Japanese government, which, despite internal divisions, agreed that the war had to be fought, under the divine protection of the emperor, for the future of Asia. Pan-Asianism, like Emperor Worship, by then had become an uncontested national religion of sorts.

As with any religion, there were bound to be skeptics and nonbelievers, however. Notably, the liberal parliamentarian Ozaki Yukio (1858–1954), who had been devoted to party politics throughout his long career, publicly sounded an alarm in protest against such a conceptually feeble and ambiguous application of Pan-Asianism to Japan's external policy. In his mind, the broad Pan-Asianist slogans such as *"Kūa"* (Construction of Asia), *"Kyūeiken"* (Co-Prosperity Sphere), and *"Ajia no Meishu"* (Asia's Alliance Leader), all pointed to the exact opposites of what they declared to achieve, since the end results were *"Tūa"* (Demolition of Asia), *"Kyūsuiken"* (Co-Impoverishment Sphere), and *"Koritsu Muen"* (Isolation and No Support).[7] But such a voice of defiance was extinguished by a more pervasive sense of enthusiastic support for Japan's war aims, leading to Ozaki's indictment for *lese-majesté* in 1943.

The direct responsibility of Japanese leaders notwithstanding, it must be said that those leaders perhaps would not have been able to reach a consensus for war without the benefit of the conceptual underpinnings and endorsement of Pan-Asianism. Moreover, in decisions relating to Southeast Asia, Japan's leaders were perhaps further blinded by opportunities for a more prominent world role for Japan, offered by the weakness and divisions in the colonial metropoles and dissatisfactions in their colonies, which indeed appeared to corroborate the claim of Japan's pre-ordained role in altering the currents of world history.

Those opportunities implied something far greater than the securing of mere war matériel, as was proven by the committed participation of many cultural recruits and educated elites in extensive occupation programs of the Sphere territories. Pan-Asianism persisted until the end of the Fifteen Years' War, even though it became increasingly clear that there was a wide gap between theory and practice. Thus in the sense that Japan continued to think of itself as fighting a war for Pan-Asianism, its Waterloo had been evaded and prolonged until August 1945 even though, theoretically speaking, it could have come much sooner if Japan's leaders had been valiant enough to admit the impossibility of winning such a war.

Broader Implications

Japan's military defeat forced the country to come to terms with the defeat of its wartime ideologies. As a consequence, postwar Japan has faced, with much reluctance and internal divisions, a discussion of those ideologies that made the war possible for nearly fifteen years. Two ideologies, as noted earlier, were decisive in the creation of Japan's expansionism. One was Emperor Worship, and the other, even more elusive and conceptually problematic, was Pan-Asianism. The readiness to dismiss Pan-Asianism as an ideology of self-serving ultranationalism, solely because of its negative consequences, has given rise to the view that anyone who claims that Pan-Asianism was a viable ideology should be categorically denounced as an apologist for Japan's war. For instance, in 2003, the cultural critic Yomota Inuhiko asserted his view of Okakura's "Asia is One" dictum as follows:

> This declaration ["Asia is One"], though unintended by Tenshin, was *exploited* as an excuse for the "Greater East Asia Co-Prosperity Sphere." Then, "the third world coalition" was proclaimed, and that too ended up as a myth. Although today's Asia is emancipated from Western colonialism, it is deeply entrenched in the maze of ethnic conflict and religious fundamentalism.[8]

The above statement is typical of the uncritical assumption that Pan-Asianism was simply an exploitative ideology. As a backlash against the unthinking moral rectitude of the left, conservative cabinet politicians express equally extreme opinions on the nature and responsibility of the war. They are then met with domestic and international—especially Asian—opprobrium, and forced to resign, or at least retract. This pattern is indeed symptomatic of the polarized and stagnant debate on the history of the Fifteen Years' War, and the uneasy position of Pan-Asianism within it.

An ideological analysis of foreign policy formulation needs to address this question on two different levels. First, it is true that some, indeed many, Japanese subscribed to Pan-Asianism and had a "sincere desire to secure Japan's self-preservation and the stabilization of Asia."⁹ Such people did not go to war believing that they were oppressing their fellow Asians. For this reason, it is impetuous to indict all Japan's wartime Pan-Asianist declarations and programs simply as hollow euphemisms for "national egoism."¹⁰

But the second layer to the argument is a more problematic and value-loaded one, as it deals directly with the consequences of those Pan-Asianist declarations and programs. The realization that many Japanese took Pan-Asianism seriously does not in the end make the Japanese wartime acts less deplorable. On the contrary, those who succumbed to the power of Meishuron Pan-Asianism must be held responsible for their recklessness and naïveté that made the actual administration of the Co-Prosperity Sphere all the more disillusioning for all the parties involved. Good intentions were never enough to compensate for Japan's lack of necessary preparations, resources, and institutions to bolster them. Moreover, such good Pan-Asianist intentions were in the end unable to prevent more devastating consequences of immoral policies, ranging from Japan's treatment of 140,000 Allied prisoners, the testing of biological weapons and other gruesome medical experiments, sex slavery, and other forms of human rights violations both at home and abroad. A further complication of this debate is the end of colonial imperialism in Asia, tempting some to argue on the purely consequentialist ground that Japanese actions produced more good than bad, without bothering to demonstrate the direct causal relationship between Japan's Pan-Asianism and the end of colonial rule.

The two related but distinct notions that Japan mobilized for the Fifteen Years' War with genuine appreciation of Pan-Asianism on the one hand and that it failed to deliver its promises in reality on the other seem to raise more questions than answers. At the very least, such an awareness makes the Fifteen Years' War more understandable. By extension, such a recognition proves that the study of Pan-Asianism is not an outlandish or unintelligible topic that has no bearings on the study of international politics at large.

Striking directly at the shortcomings of the neorealist argument that ideology is irrelevant in international politics, the case of wartime Japan suggests a general mechanism in which ideology plays a role in a country's foreign policy. The mechanism can be best summarized as an interactive process of "events," "structures," and "ideational factors." "Events," such as the Manchurian Incident, the China War, and Pearl Harbor, all constituted turning points in which other policy options might have been conceivably pursued. However, constraints stemming from "structure," such as the constitutionally backed Autonomy of the Supreme Command and the imperial institution, eliminated those policy options in reality. Such institutional constraints were no doubt reinforced by the considerations of various "ideational factors" that in turn shaped Japan's perceptions, real or exaggerated, of its external position in the world and of the notion that Asians were subjugated to substantial hardships and humiliation.

All these events, structures, and ideational factors, interacted with one another to propel a historical process that became the Fifteen Years' War. Pan-Asianism was of enduring, all-inclusive, and consistent importance in the formulation of Japanese foreign policy throughout that period. Without Pan-Asianism, the events of 1931, 1937, and 1941, among others, could not have had the legitimacy and approval they actually came to enjoy from the nation, while the Japanese government would have suffered even further internal fragmentation. Finally, Japan's cultural mobilization would not have been possible without the resounding appeal of Pan-Asianism, which shaped the mental maps of all believers of the "Greater East Asia War." Thus it is not simply certain moments that mark momentous events or policy decisions, but rather, it is longer historical processes that need to be taken into account when analyzing a country's foreign policy.

The examination of Japan's case also alerts us to the precarious position of a hegemonic power within any pan-union. As the cases of Russia in Pan-Slavism, the United States in Pan-Americanism, and Egypt in Pan-Arabism might also suggest, it is often the reaction to the hegemon that makes pan-nationalisms impracticable. Moreover, the former hegemon will always invite the suspicion of its neighbors, which then hinders the possible future development of regionalism. And yet, paradoxically, for pan-national arrangements to function, a hegemon is perhaps needed.

This brings us to what is possibly the only successful case of pan-nationalism: Pan-Europeanism. In the case of Europe, it seems valid to say that Pan-Europeanism enjoyed what every pan-nationalism—Pan-Asianism, Pan-Germanism, Pan-Slavism, Pan-Arabism, Pan-Africanism, or Pan-Islamism—lacked, which was the priority of securing a stable economic foundation. Theories of European integration abound, be they classical functionalism, neofunctionalism, federalism, and confederalism. They all emphasize common and mutual interests that mainly constitute the economic dimension of Europe's political life, while relying upon voluntary and consensual methods in expanding and deepening the community.

The last point reorients this concluding discussion back to the failure of Japan's Pan-Asianism and the significance of the ideology's unjustly overlooked and complex legacies. The preceding pages attempted to show that the notion of Pan-Asianism as a cloak disguising Japan's exclusive national interest—that of policymakers manipulating Pan-Asian rhetoric and intellectuals cleaving to theory more than practice—is too one-dimensional. The book also tried to make clear, however, how Japan was mistaken to presume that it was preordained to take on a regional leadership role without due invitation by fellow Asians.

Indeed, one cannot but help being struck by the applicability of the following Ruskinian passage set out in the preface of *St Mark's Rest* to the fate of Japanese Pan-Asianism:

> Great nations write their autobiographies in three manuscripts, the book of their deeds, the book of their words, and the book of their art. Not one of these books can be understood unless we read the two others, but of the three the only quite trustworthy one is the last. The acts of a nation may be triumphant by its good fortune; and its words mighty by the genius of a few of its children: but its art, only by the general gifts and common sympathies of the race. Again, the policy of a nation may be compelled, and, therefore, not indicative of its true character. Its words may be false, while yet the race remain unconscious of their falsehood; and no historian can assuredly detect the hypocrisy. But art is always instinctive; and the honesty or pretence of it are therefore open to the day.[11]

Japan's Pan-Asianism can best be viewed as a misguided attempt to write those three manuscripts of deeds, words, and art, but in the exact reverse order. First, there was the recognition of the richness and beauty of Asian arts. This was followed by all sorts of edifying sentiments and declarations of intent by intellectuals and politicians. Finally they were acted upon by those who were beholden to both the arts and the words of Pan-Asianism. This is why some analysts articulate, even at the risk of being misunderstood, the earnestness with which Japan fought its Pan-Asianist war. For example, Nakao Michio asserted in his study of East Asian cooperativism that "[w]hat was tragic about Japan's defeat was not that it demolished its institutions, but that Japan carried out the war at the cost of its moral values and culture. It is easy to rebuild institutions, but difficult to rebuild culture."[12]

This somewhat sentimental assessment is actually a reformulation of what the journalist Tokutomi Sohō (1863–1957), one of the most active proponents of Japanese expansionism, put forward in his postwar reflection. He wrote:

> The greatest mistake for Japan was that it was excessively impatient. Thinking that it was late and lagging behind the world's great powers, and that as things went, there was no possibility for catching up with them, Japan started running amok without being able to tell right from left, without thinking twice or thrice. For that [desire to achieve a world role], Japan could afford to be unreasonable, and for that unreasonableness, those around Japan began to hate it, and eventually it was beaten to near-death. That is the story of Japan.[13]

Ultimately, it was not the reality of war, but the ideological fantasy that mattered to Japan's Pan-Asianist fighters until the very end. It was impossible to end the Fifteen Years' War for the fantasy-struck nation, even at moments when the war could have been ended, since that would have implied sacrificing the grander war aims and the very "spirit" that made Japan a great "Asian" power and the *meishu* of Asia.

Certainly, the hopes and illusions of Japan's Pan-Asianism had been shaped long before Ishiwara's bold initiative of 1931 and continue to haunt relations with other Asian countries long after the military defeat of 1945. Not surprisingly, save for very few exceptions, Pan-Asianism of the Fifteen Years' War period never fully appealed to any Asians other than the Japanese. Japan's Meishuron Pan-Asianism made little sense to Asians, much less to those outside the "Co-Prosperity Sphere," arguably because Japan's actions betrayed its words and because Japan's one-sided interpretation of Pan-Asianism was a problematic reading of the original Teaist Pan-Asianism to start with. Already in late 1941, the British political analyst Frederick Whyte understood this imbalance of ideological appeal in and outside Japan and summarized:

> [I]t is certain that no Japanese reader would accept this appreciation as complete if it stopped short of an appraisal of the spiritual or mystical motive inspiring Japan's New Order in Asia. Doubtless, the Chinese peasant living in a world of fire and rape will not be impressed by any such plea. Nor will the European victims of Japanese competition in

colonial markets see anything more than Japan's ruthless and efficient exploitation of Opportunity. None the less, among the purpose and motives of "New Order" and "Sphere" alike, there is a missionary spirit which is neither selfish nor brutal. To describe it is a task more difficult even than to measure Japan's actual power in war on the incomplete evidence available. To appreciate it is perhaps more difficult still, for it is a peculiar Japanese manifestation of that "other worldliness" which is the outstanding characteristic of the Asiatic mind; and the Western writer would have to partake of the quality of his own European mystics in order to see it aright. But, even if it eludes definition, no one who knows the country can deny that many high-minded Japanese uphold Japan's New Order because they believe it will serve a purpose above that of military domination or material gain.[14]

Eventually, the *reductio ad absurdum* of Pan-Asianism came not because the Japanese Pan-Asian pronouncements were the cloak disguising national policy. Rather, it occurred precisely because the Pan-Asianist pronouncements came to be embraced by those Japanese who were all too willing to act upon them even without the benefit of concrete national policy.

In a manner of speaking, the Japanese embrace of Pan-Asianism ended up strangling Japan itself. The embrace was so tight that Japan was crushed until there was nothing left of its legitimacy. Japan came out of the Fifteen Years' War with no legitimacy in Asia, in the world, and above all, with no Asian union to lead. The vision of Pan-Asia as dreamt by the Japanese perished with the fate of the Empire, as did all its seeming hopes and promises. Like a mirage, Pan-Asianism deluded many intelligent minds and then disappeared. But for a mirage, it still leaves too many unacknowledged legacies for the politics of Asia and for the world. It is also hard to overstate the bloody consequences of this mirage, which cost the lives of nearly 3 million people in Japan and perhaps 15 million in China alone.

Bibliography

A. Primary Sources

1. Archives

Ajia Rekishi Shiryō Sentā [Japan Center for Asian Historical Records], Tokyo, Japan (JACAR).

Bōeichō Bōei Kenkyūjo Senshibu [War History Department, National Defense Institute, Japanese Defense Agency], Tokyo, Japan (BBKS).

Gaimushō Gaikō Shiryōkan [Diplomatic Record Office, Japanese Foreign Ministry], Tokyo, Japan (GGS).

Public Record Office at Kew, London, U.K.

2. Published Documents

In Japanese

Bōeichō Bōeikenkyūjo Senshishitsu, ed. *Senshi Sōsho Daihonei Rikugunbu Dai Tūa Sensū Kaisen Keii* [Compilation of War History: Imperial Army Headquarters and the Opening of the Greater East Asia War]. Vol. 1. Chōun Shimbunsha, 1973.

Gaimushō, ed., *Nihon Gaikū Nenpyū narabi ni Shuyūmonjo* [Chronology and Major Documents of Japan's Foreign Policy]. Vols. 1 and 2. Hara Shobō, 1965–1966.

Gendaishi Shiryū [Modern History Documents]. Vols. 1–3 and 11. Misuzu Shobō, 1962–65.

Genyōsha Shashi Hensankai, ed. *Genyūsha Shashi* [The Organizational History of the Genyōsha]. Kindaishiryō Shuppankai, 1977.

Kokuryūkai, ed. *Tūa Senkaku Shishi Kiden* [A Record of Pioneering East Asian Fighters]. Vols. 1–3. Misuzu Shobō, 1974.

Kokutai no Hongi [Cardinal Principles of the National Polity]. Monbushō, 1937.

Nihon Kokusai Seijigakkai, ed. *Taiheiyū Sensū e no Michi* [The Road to the Pacific War], updated editions. Vols. 1–7. Asahi Shimbunsha, 1987–88.

Rekishi Kagaku Kyōgikai, ed. *Shiryū Nihon Kin-Gendaishi, II, Dai-Nippon Teikoku no Kiseki* [Historical Sources of Modern and Contemporary Japanese History, Vol. 2, The Trail of the Great Japanese Empire]. Sanseidō, 1985.

Rekishigaku Kenkyūkai, ed. *Nihonshi Shiryū, [5] Gendai* [Sources on Japanese History, Vol. 5, Modern Period]. Iwanami Shoten, 1997.

———. *Taiheiyū Sensūshi* [History of the Pacific War]. Vols. 1 and 2. Aoki Shoten, 1971–72.

Shakaimondai Shiryō Kenkyūkai, ed. *Teikoku Gikaishi* [Imperial Diet Records]. Vols. 9 and 18. Tōyōbunkasha, 1976–77.

Sugiyama Hajime. *Sugiyama Memo* [Sugiyama Memoranda]. 2 vols. Hara Shobō, 1967.

In English

"The Imperial Rescript of August 14, 1945" (Japan's official translation). In *Japan's Decision to Surrender*. Edited by Robert J. C. Butow, 248. Stanford, CA: Stanford University Press, 1954.

Lebra, Joyce C., ed. and intro. *Japan's Greater East Asia Co-Prosperity Sphere in World War II*. Kuala Lumpur: Oxford University Press, 1975.

3. Contemporaneous Writings, including Diaries, Opinion Pieces, Lectures, Pamphlets, and Magazines

In Japanese

Abe Shinnosuke. "Konoe Naikaku to Shintō Undō" [The Konoe Cabinet and the New Party Movement]. *Kaizū* (November 1938): 52–59.

Dazai Osamu. *Jūnigatsu Yūka* [December 8]. In *Dazai Osamu Zenshū 5* [Collected Works of Dazai Osamu, Vol. 5], 19–31. Chikuma Bunko, 1989.

Fukuzawa Yukichi. "Jiji Shōgen" [On Current Affairs]. In *Fukuzawa Yukichi Zenshū* [Collected Writings of Fukuzawa Yukichi]. Vol. 5. Edited by Keiō Gijuku, 95–231. Iwanami Shoten, 1959.

Hamaguchi Osachi. *Nikki/Zuikanroku* [Diary/Record of Passing Observations]. Edited by Ikei Masaru, Hatano Masaru, and Kurosawa Fumitaka. Misuzu Shobō, 1991.

Harada Kumao. *Saionjikū to Seikyoku* [Prince Saionji and Political Situations]. Vols. 2–8 and *Bekkan* [Separate Volume]. Iwanami Shoten, 1950–56.

Hayashi Senjūrō. *Manshūjiken Nisshi* [Manchurian Affairs Dairy]. Misuzu Shobō, 1996.

Ibuse Masuji. *Ibuse Masuji Jisen Zenshū* [Self-Selected Collection of Ibuse Masuji's Works]. Shinchōsha, 1986.

Ishiwara Kanji. "Manmō Mondai Shiken" [Personal View on the Manchurian Problem], May 22, 1931, and "*Ōshūsenshi Kūwa*" *Ketsuron* [Conclusion: Lectures on European War History], April 1931. In *Ishiwara Kanji Shiryū: Kokubūronsaku* [Documents on Ishiwara Kanji: Theories and Policies of National Defense]. Edited by Tsunoda Jun, 76–79, 69–70. Hara Shobō, 1971.

———. *Manshūkoku Kenkoku to Shina Jihen* [The Establishment of Manchukuo and the China Incident]. Kyoto: Tōa Renmei Kyōkai, 1940.

———. *Sekai Saishū Sensū to Tūa Renmei* [The Final World War and the East Asian League]. Kyoto: Ritsumeikan Shuppanbu, 1941.

Takagi Sōkichi. *Takagi Sūkichi Nikki to Jūhū* [Takagi Sōkichi, Diary and Information]. 2 vols. Edited by Itō Takashi. Misuzu Shobō, 2000.

Kido Kōichi. *Kido Kūichi Nikki* [Diary of Kido Kōichi]. 2 vols. Tokyo University Press, 1966.

Kita Ikki. *Nihon Kaizū Hūan Taikū* [Outline of Principles for the Reconstruction of Japan (1919)]. In *Gendaishi Shiryū*. Vol. 5. Misuzu Shobō, 1964.

Konoe Atsumaro. "Dōjinshu Dōmei fu Shina Mondai Kenkyū no Hitsuyō" [Let Nations of the Same Race Unite Themselves and Discuss Chinese Questions (original title translation)]. *Taiyū* (January 20, 1898): 1–3.

———. *Keisetsu Yobun* [Untold Story of My Hard Student Years]. Vol. 1. Yōmeibunko, 1939.

———. *Konoe Atsumaro Nikki* [Konoe Atsumaro Diary]. Vol. 2. Kashima Kenkyū Shuppankai, 1968.

Konoe Fumimaro. *Sengo Ōbei Kenbunroku* [Travels in Postwar Europe and the United States]. Chūkō Bunko, 1981.

———. "Eibei Hon'i no Heiwashugi wo Haisu" [Reject the Anglo-American Dictated Pacifism]. *Nihon oyobi Nihonjin* (December 1918). In Yabe Teiji. *Konoe Fumimaro*. Jijitsūshinsha, 1958, 16–21.

———. "Taimei wo Haishite" [Upon Receiving the Imperial Mandate]. Radio broadcast speech, July 23, 1940. NHK Service Center.

Matsuoka, Yosuke. *An Address on Manchuria: Its Past and Present and Reply to Prof. Shusi-Hsu's Criticisms and Observation*. Kyoto: Institute of Pacific Relations, 1929.

———. *Economic Co-operation of Japan and China in Manchuria and Mongolia: Its Motives and Basic Significance*. Dalian: Chunichi Bunka Kyokai, ca. 1929.

Miki Kiyoshi. "Tōa Shisō no Konkyo" [The Basis of East Asian Philosophy]. *Kaizū* (December 1938): 8–20.

Miyazaki Tōten. *Sanjūsannen no Yume* [My Thirty-three Years' Dream]. Bungei Shunjū, 1943.

Morimoto (Tarui) Tōkichi. *Daitū Gappūron* [Argument for a Great Eastern Confederation], 1893.

Nakae Chōmin. *Sansuijin Keirin Mondū* [A Discourse by Three Drunkards on Government]. Iwanami Bunko, 1965.

Nakano Seigō. *Kūwakaigi wo Mokugeki shite* [On Witnessing the Peace Conference]. Tōhōjironsha, 1919.

Noguchi Yonejirō. "Indo Bunka no Taikan" [Broad View of Indian Culture]. A speech delivered on May 23, 1936, at Meiji Seimeikan, Tokyo. Compiled in a society publication *Keimeikai Dai Rokujūrokkai Kūenshū* [The Compilation of the 63rd Lecture Series].

Ozaki Hotsumi. *Aijū wa Furu Hoshi no Gotoku* [Love Is Like Falling Stars]. 2 vols. Aoki Bunko, 1953.

Ozaki Hotsumi. *Gendai Shinaron* [Discourse on Modern China]. Iwanami Shoten, 1939.

———. *Kokusai Kankei kara Mita Shina* [China as Seen from an International Relations Perspective]. Dainikokuminkai Shuppanbu, 1937.

———. *Shina Shakai Keizairon* [Social Economic Theory of China]. Seikatsusha, 1940.

Rōyama Masamichi. "Tōa Kyōdōtai no Riron" [Theory of East Asian Cooperative Body]. *Kaizū* (November 1938): 6–26.

Saionji Kinkazu. "Wan Seiei-sensei ni Yosu" [A Letter to Wang Jingwei]. *Chū Kūron* (December 1939): 168–74.

Senji Geppū. March 1942–November 1943 (The Twenty-fifth Army Publication).

Sugiyama Heisuke. "Jūgun Oboegaki" [A Memo from the Front]. *Kaizū* (December 1938): 347–60.

Tachibana Shiraki. "Watashi no Hōkōtenkan" [My Change in Direction]. *Manshū Hyūron* (August 11, 1934): 32–33.

Takayama Rinjirō. "Jinshukyōsō toshite Mitaru Gokutō Mondai" [The Far East Questions from the Point of View of the Struggle for Existence among Different Races (original title translation)]. *Taiyū* (January 20, 1898): 30–39.

Takeuchi Yoshimi. "Dai Tōa Sensō to Warera no Ketsui (Sengen)" [The Greater East Asia War and our Determination—Commitment Statement]. *Chūgoku Bungaku*. Vol. 80. January 1942, 481–84.

Yamaura Kan'ichi. "Konoe Shūhen no Henkan" [Changes in Konoe's Surroundings]. *Kaizū* (November 1938): 116–20.

Yanaihara Tadao. "Manshū Kenbundan" [Discussion on Manchurian Observations]. *Kaizū* (November 1932): 106–14.

Ōkawa Shūmei. *Ōkawa Shūmeishū* [The Collected Works of Ōkawa Shūmei]. Edited by Hashikawa Bunsō. Chikuma Shobō, 1975.

Ōkawa Shūmei. "Fukkō Ajia no Shomondai" [Various Problems Concerning Resurgent Asia]. Chūkō Bunko, 1993.

In English

Fujisawa, Chikao. *Japanese and Oriental Philosophy*. Tokyo: The Research Department of the Daito-Bunka-Kyokai, 1935.

Hakutani, Yoshinobu, ed. *Selected English Writings of Yone Noguchi: An East-West Literary Assimilation*. Vol. 2. London and Toronto: Associated University Presses, 1992.

Kipling, Rudyard. *The Ballad of East and West, Rudyard Kipling's Verse: Inclusive Edition, 1885–1932*. New York: Doubleday, Doran & Company, 1934.

Nakae Chōmin, *A Discourse by Three Drunkards on Government*. Translated by Nobuko Tsukui. Tokyo: Weatherhill Books, 1984.

Nitobe, Inazo, *Japan: Some Phases of her Problems and Development*. London: Ernest Benn, 1931.

———. *The Japanese Nation: Its Land, Its People, and Its Life, with Special Consideration to Its Relations with the United States*. New York: G. P. Putnam's Sons, 1912.

Nitobe, Inazo. *Bushido: The Soul of Japan*. Tokyo: Teibi Shuppansha, 1908.

———. "On the Dangers of Intolerance." *Pacific Affairs* 6, Conference Supplement (October 1933): 493–96.

Okakura, Kakuzo. *The Awakening of Japan*. London: John Murray, 1905.

———. *The Book of Tea*. New York: Dover Publications, 1964.

———. *The Ideals of the East: With Special Reference to the Art of Japan*. Rutland, VT: Charles E. Tuttle, 1970.

Saito, Hiroshi. *Japan's Policies and Purposes*. Boston: Marshall Jones Company, 1935.

———. "My Impressions in the Far East and Japanese-American Relations." *Annals of the American Academy of Political and Social Science* 177 (January 1935): 246–56.

Tagore, Rabindranath, and Noguchi Yonejirō. *Poet to Poet: Full Text of Correspondence between Yone Noguchi and Rabindranath Tagore on the Sino-Japanese Conflict*. Reprinted from *Visva Bharati Quarterly* 4, no. 3. Nanking & Santiniketan: The Sino-Indian Cultural Society, ca. 1940.

Van Wart, R. B. *The Life of Lieut.-General H. H. Sir Pratap Singh*. London: Oxford University Press and Humphrey Milford, 1926.

Vivekananda, Swami. *The Complete Works of Swami Vivekananda*. Vol. 1. Calcutta: Advaita Ashrama, 1977.

4. Memoirs

In Japanese

Aishinkakura Fuketsu. *Fuketsu Jiden* [Autobiography of Pu Chieh]. Kawade Shobō, 1995.

Aishinkakura Hiro. *Ruten no ūhi no Shūwashi* [Shōwa History of a Wandering Princess]. Shinchōsha, 1984.

Gotō Ryūnosuke, ed. *Shūwa Kenkyūkai*. Keizaiōraisha, 1968.

Hayashi Kyūjirō. *Manshūjihen to Hūten Soryūji* [The Manchurian Incident and the Consul General at Shenyang]. Hara Shobō, 1978.

Inukai Ken. *Yūsukū wa Ima mo Nagareteiru* [The Yang-tze River Still Flows]. Chūkō Bunko, 1984.

Inukai Michiko. *Aru Rekishi no Musume* [A Certain Daughter of History]. Chūō Kōronsha, 1990.

———. *Hanabana to Hoshiboshi to* [With Stars and Flowers]. ChūōKōronsha, 1974.

Mainichi Shimbunsha, ed. *Ichiokunin no Shūwashi* [100 Million People's Shōwa History]. Vol. 2. Mainichi Shimbunsha, 1975.

———. *Nihon Shokuminchishi (2) Manshū* [The History of Japanese Colonialism, Volume 2, Manchuria]. Mainichi Shimbunsha, 1971.

Matsumoto Shigeharu. *Shanhai Jidai: Jānarisuto no Kaisū* [Shanghai Years: Recollections of a Journalist]. 3 vols. Chūkō Shinsho, 1974–75.

———. *Shūwashi e no Ichishūgen* [A Testimony to the History of Shōwa]. Kōdansha, 1992.

Ri (Lee) Masako. *Dūran no Naka no Ōhi* [Princess amidst Great Turmoil] Kōdansha, 1968.

Saionji Kinkazu. *Saionji Kinkazu Kaikoroku "Sugisarishi, Shūwa"* [The Memoirs of Saionji Kinkazu: "Gone is Shōwa"]. Ipec Press, 1991.

Tokugawa Yoshichika. *Saigo no Tonosama* [The Last Lord]. Kōdansha, 1973.

Yamamoto Yoshimasa. *Chichi Yamamoto Isoroku: Katei de Kakonda Saigo no Yūge* [Father, Yamamoto Isoroku: The Last Family Supper]. Kōbunsha, 2001.

In English

Lee Kuan Yew. *Towards Socialism*. Vol. 5. Singapore: Government Printing Office, 1962.

Low Ngiong Ing. *When Singapore was Syonan-to*. Singapore: Eastern Universities Press, 1973.

Nehru, Jawaharlal. *An Autobiography: With Musings on Recent Events in India*. London: John Lane, 1939.

Shinozaki, Mamoru. *Syonan—My Story*. Singapore: Asia Pacific Press, 1975.

244   *Bibliography*

B. Theses and Unpublished Papers

In Japanese

Nakajima Yumiko. *Nichibei Kankei no Ichikūsatsu: Saitū Chūbei Taishi no Taibei Teian wo Chūshin ni* [An Observation in U.S.–Japan Relations—Mainly upon Ambassador Saitō's Proposals for the United States]. Master's Thesis in Politics, Keiō University, 1988.

In English

Wilson, Sandra. *Popular Japanese Responses to the Manchurian Crisis*, D.Phil. Dissertation in History, University of Oxford, 1989.

C. Secondary Sources

In Japanese

Banno Junji. *Meiji—Shisū no Jitsuzū* [Authentic Portrait of Meiji Thought]. Sōbunsha, 1977.

Corner, E.J.H. *Omoide no Shūnan Hakubutsukan* [Shōnan Museum in My Memory]. Trans. Ishii Mikiko. Chūkō Shinsho, 1981.

Eguchi Keiichi. *Jūgonen Sensū Shūshi* [A Condensed History of the Fifteen Years' War]. Aoki Shoten, 1991.

———. *Shūwa no Rekishi: Jūgonen Sensū no Kaimaku* [History of Shōwa: The Opening of the Fifteen Years' War]. Shōgakukan, 1983.

Eizawa Kōji. *"Daitūa Kyūeiken" no Shisū* [The Ideas Behind the "Greater East Asia Co-Prosperity Sphere"]. Kōdansha, 1995.

Fujioka Taishō. *Kaigun Shūshū Takagi Sūkichi: Kaigunshū Chūsaka to Minkanjin Zunūshūdan* [The Lieutenant-Captain Takagi Sōkichi: The Navy Research Unit and Civilian Brain Trust]. Kōjinsha, 1986.

Fujiwara Akira and Imai Seiichi, eds. *Jūgonen Sensūshi* [History of the Fifteen Years' War]. Aoki Shoten, 1989.

Fujiwara Akira. *Shūwa Tennū no Jūgonen Sensū* [The Showa Emperor's Fifteen Years' War]. Aoki Shoten, 1991.

Fujiwara Satoshi, Shinohara Keiichi, and Nishide Takeshi. *Ajia Senji Ryūgakusei* [Asian Students in Wartime Japan]. Kyōdō Tsūshin, 1996.

Fukuda Kazuya. *Chi Hiraku: Ishiwara Kanji to Shūwa no Yume* [The Land Opens: Ishiwara Kanji and the Dream of Shōwa]. Bungei Shunjū, 2001.

Hashikawa Bunsō, Kano Masanao, and Hiraoka Toshio, eds. *Kindai Nihon Shisūshi no Kiso Chishiki: Ishin Zenya kara Haisen made* [Basic Knowledge of the History of Ideas in Modern Japan: From the Restoration to the Defeat]. Yūhikaku, 1971.

Hata Ikuhiko. *Gun Fashizumu Undūshi* [History of the Military Fascist Activities]. Kawade Shobō Shinsha, 1962.

Hayashi Fusao. *Daitūa Sensū Kūteiron* [In Affirmation of the Greater East Asia War]. Banchō Shobō, 1964.

Hōchi Takayuki. *Harubin Gakuin to Manshūkoku* [The Harbin Academy and Manchukuo]. Shinchō Sensho, 1999.

Ienaga Saburō. *Taiheiyū Sensū* [The Pacific War]. Iwanami Shoten, 1986.

Kadono Hiroko. *Tūnanajia no Otūtotachi* [Younger Brothers of Southeast Asia]. Sankōsha, 1985.

Katō Tetsurō. "Shin-hakken no Kawakami Hajime Shokan wo Megutte" [In Reference to the Newly Discovered Correspondence of Kawakami Hajime]. http://homepage3.nifty.com/katote/2001kawakami.html.

Katō Yoshiko. *Saitū Mokichi no Jūgonen Sensū* [Saitō Mokichi's Fifteen Years' War]. Misuzu Shobō, 1990.

Kisaka Junichirō. *Shūwa no Rekishi—Taiheiyū Sensū* [History of Shōwa—The Pacific War]. Shōgakukan, 1994.

———. *Taiheiyū Sensū* [The Pacific War]. Shōgakukan, 1994.

Kobayashi Hideo. *Daitūa Kyūeiken* [Greater East Asia Co-Prosperity Sphere]. Iwanami Booklet, 1989.

———. *"Nihon Kabushiki Gaisha" wo Tsukutta Otoko—Miyazaki Masayoshi no Shūgai* [The Man Who Made "Japan Corporation"—Life of Miyazaki Masayoshi]. Shōgakukan, 1995.

Kobayashi Yoshinori. *Sensūron* [Ideas on War]. Gentōsha, 1998.

Kuroha Kiyotaka. *Jūgonen Sensūshi Josetsu* [A Prologue to the History of the Fifteen Years' War]. Sanseidō, 1979.

Matsuda Teruo. *Jūgonen Sensū-jidai Mokuroku* [Catalogue of the Fifteen Years' War Era], 2 vols. Fukuoka: Ashi Shobō, 1985–87.

Matsumoto Ken'ichi. *Kita Ikkiron* [Discourse on Kita Ikki]. Gendai Hyōronsha, 1972.

———. *Shūwa ni Shisu: Morisaki Minato to Ozawa Kaisaku.* [Dying Alongside Shōwa: Morisaki Minato and Ozawa Kaisaku]. Shinchōsha, 1988.

———. *Takeuchi Yoshimi "Nihon no Ajiashugi" Seidoku* [A Comprehensive Reading of Takeuchi Yoshimi's "Japan's Asianism"]. Iwanami Gendai Bunko, 2000.

Miyake Masaki, ed. *Shūwashi no Gunbu to Seiji* [The Military and Politics in the History of Showa]. Daiichi Hōki Shuppan, 1983.

Nakao Michio. *Nihon Senji Shisū no Kenkyū—Nihon Seishin to Tūa Kyūdūtai* [A Study of Japan's Wartime Philosophies: Japanese Spirit and East Asian Cooperative Body]. Kōseisha Kōseikaku, 2001.

Oguma Eiji. *Tan'itsu Minzoku Shinwa no Kigen: "Nihonjin" no Jigazū no Keifu* [The Origins of the Myth of the Homogenous Nation: A Genealogy of "Japanese" Self-images]. Shinyōsha, 1995.

Oka Yoshitake. *Konoe Fumimaro—"Unmei" no Seijika* [Konoe Fumimaro, a Politician of "Destiny"]. Iwanami Shinsho, 1972.

———. "Kokuminteki Dokuritsu to Kokka Risei" [National Independence and State Rationale] in *Oka Yoshitake Chosakushū* [Collected Writings of Oka Yoshitake]. Vol. 6. Iwanami Shoten, 1993, 241–308.

Okamoto Kōji, ed. *Kindai Nihon no Ajiakan* [Modern Japan's View of Asia]. Minerva, 1998.

Otabe Yūji. *Tokugawa Yoshichika no Jūgonen Sensū* [Tokugawa Yoshichika's Fifteen Years' War]. Aoki Shoten, 1988.

Satō Tetsurō. *Daiajia Shisūkatsugeki: Bukkyū ga Unda Mūhitotsu no Kindaishi* [Philosophical Action Film of Great Asia: Another Modern History Born of Buddhism]. Onbook, 2006.

Takahashi Masae. *2–26 Jiken: Shūwa Ishin no Shisū to Kūdū* [The 2-26 Incident: The Thought and Action of the Shōwa Renovation]. Chūkō Shinsho, 1965.

Takeuchi Yoshimi, ed. and intro. *Ajiashugi* [Asianism]. Vol. 9, *Gendai Nihon Shisū Taikei* [An Outline of Modern Japanese Thoughts] Series. Chikuma Shobō, 1963.

Tanaka Sōgorō. *Kita Ikki: Nihonteki Fashisuto no Shūchū* [Kita Ikki: Symbol of Japanese Fascism]. San'ichi Shobō, 1971.

———. *Nihon Fashizumushi* [History of Japanese Fascism]. Kawade Shobō Shinsha, 1972.

Tobe Ryōichi. *Pīsu Fīrā—Shina Jihen Wahei Kūsaku no Gunzū* [Peace Feeler—Sculpted Portraits of the China Incident Peace Makers]. Ronsōsha, 1991.

Tokutomi Iichirō. *Shūrisha no Hissui* [The Inevitable Fall of the Victor]. Kōdansha, 1952.

Tsubouchi Takahiko. *Okakura Tenshin no Shisū Tanbū: Meisū suru Ajiashugi* [Exploration of Okakura Tenshin's Ideas: Pan-Asianism Going Astray]. Keisō Shobō, 1998.

Ueyama Shunpei. *Daitūa Sensū no Imi: Gendai Bunseki no Shiten* [The Meaning of the Greater East Asia War: Perspective for the Analysis of Contemporary History]. ChūōKōronsha, 1964.

———. *Nippon no Nashonarizumu* [Japanese Nationalism]. Shiseidō, 1965.

Usui Katsumi. *Manshū Jihen* [The Manchurian Incident]. Chūkō Shinsho, 1974.

———. *Manshūkoku to Kokusai Renmei* [Manchukuo and the League of Nations]. Yoshikawa Kōbunkan, 1995.

Yabe Teiji. *Konoe Fumimaro*. Jijitsūshinsha, 1958.

Yamamuro Shin'ichi. *Kimera: Manshūkoku no Shūzū* [Chimera: A Portrait of Manchukuo]. Chuō Kōronsha, 1993.

Yasuhiko Yoshikazu. "Manshū Kenkoku Daigaku no Seishun" [The Youth of Manshū Kenkoku Daigaku]. *Marco Polo* (February 2, 1994): 57–64.

Yoshimoto Takaaki with Tajika Nobukazu. *Watashi no "Sensūron"* [My "Ideas on War"]. Bunkasha, 1999.

Zhai Zin. *Tūa Dūbunkai to Chūgoku: Kindai Nihon ni okeru Taigairinen to sono Jissen* [Tōa Dōbunkai and China: Ideology and Practice of Foreign Relations in Modern Japan]. Keio University Press, 2001.

In English

Ajami, Fouad. "The End of Pan-Arabism." *Foreign Affairs* 57, no. 2 (Winter 1978/79): 355–73.

Akashi, Yoji. "Japanese Policy towards the Malayan Chinese, 1941–45." *Journal of Southeast Asian Studies* 1, no. 2 (September 1970): 61–89.

Apter, David E., ed. *Ideology and Discontent*. London: Collier Macmillan, 1964.

Arendt, Hannah. *The Origins of Totalitarianism*. New York: Harcourt Brace, 1979.

Asano Tamanoi, Mariko. "Knowledge, Power, and Racial Classifications: The 'Japanese' in 'Manchuria.'" *The Journal of Asian Studies* 59, no. 2 (May 2000): 248–76.

Askew, David. "New Research on the Nanjing Incident." *The Japan Focus*. http://www.japanfocus.org/products/details/1729.

Barnhart, Michael A. *Japan Prepares for Total War: The Search for Economic Security, 1919–1941*. Ithaca, NY: Cornell University Press, 1987.

Beasley, W. G. *Japanese Imperialism, 1894–1945*. Oxford: Clarendon, 1987.

———. "Japan and Pan-Asianism: Problems of Definition." In *The Collected Writings of W.G. Beasley, The Collected Writings of Modern Western Scholars on Japan*. Vol. 5. Tokyo: Edition Synapse, 2001, 210–22.

Benfey, Christopher. "Tea with Okakura." *The New York Review of Books* (May 25, 2000): 43–47.

Best, Geoffrey. "Peace Conferences and the Century of Total War: The 1899 Hague Conference and What Came After." *International Affairs* 75, no. 3 (July 1999): 619–34.

Bix, Herbert P. *Hirohito and the Making of Modern Japan*. New York: HarperCollins, 2000.

Brooks, Barbara J. *Japan's Imperial Diplomacy: Consuls, Treaty Ports, and War in China, 1895–1935*. Honolulu: University of Hawai'i Press, 2000.

Buruma, Ian, and Avishai Margalit. *Occidentalism: The West in the Eyes of Its Enemies*. New York: Penguin Press, 2004.

Carr, E. H. *The Twenty Years' Crisis, 1919–1939: An Introduction to the Study of International Relations*. London: Macmillan, 1981.

Chang, Iris. *The Rape of Nanking: The Forgotten Holocaust of World War II*. New York: Basic Books, 1997.

Claude, Inis L., Jr. *Power and International Relations*. New York: Random House, 1962.

Coble, Parks M. *Facing Japan: Chinese Politics and Japanese Imperialism, 1931–1937*. Cambridge, MA: Harvard University Press, 1991.

Colegrove, Kenneth. "The New Order in East Asia." *The Far Eastern Quarterly* 1, no. 1 (November 1941): 5–24.

Coox, Alvin D. *Nomonhan: Japan against Russia, 1939*. 2 vols. Stanford, CA: Stanford University Press, 1985.

Crowley, James B. *Japan's Quest for Autonomy: National Security and Foreign Policy, 1930–1938*. Princeton, NJ: Princeton University Press, 1966.

Doak, Kevin M. "What Is a Nation and Who Belongs? National Narratives and the Ethnic Imagination in Twentieth-Century Japan." *American Historical Review* 102, no. 2 (April 1997): 283–309.

Dower, John W. *Embracing Defeat: Japan in the Aftermath of World War II*. London: Allen Lane, 1999.

———. *War without Mercy: Race and Power in the Pacific War*. London: Faber, 1986.

———. "Rethinking World War II in Asia." *Reviews in American History* 12, no. 2 (June 1984): 155–69.

Doyle, Michael W. *Empires*. Ithaca, NY: Cornell University Press, 1986.

Duara, Prasenjit. *Sovereignty and Authenticity: Manchukuo and the East Asian Modern*. Lanham, MD: Rowman & Littlefield Publishers, 2003.

———. "Transnationalism and the Predicament of Sovereignty: Modern China 1900–1945." *American Historical Review* 102, no. 4 (October 1997): 1030–51.

Dudden, Alexis. *Japan's Colonization of Korea: Discourse and Power*. Honolulu: University of Hawai'i Press, 2005.

Duus, Peter, Ramon H. Myers, and Mark R. Peattie, eds. *The Japanese Informal Empire in China, 1895–1937*. Princeton, NJ: Princeton University Press, 1989.

———. *The Japanese Wartime Empire, 1931–1945*. Princeton, NJ: Princeton University Press, 1996.

Duus, Peter. *The Abacus and the Sword: The Japanese Penetration of Korea, 1895–1910*. Berkeley: University of California Press, 1995.

———, ed. *The Cambridge History of Japan: Volume 6, The Twentieth Century*. Cambridge: Cambridge University Press, 1988.

Esenbel, Selçuk, and Chiharu Inaba, eds. *The Rising Sun and the Turkish Crescent: New Perspectives on the History of Japanese Turkish Relation.* Istanbul: Bogaziçi University Press, 2003.

Feis, Herbert. *The Road to Pearl Harbor: The Coming of War Between the United States and Japan.* New York: Atheneum, 1966.

Fischer, Fritz. *Germany's Aims in the First World War.* New York: W. W. Norton, 1967.

Fletcher, William Miles, III. *The Search for a New Order: Intellectuals and Fascism in Prewar Japan.* Chapel Hill: University of North Carolina Press, 1982.

Fogel, Joshua A. *Nakae Ushikichi in China: The Mourning of Spirit.* Cambridge, MA: Harvard University Press, 1989.

———. *Politics and Sinology: The Case of Naitū Konan (1866–1934).* Cambridge, MA: Harvard University Press, 1984.

Fuess, Harald, ed. *The Japanese Empire in East Asia and Its Postwar Legacy.* Munich: Indicium, 1998.

Garner, Karen. "Global Feminism and Postwar Reconstruction: The World YWCA Visitation to Occupied Japan, 1947." *Journal of World History* 15. no. 2 (June 2004): 191–227.

Garon, Sheldon. *The State and Labor in Modern Japan.* Berkeley: University of California, 1987.

Gellner, Ernest. *Nations and Nationalism.* Oxford: Blackwell, 1983.

Gluck, Carol. *Japan's Modern Myths: Ideology in the Late Meiji Period.* Princeton, NJ: Princeton University Press, 1985.

Goodman, Grant K., ed. *Japanese Cultural Policies in Southeast Asia during World War 2.* New York: St. Martin's Press, 1991.

Goto-Jones, Christopher S. *Political Philosophy in Japan: Nishida, the Kyoto School and Co-Prosperity.* London: Routledge, 2005.

Gould-Davies, Nigel. "Rethinking the Role of Ideology in International Politics during the Cold War." *Journal of Cold War Studies* 1, no. 1 (Winter 1999): 99–109.

Halliday, Jon. *A Political History of Japanese Capitalism.* New York: Random House, 1975.

Harootunian, Harry. *Overcome by Modernity: History, Culture, and Community in Interwar Japan.* Princeton, NJ: Princeton University Press, 2000.

Harvey, Robert. *The Undefeated: The Rise, Fall and Rise of Greater Japan.* London: Macmillan, 1994.

Hauner, Milan. *India in Axis Strategy: Germany, Japan, and Indian Nationalists in the Second World War.* Stuttgart: Klett-Cotta, 1981.

Heisig, James W. *Philosophers of Nothingness: An Essay on the Kyoto School.* Honolulu: University of Hawai'i Press, 2001.

Heisig, James W., and John C. Maraldo, eds. *Rude Awakenings: Zen, the Kyoto School, & the Question of Nationalism.* Honolulu: University of Hawai'i Press, 1995.

Hinsley, F. H. *Power and the Pursuit of Peace: Theory and Practice in the History of Relations between States.* Cambridge: Cambridge University Press, 1963.

Hotta, Eri. "Rash Behari Bose and His Japanese Supporters: An Insight into Anti-Colonial Nationalism and Pan-Asianism." *Interventions* 8, no. 2 (2006): 116–32.

Howland, Douglas R. *Borders of Chinese Civilization: Geography and History at Empire's End.* Durham, NC: Duke University Press, 1996.

———. *Translating the West: Language and Political Reason in Nineteenth-Century Japan.* Honolulu: University of Hawai'i Press, 2002.

Huntington, Samuel P. *The Clash of Civilizations and the Remaking of World Order.* New York: Touchstone, 1997.

———. "The Clash of Civilizations?" *Foreign Affairs* 72, no. 3 (Summer 1993): 22–49.

Iriye, Akira. *Across the Pacific: An Inner History of American–East Asian Relations.* New York: Harcourt, Brace & World, 1967.

———. *Cultural Internationalism and World Order.* Baltimore: Johns Hopkins University Press, 1997.

———. *Japan and the Wider World: From the Mid-Nineteenth Century to the Present.* Longman: London, 1997.

———. *Power and Culture: The Japanese-American War, 1941–1945.* Cambridge: Cambridge University Press, 1981.

———. *The Origins of the Second World War in Asia and The Pacific.* London: Longman, 1987.

———. "The Internationalization of History." *The American Historical Review* Supplement to 94, no. 1 (February 1989): 1–10.

James, Harold. *A German Identity: 1770 to the Present Day.* London: Phoenix Press, 1989.

Jansen, Marius B. *Japan and Its World: Two Centuries of Change.* Princeton, NJ: Princeton University Press, 1980.

———. *The Japanese and Sun Yat-sen.* Cambridge, MA: Harvard University Press, 1954.

———. *The Making of Modern Japan.* Cambridge, MA: Harvard University Press, 2000.

———. "Monarchy and Modernization in Japan." *Journal of Asian Studies* 36, no. 5 (August 1977): 611–22.

Jervis, Robert. *Perception and Misperception in International Politics.* Princeton, NJ: Princeton University Press, 1976.

Johnson, Chalmers. *An Instance of Treason: Ozaki Hotsumi and the Sorge Spy Ring.* Stanford, CA: Stanford University Press, 1964 updated in 1990.

Jones, F. C. *Japan's New Order in East Asia.* London: Oxford University Press, 1954.

Journal of Southeast Asian Studies: The Japanese Occupation in Southeast Asia 27, no. 1 (March 1996).

Kasza, Gregory J. *The State and the Mass Media in Japan, 1918–1945.* Berkeley: University of California Press, 1988.

———. "Fascism from Below? A Comparative Perspective on the Japanese Right, 1931–1936." *Journal of Contemporary History* 19, no. 4 (October 1984): 607–29.

Kedourie, Elie. *Nationalism.* London: Blackwell, 1998.

Ketelaar, James Edward. *Of Heretics and Martyrs in Meiji Japan: Buddhism and Its Persecution.* Princeton, NJ: Princeton University Press, 1990.

Li, Lincoln. *The Japanese Army in North China, 1937–1941.* Oxford: Oxford University Press, 1975.

McClain, James L. *Japan: A Modern History.* New York: W. W. Norton, 2002.

Mitter, Rana. *The Manchurian Myth: Nationalism, Resistance, and Collaboration in Modern China.* Berkeley: University of California Press, 2000.

Morley, James William, ed. *Dilemmas of Growth in Prewar Japan.* Princeton, NJ: Princeton University Press, 1971.

Morley, James William, ed. *Japan's Road to the Pacific War: Japan Erupts: The London Naval Conference and the Manchurian Incident, 1928–1932*. Selected translations from *Taiheiyū Sensū e no Michi: Kaisen Gaikūshi* [The Road to the Pacific War: The History of the Diplomacy surrounding the War Entry]. New York: Columbia University Press, 1984.

Morris-Suzuki, Tessa. "Debating Racial Science in Wartime Japan." In *Beyond Joseph Needham: Science, Technology, and Medicine in East and South East Asia*. Edited by Morris Low. *Osiris* 13 (July 1999): 354–75.

Myers, Ramon H., and Mark R. Peattie, eds. *The Japanese Colonial Empire, 1895–1945*. Princeton, NJ: Princeton University Press, 1984.

Najita, Tetsuo, and J. Victor Koschmann, eds. *Conflict in Modern Japanese History: The Neglected Tradition*. Princeton, NJ: Princeton University Press, 1982.

Nish, Ian. *Japanese Foreign Policy, 1869–1942: Kasumigaseki to Miyakezaka*. London: Routledge, 1977.

———. *Japan's Struggle with Internationalism: Japan, China and the League of Nations, 1931–1933*. London: Kegan Paul International, 1993.

Ogata, Sadako N. *Defiance in Manchuria: The Making of Japanese Foreign Policy, 1931–1932*. Berkeley: University of California, 1964.

Oguma, Eiji. *A Genealogy of "Japanese" Self-images*. Translated by David Askew. Melbourne: Trans Pacific Press, 2002.

Oka, Yoshitake. *Konoe Fumimaro: A Political Biography*. Translated by Okamoto Shumpei and Patricia Murray. Tokyo: University of Tokyo Press, 1983.

Parkes, Graham. "The Putative Fascism of the Kyoto School and the Political Correctness of the Modern Academy." *Philosophy East and West* 47, no. 3 (July 1997): 305–36.

Peattie, Mark R. *Ishiwara Kanji and Japan's Confrontation with the West*. Princeton, NJ: Princeton University Press, 1975.

———. *Nan'yo: The Rise and Fall of the Japanese in Micronesia, 1885–1945*. Honolulu: University of Hawai'i Press, 1988.

Pierson, John D. *Tokutomi Sohū, 1863–1957: A Journalist for Modern Japan*. Princeton: Princeton University Press, 1980.

Prange, Gordon W. *At Dawn We Slept: The Untold Story of Pearl Harbor*. New York: McGraw-Hill, 1981.

Reynolds, E. Bruce, ed. *Japan in the Fascist Era*. New York: Palgrave Macmillan, 2004.

Rorty, Richard. *Contingency, Irony, and Solidarity*. Cambridge: Cambridge University Press, 1989.

Ruskin, John. *St. Mark's Rest*. New York: Bryan, Taylor, 1894.

Russell, Bertrand. *A History of Western Philosophy*. New York: Touchstone, 1972.

Saaler, Sven, and J. Victor Koschmann, eds. *Pan-Asianism in Modern Japanese History: Colonialism, Regionalism and Borders*. London: Routledge, 2006.

Said, Edward W. *Orientalism*. New York: Vintage, 1978.

Sartori, Giovanni. "Politics, Ideology, and Belief Systems." *The American Political Science Review* 63, no. 2 (June 1969): 398–411.

Scalapino, Robert A. *The Foreign Policy of Modern Japan*. Berkeley: University of California Press, 1977.

Sen, Amartya. "Tagore and His India." *The New York Review of Books*, June 26, 1997.

Shimazu, Naoko. *Japan, Race and Equality: The Racial Equality Proposal at the 1919*. London: Routledge, 1998.

Snyder, Jack. *Myths of Empire: Domestic Politics and International Ambition*. Ithaca, NY: Cornell University Press, 1991.

Snyder, Louis L. *Macro-Nationalisms: A History of the Pan-Movements*. Westport: Greenwood Press, 1984.

Storry, Richard. *Japan and the Decline of the West in Asia 1894–1943*. London: Macmillan, 1979.

Sumi Barnett, Yukiko. "India in Asia: Ōkawa Shūmei's Pan-Asian Thought and His Idea of India in Early Twentieth-Century Japan." *Journal of the Oxford University History Society* 1 (Hilary 2004): 1–23.

Szpilman, Christopher W. A. "Kita Ikki and the Politics of Coercion." *Modern Asian Studies* 36, no. 2 (2002): 467–90.

Tanaka, Stefan. *Japan's Orient: Rendering Pasts into History*. Berkeley: University of California Press, 1993.

Thorne, Christopher. *The Limits of Foreign Policy: The West, the League and the Far Eastern Crisis of 1931–1933*. London: Hamish Hamilton, 1972.

Townsend, Susan C. *Yanaihara Tadao and Japanese Colonial Policy: Redeeming Empire*. Richmond, Surrey: Curzon, 2000.

Tsurumi, Shunsuke. *An Intellectual History of Wartime Japan 1931–1945*. London: KPI, 1986.

Utley, Jonathan. *Going to War with Japan, 1937–1941*. Knoxville: University of Tennessee Press, 1985.

Vinh, Sinh. *Tokutomi Sohū (1863–1957): The Later Career*. Toronto: University of Toronto-York University Joint Centre on Modern East Asia, 1986.

Whyte, Frederick. "Japan's Purpose in Asia: An Appreciation of Japan's War Potential, Strategic Position, and Foreign Policy." The Royal Institute of International Affairs, 1941.

Wilson, George. *Radical Nationalist in Japan: Kita Ikki, 1993–1937*. Cambridge, MA: Harvard University Press, 1969.

Wilson, Sandra. *Pro-Western Intellectuals and the Manchurian Crisis of 1931–1933*. Nissan Occasional Papers, Series No. 3, Nissan Institute of Japanese Studies, Oxford, 1987.

———. *The Manchurian Crisis and Japanese Society, 1931–33*. London: Routledge, 2002.

———. "The '15-Year War' in Japan." *Japanese Studies* 21, no. 2 (2001): 155–64.

Yap Pheng Geck. *Scholar, Banker, Gentleman Soldier: The Reminiscences of Dr. Yap Pheng Geck*. Singapore: Times Books International, 1982.

Young, C. Walter. *Japan's Special Position in Manchuria*. New York: Arno Press, 1979.

Young, Louise. *Japan's Total Empire: Manchuria and the Culture of Wartime Imperialism*. Berkeley: University of California Press, 1998.

Notes

Introduction

1. This follows from the age-old Japanese convention, counting the first year of war, 1931, as year one of the fifteen years, making it Fifteen Years' War rather than Fourteen Years' War. Examples of scholarship treating the period between 1931 and 1945 as a single protracted war are Kuroha Kiyotaka, *Jūgonen Sensō Josetsu* [A Prologue to the Fifteen Years' War] (Sanseidō, 1979); Otabe Yūji, *Tokugawa Yoshichika no Jūgonen Sensō* [Tokugawa Yoshichika's Fifteen Years' War] (Aoki Shoten, 1988); Fujiwara Akira and Imai Seiichi, eds., *Jūgonen Sensōshi* [History of the Fifteen Years' War] (Aoki Shoten, 1989); Fujiwara Akira, *Shōwa Tennō no Jūgonen Sensō* [The Showa Emperor's Fifteen Years' War] (Aoki Shoten, 1991); and Eguchi Keiichi, *Jūgonen Sensōshi Shōshi* [A Condensed History of the Fifteen Years' War] (Aoki Shoten, 1991).
2. *Ajia Rekishi Jiten* [Dictionary of Asian History], vol. 6 (Heibonsha, 1959), 6–7; emphasis added.
3. For various approaches to ideology, see Giovanni Sartori, "Politics, Ideology, and Belief Systems," *The American Political Science Review* 63, no. 2 (June 1969): 398–411; Roger Eatwell and Anthony Wright, eds., *Contemporary Political Ideologies* (London: Pinter, 1993); and Michael H. Hunt, *Ideology and U.S. Foreign Policy* (New Haven, CT: Yale University Press, 1987).
4. The philosopher Tsurumi Shunsuke is allegedly the first person to have used the term in 1956. See Tsurumi Shunsuke, *An Intellectual History of Wartime Japan 1931–1945* (London: KPI, 1986).
5. Sandra Wilson, "The '15-Year War' in Japan," *Japanese Studies* 21, no. 2 (2001): 155–64.
6. Some critics such as Hata Ikuhiko argue against the Fifteen Years' War on the basis that the "war" lasted only thirteen years and eleven months in total. Again, the answer to this is that many Japanese regard 1931 as the "first" year of the war and 1945 as the "fifteenth."

7. E. H. Carr, *The Twenty Years' Crisis, 1919–1939: An Introduction to the Study of International Relations* (London: Macmillan, 1981), 127.

8. Akira Iriye, *Cultural Internationalism and World Order* (Baltimore: Johns Hopkins University Press, 1997), 120.

9. Ibid., 119.

10. Carr, *The Twenty Years' Crisis*, 127.

11. The pioneering and extremely important works in this category include John W. Dower, *War without Mercy: Race and Power in the Pacific War* (London: Faber, 1986) and Akira Iriye, *Power and Culture: The Japanese-American War, 1941–1945* (Cambridge: Cambridge University Press, 1981).

12. Mark R. Peattie, *Ishiwara Kanji and Japan's Confrontation with the West* (Princeton, NJ: Princeton University Press, 1975).

13. Louise Young, *Japan's Total Empire: Manchuria and the Culture of Wartime Imperialism* (Berkeley: University of California Press, 1998).

14. Sandra Wilson, *The Manchurian Crisis and Japanese Society, 1931–33* (London: Routledge, 2002).

15. Ramon H. Myers and Mark R. Peattie, eds., *The Japanese Colonial Empire, 1895–1945* (Princeton, NJ: Princeton University Press, 1984); Peter Duus, Ramon H. Myers, and Mark R. Peattie, eds., *The Japanese Informal Empire in China, 1895–1937* (Princeton, NJ: Princeton University Press, 1989); Peter Duus, Ramon H. Myers, and Mark R. Peattie, eds., *The Japanese Wartime Empire, 1931–1945* (Princeton, NJ: Princeton University Press, 1996).

16. Rana Mitter, *The Manchurian Myth: Nationalism, Resistance, and Collaboration in Modern China* (Berkeley: University of California Press, 2000); Barbara J. Brooks, *Japan's Imperial Diplomacy: Consuls, Treaty Ports, and War in China, 1895–1938* (Honolulu: University of Hawai'i Press, 2000); Yoshihisa Tak Matsusaka, *The Making of Japanese Manchuria, 1904–1932* (Cambridge, MA: Harvard University Press, 2001); Prasenjit Duara, *Sovereignty and Authenticity: Manchukuo and the East Asian Modern* (Lanham, MD: Rowman & Littlefield, 2003).

17. William Miles Fletcher III, *The Search for a New Order: Intellectuals and Fascism in Prewar Japan* (Chapel Hill: University of North Carolina Press, 1982); Harry D. Harootunian and Tetsuo Najita, "Chapter 14: Japanese Revolt against the West: Political and Cultural Criticism in the Twentieth Century," in *The Cambridge History of Japan: Vol. 6, The Twentieth Century*, ed. Peter Duus, 711–74 (Cambridge: Cambridge University Press, 1988); Harry D. Harootunian, *Overcome by Modernity: History, Culture, and Community in Interwar Japan* (Princeton, NJ: Princeton University Press, 2000); Graham Parkes, "The Putative Fascism of the Kyoto School and the Political Correctness of the Modern Academy," *Philosophy East and West* 47, no. 3 (July 1997): 305–36; James W. Heisig and John C. Maraldo, eds., *Rude Awakenings: Zen, the Kyoto School, & the Question of Nationalism* (Honolulu: University of Hawai'i Press, 1995).

18. For solid overall accounts, see Rekishigaku Kenkyūkai, ed., *Taiheiyō Sensōshi* [History of the Pacific War], vols. 1 and 2 (Aoki Shoten, 1971 and 1972); Eguchi Keiichi, *Jūgonen Sensōshi* [History of the Fifteen Years' War], vol. 30 of *Nippon no Rekishi* [History of Japan] (Aoki Shoten, 1976); Hata Ikuhiko, *Gun Fashizumu Undōshi* [History of Military Fascist Activities] (Kawade Shobō Shinsha, 1962).

19. Yamamuro Shin'ichi, *Kimera: Manshūkoku no Shōzō* [Chimera: A Portrait of Manchukuo] (Chuō Kōronsha, 1993).

20. Matsumoto Ken'ichi, *Takeuchi Yoshimi "Nihon no Ajiashugi" Seidoku* [A Comprehensive Reading of Takeuchi Yoshimi's "Japan's Asianism"] (Iwanami Gendai Bunko, 2000).

21. For example, Inoue Toshikazu, *Ajiashugi wo Toinaosu* [Re-Questioning Pan-Asianism] (Chikuma Shinsho, 2006); Sven Saaler and J. Victor Koschmann, eds., *Pan-Asianism in Modern Japanese History: Colonialism, Regionalism and Borders* (London: Routledge, 2006); Eiji Oguma, *A Genealogy of "Japanese" Self-Images*, trans. David Askew (Rosanna, Australia: Pacific Press, 2002); Selçuk Esenbel and Inaba Chiharu, eds., *The Rising Sun and the Turkish Crescent: New Perspectives on the History of Japanese Turkish Relation* (Istanbul: Bogaziçi University Press, 2003); Dick Stegewems, ed., *Nationalism and Internationalism in Imperial Japan: Autonomy, Asian Brotherhood, or World Citizenship?* (London: RoutledgeCurzon, 2003) all deal with the formation and circulation of Pan-Asianist discourse in Japan form various perspectives.

22. See, for example, the Pulitzer-winning Herbert P. Bix, *Hirohito and the Making of Modern Japan* (New York: Harper Collins, 2000).

23. *Puraido: Unmei no Toki* [Pride: The Fateful Moment] (Tōei Film Studio, 1998).

24. Kobayashi Yoshinori, *Sensōron* [Ideas on War] (Gentōsha, 1998), 30.

25. Later revised and published in English as *Germany's Aims in the First World War* (New York: W. W. Norton, 1967).

26. The primary example of this contention is James B. Crowley, *Japan's Quest for Autonomy: National Security and Foreign Policy, 1930–1938* (Princeton, NJ: Princeton University Press, 1966).

27. Takeuchi Yoshimi, *Ajiashugi no Tenbō* [A Survey of Pan-Asianism], in *Ajiashugi* [Pan-Asianism], ed. and intro. by Takeuchi Yoshimi, vol. 9 of *Gendai Nihon Shisō Taikei* [An Outline of Modern Japanese Thoughts] (Chikuma Shobō, 1963), 13. Also reprinted as *"Nihon no Ajiashugi"* [Japan's Asianism], in Matsumoto Ken'ichi, *Takeuchi Yoshimi*, 9–10.

Chapter 1

1. Ernest Gellner, *Nations and Nationalism* (Oxford: Blackwell, 1983), 1.

2. Louis L. Snyder, *Macro-Nationalisms: A History of the Pan-Movements* (Westport, CT: Greenwood, 1984), 5.

3. Douglas R. Howland, *Translating the West: Language and Political Reason in Nineteenth-Century Japan* (Honolulu: University of Hawai'i Press, 2002).

4. Prasenjit Duara, "The Discourse of Civilization and Pan-Asianism," *Journal of World History* 12, no. 1 (2001): 99.

5. Ibid., 100–108. Also, Prasenjit Duara, *Sovereignty and Authenticity: Manchukuo and the East Asian Modern* (Lanham, MD: Rowman & Littlefield Publishers), 2003, 91–96.

6. Duara, *Sovereignty and Authenticity*, 94–96.

7. The prefix "han" here is a phonetic translation of the Greek "pan."

8. Edward W. Said, *Orientalism* (New York: Vintage, 1978), 5. This study's concern is in fact quite different from Said's in that it seeks to understand the corresponding reality of ideas about Asia from within rather than the internal consistency of Western ideas about Asia from without.

9. Stefan Tanaka, *Japan's Orient: Rendering Pasts into History* (Berkeley: University of California Press, 1993).

10. Rudyard Kipling, "The Ballad of East and West," in *Rudyard Kipling's Verse: Inclusive Edition, 1885–1932* (New York: Doubleday, Doran, 1934), 268.

11. Kipling, "The White Man's Burden," ibid., 373–74.

12. Yeats to Noguchi, June 27 [1921?], Oxford, in *Selected English Writings of Yone Noguchi: An East-West Literary Assimilation*, ed. Yoshinobu Hakutani, vol. 2 (London: Associated University Presses, 1992), 14.

13. Kakuzo Okakura, *The Ideals of the East: With Special Reference to the Art of Japan* (Rutland, VT: Charles E. Tuttle, 1970), 1.

14. Christopher Benfey, "Tea with Okakura," *The New York Review of Books* (May 25, 2000): 43–47.

15. The address was delivered at Airlie Lodge, Ridgeway Gardens, England, most likely in September 1896. Swami Vivekananda, "Vedanta as a Factor in Civilization," in *The Complete Works of Swami Vivekananda*, vol. 1 (Calcutta: Advaita Ashrama, 1977), 385–86.

16. For a comprehensive narrative of Dharmapala and his associations with Japan, see *Satō Tetsurō, Daiajia Shisōkatsugeki: Bukkyō ga Unda Mōhitotsu no Kindaishi* [Philosophical Action Film of Great Asia: Another Modern History Born of Buddhism] (Onbook, 2006).

17. *Asahi Shimbun*, August 5, 1893, reprinted in Tsubouchi Takahiko, *Okakura Tenshin no ShisōTanbō: Meisōsuru Ajiashugi* [Exploration of Okakura Tenshin's Ideas: Pan-Asianism Going Astray] (Keisō Shobō, 1998), 30–31.

18. Ibid.

19. Kakuzo Okakura, *The Awakening of Japan* (London: John Murray, 1905), 207.

20. Ibid., 207–8.

21. Ibid., 209.

22. Kakuzo Okakura, *The Book of Tea* (New York: Dover, 1964), 3.

23. Ibid.

24. Ibid., 4–5.

25. Ibid., 2–3.
26. Okakura, *The Ideals of the East*, 3–4.
27. Gaimushō Gaikō Shiryōkan and Nihon Gaikōshijiten Hensan Iinkai, eds., *Nihongaikōshi Jiten* [Dictionary of Japanese Diplomacy] (Yamakawa Shuppan, 1992), 628.
28. See Marius B. Jansen, *The Japanese and Sun Yat-sen* (Cambridge, MA: Harvard University Press, 1954).
29. Konoe Atsumaro, "Dōjinshu Dōmei fu Shina Mondai Kenkyū no Hitsuyō" [Let Nations of the Same Race Unite Themselves and Discuss Chinese Questions (original translation)], *Taiyō*(January 20, 1898): 1–3. The opinion journal *Taiyō* had a bilingual table of contents, though the articles themselves were featured only in Japanese.
30. Ibid., 1.
31. Ibid.
32. Aihara Shigeki, "Konoe Atsumaro to Shina Hozenron" [Konoe Atsumaro and the Argument for the Preservation of China] in *Kindai Nihon no Ajiakan* [Modern Japan's View of Asia], ed. Okamoto Kōji (Minerva, 1998), 71.
33. Ibid., 52–53.
34. Konoe Atsumaro, *Keisetsu Yobun* [Untold Story of My Hard Student Years], vol. 1 (Yōmeibunko, 1939), 274.
35. Konoe Atsumaro, "Dōjinshu Dōmei," 3.
36. Takayama Rinjirō, "Jinshukyōsō toshite Mitaru Gokutō Mondai" [The Far East Questions from the Point of View of the Struggle for Existence among Different Races], *Taiyō*(January 20, 1898): 30–39.
37. Ibid., 30.
38. Ibid., 36, 38.
39. Miyazaki Tōten, *Sanjūsannen no Yume* [My Thirty-three Years' Dream] (Tokyo: Bungei Shunjū, 1943).
40. For Bose's activities in Japan, see Eri Hotta, "Rash Behari Bose and His Japanese Supporters: An Insight into Anti-Colonial Nationalism and Pan-Asianism," *Interventions* 8, no. 2 (2006): 116–32.
41. Gregory Henderson, *Korea: The Politics of the Vortex* (Cambridge, MA: Harvard University Press, 1968), 67–69.
42. Uchida Ryōhei, *Nikkan Gappō* [Japanese-Korean Merger], reprinted in Takeuchi, *Ajiashugi*, 205–38.
43. Kokuryūkai, ed., *Tōa Senkaku Shishi Kiden* [A Record of Pioneering East Asian Fighters], vol. 1 (Misuzu Shobō, 1974), 10.
44. Konoe Atsumaro, "Dōjinshu Dōmei," 3.
45. Okakura, *The Ideals of the East*, 6.
46. Morimoto (Tarui) Tōkichi, *Daitō Gappōron* [Argument for a Great Eastern Confederation], 1893. Takeuchi Yoshimi's Japanese translation of the text is in Takeuchi, *Ajiashugi* [Asianism], 106–29.
47. Morimoto, 142.

48. Ibid., 117–18.
49. Ibid., 118.
50. The passage and the phrase "shakai no go" are taken from Takeuchi's translation in Takeuchi, *Ajiashugi*, 110.
51. Morimoto, 120.

Chapter 2

1. Taken from John Dower, *Embracing Defeat: Japan in the Aftermath of World War II* (London: Allen Lane, 1999), 21. Japan's mastery of the vocabulary of the international system is powerfully demonstrated in Alexis Dudden, *Japan's Colonization of Korea: Discourse and Power* (Honolulu: University of Hawai'i Press, 2005).
2. Peter Duus, "Introduction," in *The Cambridge History of Japan: Vol. 6, The Twentieth Century*, ed. Peter Duus (Cambridge: Cambridge University Press, 1988), 7.
3. Robert A. Scalapino, "Ideology and Modernization—The Japanese Case," in *Ideology and Discontent*, ed. David E. Apter (London: Collier Macmillan, 1964), 97–98.
4. Fukuzawa Yukichi, *Jiji Shinpō*, March 16, 1885.
5. Okamoto Kōji, "Joshō—'Nihon no Ajia' ka [Introduction] in *Kindai Nihon no Ajiakan* [Modern Japan's View of Asia], ed. Okamoto (Minerva, 1998).
6. Also, on varying interpretations of Fukuzawa's thesis of "Exit Asia," see Banno Junji, *Meiji—Shisō no Jitsuzō*[Authentic Portrait of Meiji Thought] (Sōbunsha, 1977).
7. Nakae Chōmin, *Sansuijin Keirin Mondō* (Iwanami Bunko, 1965). Also translated into English: Nakae Chōmin, *A Discourse by Three Drunkards on Government*, trans. Nobuko Tsukui (Tokyo: Weatherhill Books, 1984).
8. Jawaharlal Nehru, *An Autobiography: With Musings on Recent Events in India* (London: John Lane, 1939), 16.
9. From a translated excerpt given in Matsumoto Ken'ichi, *Takeuchi Yoshimi "Nihon no Ajiashugi" Seidoku* [A Comprehensive Reading of Takeuchi Yoshimi's "Japan's Asianism"] (Iwanami Gendai Bunko, 2000), 121.
10. Relevant analyses in Prasenjit Duara, *Sovereignty and Authenticity* (Lanham, MD: Rowman & Littlefield Publishers, 2003), 101–2, and "Transnationalism and the Predicament of Sovereignty: Modern China 1900–1945," *American Historical Review* 102, no. 4 (October 1997): 1030–51.
11. H. P. Ghose, "Introduction," in J. G. Ohsawa, *The Two Great Indians in Japan: Sri Rash Behari Bose and Netaji Subhas Chandra Bose* (Calcutta: Kusa Publications, 1954), vi.
12. Ibid., 33.

13. Hyung Gu Lynn, "A Comparative Study of the Tōyō Kyōkai and the Nan'yō Kyōkai," in *The Japanese Empire in East Asia and Its Postwar Legacy*, ed. Harald Fuess (Munich: Indicium, 1998), 65–95.

14. As given in Ohsawa, 27–38.

15. Milan Hauner, *India in Axis Strategy: Germany, Japan, and Indian Nationalists in the Second World War* (Stuttgart: Klett-Cotta, 1981), 104.

16. Ibid.

17. Okakura, *Ideals of the East: With Special Reference to the Art of Japan* (Rutland, VT: Charles E. Tuttle, 1970), 1.

18. Kita Ikki, *Nihon Kaizō Hōan Taikō* [Outline of Plans for the Reconstruction of Japan], in *Gendaishi Shiryō* [Modern History Documents], vol. 5 (Misuzu Shobō, 1964), 10–11; emphasis added.

19. See Najita and Harootunian, "Japanese Revolt against the West" in Duus, ed., *The Cambridge History of Japan: Vol. 6, The Twentieth Century*, 711–74; George Wilson, *Radical Nationalist in Japan: Kita Ikki, 1993–1937* (Cambridge, MA: Harvard University Press, 1969). Among numerous studies on Kita in Japanese, the benchmark works are Tanaka Sōgorō, *Kita Ikki: Nihonteki Fashisuto no Shōchō* [Kita Ikki: Symbol of Japanese Fascism] (San'ichi Shobō, 1971) and Matsumoto Ken'ichi, *Kita Ikkiron* [Discourse on Kita Ikki] (Gendai Hyōronsha, 1972).

20. Christopher W. A. Szpilman, "Kita Ikki and the Politics of Coercion," *Modern Asian Studies* 36, no. 2 (2002): 468.

21. For a sophisticated analysis of Ōkawa and His Pan-Asianism, see Christopher W. A. Szpilman, "The Dream of One Asia: Ōkawa Shūmei and Japanese Pan-Asianism," in *The Japanese Empire in East Asia and Its Postwar Legacy*, ed. Fuess, 49–63; and Yukiko Sumi Barnett, "India in Asia: Ōkawa Shūmei's Pan-Asian Thought and His Idea of India in Early Twentieth-Century Japan," *Journal of the Oxford University History Society* 1 (Hilary 2004): 1–23.

22. Jon Halliday, *A Political History of Japanese Capitalism* (New York: Pantheon, 1975), 139.

23. Bertrand Russell, *A History of Western Philosophy* (New York: Touchstone, 1972), 620.

24. Most English-language historical accounts of the conference, however, record the event as a meeting of the "Big Four," only referring to the United States, Britain, France, and Italy.

25. For an in-depth analysis of this debate, see Naoko Shimazu, *The Racial Equality Proposal at the 1919 Paris Peace Conference: Japanese Motivations and Anglo-American Responses* (London: Routledge, 1998).

26. Published in the December issue of the magazine *Nihon oyobi Nihonjin* [Japan and the Japanese], as excerpted in Yabe Teiji, *Konoe Fumimaro* (Jijitsūshinsha, 1958), 16–21.

27. Ibid., 18–19.

28. Ōkawa Shūmei, *Fukkō Ajia no Shomondai* [Various Problems Concerning Resurgent Asia] (Chūkō Bunko, 1993).
29. Ibid., 23.
30. Hannah Arendt, *The Origins of Totalitarianism* (New York: Harcourt Brace, 1979), 222–66.
31. Arendt cites Joseph Stalin's 1945 convocation of Pan-Slav Congress in Sofia as her example. Ibid., 223.
32. Noguchi Yonejirō, *"Indo Bunka no Taikan"* [Broad View of Indian Culture], a speech delivered on May 23, 1936, at Meiji Seimeikan, Tokyo, compiled in a society publication *Keimeikai Dai Rokujūrokkai Kōenshū* [The Compilation of the 66ᵗʰ Lecture Series], 10–11.
33. Ibid., 11.
34. Ibid., 30.
35. Ibid., 33–34.
36. Ibid., 32.
37. Madame de Staël observed, in the aftermath of Napoleon's defeat of Prussia, that "In literature, as in politics, the Germans show too much consideration for foreigners, and not enough national prejudices. Self-abnegation and esteem for others are qualities in individuals, but the patriotism of nations must be egotistical." Quoted from *De l'Allemagne* (1813) in Harold James, *A German Identity: 1770 to the Present Day* (London: Phoenix Press, 1989), 13. For Elie Kedourie's similar contention, see for example, *Nationalism* (London: Blackwell, 1998).

Chapter 3

1. Christopher Thorne, *The Limits of Foreign Policy: The West, the League and the Far Eastern Crisis of 1931–1933* (London: Hamish Hamilton, 1972) and Ian Nish, *Japan's Struggle with Internationalism: Japan, China and the League of Nations, 1931–1933* (London: Kegan Paul International, 1993) explore Manchuria as a test case of collective security.
2. The treaties entailed, among other things, that the nine powers of Japan, the United States, Britain, France, Italy, Belgium, the Netherlands, Portugal, and China would seek to uphold China's integrity, maintain the principle of equal opportunity, and to provide an environment for its development. See Akira Iriye, *The Origins of the Second World War in Asia and the Pacific* (London: Longman, 1987), 2.
3. Ian Nish, *Japanese Foreign Policy, 1869–1942: Kasumigaseki to Miyakezaka* (London: Routledge, 1977), 7.
4. The London Conference (1930) dealt with the rules of engagement, particularly submarine warfare, and the number of naval vessels among the United States, Britain, Japan, France, and Italy. Japan's civilian delegates achieved an

overall success in increasing Japan's allocation from the previous Washington Conference level. But Japan's Naval General Staff and the Privy Council launched an all-out campaign against the cabinet, pointing out that the achieved number was 0.025 percent short of their original target.

5. Saionji's remark on October 2, 1932, on the question of "Japan as the *meishu* of the East" and "Asiatic Monroe Doctrine," recorded in Harada Kumao, *Saionjikō to Seikyoku* [Prince Saionji and Political Situations], vol. 2 (Iwanami Shoten, 1950), 377.

6. Eguchi Keiichi. *Jūgonen Sensō Shōshi* [A Condensed History of the Fifteen Years' War] (Aoki Shoten, 1991), 19.

7. For Yoshizawa's criticism of Japan's China policy, see Barbara J. Brooks, *Japan's Imperial Diplomacy: Consuls, Treaty Ports, and War in China, 1895–1935* (Honolulu: University of Hawai'i Press, 2000), 69–70.

8. January 23, 1931, the 59th House of Representatives session, recorded in Shakaimondai Shiryō Kenkyūkai, ed., *Teikoku Gikaishi* [The Imperial Diet Session Record], vol. 9 (Tōyōbunkasha, 1976), 253.

9. See Miwa Kimitada, *Matsuoka Yōsuke, sono Ningen to Gaikō* [Matsuoka Yōsuke: His Person and Diplomacy] (Chūōkōronsha, 1971).

10. Saionji Kinkazu, *Saionji Kinkazu Kaikoroku "Sugisarishi, Shōwa"* [The Memoirs of Saionji Kinkazu: "Gone is Shōwa"] (Ipec Press, 1991), 190–91.

11. Matsumoto Shigeharu, *Shanhai Jidai: Jānarisuto no Kaisō* [Shanghai Years: Recollections of a Journalist], vol. 1 (Chūkō Shinsho, 1974), 25–29.

12. Yosuke Matsuoka, *Economic Co-operation of Japan and China in Manchuria and Mongolia: Its Motives and Basic Significance* (Dairen: The Chunichi Bunka Kyokai, ca. 1929), 5.

13. Ibid., 15.

14. James B. Crowley, *Japan's Quest for Autonomy: National Security and Foreign Policy, 1930–1938* (Princeton, NJ: Princeton University Press), 1966.

15. Sadako N. Ogata, *Defiance in Manchuria: The Making of Japanese Foreign Policy, 1931–1932* (Berkeley: University of California, 1964).

16. Ibid., 181–82.

17. The benchmark study is Mark R. Peattie, *Ishiwara Kanji and Japan's Confrontation with the West* (Princeton, NJ: Princeton University Press, 1975). In Japanese, see Fukuda Kazuya, *Chi Hiraku: Ishiwara Kanji to Shōwa no Yume* [The Land Opens: Ishiwara Kanji and the Dream of Shōwa] (Bungei Shunjū, 2001).

18. Based on the teachings of the thirteenth-century Tendai Buddhist monk Nichiren, the faith has been historically marked by its aggressive rejection of other sects and its apocalyptic dialectics. In the postwar era, it resurfaced in the organization of Ikeda Daisaku's *Sōka Gakkai* that exerts major influence on Japanese politics via the political party Kōmeitō.

19. See Ishiwara Kanji, *"Ōshūsenshi Kōwa" Ketsuron* [Conclusion: Lectures on European War History], April 1931, complied in *Ishiwara Kanji Shiryō:*

Kokubōronsaku [Documents on Ishiwara Kanji: Theories and Policies of National Defense], ed. Tsunoda Jun (Hara Shobō, 1971), 69–70, and Ishiwara Kanji, *Manmō Mondai Shiken* [Personal View on the Manchurian Problem], May 22, 1931, in ibid., 76–79.

20. Hayashi Kyūjirō, *Manshūjihen to Hōten Soryōji* [The Manchurian Incident and the Consul General at Shenyang] (Hara Shobō, 1978), 145–46.

21. Ibid., 145.

22. Ibid.

23. Hayashi, 151.

24. See Prasentjit Duara, *Sovereignty and Authenticity: Manchukuo and the East Asian Modern* (Lanham, MD: Rowman & Littlefield Publishers, 2003), 51–59, for an illuminating interpretation of this episode, in which claims made by Matsuoka Yōsuke and Chih Meng, associate director of the China Institute in America are discussed.

25. Hiroshi Saito, "A Japanese View of the Manchurian Situation," *Annals of the American Academy of Political and Social Science* 165 (January 1933): 160–61.

26. "Address Delivered by Yosuke Matsuoka, Chief Japanese Delegate, at the Seventh Plenary Meeting of the Special Assembly of the League of Nations," Matsuoka, *Japan's Case in the Sino-Japanese Dispute* (Geneva: Japanese Delegation to the League of Nations, 1933), 49–61.

27. *Teikoku Gikaishi*, vol. 18 (1977), 413.

28. "Amō Seimei" [Amō Statement], April 17, 1934, http://www.geocities.co.jp/WallStreet-Bull/6515/zibiki/a.htm.

29. Konoe Atsumaro, Konoe Atsumaro Nikki [Konoe Atsumaro Diary], vol. 2 (Kashima Kenkyū Shuppankai, 1968), 195.

30. President James Monroe in his seventh annual message to Congress, December 2, 1823, http://www.ourdocuments.gov/.

31. The Roosevelt Corollary was proclaimed over the issue of foreign debt payments by the Dominican Republic (1904). This gave rise to the fear in the United States that creditor European powers might try to occupy the Western Hemisphere under the pretext of enforcing debt collections, just at the time of the U.S. construction of the Panama Canal, in effect threatening U.S. strategic positions.

32. Tachi Sakutarō, "Monrōshugi no Tetteiteki Kentō" [A Comprehensive Study of the Monroe Doctrine], Gaikō Jihō (December 1936), vol. 770, A.2.1.0.U2, Gaimushō Gaikō Shiryōkan [Diplomatic Record Office, Japanese Foreign Ministry], Tokyo, Japan (GGS).

33. Ibid., 6.

34. Ibid., 6–7. Whitton's work is dated 1933 and Coolidge's 1909 in Tachi's text.

35. Hirota in December 1933 recorded by Harada in *Saionjikō to Seikyoku*, vol. 3 (1951): 205.

36. "Goshōkaigi Kettei no Gaikōhōshin ni kansuru Ken" [Concerning Foreign Policy Guidelines Reached at the Five Minister Conference], in *Nihon*

GaikōNenpyō narabi ni Shuyōmonjo [Chronology and Major Documents concerning Japan's Foreign Policy], ed. Gaimushō, vol. 2 (Hara Shobō, 1966), 275–77.

37. His speeches are compiled in a single volume, Hiroshi Saito, *Japan's Policies and Purposes* (Boston: Marshall Jones Company, 1935).

38. Saitō Hiroshi, "Gunshukukaigi to Kongo no Nichibeikankei" [Arms Reduction Conference and the Prospect of U.S.–Japan Relations], *Daiamondo* (August 11, 1934), as excerpted in Nakajima Yumiko, *Nichibei Kankei no Ichikōsatsu: Saitō Chūbei Taishi no Taibei Teian wo Chūshin ni* [An Observation in U.S.–Japan Relations—Mainly upon Ambassador Saitō's Proposals for the United States] (Master's Thesis in Politics, Keiō University, 1988), 96–97.

39. Ibid.

40. Nitobe's talk "Japanese Colonization" is quoted in James L. McClain, *Japan: A Modern History* (New York: W. W. Norton, 2002), 343.

41. Ibid.

42. Inazo Nitobe, *The Japanese Nation: Its Land, Its People, and Its Life, with Special Consideration to Its Relations with the United States* (New York: G. P. Putnam's Sons, 1912), 254.

43. Inazo Nitobe, *Bushido: The Soul of Japan*, revised and enlarged (Teibi Shuppansha, 1908), 23.

44. Ibid., 8.

45. For instance, Stefan Tanaka's study of Shiratori Kurakichi and others in pioneering the discipline of *Tōyōshi* in *Japan's Orient: Rendering Pasts into History* (Berkeley: University of California Press, 1993); Joshua A. Fogel's study of Naitō Konan and his contribution to the development of China studies in *Politics of Sinology: The Case of Naitō Konan (1866–1934)* (Cambridge, MA: Harvard University Press, 1984); and Kevin M. Doak, "What is a Nation and Who Belongs? National Narratives and Ethnic Imagination in Twentieth-century Japan," *The American Historical Review* 102, no. 2 (April 1997): 283–309.

46. Oguma Eiji, *Tan'itsu Minzoku Shinwa no Kigen: 'Nihonjin' no Jigazō no Keifu* [The Origins of the Myth of the Homogenous Nation: A Genealogy of 'Japanese' Self-images] (Shinyōsha, 1995). Also, Eiji Oguma, *A Genealogy of Japanese Self-images*, trans. David Askew (Melbourne: Trans Pacific Press, 2002).

47. Nitobe, *The Japanese Nation*, 256.

48. See chapter 10 of John Dower, *War without Mercy: Race and Power in the Pacific War* (London: Faber, 1986).

49. Marius B. Jansen, *The Making of Modern Japan* (Cambridge, MA: Harvard University Press, 2000), 585.

50. Inazo Nitobe, "On the Dangers of Intolerance," *Pacific Affairs* 6, Conference Supplement, October 1933: 493–96.

51. *Zentaishugi to Kōdō* [Totalitarianism and the Imperial Way], in Akira Iriye, *Cultural Internationalism and World Order* (Baltimore: Johns Hopkins University Press, 1997), 121.

52. "Manchoukuo [*sic*] and the Renaissance of Oriental Political Philosophy," in Chikao Fujisawa, *Japanese and Oriental Philosophy* (Tokyo: The Research Department of the Daitō Bunka Kyōkai, 1935), 147–52.

Chapter 4

1. Louise Young, *Japan's Total Empire: Manchuria and the Culture of Wartime Imperialism* (Berkeley: University of California Press, 1998), 13.
2. Rana Mitter, *The Manchurian Myth: Nationalism, Resistance, and Collaboration in Modern China* (Berkeley: University of California Press, 2000).
3. Peter Duus, introduction to *The Japanese Informal Empire in China, 1895–1937*, eds. Peter Duus, Ramon H. Myers, and Mark R. Peattie (Princeton, NJ: Princeton University Press, 1989), xviii.
4. *Osaka Asahi Shimbun*, January 24, 1932.
5. *"Nichiman Giteisho"* [The Japanese-Manchukuo Protocol], September 15, 1932, in Rekishigaku Kenkyūkai, ed., *Nihonshi Shiryō, [5] Gendai* [Sources on Japanese History, Volume 5, Modern Period] (Iwanami Shoten, 1997), 16.
6. Matsusaka, "Managing Occupied Manchuria," in *The Japanese Wartime Empire, 1931–1945*, eds. Peter Duus, Ramon H. Myers, and Mark R. Peattie (Princeton, NJ: Princeton University Press, 1996), 96–97.
7. Ishiwara Kanji, *Manshūkoku Kenkoku to Shina Jihen* [The Establishment of Manchukuo and the China Incident] (Kyoto: Tōa Renmei Kyōkai, 1940), 30–32. For the impact of Yu on Ishiwara's Pan-Asianist sensibilities, see Yamamuro Shin'ichi. *Kimera: Manshūkoku no Shōzō* [Chimera: A Portrait of Manchukuo] (Chuō Kōronsha, 1993), 83–99. On how Yu drew Japanese attention to the concept, see Mitter, 94–95, and Prasenjit Duara, *Sovereignty and Authenticity: Manchukuo and the East Asian Modern* (Lanham, MD: Rowman & Littlefield, 2003), 64–65.
8. See Louise Young, "Imagined Empire: The Cultural Construction of Manchukuo," in *The Japanese Wartime Empire*, 71.
9. See Matsusaka, "Managing Occupied Manchuria," 98–99.
10. Yosuke Matsuoka, "Reply to Prof. Shusi-Hsu's Criticisms and Observations," transcribed in *An Address on Manchuria: Its Past and Present and Reply to Prof. Shusi-Hsu's Criticisms and Observation* (Kyoto: Institute of Pacific Relations, 1929), 25; emphasis in the original English transcript.
11. Young, *Japan's Total Empire*, 27–28.
12. *Osaka Asahi Shimbun*, March 2, 1932.
13. For instance, see Yanaihara Tadao's contemporaneous criticism below.
14. Sōga Kensuke in Koshizawa Akira, *Manshūkoku no Shuto Keikaku* [Manchukuo's Capital Planning] (Chikuma Gakugei Bunko, 2002), 239.
15. Civilian buildings, such as department stores and theatres, had more success, especially in the structures designed by Endō Arata (1889–1951), a student of Frank Lloyd Wright, who preferred to employ local organic building materials

to concrete, in order to accommodate and pay homage to the harsh Manchurian climate.

16. Yamamuro, *Kimera.*
17. Joshua A. Fogel, *Politics and Sinology: The Case of Naitō Konan (1866–1934)* (Cambridge, MA: Harvard University Press, 1984).
18. Naitō in mid-1933, quoted in Yamamuro, 136.
19. Ibid.
20. See Susan C. Townsend, "Chapter 9: The Yanaihara Incident," in *Yanaihara Tadao and Japanese Colonial Policy: Redeeming Empire* (Richmond, Surrey: Curzon, 2000), 228–56.
21. Yanaihara Tadao, *"Manshū Kenbundan"* [Discussion on Manchurian Observations], *Kaizō* (November 1932): 107.
22. Ibid.
23. For the analysis of the highly charged romanticism among Youth League activists, see Matsumoto Ken'ichi, "Ozawa Kaisaku no Yume" [Ozawa Kaisaku's Dream] in *Shōwa ni Shisu: Morisaki Minato to Ozawa Kaisaku* [Dying alongside Shōwa: Morisaki Minato and Ozawa Kaisaku] (Shinchōsha, 1988), 117–87.
24. Mutō Nobuyoshi, "Rikyō Aisatsu" [Remark upon Departing the Capital], August 1932, 2A039-06, Ajia Rekishi Shiryō Sent-ā [Japan Center for Asian Historical Records], Tokyo, Japan (JACAR).
25. *Manshūkoku no Konponrinen to Kyōwakai no Honshitsu* [Manchukuo's Fundamental Ideals and the True Character of the Concordia Society], September 18, 1936, *Gendaishi Shiryō*, vol. 11, 909.
26. Mariko Asano Tamanoi, "Knowledge, Power, and Racial Classifications: The 'Japanese' in 'Manchuria,'" *The Journal of Asian Studies* 59, no. 2 (May 2000): 248–76.
27. Extrapolated from Young, *Japan's Total Empire*, 253.
28. Marius B. Jansen, *The Making of Modern Japan* (Cambridge, MA: Harvard University Press, 2000), 589.
29. See Takafusa Nakamura, "Depression, Recovery, and War, 1920–1945," in *The Cambridge History of Japan: Vol. 6, The Twentieth Century*, ed. Peter Duus, trans. Jacqueline Kaminsky (Cambridge: Cambridge University Press, 1988), 475, and Young, *Japan's Total Empire*, 196–97.
30. Manchukuo Government Official Announcement, "Manshūkoku Keizai Kensetsu Yōkō" [Outlines of Manchukuo Economic Construction], March 1, 1932, A-02860229, Tokyo, Japan (JACAR), 374–75. See note 24.
31. For Miyazaki's life, see Kobayashi Hideo, *"Nihon Kabushiki Gaisha" wo Tsukutta Otoko—Miyazaki Masayoshi no Shōgai* [The Man Who Made "Japan Corporation"—Life of Miyazaki Masayoshi] (Shōgakukan, 1995).
32. Taiheiyō Sensō Kenkyūkai, ed., *Manshū Teikoku* (Kawade Shobō, 1996), 109.
33. Ibid., 110.

34. Tachibana Shiraki, *"Watashi no Hōkōtenkan"* [My Change in Direction], *Manshū Hyōron*, August 11, 1934, 32–33.
35. Ibid., 31.
36. Given in Yamamuro, 114.
37. Ibid., 113.
38. Ibid., 114.
39. Aishinkakura Fuketsu, *Fuketsu Jiden* [Autobiography of Pu Chieh] (Kawade Shobō, 1995), 89.
40. Akira Iriye, *Cultural Internationalism and World Order* (Baltimore: Johns Hopkins University Press, 1997), 120.
41. Hōchi Takayuki, *Harubin Gakuin to Manshūkoku* [The Harbin Academy and Manchukuo] (Shinchō Sensho, 1999), 128, and Yasuhiko Yoshikazu, "Manshū Kenkoku Daigaku no Seishun" [The Youths of Manshū Kenkoku Daigaku], *Marco Polo* (February 2, 1994): 57.
42. Yamamuro, 281.
43. Extrapolated from ibid. More specific data available in Manshū Rōkōkai, ed., *Manshū Rōdō Nenkan* [Manchurian Labor Yearbook] (Ganshōdō, 1940 edition, published in 1941), 62–65.
44. Yamamuro, 302.
45. Ibid., 302–3.
46. Matsumoto, *Shōwa ni Shisu*, 7–115; and Asano Tamanoi, "Knowledge, Power, and Racial Classifications."
47. Matsumoto, *Shōwa ni Shisu*, 82.
48. For instance, see Duara's analysis of women as representing tradition within the discourse of the East Asian modern. "Embodying Civilization: Women and the Figure of Tradition within Modernity," in Duara, *Sovereignty and Authenticity*, 131–69.
49. Ibid.
50. Yamaguchi Yoshiko and Fujiwara Sakuya, *Ri Kōran, Watashi no Hansei* [Li Xianglan, My Life So Far] (Shinchōsha, 1987), 109–11.
51. Ibid., 117–18.
52. Ibid., 138.
53. From "Zenman Jidō Bunshū" [Writing by All Manchukuo Children] (February 1940), complied in *Nihon Shokuminchishi (2) Manshū* [The History of Japanese Colonialism, Volume 2, Manchuria] (Mainichi Shimbunsha, 1971), 255.
54. Hiroshi Saitō, "My Impressions in the Far East and Japanese-American Relations," *Annals of the American Academy of Political and Social Science* 177 (January 1935), 247.
55. Ibid., 248.
56. Aishinkakura Hiro, *Ruten no ōhi no Shōwashi* [Shōwa History of a Wandering Princess] (Shinchōsha, 1984), and Aishinkakura Fuketsu, *Fuketsu Jiden*.
57. Ri (Lee) Masako too wrote an autobiography, entitled *Dōran no Naka no Ōhi* [Princess amidst Great Turmoil] (Kōdansha, 1968).

58. Ibid., 72–73.
59. Aishinkakura Hiro, *Ruten*, 69–70.
60. Young, *Japan's Total Empire*, 13. For example, Young cites French Algeria and British India as other examples of total empires. True, the French colonial concept of *mission civilisatrice* is an indication of the reforming impetus characteristic of total imperialism and empire, but British colonial style of "divide and rule" is more indicative of informal, rather than total, imperialism.
61. Jansen, *The Making of Modern Japan*, 589.
62. Ibid., 590.
63. Young, "Imagined Empire," 71.
64. Ibid.

Chapter 5

1. Rōyama Masamichi, "Tōa Kyōdōtai no Riron" [The Theory Behind East Asian Cooperative Body], *Kaizō* (November 1938): 7.
2. Shiraki Tachibana, "Watashi no Hōkōtenkan" [My Change in Direction], *Manshū Hyōron* (August 11, 1934): 33.
3. William Miles Fletcher III, *The Search for a New Order: Intellectuals and Fascism in Prewar Japan* (Chapel Hill: University of North Carolina Press, 1982).
4. See Miyake Masaki, ed., *Shōwashi no Gunbu to Seiji* [The Military and Politics in the History of Showa] (Daiichi Hōki Shuppan, 1983), and Hata Ikuhiko, *Gun Fashizumu Undōshi* [History of Military Fascist Movement] (Kawade Shobō Shinsha, 1962).
5. Tanaka Sōgorō, *Nihon Fasizumushi* (Kawade Shobō Shinsha, 1972), 131–34.
6. Monbushō, ed., *Kokutai no Hongi* [Cardinal Principles of the National Polity], 1937.
7. The Takigawa Affair (1933) in which Professor Takigawa Yukitoki and his colleagues were forced out of the law faculty of Kyoto Imperial University and Tokyo Imperial University's red purge of its economic professors (1939) were also part of this larger "sacralization" trend.
8. Sano Manabu and Nabeyama Sadachika, "Kyōdō Hikoku Dōshi ni Tsuguru Sho" [An Announcement to the Convicted Fellow Colleagues], in Rekishigaku Kenkyūkai, ed., *Nihonshi Shiryō* [Sources on Japanese History], vol. 5 (Iwanami Shoten, 1997), 63–64. Originally appeared in *Tokkō Geppō* (July 1933): 91–95.
9. Ibid., 63.
10. Ibid., 64.
11. Ibid.
12. For a classic analysis of the phenomenon of *Tenkō*, and its semantics, see Shunsuke Tsurumi, *An Intellectual History of Wartime Japan 1931–1945* (London: KPI, 1986), 5–14.
13. Ozaki Hotsumi, "Ozaki Hotsumi no Shuki (1)" [*Ozaki Hotsumi's Shuki* (1)], June 1943, *Gendaishi Shiryō*, vol. 2, 9.
14. Ibid., 9–10.

15. Haruhiko Fukui, "Chapter 4: Postwar Politics, 1945–1973," in *The Cambridge History of Japan: Vol. 6, The Twentieth Century*, ed. Peter Duus (Cambridge: Cambridge University Press, 1988), 146; and Kisaka Junichirō, *Taiheiyō Sensō* [The Pacific War] (Shōgakukan, 1994), 93.

16. Taken from: "My political intentions were rather complex. That is because I was not a simple Communist." Ozaki, *Gendaishi Shiryō*, vol. 2, 32.

17. Ibid., 34.

18. "Kokusaku no Kijun" [Fundamental Principles of National Policy], The Five Ministers' Conference, August 7, 1936, *Shuyōmonjo*, vol. 2, 344–45.

19. Though the "Nanking Incident" has been a perennial issue, the polemics and emotional stakes with it have been markedly heightened by the publication of Iris Chang's *The Rape of Nanking: The Forgotten Holocaust of World War II* (New York: Basic Books, 1997). David Askew's "New Research on the Nanjing Incident" in *The Japan Focus* best summarizes the origins and the present state of this debate, http://www.japanfocus.org/products/details/1729.

20. Matsumoto Shigeharu, *Shanhai Jidai: Jānarisuto no Kaisō* [Shanghai Years: A Recollection of a Journalist], vol. 2 (Chūkō Shinsho, 1974), 209.

21. Ibid.

22. Sugiyama Heisuke, "Jūgun Oboegaki" [A Memo from the Front], *Kaizō* (December 1938): 347–60.

23. Ibid., 357.

24. Ibid., 358.

25. Ibid., 358–60.

26. Ibid., 360.

27. For example, the ambivalent position of some Japanese Christian women during and after the war is explored in Karen Garner, "Global Feminism and Postwar Reconstruction: The World YWCA Visitation to Occupied Japan, 1947," *Journal of World History* 15, no. 2 (June 2004): 191–227.

28. From Noguchi to Tagore, July 23, 1938, *Poet to Poet: Full Text of Correspondence between Yone Noguchi and Rabindranath Tagore on the Sino-Japanese Conflict*, reprinted from *Visva Bharati Quarterly* 4, no. 3 (Nanking and Santiniketan: The Sino-Indian Cultural Society, ca. 1940), 3.

29. From Tagore to Noguchi, September 1, 1938, ibid., 6–7.

30. Ibid., 8.

31. Ibid.

32. The benchmark study on Nomonhan is Alvin D. Coox, *Nomonhan: Japan against Russia, 1939*, 2 volumes (Stanford, CA: Stanford University Press, 1985).

33. His first premiership ran from June 1937 to June 1939; second, from July 1940 to July 1941; and finally, from July 1941 to October 1941.

34. Marius B. Jansen, *The Making of Modern Japan* (Cambridge, MA: Harvard University Press, 2000), 618.

35. Ibid., 613, 618.
36. In an interview with Yamaura, given in Yamaura Kan'ichi, "Konoe Shūhen no Henkan" [Changes in Konoe's Surroundings], *Kaizō* (November 1938): 120.
37. Konoe Fumimaro, *Sengo Ōbei Kenbunroku* [Travels in Postwar Europe and the United States] (Chūkō Bunko, 1981), 138.
38. Ibid., 140.
39. Ibid., 141.
40. Ibid.
41. His thesis was initially propounded in the co-authored book, Ishihara Shintarō and Morita Akio *"No" to Ieru Nihon* [Japan that can say "No"] (Kōbunsha, 1989).
42. Kenneth Colegrove, "The New Order in East Asia," *The Far Eastern Quarterly* 1, no. 1 (November 1941): 6.
43. For an excellent account of this debate, see Gregory J. Kasza, "Fascism from Below? A Comparative Perspective on the Japanese Right, 1931–1936," *Journal of Contemporary History* 19, no. 4 (October 1984): 607–29. Also on the theme of fascism, see E. Bruce Reynolds, ed., *Japan in the Fascist Era* (New York: Palgrave Macmillan, 2004). In Japanese, the benchmark study is Tanaka, *Nihon Fashizumushi.*
44. In some interpretations, "Four directions and for corners of the world" rather than "eight corners."
45. "Kokuminseifu wo Aite to sezu" [No longer to deal with the Kuomintang government], January 16, 1938, *Shuyōmonjo*, vol. 2, 386.
46. Saionji, 141–50.
47. Ibid., 160.
48. Yamaura, "Konoe Shūhen no Henkan," 120.
49. In addition to Fletcher, also see James B. Crowley, "Intellectuals as Visionaries of the New Asian Order," in *Dilemmas of Growth in Prewar Japan*, ed. James William Morley (Princeton, NJ: Princeton University Press, 1971), 319–73.
50. Yamaura, "Konoe Shūhen no Henkan," 120.
51. Itō Nozomi, "Shōwa Kenkyūkai ni okeru Tōa Kyōdōtairon no Keisei" The Formation of the Theory of East Asia Cooperative Body in the Shōwa Research Association], in Okamoto, ed., *Kindai Nihon no Ajiakan*, 228.
52. Given in Shōwa Kenkyūkai, ed. Gotō Ryūnosuke (Keizaiōraisha, 1968), 63.
53. "Tōa Shinchitsujo Seifu Seimei" [Governmental Declaration on the New East Asian Order], November 3, 1938, *Shuyōmonjo*, vol. 2, 401.
54. Ibid.
55. Here I have translated the term "tōitsuteki rinen" as "unifying principles" rather than "global ideas" or "universal ideas" as others might have. Miki Kiyoshi, "Tōa Shisō no Konkyo" [The Basis of East Asian Philosophy], *Kaizō*(December 1938): 9–10.
56. Ibid., 9.
57. Ibid., 12.

58. Ibid., 18.
59. See Ian Buruma and Avishai Margalit, *Occidentalism: The West in the Eyes of Its Enemies* (New York: Penguin Press, 2004).
60. See Fletcher for a focused account on these three characters.
61. Kanokogi (1884–1948) famously coined the term *"Sumera Ajia"* [Imperial Asia], in which he propounded the vision of totalitarian Asia under Japan's imperial rule. See Kanokogi Kazunobu, *Sumera Ajia* [Imperial Asia] (Dōbun Shoin, 1937).
62. The Berlin Anti-Imperialist Group is Katō Tetsurō's long-term research project. For the discussion of the group, see for example, "Shinhakken no Kawakami Hajime Shokan wo Megutte" [In Reference to the Newly Discovered Correspondence of Kawakami Hajime], http://homepage3.nifty.com/katote/2001kawakami.html.
63. Rōyama, "Tōa Kyōdōtai no Riron," 18.
64. Ibid., 18–19.
65. Ibid., 20.
66. For Tokyo's effort to create a Chinese regime independent of Chiang Kai-shek and the Kwangtung Army, see Tobe Ryōichi, *Pīsu Fīrā—Shina Jihen Wahei Kōsaku no Gunzō* [Peace Feeler—Sculpted Portraits of the China Incident Peace Makers] (Ronsōsha, 1991).
67. "Kokuminseifu wo Aite to sezu," 386.
68. See Emiko Ohnuki-Tierney, *Kamikaze, Cherry Blossoms, and Nationalisms* (Chicago: University of Chicago Press, 2002).
69. Rōyama, "Tōa Kyōdōtai no Riron," 6. Such material considerations might be there, he concedes, but they are of "a secondary consideration."
70. The statement was taken from: "The only thing that can defeat the United States when it comes to the global war on terror is America itself, if we lose the courage of our convictions, if we simply give up." Attributed to the Republican Senator from Texas, John Coryon. Given in "Senators Begin Debate on Iraq, Visions in Sharp Contrast," *The New York Times*, June 22, 2006.

Chapter 6

1. For instance, an August 1941 report from an information-gathering mission indicated that the United States had a far greater industrial capacity than Japan (12 times its GNP and 527.9 times its petroleum production). See Jack Snyder, *Myths of Empire: Domestic Politics and International Ambition* (Ithaca, NY: Cornell University Press, 1991), 113.
2. Although commonly regarded as an effective Japanese decision to enter war, the September 6, 1941 "Teikoku Kokusaku Suikō Yōryō" [Essentials for Carrying Out the Empire's Policies], *Shuyōmonjo*, 544–45, nonetheless intensified divisions within the government. Hirohito himself was profoundly

doubtful of the feasibility of such a plan, drawing analogies to the disastrous China War.

3. See Jack Snyder, 112–52, for more.

4. Hard-liners, such as General Sugiyama Hajime, Chief of the General Staff and Admiral Nagano Osami, Navy Chief of Staff, repeatedly pleaded their cases in terms of opportunity cost. Sugiyama impetuously responded to his opponents, who suggested that more thorough research of strategic alternatives was needed, with a remark, "It is impossible to research the surrounding situation in just four or five days. So let's do it!" Nagano, too, announced that "Every hour, as we speak, we are consuming 400 tons of oil. The matter is rather urgent. We must promptly decide 'either-or.'" The Liaison Conference of October 23, in Nihon Kokusai Seijigakkai, ed., *Taiheiyō Sensō e no Michi* [Road to the Pacific War], *Bekkan Shiryōhen* [Separate Volume on Sources] (Asahi Shimbunsha, 1988), 537.

5. Given in Yui Masaomi, "Taiheiyō Sensō" [The Pacific War], in *Jūgonen Sensōshi* [History of the Fifteen Years' War], eds. Fujiwara Akira and Imai Seiichi (Aoki Shoten, 1989), 21.

6. Recorded in "Dai Nanakai Gozenkaigi Shitsugi ōtō no Gaikyō" [The Seventh Imperial Conference—Proceedings of Q & A], November 15, 1941, *Sugiyama Memo* [Sugiyama Memoranda], vol. 1 (Hara Shobō, 1967), 406–16.

7. Ibid., 414.

8. Ibid., 415.

9. Ibid.

10. Ibid., 416.

11. It outlined (1) that Japan has decided to enter war; (2) that the war shall start at the beginning of December; and (3) that diplomatic means will be employed until 12:00 a.m. of December 1, and if diplomacy were to succeed, the war option shall be suspended. "Teikoku Kokusaku Suikō Yōryō" [Essentials for Carrying Out the Empire's Policies], *Shuyōmonjo*, vol. 2, 554–55.

12. "Gaimudaijin Setsumei Jikō" [Items for Explanation by the Foreign Minister], at the Seventh Imperial Conference, November 5, 1941, *Sugiyama Memo*, vol. 1, 420.

13. *Shuyōmonjo*, vol. 2, 573–74.

14. "Konji Sensō no Koshō narabi ni Senji no Bunkai Jiki ni Tsuiite" [Concerning the Official Name of this War and the Delineation of the War Zones], December 10, Liaison Conference, *Sugiyama Memo*, vol. 1, 568.

15. *Asahi Shimbun*, December 13, 1941.

16. *The Syonan Times*, March 17, 1942.

17. "Daitōa Kyōeiken Kakuritsu—Dōchō Yūhō to Teikei" [Establishing the Greater East Asia CoProsperity Sphere—Friendship and Alliance], *Tokyo Asahi Shimbun*, Evening Edition, August 2, 1941.

18. Rabindranath Tagore to Yonejirō Noguchi, September 1, 1938, in *Poet to Poet: Full Text of Correspondence between Yone Noguchi and Rabindranath Tagore on the*

Sino-Japanese Conflict (Nanking & Santiniketan: The Sino-Indian Cultural Society, ca. 1940), 8.

19. Yasuda Takeshi, "Sekaishi no Tetsugaku" [Philosophy of World History], in *Kindai Nihon Shisōshi no Kiso Chishiki: Ishin Zenya kara Haisen made* [Basic Knowledge of the History of Ideas in Modern Japan: From the Restoration to the Defeat], eds. Hashikawa Bunsō, Kano Masanao, and Hiraoka Toshio (Yūhikaku, 1971), 443.

20. The Kyoto School has attracted much scholarly attention, with ramifications for some interesting revisionist debates. For example, Graham Parkes, "The Putative Fascism of the Kyoto School and the Political Correctness of the Modern Academy"; Christopher S. GotōJones, *Political Philosophy in Japan: Nishida, the Kyoto School and Co-Prosperity* (London: Routledge, 2005).

21. Entitled "Kaisen" [The War Begins] and published in the New Year issue of the magazine *Bungei* in 1942.

22. Katō Yoshiko, *Saitō Mokichi no Jūgonen Sensō* [Saitō Mokichi's Fifteen Years' War] (Misuzu Shobō, 1990), 124.

23. "Dōbasanbō Yawa: Kaiin Shokun ni Tsugu" [A Night Chat at Dōba Mountain Hut—An Announcement to the Members], *Araragi* 35, no. 1 (January 1942): 22.

24. *Asahi Shimbun*, February 16, 1942.

25. For more on this thesis, see Richard Rorty, *Contingency, Irony, and Solidarity* (Cambridge: Cambridge University Press, 1989).

26. Yasuda, "Sekaishi no Tetsugaku," 441.

27. Yoshimoto Takaaki with Tajika Nobukazu, *Watashi no "Sensōron"* [My "Ideas on War"] (Bunkasha, 1999), 32–34.

28. "Dai Tōa Sensō to Warera no Ketsui (Sengen)" [The Greater East Asia War and our Determination - Commitment Statement], *Chūgoku Bungaku* 80 (January 1942): 481–84.

29. "Overcoming modernity" was the main theme of a roundtable discussion attended by Takeuchi, along with some of the Kyoto School scholars mentioned above. The proceedings were featured in the journal *Bungakukai* (September/October 1942).

30. Harry Harootunian, *Overcome by Modernity: History, Culture, and Community in Interwar Japan* (Princeton, NJ: Princeton University Press, 2000), 46.

31. Yasuda Takeshi, "Jūnigatsu Yōka no Shisō" [The Ideology of 8 December], in Hashikawa, Kano, and Hiraoka, eds., *Kindai Nihon Shisōhi*, 441.

32. Samuel P. Huntington, "The Clash of Civilizations?" *Foreign Affairs* 72, no. 3 (Summer 1993): 22–49.

33. Yoshimoto with Tajika, 32–34.

34. Although sometimes regarded as a Kyoto School scholar because of his education at the university, Tanaka self-consciously detached himself from the clique and devoted himself to the studies of classical Greek philosophy.

35. Yasuda, "Sekaishi no Tetsugaku," 444.

36. Ibid.
37. Watsuji as recorded in the transcript of the proceedings of Takagi's meetings, "Rinsen Shisō Taisaku Kondankai" [Discussion on Ideology for War Entry] Bōeichō Bōei Kenkyūjo Senshibu [War History Department, National Defense Institute, Japanese Defense Agency], Tokyo, Japan (BBKS), 79; emphasis retained from the original.
38. Ibid.
39. Yoshimoto with Tajika, 34.
40. Dazai Osamu, *Jūnigatsu Yōka* [December 8] in *Dazai Osamu Zenshū* 5 [Collected Works of Dazai Osamu, Volume 5] (Chikuma Bunko, 1989), 19–31.
41. Ibid., 19.

Chapter 7

1. Jon Halliday, *A Political History of Japanese Capitalism* (New York: Random House, 1975), 141.
2. Marius B. Jansen, *The Making of Modern Japan* (Cambridge, MA: Harvard University Press, 2000), 648.
3. *The Journal of Southeast Asian Studies* 27, no. 1 (March 1996) deals with various aspects of different parts of Southeast Asia under the Japanese occupation.
4. Grant Goodman, ed., *Japanese Cultural Policies in Southeast Asia during World War 2* (New York: St. Martin's Press, 1991), 3.
5. "Nanpō Senryōchi Gyōsei Jisshi Yōryō" [The Outlines of the Administration of Southern Occupation], *Shuyōmonjo*, vol. 2, 562–63.
6. Ibid.
7. "Senryōchi Gunsei Jisshi ni Kansuru Rikukaigun ChūōKyōtei" [The Central Army/Navy Agreement on the Execution of the Military Administration of the Occupied Territories], November 26, 1941 (BBKS).
8. For instance, the Imperial Navy's "Senryōchi Gunsei Shori Yōkō" [The Outlines for the Military Administration Management of the Occupied Territories] on March 14, 1942 (BBKS).
9. January 21, 1942, at the Seventy-ninth Imperial Conference, in Ibid.
10. Joyce C. Lebra in Lebra, ed. and intro., *Japan's Greater East Asia Co-Prosperity Sphere in World War II* (Kuala Lumpur: Oxford University Press, 1975), xiv.
11. Ibid., x.
12. Yoji Akashi, "Japanese Cultural Policy in Malaya and Singapore," in Goodman, ed., 118.
13. Motoe Terami-Wada, "Japanese Propaganda Corps in the Philippines," in Goodman, ed., 175.
14. "Genjūmin Shidō Hōshin" [Guidelines for Instructing the Native Population], in *Senji Geppō*, March 1942.
15. *Senji Geppō*, October 1942, 8.
16. *The Syonan Times*, February 28, 1942.

17. Yoji Akashi, "Japanese Cultural Policy," 153.
18. Ibuse Masuji, "Chōyōchū no Kenbun" [Experiences during Military Service], in *Ibuse Masuji Jisen Zenshū* [Self-Selected Collection of Ibuse Masuji's Works] (Shinchōsha, 1986), 176–77.
19. As given in Akashi, "Japanese Cultural Policy," 153.
20. *The Syonan Times*, June 1, 1942; emphasis added.
21. An attachment file to *Senji Geppō*, June 1942.
22. Mamoru Shinozaki, *Syonan—My Story* (Singapore: Asia Pacific Press, 1975), 76–77.
23. Yoji Akashi, "Japanese Policy towards the Malayan Chinese, 1941–45," *Journal of Southeast Asian Studies* 1, no. 2 (September 1970): 76.
24. "Tenchōsetsu Hōshuku Gyōji Yōkō" [Guidelines for the Imperial Birthday Celebration], complied in *Senji Geppō*, April 1942.
25. Ibid.
26. Otabe Yūji, *Tokugawa Yoshichika no Jūgonen Sensō* [Tokugawa Yoshichika's Fifteen Years' War] (Aoki Shoten, 1988), 163–64.
27. Taken from lectures by Ibuse Masuji as quoted in Akashi, "Japanese Cultural Policy," 131.
28. As given in ibid., 146.
29. Ibid.
30. "Gunseibu no Kunrenjo Kaikō Mokuteki" [The Military Administration's Objectives for the Establishment of the Training Schools] as quoted in Otabe, 158.
31. *Senji Geppō*, August 1942.
32. Akashi, "Japanese Cultural Policy," 141.
33. Ibid., 145–46.
34. Fujiwara Satoshi, Shinohara Keiichi, and Nishide Takeshi, *Ajia Senji Ryūgakusei* [Asian Students in Wartime Japan] (Kyōdō Tsūshin, 1996), 116–18.
35. Akashi, "Japanese Cultural Policy," 141.
36. "Nanpō Bunka Kōsaku Tokubetsu Shidōsha no Kyōiku Ikusei Jigyō" [Education Scheme of the Special Leaders for the Cultural Engineering of the South] in ibid., 118.
37. Fujiwara, Shinohara, and Nishide, 200.
38. As quoted in Kadono Hiroko, *Tōnanajia no Otōtotachi* [Younger Brothers of Southeast Asia] (Sankōsha, 1985), 259–60.
39. Given in Akashi, "Japanese Cultural Policy," 150.
40. Diasis in Fujiwara, Shinohara, and Nishide, 274–75.
41. Ibid.
42. Ibid., 276–77.
43. Tran My-Van, "Japan and Vietnam's Caodaists: A Wartime Relationship (1939–45)," in *Journal of Southeast Asian Studies* 27, no. 1 (March 1996): 183.
44. "Daitōa Seiryaku Shidō Taikō" [The Outlines for the Political Guidance of Greater East Asia], issued on May 13, 1943, *Shuyōmonjo*, vol. 2, 583–84.

45. Ibid.
46. Ibid.
47. Ibid.
48. An important work on Bose is Milan Hauner, *India in Axis Strategy: Germany, Japan, and Indian Nationalists in the Second World War* (Stuttgart: Klett-Cotta, 1981).
49. "A Secret Memorandum from Councilor Asada to FM Shigemitsu," September 25, 1943, (GGS).
50. The "F" represented Fujiwara, Friendship, and Freedom.
51. Eunice Thio, "Singapore under Japanese Rule," in Ernest C. T. Chew and Edwin Lee, eds., *A History of Singapore* (Singapore: Oxford University Press, 1991), 101.
52. In Burma, Colonel Suzuki Keiji founded the "Minami Kikan" [Southern Agency] to support the formation of the Burmese Independence Army. John Dower, *War without Mercy: Race and Power in the Pacific War* (London: Faber, 1986), 285.
53. Thio, 101.
54. Ibid.
55. Kisaka, 244–45.
56. "Daitōa Kaigi Kanren Shiryō" [Documents concerning the Greater East Asia Conference] (GGS) and "*Dai Tōa Kyōdōsengen*" [Greater East Asian Joint Declaration], 2–3.
57. The Atlantic Charter, August 14, 1941, http://www.yale.edu/lawweb/avalon/wwii/atlantic.htm.
58. Ibid.
59. Yoshimoto in the TV program *Miyoshi Jūrō: ETV 2001 Honoo no Hito Miyoshi Jūrō* [Miyoshi Jūrō, a Person of Fire], April 23, 2001, NHK/ETV.
60. Takeuchi, "Nihon no Ajiashugi," 10–11.
61. The Times (London), February 13, 1942.
62. Lee Kuan Yew, *Towards Socialism*, vol. 5 (Singapore: Government Printing Office, 1962), 10–11.
63. See Otabe, 134–60 for more anecdotes.
64. E. J. H. Corner, *Omoide no Shōnan Hakubutsukan* [Shōnan Museum in My Memory], trans. Ishii Mikiko (Chūkō Shinsho, 1981), 4–5.
65. Tokugawa Yoshichika, *Saigo no Tonosama* [The Last Lord] (Kōdansha, 1973), 74–75.
66. Frederick Whyte, "Japan's Purpose in Asia: An Appreciation of Japan's War Potential, Strategic Position, and Foreign Policy" (The Royal Institute of International Affairs, 1941), 30.
67. Ibid.
68. *The Syonan Shinbun*, August 21, 1945.

Conclusion

1. Japan's official translation of the *Imperial Rescript of August 14, 1945*, in Robert J. C. Butow, *Japan's Decision to Surrender* (Stanford, CA: Stanford University Press, 1954), 248. For the original, see *Nihon Gaikō Nenpyū narabi ni Shuyōmonjo* [Chronology and Major Documents of Japan's Foreign Policy], ed. Gaimushō (Hara Shobō, 1965–1966), vol. 2, 573–74.

2. Low Ngiong Ing, *When Singapore Was Syonan-to* (Singapore: Eastern Universities Press, 1973), 132.

3. Fouad Ajami, "The End of Pan-Arabism," *Foreign Affairs* 57, no. 2 (Winter 1978/79): 357.

4. See Geoffrey Best, "Peace Conferences and the Century of Total War: The 1899 Hague Conference and What Came After," *International Affairs* 75, no. 3 (July 1999): 619–34.

5. "*Tōa Shinchitsujo Seifu Seimei,*" *Shuyōmonjo*, vol. 2, 401.

6. Arika Iriye, *Cultural Internationalism and World Order* (Baltimore: Johns Hopkins University Press, 1997), 121.

7. Ozaki at the 76th Debating Session, as given in Eizawa Kōji, "*Daitōa Kyōeiken*" *no Shisō* [The Ideas Behind the "Greater East Asia CōProsperity Sphere"] (Kōdansha, 1995), 211.

8. Yomota Inuhiko, "*Ajia wa Ima Sendake Aru*" [Now, There Are a Thousand Asias], *Asahi Shimbun*, February 4, 2003; emphasis added.

9. Butow, 248.

10. This tautological phrase "*kokka egoizumu*" is often used as an alternative term for "national interest" in leftist accounts of the Fifteen Years' War.

11. John Ruskin, St. Mark's Rest (New York: Bryan, Taylor, 1894), 3.

12. Nakao Michio, *Nihon Senji Shisō no Kenkyū—Nihon Seishin to Tōa Kyōdōtai* [A Study of Japan's Wartime Philosophies: Japanese Spirit and Greater Asia Cooperative Body] (Kōseisha Kōseikaku, 2001), ii.

13. Tokutomi Iichirō, Shōrisha no Hissui [The Inevitable Fall of the Victor] (Kōdansha, 1952), 52.

14. Frederick Whyte, "Japan's Purpose in Asia: An Appreciation of Japan's War Potential, Strategic Position, and Foreign Policy" (The Royal Institute of International Affairs, 1941), 46.

Index

Made in the USA
Las Vegas, NV
22 July 2021

26864057R00174